anglistik & englischunterricht

Reading the Caribbean

Reading the Caribbean

Verantwortlicher Herausgeber
für den thematischen Teil des Bandes:
Klaus Stierstorfer

UNIVERSITÄTSVERLAG WINTER
HEIDELBERG

Gabriele Linke · Erwin Otto · Holger Rossow
Gerd Stratmann · Merle Tönnies (Hg.)

anglistik & englischunterricht

Band 67

Reading the Caribbean: Approaches to Anglophone Caribbean Literature and Culture

UNIVERSITÄTSVERLAG WINTER
HEIDELBERG

Bibliografische Information Der Deutschen Bibliothek
Die Deutsche Bibliothek verzeichnet diese Publikation in der Deutschen Nationalbibliografie; detaillierte bibliografische Daten sind im Internet über *http://dnb.ddb.de* abrufbar.

ISBN 978-3-8253-5358-2
ISSN 0344-8266

Anschrift der Redaktion:
Universität Rostock, Institut für Anglistik und Amerikanistik
18051 Rostock

Imprimé en Allemagne · Printed in Germany
Druck: Memminger MedienCentrum AG, 87700 Memmingen
Gedruckt auf umweltfreundlichem, chlorfrei gebleichtem und alterungsbeständigem Papier
Den Verlag erreichen Sie im Internet unter: www.winter-verlag-hd.de

Contents

Introduction

The time-honoured a&e series (anglistik & englischunterricht) published by Winter, Heidelberg University Press, has developed its very specific mission of providing material and inspiration for teachers of English in the German-speaking countries into a broad, international approach of authoritative introductions to the hot spots in literary, linguistic and cultural research in the wider field of the English-speaking world.

Within the series profile this volume on Caribbean literature and culture is intended to provide discussions and analyses of those issues and approaches which have emerged as particularly important or, indeed, contentious in literary and cultural scholarship in the field. Obviously, no attempt at completeness is possible within the circumference of this book, and a number of gaps and elisions must remain painfully obvious. While these had better not be identified all at once so that they take the shape of a great, gaping and discouraging void at the outset of this book, the fact that the following essays are almost exclusively focused on what is sometimes called the 'Anglophone' Caribbean, should be immediately pointed out. While productions and texts from the other important languages in the region occasionally put in an appearance, these rare references can at best begin to establish a cross-disciplinary link-up to the other important languages, notably Spanish and French, in the area. The Hispanic, Francophone Caribbean merits its own volume(s) and the interchanges and productive crossings between the various languages and the cultures they inform will again call for further, special attention. The main reasons for this reductionist approach to what is admittedly one of the most productively multi-cultural contexts to be found in recent history, is, first, the general focus on English of the series to which this volume belongs, and, second, the simple truth that, hermeneutically speaking, insight will accrue in cycles and by crossing and re-crossing borders of cultures, periods and languages – and beginning this hermeneutic approach to the Caribbean from an Anglophone perspective will certainly be as good as any other. Beyond these apologetic remarks readers should, however, remain aware that Anglophone Caribbean culture has developed its own, specific profile. This profile will, of course, ultimately not be fully intelligible without due consideration of the other languages in the area; and the Caribbean as a shared cultural space will not be understood without taking its various literatures, languages and cultures into account; still, the Anglophone Caribbean has its own historical linkages and its specific cultural connectedness and relationship even beyond the Western, dominantly Anglophone world today which makes its focused study as set out in the present volume well worth such differentiated attention. It is perhaps the almost paradoxical combination of the local with the global so typical of the Caribbean which produces different impressions and new vistas with each new context in which it is perceived, be it in its linkage to Africa as in Irele and Gikandi's *Cambridge History* mentioned below; be it in relation to 'Latin America' as in Balderston and Gonzalez's *Encyclopedia of Latin American and Caribbean Literature*,[1] or, to add only the most obvious with many more to consider, in the well-established connections to the USA and to Europe.

As for the choice of its format, this book is best considered in reference to existing work in this field, in the context of which it can hopefully find its useful position. If we look to one side of this projected position, there are now, after many years of a dearth in substantial surveys, such important maps of the territory of Caribbean Writing as Louis James's by now classic *Caribbean Literature in English* in the *Longman Literature in English Series*[2] and the even wider-ranging, magisterial *Cambridge History of African and Caribbean Literature*, competently put together by F. Abiola Irele and Simon Gikandi (2004)[3]. There are also surveys of individual genres, such as Booker and Juraga on the novel or Breiner on poetry[4], albeit by no means in the variety and scope which their subject might warrant. With the publication of Greenwood Press' s massive *Encyclopedia of Caribbean Literature*, edited by D. H. Figueredo (2005),[5] those looking for an alphabetical work of reference will be well and copiously served.

Looking to the other side of the present volume, there is some rare and exceptional work which directly addresses the concrete needs of those involved in teaching Caribbean Literature and Culture. Clearly, David Dabydeen's *A Handbook for Teaching Caribbean Literature* (1988)[6] is here the pioneering work. In this book,

Dabydeen had not only collected important readings and teaching aids to major texts in Caribbean writing by outstanding experts in the field; he was also able to show how much Caribbean writing had entered the curricula of British universities and schools by the 1980s, thus generating the need for precisely the kind of work he provided. This was two decades ago and it is clear that the progress of Caribbean writing, both on the wider stage of world literature and in the more specialized confines of the English and EFL classrooms and seminar rooms around the world, has been constant and remarkable.

This notable increase in the importance of Caribbean writing is also part of the rationale behind *Reading the Caribbean*, which could then be seen to cover the middle ground between, say, Dabydeen's *Handbook* and the august *Cambridge History*. The rationale of *Reading the Caribbean* is to open major themes of Caribbean literature and culture rather than provide a historical survey in a continuous narrative or a reference work for readers with particular queries or specific, detailed interests – or a manual and study or teaching aid for specific texts or writers.

The themes covered open a wide survey of prominent topics currently discussed in Caribbean studies, but also those which students will find particularly accessible or stimulating. The essays are usually constructed in such a way that they address a general issue of outstanding significance, but then deal with it by engaging with one or a few examples considered particularly important or illustrative of the general issue. Thus, the first four essays deal with aspects of Caribbean literature. Silvio Torres-Saillant opens the discussion with a reflection on the question of a specific Caribbean poetics and how this is continually adjusted to the changing requirements to which Caribbean writing responds. Jana Gohrisch then provides a wide survey of the content side of Caribbean literature and highlights its most noteworthy themes and narratives, while Helge Nowak's contribution explores generic forms, paying special attention to the European cross-over in poetry. Curwen Best takes up this cue by including the recent impact of cyberculture in his assessments of orality and orature as particularly important forms of artistic expression in the Caribbean, both traditionally and, as he suggests, with good prospects in the cyberworlds still to come in the future. Gail Low provides indispensable insight into the specific forms of literary and cultural production in the Caribbean, adding a line of ‘material’ culture and its history to the discussion. Hubert Devonish introduces the impressive linguistic clout of the Caribbean which has made the region one of the preferred prospecting fields for linguists world-wide, and Sabine Sörgel shows the vitality of Caribbean theatre by focusing on the staging of its most famous representative, Derek Walcott. Denise deCaires Narain’s essay is most helpful in introducing the gender perspective on Caribbean literature and culture. Taking an early historical instance in Ligon’s map and history of Barbados, Keith Sandiford gives a lasting impression of the significance of maps, mapping and mapmaking which is particularly valuable in a contested space such as the Caribbean. In a focus on the connections between the Caribbean and South Africa, Miki Flockemann widens the view on the Caribbean by pointing out the global connectedness of its diverse cultural traits and histories, an aspect further elaborated on another level by Monika Gomille’s exploration of issues of literary and cultural translation. Mike Alleyne provides a good grounding in Caribbean music as one of the most important mainstays of Caribbean culture and one of its most prominent ‘exports’ world-wide. Klaus Stierstorfer then rounds off the survey by analysing the specifically Caribbean brands and uses of humour as another outstanding feature of what could be called the Caribbean ‘way of life’.

Between them, the contributors hope to be able to convey something of the inspiring vitality and the spirit of abounding artistic creativity which pervades the Caribbean as a region, but which can also be observed to spring up vigorously wherever Caribbean culture finds a foothold in its various diasporas around the globe. With the grounding to be derived from the pages of this volume, readers will hopefully find themselves well equipped and, indeed, stimulated, to explore further this rewarding and engaging field of literary, linguistic and cultural study.

The editor takes this opportunity to thank all the contributors for their patience and forbearance with what has, for some of them, been a long and arduous process of germination and growth before the book could reach its present format. An equal share of gratitude is due to the series editors of a&e, for backing this volume without qualifications and with all their expert advice and support.

Münster, February 2007 *Klaus Stierstorfer*

Notes

1 Daniel Balderson & Mike Gonzalez (Eds.): *Encyclopedia of Latin American and Caribbean Literature, 1900-2003*, Encyclopedias of Contemporary Culture, London, 2004.
2 Louis James: *Caribbean Literature in English*. Longman Literature in English Series, London & New York, 1999.
3 F. Abiola Irele & Simon Gikandi (Eds.): *The Cambridge History of African and Caribbean Literature*, 2 vols, Cambridge, 2004.
4 N. Keith Booker & Dubravka Juraga: *The Caribbean Novel in English. An Introduction*, Portsmouth, NH a.o., 2001; Laurence A. Breiner: *An Introduction to West Indian Poetry,* Cambridge, 1998.
5 Danilo H. Figueredo (Ed.): *Encyclopedia of Caribbean Literature*, 2 vols, Westport, CT, 2005.
6 David Dabydeen: *A Handbook for Teaching Caribbean Literature*, London, 1988; specific discussions of the 'teachability' of contemporary Caribbean Writing also forms an integral part of the *Teaching Contemporary Literature Series*, edited by Susanne Peters & Klaus Stierstorfer & Laurenz Volkmann; appeared so far: *Teaching Contemporary Drama*, 2 vols, Trier, 2005, see esp. pp. 295-311 and pp. 527-544.

Silvio Torres-Saillant (Syracuse, NY)

Caribbean Literature III: Towards a New Caribbean Poetics in the 21st Century

1. Preamble

The difficult location of Zadie Smith's first novel, *White Teeth* (2000), in relation to the corpus of writings we think of as Caribbean literature, offers a useful starting point to attempt to prefigure the emphases, texture, and dominant direction of this corpus in the twenty-first century. Based on the intellectual and artistic trends we have witnessed since the last decade, and given the close ties between the literary act and the history of thought in the region, I would like to suggest at the outset that Caribbean writers will for the most part continue to distance themselves exponentially from the features that typified their predecessors. Rather than the affirmation of Caribbean identity that we find in the foundational documents of twentieth-century literature from the region, we have begun to see a growing tendency to challenge identitarian fixities. Similarly, evocations of the uniqueness of the Caribbean person, as a peculiar product of a distinct homogenizing historical experience, has tended to give way to the habit of investigating the creases within Caribbean personhood by stressing the diverse tensions borne out by internal differences of class, language, race, sexuality, gender, and ethnic ancestry. The popular in music, social practices, dance, and non-literate figurations has risen in prominence, at times competing with the power of the intellectual to promote the upliftment of the less empowered and to shed light on the intricacies of Caribbean life. By the same token, along with a widespread critique of nationalism, texts that engage the past, the present, and the future of Caribbean communities have increasingly stressed the long history of transnational exchange that has shaped the lives of the populations in question. They have tended to foreground diasporic locations as integral to the Caribbean experience from the very start of the colonial transaction. They thus show the extent to which the very geography within which Caribbean writing may be said to exist can hardly correspond to the national contours of given nation-states. This is hardly new in Caribbean literary history, as the binational locations of Saint-John Perse and Jean Rhys would indicate, but today the translocal spread of the Caribbean experience in literary practice and representation has attained a formerly unseen centeredness.

2. Inhabiting a Diverse World

The spectacular success of *White Teeth*, a novel that became a sensation the instant it appeared in print in the last year of the twentieth century, further increasing its popularity through an adaptation for the small screen as a BBC-TV miniseries, meaningfully brought Jamaican characters to the average British household. The characters are Clara Bowden, a beautiful black Jamaican woman with false teeth who immigrated to England at age seventeen, arriving in 1972 in the company of her mother Hortense, a vociferously fanatic Jehovah's Witness whose husband, Darcus Bowden, had failed in his plan to save enough money to bring his wife and daughter to Britain. As soon as Darcus arrived in London from Jamaica in 1958, a mysterious illness debilitated him and confined him to an armchair from which he never again removed himself for the rest of his life, a life that he spent in total silence except for the occasional utterance of one single word, "Hmph", and watching British television.[1] Clara married Archibald Jones, a lower-middle class white Englishman who "folds things" for a living, and they had one daughter, Irie Jones, a bright but impressionable young woman who, in the words of a commentator, holds "the novel together"[2]. Clarence and Denzel, two old Creole-speaking Jamaicans, regulars at O'Donnell's Café, a site to which the scene of the action recurringly returns throughout the novel, complete the Caribbean *dramatis personae*.

One might hasten to classify *White Teeth* as a Caribbean text given the prominence of characters, situations, and historical memories linking London institutions to the Caribbean. Witness the case of Glenard Oak, the school the young characters attend, which is named after Sir Edmund Flecker Glenard (1842-1907), a benefactor who had made his wealth in the malefaction of colonial exploitation on the islands.[3] However, such a classification would not exhaust the book's entire identity. The characters in the novel inhabit the urban arena of northwest London in the last three decades of the twentieth century, and they share their time and space with members of other branches of the human family. Archibald and Clara live in intimate proximity with Bangladeshi Muslim immigrant Samad Miah Iqbal, his self-assertive wife Alsana, and their two sons Magid and Millat. The two families, in turn, interact intensively with Jewish-descended Oxford University scientist Marcus Chalfen, his devoted Irish wife Joyce, and their willful son Joshua. In the collage of heritages that the novel ventures to interweave for its interethnic tapestry, *White Teeth* "jumps across walls of race and class in a manner typical of late twentieth-century multicultural youth culture in London", making it unwise to attempt "to fit it neatly and entirely into any past or present literary tradition", says critic Jan Lowe, who nonetheless recognizes the way "Caribbean culture and its legacy" emerge in the text as the primary source of resistance in "the melting pot of Britain's multicultural youth culture".[4] The novelist herself would seem to stress the currency of the Caribbean in the London cosmos that her characters inhabit. At one point the narrator comments thus when describing an exchange between Samad's two boys: "'*Cha*, man! Believe, I don't want to tax dat crap,' said Millat with the Jamaican accent that all kids, whatever their nationality, used to express scorn".[5]

Though left unglossed by the author, the title of Jan Lowe's review of *White Teeth*, "No More Lonely Londoners", evidently alludes to the title of the 1956 novel by Samuel Selvon to suggest that the Caribbean immigrants and their children who populate Smith's novel are not "lonely". Unlike the characters in *The Lonely Londoners*, who inhabit a West Indian enclave, in virtual isolation from other ethnically differentiated segments of the city population, they regularly interact, influence, are influenced by, and intermarry with people of Asian, Jewish, Irish, Arab, and white English descent. They, in other words, form part of the fabric of which London society is made. Smith probably had this in mind when answering the question "How were you trying to approach multiracial London?" during her stint as a Radcliffe Fellow at Harvard University for the 2002-2003 academic year. She simply said: "I was just trying to approach London. I don't think of it as a theme, or even as a significant thing about the city. This is what modern life is like. If I were to write a book about London in which there were only white people, I think that would be kind of bizarre".[6] We might be justified in deducing from this pithy remark that the literary instinct to do justice to the interracial and multicultural tapestry of modern London carries more weight in the novel than the desire to tell the story of Caribbean people. Her Jamaicans represent only one of the colors that give London its polychromatic hue.

Ironically, many of the features that render *White Teeth* problematic as a member of the Caribbean family of literary texts correspond dynamically to the emphases that set the most recent literary developments in the Caribbean apart from the works of earlier generations. Indeed, the novel consistently invites reflection on the most recurring issues surfacing in the body of utterances that one might generically describe as the 'new' Caribbean thought, namely the formulations interpretive of the region's past, present and future voiced by the generation of writers, scholars, and thinkers that began their publishing career starting in the 1980s. Brian Meeks places the emergence of new paradigms for the study of the Caribbean in the context of the deleterious consequences of three decades of economic decline, structural adjustment, and the failure of development projects in the region that signaled "the demise of an entire notion of sovereignty and non-alignment".[7] The economic and political futility ushered in by the 1980s brought about "the debilitating retreat of the intellectual both from politics and the project of serious inquiry".[8] Concomitantly, a new generation of Caribbean academics, made up of younger scholars formed in Canada, the United States, and Europe who, by virtue of their emigration had escaped the "corrosive effect of economic decline" in the region, engaged in an eclectic interdisciplinary search for fitting approaches to understanding the human drama of their homelands.[9] Meeks regards their development as one that amounts to "a renaissance" in Caribbean social, economic, and political thought.[10] Salient emphases among the representatives of these new voices on the horizon of Caribbean thought include critiques of nationalism, post-Marxist formulations, deployment of postmodernist and postcolonial axes of analysis, and problematizations of previously established ways of imagining the Caribbean community.

In a study that approaches the Caribbean as a site within the larger global geography of postcolonialism, anthropologist David Scott deploys a sensitive critique of Afrocentric interpretations of Caribbean culture as represented by the work of Kamau Brathwaite.[11] He thus allies himself conceptually, though not uncritically, with Paul Gilroy's adamant rebuke against cultural nationalists and racial essentialists, crediting him with breaking with rationalist historiography and cultural nationalism in black diaspora criticism.[12] Scott's non-chalant advice, however, that we read Frantz Fanon 'with' Michel Foucault reveals a willingness to relinquish from the outset the ambition to assert the Caribbean as a self-sustaining site of intellectual production.[13] As it relates to the overall movement of society, he envisions a political scenario in which "Jamaica would no longer be about political parties, periodic elections, or even Parliament", but it would be refashioned so as to "multiply the relational identities that can be enacted or practiced, the subjectivities that can appear as constituent members of a pluralizable, public sphere".[14] In thinking the Caribbean, Scott occupies himself with decentering and departiculiarizing so as to arrive at a new conceptualization of "postcolonial politics"[15]. Anthropologist Charles V. Carnegie, a Caribbeanist of the same generation, shares the impetus to decenter but retains the commitment to particularize the Caribbean experience as an instance with the capability to contribute meaningful knowledge to the rest of the human family. Convinced that the nation-state neither assures well-being nor is amenable to reform, Carnegie represents the Caribbean as a region that, expressly formed on the orbit of the nation state, has continuously breached its "ideological and political claims and reach", thus assigning to the region an exemplary position in world affairs.[16] The Caribbean, in his view, leads other parts of the world in the practice of "transnational modes of dwelling", making available potential models for "new modes of belonging".[17]

In keeping with the complex manner of figuration reflected in the interventions of Scott and Carnegie, the evocation of Caribbean life penned by the literary artists since the 1980s have leaned toward the decentering of national belonging, ethnicity, and identity as a whole. The Jamaican poet, fiction writer, and cultural historian Olive Senior has asserted her hybrid ancestry by taking a decentering view of identity. She has said "I represent many races and I'm not rejecting any of them to please anybody".[18] The title story in her second collection of short fiction, *Arrival of the Snake-Woman* (1989), creates the character of an Indian woman as the protagonist who confronts and subverts the structure of patriarchal abuse by exerting herself in her ethnic difference and sexual subjectivity. Senior's foregrounding of an Indian woman to enact a stance of Caribbean womanhood undeniably contributes to inscribing the memory of rural India "on the Caribbean landscape", evincing "the Indian indentured experience as an integral part of a larger historical experience, sharing a common language of both disinheritance and self-determination with the Afro-Caribbean majority and other ethnic and mixed-race minorities".[19] Caribbean writers who themselves trace their ancestry back to India have compellingly voiced the urgency of moving beyond "conventionally defined paradigms of Caribbean-ness" that have relegated the Indo-Caribbean heritage to a rank of invisibility.

One can easily see the urgency to assert a presence in characteristic lines from David Dabydeen's *Coolie Odyssey* (1984): "We mark our memory in songs / Fleshed in the emptiness of folk, / Poems that scrape bowls and bone / In English basements far from home".[20] Having left Guyana for England at age 12, Dabydeen speaks largely for the Indo-Caribbean experience in Britain. Literary efforts to mark the presence in the countries of the region go back at least to the 1934 Guyanese compilation *Anthology of Indian Verse*, edited by C. E. J. Ramcharitar-Lalla.[21] None of the poets included seems to have achieved enough distinction to be remembered today, but in recent decades few could ignore the talent of the late Mahadai Das, a native of Guyana committed to bearing witness to the endurance of her Indian heritage. Her first collection of poems, tellingly entitled *I Want to be a Poetess of My People* (1977), traces the roots of her community from indentureship to independence. Included in that volume, the memorable poem "They Came in Ships" contains lines that effectively weave her gender and ethnic self-affirmation: "I stand 'twixt posterity's horizon / And her history. / I, alone today, am alive, / Seeing beyond, looking ahead".[22] That the compulsion to bear witness is hardly circumscribable to English-speaking writers is clear from the estimable work of the Surinamese Jit Narain, whose verse, in Dutch as well as in Sarnami, memorializes the Hindustani immigrant experience in Surinam. "Why he left India, that I can fathom; / that India never left him, is the burden I bear," says a poem of his that meditates on the parental origins of his ethnic awareness.[23] On the whole, Indo-Caribbean writers, and particularly the women, have demonstrated ideological sophistication in exalting their Indian roots while simultaneously "exposing the perniciousness of Hindu racial, class, and gender prejudice".[24] Though each in her own distinctive voice, such authors as Mahadai Das, Ramabai Espinet, Jan Shinebourne, Rosanne Kanhai, Shani Mootoo, Michelle Mohabeer, Kamala Kempadoo, Laksmi Persaud, Lelawattee Manoo-Rahming, Rajandaye Ramkisoon-Chen, Oony Kempadoo, and Narmala Shewcharan seem jointly to aspire to a capacious understanding of Caribbean identity that facilitates the natural recognition of ethnoracial difference, the equitable partnership of males and females in the public and private domains, and the necessarily transnational space of belonging.[25] That the overwhelming majority of these Indo-Caribbean women writers have taken up residence elsewhere makes the separation of their identitarian space and the discrete geography of their ancestral homeland particularly relevant.

3. Multiple Origins, Destinations, Visions

Invested in disrupting conventional fixities regarding ancestry and geography as determinants of identity, the Guyanese-born short fiction writer, novelist and actress Pauline Melville seems to relish in the difficulty that her own origins presents to those requiring homogeneity. She reminds us that reggae legend Bob Marley chose to identify with his black roots inherited from his mother, but he could have conceivably leaned toward his father's Anglo-Scottish ancestry.[26] The title story in Melville's memorable collection of short fiction *The Migration of Ghosts* features a couple made up of Guyanese landowner Vincent Dawes and his Amerindian wife Loretta, as they, five years into their marriage, travel to London and Prague prior to returning to Brazil, where Victor has a small holding. Walking across a bridge in Prague they come upon a band of six young musicians playing traditional Slovakian songs on fiddles and a drum. When Loretta looks at the drummer in the face, she catches her breath in astonishment: "He was unmistakably a native Indian like her: the same jet-black straight hair, the same brown face and flat features and fat brown eyelids over black pebble eyes".[27] Sharing his wife's impression of the drummer as "an Amerindian boy", Vincent approaches the young man in search of confirmation. After an exchange in which the speakers tried to overcome their language barriers, Vincent comes back with a negative finding. Apparently, a native of Mongolia in the former USSR, the young man immigrated to Prague with his parents only a few years before. Vincent, an educated man, the child of communist parents, who "always went somewhere in the Eastern bloc for our summer holidays" during his childhood, knows enough history to offer a plausible explanation of the intriguing resemblance: "your people are supposed to have come over from Mongolia originally, across the Bering Strait".[28] The daughter of a Macusi Indian from the Guyanese side of the Brazilian border, Loretta, in Prague, a world away from home, comes face to face with a distant relative. The scene closes as the young man slings the drum across his shoulder, eyeing Loretta with curiosity, nodding acknowledgement, and giving a little bow, while she smiles back at him: "They faced each other across tens of thousands of years".[29]

Melville has described her own ancestry in a way that perhaps explains her interest in investigating the elasticity and complexity of roots as they extend over vast expanses of space and time:

> I look completely English. My mother is English, second of ten children from a London family, a tribe of Anglo-Saxons if ever there was one, blonde and blue-eyed. The photographs show St. Augustine's angels in hand-me-down clothes. My father was born in Guyana (or British Guiana as it was then), also the second of ten children. The photographs show a genetic bouquet of African, Amerindian and European features, a family gazing out from dark, watchful eyes – all except one, who turned out with the looks of a Dutchman. But then, Berbice, their birthplace, was a Dutch colony in the eighteenth century. I am the whitey in the woodpile.[30]

A document kept safely in a drawer at home, her great-great-grandmother's baptism certificate, dated 13 June 1832, which identifies her ancestress as "Slave of D. Melville", enables her to remain mindful of her loaded identity: "White present, black past, a good position for […] shifting boundaries and unfixing fixities".[31] "I think of my Amerindian forbears," she says, recalling their presumed arrival "originally from Mongolia", to ask rhetorically: "Do I have a Mongolian herdsman galloping along the spidery pathways of my DNA?"[32] Melville, of course, did not expect an answer when she wrote those words in 1991. But her own literary insight, as captured in the encounter of Loretta with her distant relative in Prague, would seem to venture an answer: that the Mongolian herdsman will have by now been transformed, appearing not as a horseman but as a displaced worker who has ended up in the land of the Czechs, whose culture (beginning with traditional Slovakian songs) he has begun to internalize in order to eke out a living.

Another aspect of Melville's fiction relevant to the present discussion is her character's often unproblematic location in more than one national geography as they smoothly straddle disparate polities and class locations. The scene of the action in the story "English Table Wuk", for instance, takes places in Georgetown, Guyana, but Auntie May, the owner of the house, is on her way to take a flight to Miami that afternoon, and she, thus, cannot afford the time to mind the guests her niece Adriana has brought to the house. Home "from studying sociology at university in England", where her radical classmates disapproved of her upbringing, namely her coming from a middle-class family which employed servants, Adriana must negotiate different social sensibilities, leading at times to awkward moments.[33] Her aunt gone to the airport, Adriana mistakes for a theft a loan of china, antique silver knives and forks by Gita, one of the maids. Her initial distrust gradually turns into curiosity and she learns about the annual ceremony near the burial ground opposite a former orange plantation where the descendants of slaves, people at the bottom rung of the social ladder, set an elegant and abundant banquet ("the wealth of the display" in sharp contrast "to the appearance of the people") for the purpose of appeasing "the spirits of the English dead who bury across de road right here", as Gita explains.[34] The ceremony's cross-cultural and inter-class displacement is perhaps foreshadowed by the interest with which Adriana's guests in the opening scene follow every detail in the televised funeral of the late Diana, Princess of Wales, in the middle of a Georgetown in which power failures can interrupt the simple pass-time of watching TV in the house. The scene happens in the same Guyana where, as the speaker in a poem by Grace Nichols would put it: "Blackout is endemic to the land. / People have grown sixth sense and sonic ways, like bats, / emerging out of the shadows / into the light of their own flesh".[35]

With her tendency to foreground the varied and hybrid texture of life for Caribbean people in terms of the ethnoracial, geographical, social, and cultural location of her characters, Melville belongs to a generation of writers that abhors homogeneity in the dissection of their societies of origin. Among the most provocative manifestations of that outlook is afforded by the dynamic fiction writer Robert Antoni, whose books explore the multilocality of Caribbean life that he himself embodies. Born in Detroit, Michigan, to Trinidadian parents, Antoni spent many of his formative years in Bahamas and studied creative writing in U.S. universities. A biographical sketch attached to one of his widely circulated stories highlights the fact that he "carries three passports: US, Trinidad and Tobago, and the Bahamas".[36] His award-winning first novel *Divina Trace* (1991) introduced readers to his fictional island of Corpus Christi, the ground on which his characters congregate across several books. Stylistically the novel enacts a festival of multiplicity as all of eight characters – the unifying narrator Johnny Domingo, Jr. and seven additional speakers who share with him their recollections – contribute to assemble the assorted account of Magdalena Divina. Consistent with their diverse origins, experiences, perspectives, and desires, their testimonies are conveyed through a variety of genres, narrative techniques, and expressive forms to suit the distinct voice of each individual speaker. Antoni's second novel, *Blessed is the Fruit* (1997), turns on the initially distant and ultimately tender relationship between a white mistress, Lilla, and her longtime black servant, Vel. Stemming from the race and class divide that set them socially apart, their distance crumbles under the weight of the tenderness brought about by the gender solidarity that the latter's pregnancy triggers.

Carnival (2005), the author's third novel, adds complexity of outlook to the Caribbean's difficult interweavings of class, race, and gender. The white Trinidadian narrator, William Fletcher, an economically well-off expatriate, reunites by chance at a bar in New York City with his childhood friends Lawrence and Rachel, his boyhood love for the latter quickly rekindled. There they resolve to return to their country together during carnival time to reconnect with their homeland. Rather than experiencing their country's amiable embrace, the three expatriates endure the frenzy of dance, music, drunkenness, and uninhibited sensuality, followed by an eventful foray deep into the island's mountainous interior, in a manner that further exacerbates their disconnection from Trinidad. The tensions borne of the interplay of racism, sexuality, and violence prove too conspicuous for the equalizing masks of carnival to mitigate them. David Dabydeen, whose review of *Carnival* stresses the novel's intertextual rapport with Ernest Hemingway's *The Sun Also Rises* (1926), finds that Antoni weaves into the story a "desperately tender and hopeful" outlook communicated through "a beauty" that is "always within human reach, however slowly we move towards it, hobbled by the self-inflicted wounds of race, class, and gender".[37] It remains true, however, that the novel refrains from endorsing a view of Caribbean self-affirmation insofar as the Trinidadian expatriates end up flying back to their deracinated lives in Europe and the United States.

The closing of *Carnival*, though perhaps 'hopeful' at some generically human level, may be said to represent the ambivalence of the latest generation of Caribbean writers to commit themselves to a particularly salutary and specifically Caribbean vision of the future. It will perhaps not be deemed excessive extrapolation to detect a less than cheerful sense of possibility in the lines "I am gathering the relics of a broken threnody, / lisping psalms – all I have – and crying salt and wet" from the poem "Liminal" by the Ghanaian-born Jamaican poet Kwame Dawes or to discern a despondent outlook in the Heather Royes poem whose speaker sees no point in continuing to read poetry: "Mesmerised by the present, / forsaking the past, my mind / a jealous lover holds each moment / much longer than it lasts. / Time slips away and with it/dreams. / I no longer read poetry".[38] On the whole, present-day formulations of Caribbean prospects will at best convey a sense of ambivalence about the good that may come. At one level the ambivalence may reflect the pervasiveness of a Western postmodern sensibility that has influenced writers and intellectuals internationally in light of the increased currency of Western thought globally. A critical observer of this phenomenon has noted that postmodernism developed in the industrialized consumer-driven societies where thinkers have rendered class an antiquated concept and that it is mostly through an act of intellectual mimicry that the post-modern sensibility has found echo in non-industrialized Caribbean societies.[39] But irrespective of the influence of postmodernism, especially as it relates to its widespread reticence to conceive of any notion of history that might hearken to the certainties espoused by Enlightenment thinkers about the future of the species, the new generation of writers and thinkers chronicling the Caribbean experience and conceptualizing the structure of life there have reasons of their own to flaunt their distance from the formulations of their elders regarding the representation and the prospects of the Caribbean community.

Admittedly, figurations of the Caribbean person in the literature and thought of the region often assumed a monolithic form. Evincing a homogeneity that today we would regard as alarming in light of its known record of exclusion, earlier generations of authors tended to envision the Caribbean person through the recurring image of a black male of humble extraction endowed with a revolutionary vision or a state of mind conducive to liberatory missions. One thinks of Jacques Roumain's Manuel in *Gouverneurs de la rosée* (1944), the archetypal Caliban conceptualized by Georges Lamming in *The Pleasures of Exile* (1960), the generic Maroon in Anton de Kom's *We, Slaves of Surinam* (1934), or the ex-slave turned independence warrior in the character of Esteban Montejo from Miguel Barnet's *Autobiografía de un cimarrón* (1968), to name only a few of the most prominent texts. By stark contrast, the menu of race, class, gender, and ideological options currently available to writers to epitomize the human drama in the Caribbean appears to have considerably expanded. The cast of characters who at present serve literary artists as props to evoke or remember their region's past need not follow the moral or political prescriptions discernible in the texts of their predecessors. A widely circulated heralding of Cuba's future possibilities may come via the sex-driven Cuca Martínez whose life in Havana follows the call of the wild as she holds on to her obsessive and unrequited love for the unreliable and hardly corrigible Juan Pérez in *Te di la vida entera* (1998) by Zoé Valdez. The protagonist may take the form of a cross-dresser such as Lowe, the Chinese woman who for decades has had to pass for a male shopkeeper in rural Jamaica, from Patricia Powell's novel *Pagoda* (1998). Similarly, writers may select to draw on the historical memory to imagine what it may have felt like for a white heiress of her father's Caribbean plantation to travel from the safety of England to take stock of her property of business, land, and slaves, as does Emily in Caryl Phillips' novel *Cambridge* (1991) or for a free black, slave-owning businesswoman in eighteenth–century Surinam to compete successfully in the white male-controlled plantation economy as does Elisabeth

Samson in *De vrije negerin Elisabeth: Gevangene van Kleur* (2000) by Cynthia McLeod.

Apart from a greater flexibility of sexual mores, an ampler recognition of the multiplicity of ethnic and cultural roots of the population, a quicker willingness to acknowledge class differences, and a wider recognition of ideological diversity informing the sensibility of people in the region, the texts of the newer generation of Caribbean writers also seem to reflect a keener observation of the mobility of the Caribbean person not only from the region to elsewhere in the globe but also within societies in the region itself. For instance, the site where the clash between the clairvoyant Zule and her murderous foe Simila in Mayra Montero's *Del rojo de su sombra* (1996) takes place is the Dominican Republic, but the characters are mostly Haitian as a result of decades of labor migration that resulted in the spreading of bateyes and immigrant settlements along the border dividing the two countries that share the island of Hispaniola. A Cuban who, born in Havana in 1952, has lived in Puerto Rico since settling there in 1972, Montero has first-hand knowledge of intra-Caribbean mobility. We se Leocadio, the main character in *Sirena Selena vestida de pena* (2000) by Mayra Santos Febres, start out in San Juan, Puerto Rico, where his life at age 15 already shows dim prospects given his drug habit and social destitution. Enchanted by his beauty and luring singing voice, Martha Divine, the transsexual owner of the cabaret the Blue Danube, resolves to rescue him from the streets and turn him into a transvestite diva. Leocadio's success secured in Puerto Rico, Martha then engineers his foray into the entertainment circles of Santo Domingo, Dominican Republic, where the young man's beauty, voice, and magnetism gain him the adoration of an affluent businessman in an elite circle. That Martha should think of Santo Domingo as a destination for Leocadio, despite the young man's Dominican origins, to move up in his line of work might seem odd in view of the place of otherness that things Dominican often occupy in Puerto Rican society. There the migratory flow of devalued workers from the Dominican Republic tends to locate the immigrants in a position of social marginality in the host country. Perhaps the author's interest in margins and in destabilizing the very notion of marginality might explain her exploration of transvestism and transsexuality as well as her resignification of the Dominican space. Elucidating her attraction for the subject of her novel, Santos Febres has said:

> I do not believe in fixed marginalities, perhaps because several apply to me. I am a woman, black, Caribbean, and who knows which other things that relegate me to a margin. But I have seen that this margin is always mobile. Sometimes I find myself at the center (by reason of education, perhaps of class), and sometimes I am despised (by reason of skin color, or for coming from a country colonized by the United States). Precisely because of that mobility I allow myself to travel through various worlds, various margins, and sometimes even through the center. I thus get connected with the people who, like me, walk around the place transgressing social boundaries".[40]

The intra-Caribbean mobility of people that has emerged among the features emphasized by younger writers in their representation of the region has also been noted by George Lamming who has upheld "a concept of Nation that is not defined by specific territorial boundaries", precisely because of his awareness of the historical scattering of Caribbean peoples across various latitudes within and beyond the region.[41] Lamming points to the advent of "the transnational family", a phenomenon "which does not allow a funeral in Barbados to take place for over a week after the death" for the sake of completing the cortege with relatives arriving "from Jamaica, Trinidad, Guyana, Toronto, Birmingham, Brooklyn".[42] Lamming contends that the rise of "the transnational household" results from two factors, "the political and cultural consequences of sexual intercourse" and "the economic compulsion to migrate".[43] He recalls his first sojourn in Trinidad in 1946 when he took up residence in Belmont: "I discovered that in every family I got to know, the only Trinidadians by birth were the children. Mothers, fathers, aunts, uncles had originated elsewhere."[44] Regarding labor mobility, he notes that "from the middle of the nineteenth century to the second decade of the twentieth, Barbados provided over fifty thousand workers to Guyana and Trinidad", and that the population of Trinidad and Tobago doubled from 1844 to 1881 owing to "this movement of our peoples from St. Vincent, Grenada, and as far as St. Martin in the northeast".[45] The gradual intermingling of people in the region, which in Lamming's view gives credence to the contention by his friend George Beckford that it is only the governments that remain aloof to the already existing integration, continues a process that began over one hundred years ago.[46] Scholars looking at the border crossing of slaves from one colonial domain to another or between territories in order to enhance their chances of freedom would extend Lamming's chronology to some two centuries earlier. Until 1790 slaves from Danish, French, English, and other colonies could escape to Spanish colonial domains and generally count on receiving succor and winning their freedom. By the same token, runaways fled from St. Croix and St. Thomas to Puerto Rico and the smaller island of Vieques, from St. Domingue across to the mountainous Santo Domingo border, from Jamaica's northern coast to Cuba, and from eastern Caribbean islands to Trinidad, creating a long pattern of "transfrontier marronage throughout the region".[47]

4. Diaspora as Locus of Identity

The history of transnational life may actually be coterminous with the chronology of colonialism and its aftermath in the Caribbean, which has been a cradle of cross-cultural marriages, widening and intertwining of intraregional family networks, and the multiplicity of identities that ensue from such relations. The mobility of Caribbean slaves also involved overseas relocations. We may gather this from the fact that up to 1700 "all slaves in South Carolina came from the Caribbean and Barbados in particular", and that throughout the eighteenth century from 15 to 20 percent of all enslaved workers came from the same origin.[48] Early in the seventeenth century slaves from Barbados made up a substantial portion of Virginia's black population, and as late as 1860 one in five black Bostonians had come from Barbados or elsewhere in the Caribbean.[49] The heavy flow of intra-Caribbean and centrifugal migration normally followed the fluctuations of the plantation economy. For instance, between 1924 and 1940 workers from Grenada, Barbados, Antigua, and St. Kitts gravitated to employment opportunities available to them in the oil refineries of Aruba and Curaçao, whereas in the period roughly from 1945 to 1965 the European metropolises and the United States emerged as predominant destination for mass Caribbean emigration.[50] During the mid 1960s, with the removal of racially discriminatory biases in the immigration legislation, Canada began to rival the other major destinations for migrants from the Anglophone Caribbean, leading to today's substantial immigrant settlements in Toronto, Montreal, and Quebec.[51]

Consistent with the momentum bequeathed by the long history of mobility, intra-regional migration and emigration from the region have continued to grow, with nearly 5.5 million people leaving the Caribbean between 1950 and 1989, an exodus that has turned the émigré population into "an important source of household income" in many Caribbean "societies as well as a major aspect of people-based integration within the social life of the region".[52] Since the conquest and colonization that started in 1492 mobilized large masses of people from Europe, Africa, and Asia, and since the colonial transaction itself promoted the regular flow of humans between Western metropoliscs and their overseas territories, the historical experience of the Caribbean may be said to have revolved around the constant rapport between "here and elsewhere". Glancing at the past 500 years, demographer Aaron Segal maintains that "the Caribbean region has borne the deepest and most continuous impact from international migration of any region in the world".[53] "Everybody in the Caribbean comes from somewhere else", says Stuart Hall, a thought which, compounded by the awareness of the historical forces that have caused people from the region to go elsewhere, probably explains his understanding of the Caribbean as "the first, the original, and the purest diaspora".[54] By the same token, relying on his literary insight, sociologist and novelist Orlando Patterson decades ago encouraged a view of the Anansi legend as a representation of migrancy: "The spider is a migrant. It can live anywhere, in trees or houses or caves or nowhere in particular, for the spider carries its home, its only real home, buried in its belly".[55]

A meaningful consequence of the intense involvement of Caribbean people in migratory movements is the creation of a literary tradition with tributaries spreading across different polities, geographies, languages, and cultural heritages. Increasingly, the makers of the corpus of Caribbean letters seem to live and work elsewhere. To illustrate this point, let it suffice to observe that in the volume of interviews of fourteen Anglophone Caribbean poets put together by Kwame Dawes only three – St. Lucians John Robert Lee and the married couple Jane King and Kendel Hyppotyte – reside in the region. The remainder make their home elsewhere:

Trinidadian Claire Harris in Calgary, Jamaican Olive Senior mostly in Toronto, Guyanese Cyril Dabydeen in Ottawa, Jamaican Lorna Goodison in Michigan, Trinidadian Ramabai Espinet in Canada, Guyanese Grace Nichols in Britain, Jamaican Lillian Allen in Canada, Jamaican Opal Odesa Palmer in Oakland, California, Guyanese David Dabydeen in the United Kingdom, Jamaican Afua Cooper in Toronto, and Guyanese-descendant, English-born Fred D'Aguiar in Florida.[56] Consistent with the foregoing scenario, one notes a tendency among literary scholars and compilers of anthologies to erase the boundary between literature produced in the region and the writings crafted by the emigres and their children even when, as a result of an education and a literary training taking place elsewhere, language differences have emerged. Seeking to conceptualize their grouping of poets from the region and the diaspora in their anthology of Caribbean verse, editors Stuart Brown and Mark McWatt have posited that, not only does migration exist as "the defining experience of Caribbean 'being'", but that, unlike those of earlier generations, migrations today no longer entail "a breaking of ties" with the sending homelands, making it hard to draw a rigid line between here and there. Applying that scenario to literary production, they have the following proposition:

> The twenty-first century Caribbean aesthetic depends less on a lived geography than on a distinctive perspective on history, a perspective that reflects the creole nature of Caribbean societies.[57]

The merging of here and there that Brown and McWatt articulate seems to be assumed as self-evident in the literary compendia of others. In a recent compilation Haitian-American fiction writer Edwidge Danticat, who was raised in the United States and writes in English, and Myriam Chancy, who grew up in Anglophone regions of Canada, appear considered in the same breath with authors based in Haiti such as Yanick Lahens and Jan J. Dominique, who write in French, and the Creolophone poet and novelist Franketienne without any apparent compulsion on the part of the editors to draw distinctions.[58] Similarly, a study of the poetry of "contemporary Caribbean women" focusing on poets from the Anglophone region makes no distinction between poets based in the native land, such as the late Mahadai Das, who stayed in Guyana until her death in 2003, those based in Canada, such as M. Nourbese Phillip, and longtime residents of Britain such as Amryl Johnson, Valerie Bloom, and Grace Nichols.[59] Showing that the tendency to fuse the diasporic with the homeland space as one seamless literary terrain applies to the various language origins of Caribbean writers, a recent study concentrates on the works of Michele Cliff, Jamaica Kincaid, Edwidge Danticat, Jan J. Dominique, Julia Alvarez, and Rosario Ferre for an examination of questions related to body, nation, and empire in "Modern Caribbean Literature by Women", evincing a predominance of diaspora voices in representing the Caribbean experience to the world.[60] Perhaps as a result of the increasing binationality of the corpus of Caribbean writing, the practical normalizing of its straddling geographies and nations, the tension between 'exile and return' that many scholars have recognized as a motif in the region's seminal texts had begun to lose currency.[61]

While writers in the diaspora today may still echo the yearnings of migrant voices stretching back at least to Mary Prince, the West Indian slave who escaped to London and there published her *History* in 1831, the relative ease with which they have owned to their binationality as inhabitants of a diasporic space would seem to suggest an overcoming of "the anxiety and polemics" that formerly "marked the issue of a Caribbean writer's physical location".[62] Whether or not we might agree with Louis James' claim that the deterritorializing of Caribbean writing grants it "global significance", placing it "in a central position within world literature", one must recognize the value of his observation concerning the "shadowy borders between Caribbean writing in English, and British, black United States and Black Canadian writing".[63] Indeed, one can discern among diasporic voices of the current generation a propinquity to occupy an identitarian location that transcends the contours of Caribbeanness. The collection *Empire Windrush*, whose title evokes a distinct moment in the history of West Indian mobility to the British Isles, groups Caribbean-descended writers like Beryl Gilroy, Meiling Jin, Andrea Levy, Victor Headley, and Merle Collins with authors originating from Africa and other parts of the 'Commonwealth', the organizing principle of the volume centering around "writing about Black Britain".[64] Another collection brings the texts of six Caribbean authors together with similar numbers of Asian and African ones, focusing on "the impact of Britain" on them as the overreaching theme.[65] These collections for the most part choose to rely on reactive identity formulations by stressing the blackness of the writers in contradistinction of the whiteness of the mainstream, in one case, and the cultural otherness of the writers included in contradistinction to the Englishness that defines the center, in the other. Since Anglophone Caribbean writers share with writers from other corners of the 'Commonwealth' a difficult rapport with whiteness and the cultural values of Englishness, they have generally come to share with them also the embrace of the new geopolitics of identity that, renaming the domain of the British Commonwealth and extending its nomenclatural reach to territories dominated by the other imperial powers as well, has denominated nearly two thirds of the globe with the rubric of the 'postcolonial world'. Blackness, cultural otherness with respect to a Western mainstream, and now postcoloniality have become available to Caribbean writers as large identitarian spaces that subsume their region-specific Caribbeanness.

5. Change of Gender Guard

With the rise of women as a predominant presence among the makers of Caribbean literature starting in the 1970s, significant new paradigms have entered the conversation regarding the nature and texture of Caribbean people and their relationship with other branches of the human family.[66] Often the very notion of travel, the existential gliding over large expanses of culturally or politically marked soil, has provided the thematic basis for reading the works of contemporary Caribbean women authors.[67] Trinidadian literary scholar Rhonda Cobham and Grenadian fiction writer and poet Merle Collins chose the intersection of gender, race, and cultural otherness, namely the markers afforded by the category 'Black women in Britain', as the identitarian space within which to place the works of six Anglophone Caribbean writers in their anthology *Watchers and Seekers*.[68] Similarly, her exploration of the "migratory subject" in the works of Afro-Caribbean women authors along with the texts of African American, Black British, and African women writers by critic Carole Boyce Davies stems from her understanding of the literature produced by black female authors "not as a fixed, geographical, ethnically or nationally bound category of writing", but as one whose study requires "cross-cultural, transnational, diasporic perspectives".[69] Haitian-Canadian fiction writer and scholar Myriam J. A. Chancy too draws on a combination of blackness and migration to organize an understanding of the works of Afro-Caribbean women writers based in Britain (Joan Riley and Beryl Gilroy), Canada (M. Nourbese Phillip, Dionne Brand, Makeda Silvera and Afua Cooper), and the United States (Audre Lorde, Rosa Guy, Michelle Cliff, and Marie Chauvet). Chancy's study, however, retains the commitment to organizing a Caribbean literary knowledge, and her expanding the inquiry into the African-American literary terrain of the United States finds conceptual justification in the strong cross-cultural ties that have historically linked the U.S. black and Afro-Caribbean communities.[70] She strengthens this point by stressing the African American women writers who traced their origin back to the Caribbean and wrote about it, such as Audre Lorde, Paule Marshall, and June Jordan, as well as by arguing that Afro-Caribbean women writers generally adopt the tenets of U.S.-based black feminism in forging their own feminist theories pertinent to their particular geopolitical situation.[71] The inclusion of Francophone Haitian novelist Marie Chauvet in a study that focuses primarily on the writings of Anglophone Afro-Caribbean women can be explained by the time Chauvet spent writing in exile in the United States insofar as exile, along with blackness, provides the key axis of analysis in Chancy's monograph.[72] The experience of exile actualizes what Chancy refers to as "the paradox of home", namely the existential scenario whereby the ancestral homeland can alternate, simultaneously occur, or offer a choice between "the site of self-discovery and the point of no return" in the writer's imagination.[73]

As the foregoing would suggest, then, Caribbean women follow diverse routes to chart their identitarian path in representing the world to which they belong. They do not collectively adhere to one single metadiscourse to evoke their human experience in the Caribbean and its corresponding diaspora. Womanist and Third World perspectives along with Postcolonialism and Afrocentrism appear in their formulations in varying degrees of emphasis, making for a variegated figuration of the structure of Caribbean life. Even the renunciation of the idea of homeland as a stable dwelling space may find expression in their texts, as we gather from the exile Cuban poet Belkis Cuza Malé's poem "My Mother's Homeland", which, among other things, says: "My mother always said / your homeland is any place, / preferably the place where you die".[74] This matters a great deal in light of the predominant role of women among the literary figures who have achieved distinction since the 1980s. In the late 1970s women poets from the Anglophone Caribbean began to show a distinct leadership, clearly indicating their reticence to satisfy themselves with playing a supporting role in relation to the men who formerly dominated the literary scene.[75] Few documents of feminist dissidence have articulated their sense of protest against the traps of patriarchy's deference toward the disempowered feminine more cogently than these lines from "Woman Descendant" by Cynthia James: "this is your daughter / […] / my womb is eternity / my backbone is history / […] / to be free from fixations / that commend me and degrade me, / disrespect me in respect".[76] The literary emergence of women manifested itself in a series of memorable compilations that evidently intended to mark their presence, from *Jamaica Woman* (1980), edited by Mervyn Morris and Pamela Mordecai, to *Creation Fire* (1990), assembled by Ramabai Espinet. As the 'demography' of West Indian poetry shifted, with diaspora and region-based authors contending for predominance in the continued construction of the Caribbean corpus, women again seemed to lead the way. The names of Jean 'Binta' Breeze, Mahadai Das, Opal Odesa Palmer, Claudia Rankine, Claire Harris, Dionne Brand, M. Nourbese Phillip, Merle Collins, Christine Craig, Gloria Escoffery, Lorna Goodison, Judith Hamilton, Jane King, Meiling Jin, Jennifer Raheem, Beverly Brown, and Cynthia James, among various others, achieved considerable distinction.[77] In the extent to which diaspora voices, particularly in the United States, increased in number and significance, the centrality of women became further accentuated. The overwhelming majority of the truly successful U.S. Caribbean diaspora writers are indisputably women: Paule Marshall, Edwidge Danticat, Julia Alvarez, Cristina Garcia, Esmeralda Santiago, Rhina P. Espaillat, to name only the most highly regarded, best-selling, and award-winning literary figures who have conquered the book market in recent decades. Given the efflorescence of women in the region and in the vast geography of the diaspora, one must concede that at present they bear on their shoulders the maintenance and advancement of the literary tradition. With that change of gender guard has come necessarily a greater degree of aesthetic, social, ideological, thematic, and formal diversity than the Caribbean corpus seemed to show in earlier decades.

6. Enduring Visions of the Popular

Contemporaneous with the rise of women writers, Caribbean literature has seen a foregrounding of formerly devalued expressive forms from the realm of popular culture. To be sure, Caribbean writing never alienated itself from popular and folk expressive forms. We can tell, among other things, from Kamau Brathwaite's early effort to formulate the emergence of the 'jazz novel' in the Caribbean, suggesting *Brother Man* by Roger Mais and *A Quality of Violence* by Andrew Salkey as illustrations.[78] Similarly, the momentous 1963 autobiographical essay *Beyond a Boundary* by the Tridinadian thinker C. L. R. James, which offers a sociocultural meditation on cricket, and Gordon Rohlehr's *Calypso and Society in Pre-Independence Trinidad* (1990), which provides an engaging cultural history of a now highly esteemed musical form from the region, give a clear sense of the proximity that learned discourse has maintained to the expressions and social practices of the popular masses. Three of the central novels in the literary histories of Cuba, Puerto Rico, and the Dominican Republic—respectively *Tres tristes tigres* (1968) by Guillermo Cabrera Infante, *La guaracha del macho Camacho* (1976) by Luis Rafael Sánchez, and *Solo cenizas hallarás* (1980) by Pedro Vergés—are steeped in the evocation of each society's habits of musical consumption and popular speaking patterns. By the same token, were one to peruse the key authors in the national corpus of Haitian literature, say René Depestre, Jacques Stephen Aléxis, Marie Viau Chauvet, and Frankétienne, one could not go very far before encountering their invariable engagement with, discussion of, or position on voodoo, the religion of the Haitian masses, or Creole, the language with which they communicate. Attention to popular cultural expressions and folk practices have for so long pervaded Caribbean writing that one could dismiss the relatively recent importation of 'cultural studies' – with its enhanced attention to the expressive arts and social practices of the lower strata of society – as a paradigm that really contributes nothing new to the Caribbean other than the naming of a practice that had existed all along.

Considered in function of degrees, however, one can probably still speak of the rise of the popular as an accentuated emphasis in recent decades. Louise Bennett's pioneering precedent as a performance artist and poet writing exclusively in Jamaican dialect from the 1930s onward had to wait several decades to gain acceptance as a form offering anything other than carefree merriment. Brathwaite's poetic praxis that conceptualized the Creole language as fundamental to the Caribbean's worldview lent added weight to Bennett's precedent beginning with *Rights of Passage* (1967), the first volume of his famous verse trilogy *The Arrivants*. Since the 1970s, we have seen the striking development of oral or 'dub' poetry as a major expressive art form with great public appeal. The performance poets in this form differ from earlier generations of reciters and storytellers in that their language closely follows the rhythms of reggae music. Although generally concentrating on composing their words strictly for the ear and for sound recordings, their performances especially in Europe often gaining them a popularity similar to that of reggae musicians, several among them have successfully made the passage into print. These include the island-based Jamaican poets Oku Onuora, Mutabaruka, Jean 'Binta' Breeze, and the late Michael Smith, the Canadian-based Lillian Allen, and the renowned Linton Kwesi Johnson, who lives and works in London.[79] Scholar and poet Edward Baugh has also highlighted the accomplishments of Paul Keens-Douglas, whose *Tim Tim* (1976) dexterously displayed a storyteller's folk art element in poetry, as well as John Agard, who made a mark with his *Man to Pan* (1982).[80] Significantly, *Wheel and Come Again* (1998), an anthology of 'reggae poetry' compiled by the Ghanaian-Jamaican poet Kwame Dawes,[81] features many of the best known West Indian scribal poets comfortably standing side by side with some of the salient dub poets. That the turn to dialect has captivated the prose no less than the poetry is evinced by Merle Collins in her novel *Angel* (1987), written almost entirely in Grenadian Creole. The characters in that text reflect an understanding of the politics and the economics of language in their awareness that a command of the Standard rather than the vernacular matters for material advancement, as when Angel's mother Doodsie discourages her from learning to talk 'stupidness'.[82]

One popular expressive art form in which the current generation of performers seems to have continued rather than diverged from the precedent of their predecessors is calypso. Tracing the commentaries of calypsonians and folk poets from the 1930s through the 1990s, Trinidadian critic Gordon Rohlehr has noted their consistent awareness of the obstacles and perseverance that have attended all efforts at regional integration.[83] The voice of the calypsonians was there in 1958 cheering the formation of the West Indies Federation, with such songs as "We All Is One" and "Federation" by the legendary Mighty Sparrow, and Louise Bennett's "Dear Departed Federation" would sing its demise when it floundered in 1962.[84] They sang to applaud the formation of an intergovernmental regional body to regulate trade and promote economic development in memorable musical utterances such as "CARICOM" by Chalkdust and "Caribbean Unity" by Stalin, both in 1979, and as late as the 1990s calypsonian David Rudder's "One Caribbean" still invoked an undaunted vision of regional unity: "One Caribbean, One Caribbean / One heart together in a changing world / One Caribbean, One Caribbean / One love, one heart, one soul / Reaching for a common goal".[85] Rohlehr attests to the survival of the dream of Caribbean unity and regional integration among calypsonians, whose unitarian hope is not deterred by the grimness that surrounds them.

7. The Micro-Spatial Gaze

Concomitant with the survival of the centuries-old dream of Caribbean integration, contemporary Caribbean discourse reveals also the contrasting compulsion to assert the specificity of discrete nations and societies in the region. Perhaps consistent with the precedent established by the works of Luis Rafael Sánchez, Puerto Rican fiction, as illustrated by such salient younger practitioners as Mayra Santos Febres, displays a distinct micro-spatial quality, its action concentrated on minute localities even while the texts aspire to evoking a representative Caribbean milieu. Edgardo Rodríguez Juliá's *San Juan, ciudad soñada* (2005), a moving autobiographical evocation of the Puerto Rican capital, the author's native city, reflects the microscopic gaze of much recent writing from the region. The affirmation of the differentiated space of the author's cultural experience often supposes an attitude of refusal to embrace a reactive identity, a derivative ontology such as anti-colonialist formulations often seemed to espouse. Many young writers today proceed as if unencumbered by the urgency to define themselves in contradistinction to a Western subject or to 'write back' to a metropolitan mainstream. The erotic novels and short fiction of Dominican writer Ligia Minaya, such as *Cuando me asalta el recuerdo de tí* (2003), deal with the marital or romantic conflicts of couples specifically in the city of Santo Domingo. *La isla del Cundeamor* by Sweden-based Cuban writer René Vázquez Díaz evokes the very specific cosmos of Cuban exiles in Miami to shed light on some of the homeland's historical avatars, and the short story by Senel Paz "Strawberries and Chocolate", later turned into a successful film, ascribes to discrete spaces within the city of Havana the exploration of the problem of diverse sexual orientations against the backdrop of traditional Cuban mores.

Consistent with the emphasis to write small, geographically speaking, one notes a tendency to unearth, highlight, or mythicize very particular historical moments from the writers' countries of origin. Olga Nolla's *El castillo de la memoria* (1996) thus chronicles the arrival of Juan Ponce de León in sixteenth-century Puerto Rico as the explorer, seen through the eyes of Lope López de Villalba, engages in a quest for the fountain of youth. The novel *De langste maand* (The longest month) by Diana Lebacs examines urban violence in Curaçao during the 1980s, and Edwidge Danticat's *The Farming of Bones* (1998) memorializes the massacre of Haitian immigrants and Haitian-Dominican residents of the border regions in October 1937. The horrendous murder of the Mirabal sisters in 1960 by the Trujillo dictatorship gave Julia Alvarez the material to weave the plot of her novel *In the Time of the Butterflies* (1994), and post-blitz London gave Andrea Levy the place of convergence for her Jamaican and English characters to negotiate the racial and social divide they inherit from their colonial past in her award-winning novel *A Small Island* (2005). Another dimension of that tendency to represent the Caribbean experience by targeting a slice of history in a differentiated site could be the unabashed affirmation of one's locality that Daniel Maximin voices in the extolment of his native Guadeloupe:

> You dare to write that your love for your island is not a reflection of the foreigner's gaze. And if you dare to write it and describe it yourself in the present, without guilt and without recourse to courts of the past nor

> to juries of the future, […] then you will dare to let your writing body lovingly mold its wayward path to the future, as its uprooted sap nourishes your store of spirit.[86]

Ironically, that sense of comfort in the validity of one's locality harmonizes beautifully with the complementary vision of one's place as merely a point within a larger spectrum to which one remains inexorably connected. At the end of *Caraïbe sur Seine*, the novel for young readers by Gisèle Pineau, Lindy, the girl whose immigrant experience in Paris the novel recounts, derives consolation for the separation from her best friends from a conviction of her profound connectedness to the rest of the globe:

> [T]hough very far from one another, we are not dispersed. We are on the same earth, and our dreams have no limit, because the earth is an island.[87]

8. Queering the Literary Space

We have already made references to the novel by Santos Febres *Sirena Selena*, which explores the reality of homoerotic desire, cross-dressing, and trans-sexuality in both Puerto Rico and the Dominican Republic. These, along with the story by Paz, which daringly investigates same-sex love in the proverbially hetero-normative context of socialist Cuba, point to pioneering instances of what we might call the queering of the literary space in the Caribbean. This is clearly another meaningful emphasis we find in various writers of the newer generations, but these interventions still tread the arena of the eccentric and the socially exceptional, and that most likely has to do with the marginal location that non-heterosexual individuals continue to occupy in Caribbean societies. Suffice it to say that in the Dominican Republic a public gathering of gays and lesbians did not occur until 1 July 2001 after the coordinators received several rejections to their application for preferred city locations wherein to hold their assembly, the authorities presumably justifying their denial on grounds of protecting public morality. Five years later, one could still read the news of discotheques, bars, and other entertainment establishments in Santo Domingo's "Zona Colonial" that were closed down by local authorities and their patrons arrested for serving as meeting points for a homosexual clientele.[88] During the April 2001 Santo Domingo Book Fair, the Minister of Culture himself, a politician named Tony Raful, barged in the company of several police officers into the kiosk sponsored by a Dominican gay and lesbian advocacy group known as Gaylesdom. He showed up to forcibly remove all display or publicity items that he might judge offensive to the rabidly homophobic sensibility of Nicolás de Jesús Cardinal López Rodríguez, who had days before imprecated vociferously against the Ministry of Culture for granting space in the Book Fair to a gay and lesbian kiosk, urging that the Gaylesdom exhibit should be burned instead of displayed. The embodiment of bigotry, Cardinal López Rodríguez habitually uses the power of his pulpit to cast aspersions on gays and lesbians with an occasional barrage of scorn launched against single mothers and peasants fighting against abusive landlords in the rural areas. The tolerance that Dominican society shows toward the ideological obscurantism of this prelate suggests that it has not yet made great progress toward the goal envisioned by a few of recognizing diversity as a fundamental democratic value and ensuring the protection of the entire population's civil rights.

That adverse reality notwithstanding, the yearly parade of the homosexual community has continued with an increasing number of self-identified heterosexuals advocating respect for people with different sexual orientations. The launching in 2004 of the collection *Desde la Orilla: hacia una nacionalidad sin desalojos*,[89] a compilation of conference addresses on various aspects of Dominican diversity which devoted three chapters to sexual orientation, challenged the scholarly community to take the matter seriously. Later the same year, the fiction writer Mélida García and the Santo Domingo publisher Miguel de Camps teamed up as co-editors of the first Dominican anthology ever that sets out to bring together "gay writings" from the country's literature.[90] Finally, at the March 2006 International Congress of the Latin American Studies Association, which took place in San Juan, Puerto Rico, sociologist Ginetta Candelario, cultural studies scholar Carlos Decena, and literary critic Maja Horn, successfully introduced the topic of Dominican sexuality in a panel suggestively entitled "Queering Quisqueya". Apart from examining the extent to which a gay man living under the auspices of a traditional middle-class household can find himself implicated in the maintenance of patriarchal paradigms as they pertain to the construction of masculinity, the panel ventured a re-examination of the legacies of early Dominican feminist thinkers, activists, and writers such as Evangelina Rodríguez Perozo, Petronila Gómez, and Hilma Contreras with an eye on identifying the foundational elements of a discourse that more than half a century ago had the courage to challenge hetero-normative assumptions in Dominican society. Different Caribbean societies will reveal different scenarios regarding the struggle against entrenched homophobia, but, as with the Dominican case, the queering of the literary space will most likely come about as a result of both the emergence of a new sexual ideology made current by writers and thinkers of the newer generations as well as through a concentrated effort to unearth the submerged legacies of dissi-dencc owed to earlier generations and which we only now can boast the sensibility to appreciate.

9. Expanding the Internal Geography

Perhaps the one area in which the newer generations of Caribbean writers and thinkers have done the least to distinguish themselves from their predecessors has been the continued configuration of a geographically, culturally, and linguistically narrow image of the region. The new voices continue to deploy the term 'islands' to invoke the region despite the indisputable geographical fact that countries located smack dab in the middle of the Caribbean experi-ence such as Belize, French Guiana, Guyana, and Surinam lie firmly on the South American continent. To these we should add the Atlantic portions of such Latin American republics as Colom-bia, Costa Rica, Panama, and Venezuela, whose ecological and cultural traits resemble the core Caribbean societies as much as they differ from the overall texture of life in the non-coastal areas of the republics in question. The word 'archipelago' recurs fre-quently in the language with which Edouard Glissant conceptual-izes the region, just as it does in the formulations of the late Anto-nio Benítez Rojo, who conceived of the region figuratively as a "repeating island". But any terminology that homogenizes the geo-graphical visage of the region on the basis of its insular facet not only diminishes its magnitude but it enfeebles its cultural vastness. The Atlantic rimland regions of continental Latin America and the mainland Caribbean societies have contributed greatly to the over-all literary corpus. The mention of Belize's Zee Edgell, Guyanas's Wilson Harris, and Surinam's Albert Helman should suffice to illustrate this point. We can see the limits of the insular vision in a recent volume of scholarly essays on the "cultures of the Hispanic Caribbean" that focuses almost exclusively on Cuba, the Dominican Republic, and Puerto Rico.[91] In three chapters out of seventeen, the volume makes gestures to Colombia and Venezuela: Jorge Marbán's look at representations of the African heritage in four Venezuelan novels published between 1931 and 1950, Lancelot Cowie's survey of the recurrence of the cult of Reina María Lionza in Venezuelan fiction of various periods, and Gilberto Gómez Ocampo's comparative reading of Colombian novelist Héctor Rojas Herazo and Cuban writer Virgilio Piñera as they both confronted the problematic of modernity. Yet, while both the general editor of the series and the compilers of the volume refer to the "*circum*-Caribbean", their project remains overwhelmingly insular. They concern themselves primarily with the problem of reconciling the presumably disparate literary and intellectual products of societies marked by differing sociopolitical systems, namely a "revolutionary dictatorship in Cuba, democratic authoritarianism in the Dominican Republic, and the continued colonization of Puerto Rico by the United States".[92]

Evidently much gets lost in any conceptual configuration of the Caribbean that reduces the region to its insular part particularly as it relates to the literary corpus. The insular prism truncates the region's literary history, killing the hope that we might get closer to chronicling it in its entirety, an enterprise that we have only poorly begun and which cries for satisfactory execution. The map of Caribbean writing will change significantly once we learn to factor in the literary activity taking place on the coastal regions of South America; Veracruz, and the Yucatan Peninsula of Mexico in the North; and the riverine zones of Central America. I would contend that the tabulation of literary texts will become more difficult, almost unwieldly, and therefore truer since simplification of reality always involves a falsification. I would envision a map of Caribbean writing that recognizes the remarkable literary career of Oscar Collazos, the author of numerous works of fiction and expository prose, including *Los días de la paciencia* (1976), *Todo por nada* (1980), and *Jóvenes pobres amantes* (1983); the accomplished poetry of Romulo Bustos Aguirre, whose collected verse entitled *Oración del impuro: Obra reunida* (2004) appeared under the university press of Colombia's Universidad Nacional; the outstanding contributions of short fiction writer and novelist Roberto Burgos Cantor, author of compelling texts such as *Lo amador* (1981) and *Quiero es cantar* (1998); and the equally distinguished legacy of novelist and playwright Fanny Buitrago, whose novel *Los pañamanes* (1979) occupied Benitez Rojo's attention for a chapter of *The Repeating Island*. This is only a minute sampling of the literary artists who would have to come to the fore if we considered merely the most salient figures from the Caribbean region of Colombia, where cities such as Santa Marta, Cartagena, and Barranquilla have for generations been vibrant sites of artistic and intellectual production. Imagine if we looked into the Caribbean coasts of the other Latin American republics that qualify! For one thing, an exploration of the 'Hispanic Caribbean' literature that chooses to limit its search to the islands of the Greater Antilles would at best seem bizarre.

A native of Barranquilla, Buitrago drew her plot for *Los pañamanes* from the colonial history of the archipelago made up of San Andrés, Santa Catalina, and Providencia, a cluster of islands that from 1822 have formed part of Colombia, having previously been claimed by English colonists. The Colombian government in 1868 placed the archipelago under the administrative control of Bogota as 'territories', but the islands continued to suffer isolation not only from the rest of the Hispanic Caribbean but also from mainland Colombia itself. Situated over 480 km off the Caribbean coast of Colombia and only some 180 km from the Nicaraguan coast, the islands do not show up in most general maps of the Caribbean. Because of an original colonization by English Puritans and their economic linkage to the plantation system that spread throughout what later became the British West Indies, before and after emancipation the islands for a long time had greater commercial and cultural contact with Cayman Islands and Jamaica than with mainland Colombia. The conflict between Britain and Spain over the colonial control of the islands lasted from 1632 to 1822, but the estrangement of the archipelago from Colombia survived the era of conflict.[93] In fact, Colombia waited until well into the twentieth century to attempt the integration of the archipelago culturally and socially to the unifying nation through a campaign of

'Colombianization', presumably not an easy feat if we considered that until the beginning of the twentieth century only the government personnel in the archipelago spoke Spanish, the majority of the population speaking primarily English and the Creole that served as the common language to the uneducated folk.[94] Today the Colombian State recognizes both Spanish and English as official languages of the archipelago.

The body of utterances produced by the residents of San Andrés, Providencia, and Santa Catalina, an archipelago that necessarily ought to fit within an inclusive understanding of the 'Hispanic Caribbean', will ideally figure among the tributaries that make up the large corpus we end up acknowledging as Caribbean literature. The San Andrés native Hazel Robinson Abraham, interested in recovering the submerged history of the formation of Creole societies on the islands, has dedicated two novels toward that end. *No Give Up, Maan* (2002) tells the story of the islands prior to Colombia's attempt to incorporate them into the nation, and *Sail Ahoy* !!! (¡Vela a la vista!) (2004) evokes the process whereby the islanders developed a mastery of the sea and turned it into their principal source of sustenance. Beginning to facilitate the availability of the words of the islanders to the overall region, the Caribbean Studies Institute at the San Andrés Campus of the Universidad Nacional de Colombia has devoted several issues of its *Cuadernos del Caribe* to capturing the ideas, life stories, voices, and yearnings of the residents of the archipelago. Issue No. 4 consists of 36 first-person texts composed by the editors on the basis of long interviews conducted with "people who have a visible role in the life of the islands and who, in various ways, have contributed and continue to contribute to shaping their future", representing the voices of ordinary people, differing from an earlier cohort of local government and community leaders convened by the Institute to hear their perception of the condition of life on the archipelago and the most pressing needs of the local population.[95] Coming from different walks of life, levels of schooling, professional training, and ways of participating in community advancement, the speakers in the collection bear predominantly English names, the majority being 'raizales' (natives), those residents who trace their origins back to the enslaved workers brought in the eighteenth century from Belize, Cayman Islands, and Jamaica by settlers under authorization by the Spanish colonial authorities. In sum, a vision of the Caribbean that views the region through an insular prism will most likely be less ready to perceive the human experience – hence the works and the words – of continental Caribbean societies as well as of the numerous Caribbean communities inhabiting the rimland areas. Furthermore, since the idea of 'islands' or 'archipelago' that informs the learned discourse on the Caribbean is really not geographical but political, island clusters that exist within a differentiated polity will tend to stay out of consideration by proponents of panoptic visions of the Caribbean. That is, the island nation-states such as Jamaica or Cuba or the non-independent insular territories that answer juridically to a colonial metropolis overseas will monopolize the name. The Colombian archipelago is hardly the only one that could enter this discussion, but it suffices to show that insular visions of the Caribbean do injustice to the region's numerous continental sites as well as to those islands that by virtue of their small size and their inconvenient location have trouble attracting the attention of the cartographers who design the Caribbean region's general maps.

10. Present Aboriginals and Future Cross-Linguals

A more attentive focus on the continental Caribbean will bring into clearer view those spaces within the region's geography whose population is predominantly aboriginal, tracing their origins directly to the communities that inhabited the Americas prior to the conquest and colonization over five centuries ago. Despite insightful evocations found in the works of Wilson Harris, literary representations of the Caribbean generally seem to reflect the enduring legacy of the myth of 'the absent aboriginal' that the contributors to *Indigenous Resurgence in the Contemporary Caribbean* aim to interrupt.[96] With the work of sociopolitical organizing and the cultural self-affirmation launched in the last two decades by Amerindian advocates in Belize, French Guiana, Guyana, and Surinam, new figurations of the Caribbean will necessarily have to account for the aborigines, with their culture, their works, and their words, as an inescapable presence within the region's pan-ethnic human family. Similarly, mixed ancestry Afro-Amerindian groups like the Black Caribs of Belize, St. Vincent, and the Grenadines, as well as the Garifuna of Honduras, Guatemala, and Nicaragua will enter the sphere of utterances in a truly holistic vision of Caribbean literature and thought.

The new Caribbean poetics, in other words, is called upon to make a greater attempt than has been made thus far to circumvent the region's historic fragmentation as reflected in the combined geographical and political complications that impinge on the lesser visibility of isolated territories such as those of San Andrés, Providencia, and Santa Catalina. But it has to make an even greater attempt to circumvent the truly debilitating linguistic balkanization that has historically impeded appropriate intraregional exchanges of words, knowledge, and thought. Some twenty indigenous languages, as many as fifty Creoles, the four major European tongues that the colonial powers brought with them, and the Asian languages that came with the indentured workers after the 1838 emancipation render the Caribbean region a virtual Tower of Babel. The linguistic barriers to those aspiring to apprehend the region holistically are practically insurmountable, in the worst-case scenario discouraging intra-Caribbean literary and intellectual conversation. The awareness of that insurmountability perhaps explains the tendency of many in the learned community to cultivate their monolingual garden, each in their distinct subsection in isolation from the rest of the polyglot region. That tendency shows up in the otherwise impressive collection *New Caribbean Thought: A Reader*[97] and the compelling monograph *The Caribbean: An Intellectual History 1774-2003*[98] whose use of the holistic term 'Caribbean' in the titles might raise cross-lingual hopes which he Anglophone-centric nature of their contents immediately frustrates.

Elsewhere I have noted the intellectual self-sufficiency of the view of creolity as a quintessence of Caribbean identity posited by the celebrated Martinican authors Jean Bernabé, Patrick Chamoisseau, and Raphael Confiant in function of the exclusively Francophone origin of the sources used by the authors.[99] That linguistic isolationism causes a scenario in which, for instance, the major contributions of Anton de Kom, Boeli van Leeuwen, and Astrid Roemer, coming from the Dutch-speaking side, will seldom succeed at crossing the linguistic border to Anglophone, Francophone, or Spanish-speaking literary conversation, just as the seminal essay *Tres leyendas de colores* by Pedro Mir will fail to join the company of the better-known essential books of Caribbean thought, such as *The Black Jacobins* by C. L. R. James and *Peau noire, masques blancs* by Frantz Fanon. Such is the scenario in which one finds the venerable George Lamming lamenting the possibility "that a generation of graduates from the University of the West Indies, including the History Department, would have left that institution knowing little or nothing about Martí, perhaps the most creative thinker the region has produced".[100] Interestingly, the essay in which Lamming conveys this sorrow has become available in Spanish and French in addition to the English original thanks to the visionary intiative of Lesana M. Sekou, a publisher and poet from St. Martin, whose House of Nehesi Publishers seems to have taken on, at a much more modest scale, the unprecedented cross-lingual project that Cuba's Casa de las Américas kept alive from the start of the socialist government to the 1980s.

During the golden years when the Cuban Revolution enjoyed economic stability, Casa de las Américas encouraged literary creativity in the region by opening the prestigious Casa Award to participants writing in any of the languages of the Americas while sponsoring Spanish translations of numerous literary texts from across the language spectrum. For instance, the existing Spanish versions of Lamming's novels *In the Castle of my Skin* and *Natives of my Person* came out in 1979 as part of the Casa initiative. Similarly, the literary and intellectual productions of Anton de Kom, Aimé Césaire, Kamau Brathwaite, René Depestre, and Jacques Roumain, to name only a few, first entered the sphere of the Hispanophone world through Casa's invaluable enterprise. Today the socialist government that supported that initiative no longer enjoys its former prosperity and the neoliberal states that abound in the rest of the region have not exhibited a comparable commitment to ameliorating the bane of Caribbean fragmentation by forging bridges of artistic and intellectual communication across the various divides of language and recondite geography. Therefore, it may have to fall upon enlightened private advocates like Sekou to endeavor to create structures, their magnitude notwithstanding, that may contribute to bringing the multilingual voices of the Caribbean to speak within hearing range of one another, thereby affording us a fuller, more complex – hence truer – view of the body of utterances we call Caribbean literature. One could envision here an inclusive corpus of texts brought together by the force of a chaos as beautiful and real as that coloring the polychromatic texture of the variegated cosmos inhabited by Zadie Smith's characters in *White Teeth.*

Notes

1 Zadie Smith: *White Teeth*, London, [2000], 2001, p. 31.
2 Jan Lowe: "No More Lonely Londoners", *Small Axe* 9, 2001, 166-180, 179.
3 Smith: *White Teeth*, pp. 303-307.
4 Lowe: "No More Lonely Londoners", 175, 171.
5 Smith: *White Teeth*, p. 167.
6 Zadie Smith: "An Interview", <www.pbs.org/wgbh/masterpiece/teeth/ei_smith_int.html>, accessed 15 February 2007.
7 Brian Meeks: "On the Bump of a Revival". – In B. M. and Folke Lindahl (Eds.): *New Caribbean Thought: A Reader*, Kingston, 2001, pp. viii-xx, ix.
8 *Ibid.*, 14.
9 *Ibid.*, xv.
10 *Ibid.*, xiii.
11 David Scott: *Refashioning Futures: Criticism after Postcoloniality*, Princeton, 1999, p. 107.
12 *Ibid.*, 110-111, 118.
13 *Ibid.*, 195.
14 *Ibid.*, 218.
15 *Ibid.*, 224.
16 Charles V. Carnegie: *Postnationalism Prefigured: Caribbean Borderlands*, New Brunswick, New Jersey, and London, 2002, p. 83.
17 *Ibid.*, 65.
18 Laura Tanna: "One-on-One with Olive Senior", Interview. (Part 3), *The Gleaner*, 7 November 2004.
19 Brenda Mehta: *Diasporic (Dis)locations: Indo-Caribbean Women Writers Negotiate the "Kala Pa"*, Kingston, 2004, p. 228.
20 David Dabydeen: *Coolie Odyssey* (excerpt). – In Start Brown and Mark MacWatt (Eds.), *The Oxford Book of Caribbean Verse*, Oxford, 2005, pp. 299-303, 302-303.
21 Brown & MacWatt (Eds.), *The Oxford Book of Caribbean Verse*, p. xxxiii.
22 Mahadai Das: "They Came in Ships". – In Brown & MacWatt (Eds.), *The Oxford Book of Caribbean Verse*, pp. 290-291.
23 Jit Narain: "Working All Day, Dreaming All Night". – In Brown & MacWatt (Eds.), *The Oxford Book of Caribbean Verse*, p. 240.
24 Mehta: *Diasporic (Dis)locations*, p. 228.
25 *Ibid.*, 229.
26 Pauline Melville: "Beyond the Pale." *Daughters of Africa: An International Anthology of Words and Writings by Women of African Descent from the Ancient Egyptian to the Presen*t. Ed. Margaret Busby, New York, 1992, pp. 739-743, 742.
27 Pauline Melville: *The Migration of Ghosts*, London, 1999, p. 186.
28 *Ibid.*, 187.
29 *Ibid.*
30 Melville: "Beyond the Pale", p. 740.
31 *Ibid.*

32 *Ibid.*, 742.
33 Melville: *The Migration of Ghosts*; p. 198.
34 *Ibid.*, 206, 208.
35 Grace Nichols: “Blackout.” – In Brown & MacWatt (Eds.), *The Oxford Book of Caribbean Verse*, pp. 258-259, 258.
36 Robert Antoni: “The Tale of How Iguana Got Her Wrinkles or the True Tale of El Dorado”, *Barcelona Review* 20, 2000, <www.barcelonareview.com/20/ e_ra.htm>, accessed 12 February 2007.
37 David Dabydeen: “Carnival by Robert Antoni: Dances with Bulbs and Turtles”, *The Independent*, 19 May 2006.
38 Kwame Dawes: “Liminal.” – In Brown & MacWatt (Eds.), *The Oxford Book of Caribbean Verse*, pp. 332-333, 333; Heather Royes: “I No Longer Read Poetry.” – In Brown & MacWatt (Eds.), *The Oxford Book of Caribbean Verse*, p. 197.
39 Thomas Cline: “On Reconstructing A Political Economy of the Caribbean.” – In Meeks & Lindahl (Eds.): *New Caribbean Thought: A Reader*, pp. 498-520, 499.
40 Marcia Morgado: “Literatura para curar el asma: Una entrevista con Mayra Santos Febres”, *Barcelona Review* 17, 2000, <www.barcelonareview.com /17/s_ent_msf.htm>, accessed 12 February 2007.
41 George Lamming: *Coming, Coming Home: Conversations II*, Philipsburg, 2000, p. 32.
42 *Ibid.*
43 *Ibid.*, 33.
44 *Ibid.*
45 *Ibid.*
46 *Ibid.*
47 Carnegie: *Postnationalism Prefigured*, pp. 118-119.
48 Winston James: “New Light on Afro-Caribbean Social Mobility in New York City: A Critique of the Sowell Thesis”. – In Meeks & Lindahl (Eds.): *New Caribbean Thought: A Reader*, pp. 395-427, 396.
49 *Ibid.*, 396-397.
50 Dennis Conway: “The Caribbean Diaspora.” – In Richard S. Hillman and Thomas J. D. D’Agostino (Eds.): *Understanding the Contemporary Caribbean*, Boulder et al., 2003, pp. 333-353, 340-341.
51 *Ibid.*, 344, 348.
52 Norman Girvan: “Reinterpreting the Caribbean” – In Meeks & Lindahl (Eds.): *New Caribbean Thought: A Reader*, pp. 3-23, 14-15.
53 Cited in Carnegie: *Postnationalism Prefigured*, p. 99.
54 Stuart Hall: “Negotiating Caribbean Identities”. – In Meeks & Lindahl (Eds.): *New Caribbean Thought: A Reader*, pp. 24-39, 27-28.
55 Orlando Patterson: “Migration in Caribbean Societies: Socioeconomic and Symbolic Resource.” – In William H. McNeill & Ruth S. Adams (Eds.): *Human Migration: Patterns and Policies*, Bloomington, Indiana, 1978, pp. 106-145, 134.

56 Kwame Dawes (Ed.): *Talk Yuh Talk: Interviews with Anglophone Caribbean Poets*, Charlottesville & London, 2001.

57 Brown & MacWatt (Eds.), *The Oxford Book of Caribbean Verse*, p. xxii.

58 Marie-Agnès Sourieau & Kathleen M. Balutansky (Eds.): *Écrire en pays assiegé: Haiti / Writing Under Siege*, Amsterdam & New York, 2004.

59 Denise de Caires Narain: *Contemporary Caribbean Women's Poetry: Making Style*, London & New York, 2002.

60 M. M. Adjarin: *Allegories of Desire: Body, Nation, and Empire in Modern Caribbean Literature by Women*, Westport, 2004.

61 J. Michael Dash: "Exile and Recent Literature." – In A. James Arnold (Ed.): *A History of Literature in the Caribbean*, vol. 1: *Hispanic and Francophone Regions*, Amsterdam and Philadelphia, 1994, pp. 451-461, 451.

62 Kevin Meehan & Paul B. Miller: "Literature and Popular Culture". – In Hillman & D'Agostino (Eds.): *Understanding the Contemporary Caribbean*, pp. 305-332, 329.

63 Louis James, *Caribbean Literature in English*, Longman Literature in English Series, London & New York, 1999, pp. 212-214.

64 Onyekachi Wambu (Ed.): *Empire Windrush: Fifty Years of Writing about Black Britain*, London, 1998.

65 Ferdinand Dennis & Naseem Khan (Eds.), *Voices of the Crossing: The Impact of Britain on Writers from Asia, the Caribbean and Africa*, London, 2000.

66 James, *Caribbean Literature in English*, p. 199; Meehan & Miller: "Literature and Popular Culture", p. 328.

67 Isabel Hoving: *In Praise of New Travellers: Reading Caribbean Migrant Women Writers*, Stanford, 2001.

68 Rhonda Cobham & Merle Collins (Eds.): *Watchers and Seekers: Creative Writing by Black Women*, New York, 1988.

69 Carole Boyce Davies: *Black Women, Writing, and Identity: Migrations of the Subject*, London & New York, 1994, p. 4.

70 Myriam J. A. Chancy: *Searching for Safe Spaces: Afro-Caribbean Women Writers in Exile*, Philadelphia, 1997, p. xviii.

71 *Ibid.*, 17.

72 *Ibid.*, 168.

73 *Ibid.*, xi.

74 Belkis Cuza Malé: "My Mother's Homeland". – In Brown & MacWatt (Eds.), *The Oxford Book of Caribbean Verse*, p. 191.

75 Edward Baugh: "A History of Poetry". – In A. James Arnold (Ed.): *A History of Literature in the Caribbean*, vol. 2: *English- and Dutch-Speaking Regions*, Amsterdam & Philadelphia, 2001, pp. 227-282, 264.

76 Cynthia James: "Woman Descendant". – In Brown & MacWatt (Eds.), *The Oxford Book of Caribbean Verse*, pp. 233-234, 233.

77 Baugh: "A History of Poetry", pp. 270-272.

78 Kamau Brathwaite: "Jazz and the West Indian Novel", *Bim* 12:46 (1968), 115-126, 124-125.

79 Olive Senior: *Encyclopedia of Jamaican Heritage*, St. Andrew, Jamaica, 2003, p. 289.
80 Baugh: "A History of Poetry", pp. 269-270.
81 Kwame Dawes (Ed.): *Wheel and Come Again: An Anthology of Reggae Poetry*, 1998.
82 Merle Collins: *Angel*, Seattle, 1988, p. 91.
83 Gordon Rohlehr: "A Scuffling of Islands: The Dream and Reality of Caribbean Unity in Poetry and Song". – In Meeks & Lindahl (Eds.): *New Caribbean Thought: A Reader*, pp. 265-305, 265.
84 *Ibid.*, 276.
85 *Ibid.*, 276, 290, 304.
86 Daniel Maximin: "Antillean Journey". – In Kathleen Balutansky & Marie-Agnès Sourieau (Eds.): *Caribbean Creolization: Reflections on the Cultural Dynamics of Language, Literature, and Identity*, Gainesville, 1998, pp. 13-19, 19.
87 Gisèle Pineau: *Caraïbe sur Seine*, Paris, 2003, p. 171.
88 Redacción: "Batida contra los sitios gays: Cierran discoteca Arena, bar Punto y Colmadón Omar en la Zona Colonial", *Clave Digital*, 19 June 2006, <www.clavedigital.com>, accessed 2 February 2007.
89 Silvio Torres-Saillant & Ramona Hernández & Blas R. Jiménez (Eds.): *Desde la Orilla*: *hacia una nacionalidad sin desalojos*, St Domingo, 2004.
90 Mélida García & Miguel de Camps Jiménez (Ed.): *Antología de la literatura gay en la República Dominicana*, Santo Domingo, 2004.
91 Conrad James & John Perivolaris (Eds.): *The Cultures of the Hispanic Caribbean*, Warwick University Caribbean Studies, London & Oxford, 2000.
92 Conrad James: "Introduction". – In J. & Perivolaris (Eds.): *The Cultures of the Hispanic Caribbean*, pp. 1-8, 2.
93 Gerhard Sandner: *Centroamérica y el Caribe occidental: coyunturas, crisis y conflictos 1503-1984*. Trans. Jaime Polania, San Andrés, 2003, pp. 36, 267.
94 Beate M. W. Ratter: *Redes Caribes San Andrés y Providencia y las Islas Cayman: Entre la integración económica mundial y la autonomía cultural regional*. Trans. Jaime Polania. San Andrés, 2001, p 56.
95 Socorro Ramírez & Luis Alberto Restrepo. "Por qué leer estas entrevistas". – In R. S. & L. A. R. (Eds.): *Cuadernos del Caribe: Textos y testimonios del archipiélago*, 4, San Andrés, 2002, pp. 13-15, 13.
96 Maximilian Christian Forte (Ed.): *Indigenous Resurgence in the Contemporary Caribbean: Amerindian Survival and Revival*, New York, 2006.
97 Meeks & Lindahl (Eds.): *New Caribbean Thought: A Reader.*
98 Denis Benn: *The Caribbean: An Intellectual History 1774-2003*, Kingston, 2004.
99 Silvio Torres-Saillant: *Caribbean Poetics: Toward an Aesthetic of West Indian Literature*, Cambridge, 1997, pp. 29-30.
100 Lamming: *Coming, Coming Home*, p. 46.

Jana Gohrisch (Hannover)

Literary Literature II: Themes and Narratives

1. Introduction: Caribbean Themes and Narratives

Writing about Caribbean literature, its themes and narratives involves at least two paradoxes. First of all, 'the Caribbean' does not really exist. Rather, it is a construct serving as a cover term for a number of islands and mainland territories between the Caribbean Sea and the North Atlantic Ocean. The term may be convenient but at the same time it tends to obscure the region's considerable diversity of natural surroundings as well as its heterogeneous racial and ethnic groups with their specific histories, cultures and languages. Linguistically, English and English-based Creoles coexist along with Spanish as well as French and Dutch and their Creole versions. To give an example: ethnically, half of the population of Trinidad and Tobago and of Guyana is African and half is Indian. Portuguese Creoles and Chinese and, in Guyana, Amerindians, are added to the mixture. Compared with this, Jamaica is populated mainly by people of African descent but has a sizeable light-skinned population as well. Race and ethnicity in the Caribbean are always markers of social status shaping the region's literature and its themes to the same extent as do its physical conditions, landscapes, histories and cultures.

Secondly, at the beginning of the 21st century there is very little literature that is actually produced by authors resident in the Caribbean who publish with Caribbean publishing houses and rely on local distribution networks. Along with its representatives, Caribbean literature has long since migrated to Britain, the United States and Canada. Speaking of the most recent developments Sarah Lawson Welsh even diagnoses a paradigm shift away from Caribbean or national literature towards a post-colonial literature occupied with hybridity and migration.[1] However, the Caribbean produced two Nobel Prize winners, Derek Walcott in 1992 and V. S. Naipaul in 2001 who, in addition, was knighted by the Queen in 1990 for his services to British literature.[2]

What, then, is Caribbean literature? What are Caribbean themes? Does it make sense to search for a regional literature in an age of globalization? Why should almost all the major writers live in the metropolis thus constructing the Caribbean as a place only worth leaving?

Let me suggest a preliminary contention concerning Caribbean themes and narratives that takes into account these paradoxes and questions: since its massive emergence in the 1950s, issues of migration, both geographical and social, of exile and displacement have been dominant themes in Caribbean fiction.[3] They are aesthetically reflected in the recurrent motif of the journey. The self is very often portrayed as divided and alienated due to the lack or loss of a supporting community. But equally important, especially in the fiction from the 1930s onwards (a period of social and political unrest in the region), are the socially and locally specific interactions of gender, race, ethnicity and class. The earlier writers were often political activists as well. They use fiction to investigate ways of achieving individual wholeness and to delineate political solutions to racial and social tensions in their fragmented societies. The representation of the region's history with its specific ethnic and social cultures of resistance against colonialism and oppression is especially prominent in the narrative texts written before and around independence in the 1950s and 1960s. Fiction with a Caribbean background published since the 1990s, however, tends to see the Caribbean as an integral part of a world history of displacement imagined as a shared history. Writers are primarily concerned with the politics of representation and, in their historical fiction, treat language as the most oppressive feature of colonialism. A theme that can be discerned in all Caribbean fiction is the search for a Caribbean aesthetics. Writers use both modified versions of social realism and experiment with the region's varieties of English, with magic realism and with textual strategies influenced by postmodernism.

My essay focuses on narratives that are connected to the Caribbean by their authors' biographies and their choice of settings to demonstrate how place and social context, race, ethnicity and gender influence the choice of themes. I shall first outline some models of cultural production which provide the interpretive background to my examples of imaginative writing.

2. Models of Caribbean Cultural Production

Edward Kamau Brathwaite, Derek Walcott and Stuart Hall stand for the older generation leaving aside for the moment such important figures as Wilson Harris or V. S. Naipaul. The younger generation's coming to terms with their Caribbean heritage shall be illustrated briefly by taking Paul Gilroy as an example who follows Hall in many ways. The two groups differ according to their emotional identification with the Caribbean: the writers Brathwaite and Walcott stick to the Caribbean despite living elsewhere while the scholars Hall and Gilroy identify themselves with Britain and an international black diaspora, respectively. As for the writers, emotional commitment and identification reverberate in the choice of themes and aesthetics.

Both Brathwaite (born in Barbados in 1930) and Walcott (born in St Lucia in 1930), base their models on Caribbean history. It is characterized by colonialism and neocolonialism, slavery and indenture, by the miscegenation of races and the development of linguistic and other cultural strategies of resistance. Instead of subscribing to the dominant reading of this history as one of annihilation and destruction (which is very strong in Naipaul) they stress its inherent potential for the creation of something new.

In his seminal historical study on *The Development of Creole Society in Jamaica 1770-1820* (1971), Brathwaite characterizes this creative process as "creolization" and defines it as "an historically affected socio-cultural continuum".[4] He stresses the importance of African and Amerindian elements for Caribbean folk culture. Later on he adapted this concept to literature and added the role of place in the formation of a regional identity as expressed in what he calls "nation language". "Nation language is the language that is influenced very strongly by the African model, the African aspect of our New World / Caribbean heritage."[5] According to Brathwaite, employing Creole in literature helps writers to develop an aesthetics that does not imitate the literature of the colonizers.

Walcott claims the Western poetic traditions as equally relevant sources for modern Caribbean writers. In his 1992 Nobel Lecture, he restates earlier observations, taking the Nobel Prize as a proof for the literary success of his theoretical model. "Antillean art", he writes, "is this restoration of our shattered histories, our shards of vocabulary, our archipelago becoming a synonym for pieces broken off from the original continent."[6] Echoing John Donne's prose text "Meditation No. 17" (1624), Walcott sees these historical fragments and pieces as parts of a whole comprising both American and European elements. He provides an analogy between the people in the region and poets who both find themselves in a "process of renaming, of finding new metaphors"[7] for their natural and social surroundings. Both redefine and create using the chance of a new beginning that lies in shattered and fragmented histories. Walcott sees "at last, islands not written about but writing themselves",[8] serving as their own standards of evaluation.

Stuart Hall (born in Jamaica in 1932) reflects on the role of the intellectual based on the black British experience. He studied in Britain and later served as the director of the famous Centre for Contemporary Cultural Studies at the University of Birmingham. Hall points to ethnicity as "the necessary place or space from which people speak"[9] and claims that "the aesthetics of modern popular music is the aesthetics of the hybrid, the aesthetics of the crossover, the aesthetics of the diaspora, the aesthetics of creolization".[10] Together with others of his generation, Stuart Hall has helped to institutionalize a politicized discourse on race relations that influenced British legislation and politics as well as the media coverage of black issues.

Paul Gilroy (born in London in 1956) is the son of Guyanese writer and teacher Beryl Gilroy. He continues Hall's efforts to set up Black Cultural Studies as a discipline in its own right and emphasizes the necessity to re/construct a global black history. He proposes *The Black Atlantic* (1993) as a counterculture of modernity, developing ideas about the cross-Atlantic black diaspora and its aesthetics of hybridity, exemplified especially in music. He is now based in the American academy and shares the desire to establish common ground between African Americans and Black Britons with such Caribbean-British writers as Caryl Phillips and Fred D'Aguiar who teach in the US as well (as does Edward Brathwaite for that matter). Both Hall and Gilroy echo the influential Indian critic Homi Bhabha, who lived in Britain and now teaches at the prestigious University of Chicago. Bhabha's concept of the "third space of enunciation"[11] locates the meaning of cultures in "the 'inter' – the cutting edge of translation and negotiation, the in-between space".[12]

Over the last 50 years the models of Caribbean cultural production have clearly shifted in terms of their focus and inspiration. While Brathwaite and Walcott proceed from Caribbean histories, Hall's and Gilroy's starting point as critics is the Black experience in Britain. The latter have influenced transnational writers of Caribbean descent in Britain who are now paying increased attention to shared or entangled histories of exile and migration across continents and cultures. Both groups are united, however, in their search for future options that will transcend the destructive elements of a Caribbean history of slavery and indenture, colonialism and neocolonialism and a history of immigration characterized by racial discrimination and exclusion.

3. From Herbert De Lisser to Andrea Levy: Continuity and Change in Caribbean Themes

In order to be able to demonstrate the historical changes and continuities of Caribbean themes and narratives I shall discuss them chronologically following James A. Arnold's *History of Literature in the Caribbean*. He divides Caribbean fiction into three periods: the novel before 1950, the novel from 1950 to 1970 and the novel since 1970.[13]

The major precondition for a functioning and self-perpetuating literary culture in the Caribbean and elsewhere is the existence of an urban middle-class. It has to be large and prosperous enough to want to buy and read books and to sustain and need (or at least, tolerate) an intellectual elite that serves as a political and cultural think-tank and critical consciousness. Despite the regional differences of the islands and mainland territories in the Caribbean this has always been one of the problems for aspiring writers. Both under colonialism and after independence, they have found it very difficult to live off their profession. Therefore, they have left the Caribbean in search of an audience and an income similar to their fellow Caribbeans of all classes who went away in search of paid employment and better living conditions. While earlier in the century workers went to Panama to build the canal, they later migrated to Great Britain to work in factories and the public services after the Second World War as well as to the United States and Canada to seek employment there.

3.1. The novel before 1950

The earliest literary texts of the region were produced in Jamaica and in British Guiana[14] which were Britain's largest and most populous territories in the Caribbean in the nineteenth century. Kingston, Jamaica, and the two urban centres of Guyana, New Amsterdam and Georgetown, offered white immigrant writers both a market and a readership for poetry and short fiction that mainly followed Victorian models. In Guyana, the interior of the country furnished them with an intriguing new subject. The almost inaccessible tropical jungle has remained a central topic and powerful symbol for later authors with a Guyanese background such as Wilson Harris and Fred D'Aguiar, David Dabydeen and Pauline Melville (born in 1948). In colonial Jamaica, Herbert G. De Lisser (1878-1944) and Thomas H. MacDermot (1870-1933) worked to establish a reading public on the island around the beginning of the twentieth century.[15] At that time middle-class Jamaicans began to perceive of themselves as a nation and started to take an interest in local history and culture.[16] MacDermot published his novels in Jamaica under the pen name of Tom Redcam and in the famous preface to *One Brown Girl and –* (1909) encouraged his readers to read more Jamaican literature and thus to enable a local literature to develop. Both De Lisser and Redcam focused on socially disadvantaged groups such as blacks, women and peasants with De Lisser using a Jamaican upper-class family in his later fiction to examine how gender and race influence class mobility. From the 1920s onwards, the local reading public recedes into the background of the writers' attention because they increasingly publish in the United States and Great Britain, setting a pattern that has lasted until today.

Claude McKay (1890-1948) was born in Jamaica but is generally treated as an American author due to his contribution to the Harlem Renaissance. He published his third novel *Banana Bottom* in 1933 which, unlike his two earlier novels, is set in Jamaica and explores the issue of the divided self using a young black girl as a main character. She is raped as a young country girl and sent to Britain by well-meaning white missionaries. She later returns to her native village Banana Bottom where she tries to reconcile her English middle-class values with life in rural and colonial Jamaica. McKay presents the vitality of Jamaican hill culture with its local language, music and festivals as the main source of the central character's ability to survive.

C. L. R. James (1901-1989) was a political activist, sports journalist, critic and writer from Trinidad who lived in both Britain and the United States. His novel *Minty Alley* (1936) inaugurated the tradition of the yard novel, a genre which sympathetically deals with the impoverished lower classes of Caribbean urban society. *Minty Alley* centres on a young black middle-class man in Trinidad to examine the interrelation of race, gender and class set against the background of yard life. Alfred H. Mendes (1892-1991) was a white Trinidadian of Portuguese Creole descent who later went to the United States. In *Pitch Lake* (1934) he explores sexual relationships between white men and African and Indian women from the point of view of the white man. *Black Fauns* (1935), a yard novel with a strong didactic flavour, shows how black women keep life going despite their extreme poverty. Roger Mais (1905-1955), a radically anti-colonial journalist and writer from Jamaica who was even jailed for sedition, sets his ironically titled novel *The Hills Were Joyful Together* (1953) in the run-down slum areas of colonial Kingston. His provocative book shows that yard life is rife with criminality and violence but does not offer a way out of the misery despite the occasional goodness of even the most depraved of the characters.

In the late 1920s, Albert Gomes, Alfred Mendes and C. L. R. James formed the influential '*Beacon* Group' of left-wing writers and intellectuals which was based in Port-of-Spain, Trinidad. *The Beacon*, published from 1931 to 1933, was the first openly anti-colonial literary journal in the Caribbean, followed in the 1940s by similar projects in Barbados, Jamaica and Guyana. The journals served as catalysts for a Caribbean literary culture that gained in scope until it reached international dimensions in the 1950s with the publication of an increasingly large number of novels by Caribbean writers who had gone to Britain.

The first novels and short stories are mainly in the mode of social realism and explore the psychological implications of life in a colonial situation characterized by permanent biological, cultural and linguistic creolization processes as outlined by Brathwaite. The absence of indigenous literary role models to carry their specifically Caribbean experience encouraged authors to experiment with local story-telling traditions and (non-codified) Creole as a language of serious fiction. They sought to transcend its stereotypical devaluation as a non-standard variety associated with backwardness and a lowly social position by using it for the speech of characters according to their social context. The next generation of writers takes these experiments further by introducing Creole as the language of both characters and narrators as pioneered in Vic Reid's *New Day* (1949) and Samuel Selvon's *The Lonely Londoners* (1956). The novels published since the 1950s are read by a fairly large metropolitan readership compared to the rather small literate elite resident in the Caribbean. In the metropolis, however, writers have to negotiate the paradox of wanting to be appreciated by an audience unfamiliar with the languages and cultures of the Caribbean and wanting to be true to their linguistic and cultural as well as political heritage.

3.2. The novel from 1950 to 1970

One of the writers who arrived in Britain in 1950, accidentally on the same boat as Samuel Selvon from Trinidad, was George Lamming (born in 1927) from Barbados. Looking back on several decades of fictional production, Lamming observed that "one of the functions of the novel in the Caribbean is to serve as a form of social history".[17] To him, it is first and foremost the history of labour that needs exploration because it gave rise to a concept of the region that resisted the perception of the Caribbean as an imperial frontier. The concept unites the Caribbean because it perceives the region as "a landscape remade by the labour force of all those who had been brought to it".[18] The culture of labour that originated in colonial plantation society is the "common historical experience" shared by Africans and Indians and is reinforced by the literature of the region.[19]

Despite this common history, post-independence political divisions (especially violent in Guyana and Trinidad) set the ethnic groups against each other in their struggle for economic resources and political power.[20] These divisions, however, became less important in Britain where the immigrants shared the same fate of racial discrimination. Authors fared rather well, though, because they found publishers ready to print their manuscripts and fellow writers and intellectuals to discuss politics and aesthetics. Andrew Salkey (1928-1995), a writer and editor from Jamaica, was at the centre of the Caribbean literary community in London which formed the Caribbean Artists' Movement in Salkey's London apartment in 1966.

But it was through the BBC programme *Caribbean Voices* set up in 1946 that these writers were heard in the Caribbean itself and that a 'Caribbean literature' took shape. It succeeded *Calling the West Indies* founded by the Dominican poet, playwright and politician Una Marson in 1938. As a spoken programme, *Caribbean Voices* further encouraged experiments with Creole and oral folk culture. Moreover, it helped to create a common Caribbean identity both within the Caribbean and among those in Britain. The careers of V. S. Naipaul (who edited the programme for some years), Edgar Mittelholzer, Samuel Selvon, George Lamming and Andrew Salkey began with their involvement in *Caribbean Voices*.[21] As George Lamming repeated in a recent interview "my generation's West Indian and Caribbean formation was, to a large extent, if not initiated, directed and reinforced in London, not before. Most of us were not West Indians until the London experience."[22]

3.2.1. Novels of Childhood and Transition

Writers remained connected to the Caribbean not only through *Caribbean Voices* but through the experience of having grown up there. Caribbean childhood and adolescence under colonialism thus became one of the major themes of the novel from the 1950s to the 1970s[23] along with the representation of migration and life in exile and the negotiation of narrative form. The socially contextualized representation of growing up in the Caribbean very often metaphorically suggests an increasing self-awareness of the region in the period of transition from colonial dependence to post-colonial independence. Since the 1970s, women writers like Merle Hodge from Trinidad (born in 1944), Zee Edgell from Belize (born in 1944) and Jamaica Kincaid from Antigua (born in 1949 and now, like Edgell, living in the United States) have introduced a critical female perspective on the issues. They highlight sexual discrimination and exploitation as well as the losses that come with the region's transition to western modernity. Their fictional characters have to survive in a modern capitalist economy whose destructive effects on the socially underprivileged are not alleviated by state intervention.

The first of these novels of childhood is George Lamming's semi-autobiographical *In the Castle of my Skin* (1953) in which he tells the story of a boy growing up in rural Barbados. He experiments with plot structures, focalization and symbolism transcending the generic conventions by introducing a chorus-like element to highlight the role of the community. The main character of the text is this village community which is slowly disintegrating as plantation economy collapses and colonialism draws towards its end amidst a climate of social unrest and confusion. The major themes are alienation and the loss of wholeness due to political and personal changes. The narrator finally exchanges his rural background for a middle-class existence by moving to Trinidad and becoming a teacher. Lamming's novel ends on a note of vague expectation for a new life to supplant the old one that is slowly coming to an end. The limitations of rural island life feature similarly in Michael Anthony's childhood novel *The Year in San Fernando* (1965). It is set in Trinidad and focuses on a young boy who spends a year in the city and experiences this as a process of personal growth.

The first novel of childhood and adolescence written by a woman is Merle Hodge's *Crick Crack Monkey* (1970) which presents rural and urban Trinidad from the perspective of a young black girl. Hodge skilfully employs varying registers of Trinidadian Creole and derives the title of her open-ended narrative from a folk rhyme. The conflict between the two worlds is exemplified in the values that are attached to them. The country stands for the African-based and community-oriented values of the working and peasant classes. The city represents the social rise through a Eurocentric colonial education, the denial of the 'backward' African and Creole heritage and immersion into the city's urban middle-class culture. The protagonist ends up with a divided and alienated self and, with her migration to Britain, adds a geographical dimension to her cultural dislocation.

V. S. Naipaul (born in 1932), similar to Samuel Selvon, has an Indo-Trinidadian background but has lived in Britain since 1950. Naipaul's immense productivity establishes him as the perhaps best known and most widely read of all the Caribbean writers discussed here. The settings of his more than twentyfive narrative texts span the entire post-colonial world and show the development of an individual style that consists of a mixture of realism, autobiography and travel writing. According to critic Bruce King, "Naipaul's early fiction brought to West Indian writing the social awareness and comedy characteristic of British fiction, the sense of form and economy found in the early fiction of James Joyce and a Proustian awareness of change, time and memory."[24] *A House for Mr Biswas* (1961) attempts a social history of the Indian community in Trinidad, both rural and urban, which also features in Selvon's *A Brighter Sun* (1952). Naipaul's novel tells the story of a young Trinidadian Indian coming of age and negotiating his relationship with his father modelled on Naipaul's own difficulties with his father. The house the title alludes to symbolizes more than just a narrow family problem or the stereotypical middle-class desire for property and status. Rather, it stands for the precarious position of colonial Trinidadian Indians in an impoverished and unstable society. They appear to be caught between the material and psychological security a family may offer and its overwhelming power over the individual who is subsequently denied to develop his own personality. But as always in Naipaul's fiction, the individual is shown as flawed and unable to reliably translate the chances life offers into reality. This does not diminish the social criticism of the text but transposes it onto another level. By pointing out reasons for past failure it indicates an agenda for future action. In *The Mimic Men* (1967) this move gives way to a rather nihilistic image of Caribbean society as uncreative and imitative, a view for which Naipaul has often been criticized.

3.2.2. Negotiating Narrative Form

In *A House for Mr Biswas* Naipaul alludes to Shakespeare's tragedy *King Lear*, a strategy that other Caribbean writers employ as well:

George Lamming uses the Shakespearean characters Prospero and Caliban from *The Tempest* in his essay *The Pleasures of Exile* (1960) as well as in his experimental *Water with Berries* (1971). With *Wide Sargasso Sea* (1966) Jean Rhys writes back to Charlotte Brontë's *Jane Eyre* (1847) in order to redress the Eurocentric colonial perspective inherent in the earlier novel.

As reader-oriented strategies, these allusions to English literature facilitate the texts' reception by a western-educated intellectual audience. Being familiar with the English pre-texts enables these readers to concentrate on the unfamiliar elements of Caribbean folk cultures and to appreciate the integration of the two modes. The resulting aesthetic hybridity supports Walcott's model of Caribbean cultural production which stresses the contribution of the ethnically diverse heritage to the making of the Caribbean and its literatures. On the level of the stories told, the experience of the hitherto excluded Other is being inscribed into English culture.

In her most famous novel, *Wide Sargasso Sea*, Jean Rhys (1890-1979) relies on modernist techniques to generate coherence, among them non-chronological narration with varying focalizers, juxtaposed interior monologue, metaphors and the extended use of imagery. The impression of sensuousness is achieved by colour, plant and animal symbolism and the recurrent image of the fire. Renouncing guidance through an omniscient narrator the author tells the Caribbean pre-history of Bertha Mason Rochester who, in Brontë's novel, embodies the dangers of uncontrolled passion. Rhys's complex and open-ended narrative intertwines social and individual reasons to explain Bertha's alleged madness: the disintegration of plantation society after emancipation, the struggles of the different races and classes against each other, the continued greed for profit to be gained by importing indentured labourers or marrying for money as well as male abuse of power. These forces combine to deny women in particular, but not exclusively, individual development and a fulfilled emotional life.

Similarly, the motif of decay and destruction runs through Phyllis Shand Allfrey's novel *The Orchid House* (1953) set after World War One. Allfrey (1915-1986), like her friend Rhys a native of Dominica, combines family and national history but ends her novel on a more hopeful note than Rhys: the decay is offset by the seeds of a new beginning involving whites and blacks alike.

Far more difficult to read than Allfrey or Rhys are the novels by Wilson Harris (born in Guyana in 1921) because his idiosyncratic and self-reflexive experiments with narrative form reach out into the mythic and unconscious. In his non-fiction Harris has repeatedly explained his distrust in both European realism and modernism which, to him, always suggest order and solution while he prefers an unending search for meaning. In his tellingly titled *The Infinite Rehearsal* (published in 1987 as the second novel in the Carnival Trilogy) Harris once again champions his model of cultural production in the Caribbean: it consists of the continual rewriting of Caribbean history to extract from it elements that may constitute the region's cross-cultural future. In this process, which rests on the belief in regeneration through catastrophe, the writer seeks to liberate language from disabling ideas and attitudes by dissolving conventional metaphors and images. The infinite rehearsal results in a creative syncretism which merges and preserves the seemingly lost cultures and histories of Guyana through the transformative powers of the imagination.

These powers are the major theme in *The Palace of the Peacock* (1960). Modelled on the search for an Eldorado, the novel describes an allegorical journey into the interior of Guyana where Europeans and Amerindians meet. One of the characters is called Donne after the seventeenth century poet and divine to whom Derek Walcott also repeatedly alludes in his work. Harris's choice evokes the early modern spirit of exploration, as well as the power of poetic imagination and the visionary realization of one's actions. The novel ends when Donne finally understands the catastrophic results of his search. Donne's death is refracted into different versions and rendered in highly ambiguous images and metaphors of which the title-giving palace of the peacock is one.

Harris' stress on change through language endears him especially to academics who, in the wake of post-structuralism, have placed prime importance on language themselves. While such critics have treated Harris as a model for post-colonial literatures[25] he is not much read outside academic circles. Younger writers such as Caryl Phillips and David Dabydeen, however, continue to appreciate Harris's insistence on experiment to validate their own endeavours. The younger writers' concern with the power of language is certainly related to Harris. This move reinforces the perception of Harris' model as central to Caribbean and post-colonial literatures.

Equally experimental but less widely acclaimed by critics is Erna Brodber (born in Jamaica in 1940). Living in Jamaica (with extended periods of lecturing in the United States) she combines a career as a sociologist and anthropologist with writing fiction. Her research into Jamaican religious cults and beliefs informs her first two novels which centre on black women's lives. Using techniques derived from oral story-telling and music, Brodber (sister of linguist, novelist and poet Velma Pollard, born in 1937) experiments with non-linear plots and merges individual and collective narrative voices speaking in various registers of Standard English and Creole. In her recent novel *Louisiana* (1994) Brodber investigates the common cultural heritage of Caribbean and American blacks across "the Black Atlantic" reminiscent of Gilroy's model of cultural production.

3.2.3. Novels in and of Exile

In his non-fictional book *The Pleasures of Exile* (1960), George Lamming uses Shakespeare's *Tempest* to explore the ambiguous inheritance of the English language for a Caribbean writer in exile. Compared to the sombre tone in Lamming's extended essay and his three novels that deal with immigration, Samuel Selvon's classic *The Lonely Londoners* (1956) relies on humour as its central strategy to convey the otherwise depressing experience of exile. Highly innovative, Selvon (1923-1994) devises a Caribbean Creole that provides his fictional immigrants with a group identity as well as with strategies of survival and resistance. The author experiments with the form of the novel blending the Bible and European literary traditions such as the picaresque novel and medieval romance with Caribbean Calypso and oral story-telling. The episodic structure of the narrative creates the impression of unending movement rather than of conflict and solution. Selvon's West Indians are working-class men in search of a better life in the metropolis whose mock-heroic names ironically comment on their personalities. Despite their disappointment, alienation and isolation they are here to stay and create a black urban subculture to support each other in a racist society. With this set-up Selvon translates the social structures of the Caribbean village community into an urban context in which women appear as marginal characters only. White women figure as objects of sexual desire and as status symbols while elderly black women organize the everyday life of the community. The focalizers are all male and it is only in the 1980s that more black women begin to speak about their specifically female experience of racial and class oppression both in the Caribbean and in Britain.

3.3. The Novel since 1970: Novels in and of Exile Continued

Generally, the 1970s and 1980s are dominated by Wilson Harris and V. S. Naipaul. While Naipaul explores the post-colonial world Harris returns time and again to Guyanese history blending it with Western and indigenous myth to unearth the seeds of regeneration. George Lamming and Samuel Selvon continue to investigate the themes of exile and displacement. In the 1980s, however, young black men and women begin to tell the story of migration and settling in Britain from different points of view. While the male writers, especially David Dabydeen (with five novels so far) and Caryl Phillips (with eight novels), have become prominent, women writers from the Caribbean tend to publish less in number and in thematic scope. Sometimes they disappear from the literary scene after an acclaimed first novel or write only minor second and third novels, afterwards continuing with their careers as poets or professionals. Often, their fiction is didactic in purpose and less formally innovative than fiction by men. In the 1990s and early 2000s, Andrea Levy and Zadie Smith have developed narrative modes they share with the many transnational women writers in Britain who write for the ever-expanding market for transcultural fiction.

3.3.1. Unbelonging

One of the most prolific black women writers in the 1980s, along with Beryl Gilroy (1924-2001), is Joan Riley (born in Jamaica in 1958) who published four novels between 1985 and 1992.[26] Riley explicitly writes for people like her herself, working- or lower-middle class in origin and with a standard education in English. Therefore, she does not experiment with narrative form but relies on social realism in her accounts of black women's lives in exile. In *The Unbelonging* (1985) she focuses on a young black girl whose story of growing up is complicated by having to live in a racist society, in poverty and with a father who abuses her sexually. The reader is invited to identify with the protagonist of this novel which is told chronologically and ends with the protagonist's abortive return to Jamaica. The realist mode makes it easier for Riley to point out reasons for misbehaviour and to suggest to her readers how the condition of the alienated and abused black woman in Britain may be alleviated.

3.3.2. In-Betweenness

While Riley represents the unbelonging of her main character through the story line, Caryl Phillips's novels of the 1990s do so through their narrative structure. Beginning with *Cambridge* (1992) Phillips (born in St Kitts in 1958) narrates several novels from two, or three, points of view. This metaphorically marks the in-between status of the texts' displaced protagonists reminiscent of Bhabha's theoretical model of the third space. *Cambridge* juxtaposes the observations of the daughter of an absentee plantation owner who travels to Jamaica with the life account of a slave who once lived in England as an educated Christian. Their shared histories are rendered in carefully recreated 19th-century prose and, by comparison, reveal the silences and discords in each version of the past. Phillips concentrates on the power of language and demonstrates the contradictions of colonialist discourse along with its capacity to distort the individual's perception of reality irrevocably.

Where the earlier authors write back to the Caribbean in search of alternative visions, Phillips writes back to Britain engaging her in a dialogue about her colonial past. The political urgency with which writers like Lamming discussed the history of the Caribbean looking at its future is gone from Phillips's texts. They are intellectually challenging and transpose political commitment to the realm of language and discourse in their polyphonous critique of misrepresented history.

As George Lamming recently observed: while the Caribbean writers of his generation "came out of strong community living, strong village living", black British people are "the products of an urban culture, [...] the products of a very atomized kind of urban life".[27] Despite their sometimes rather aggressive claims to be part of Britain, they have not yet solved the question of belonging in the sense that they have not decided yet "whether they are going to be of the society, as distinct from simply being in the society".[28] While his generation "never broke [its] deepest sentimental links with where [it] had come from"[29] black British people have to negotiate living in a country that only reluctantly acknowledges their presence. They have to decide whether they want to insert themselves into British institutions, a decision which will finally influence their post-migratory self-definition and sense of belonging.

That this process, at least for intellectuals, has been long under way may be proved by David Dabydeen (born in Guyana of Indian descent in 1956). He is an art historian and professor at the Centre for Caribbean Studies at the University of Warwick as well as a renowned poet and novelist. Dabydeen, like Fred D'Aguiar (born in 1960), returns in his fiction to the colonial past of Guyana to heal its wounds and redeem the migrant's split self. D'Aguiar's themes circle around slavery and the Middle Passage (i. e. the crossing of the Atlantic Ocean) offering a fictional version of Paul Gilroy's "Black Atlantic". Dabydeen's novel *A Harlot's Progress* (1999) parodies the conventions of 18th-century art and fiction and the history of Otherness. The protagonist, a freed slave and former servant once painted by Hogarth and Reynolds, is paid by abolitionists to tell his story to serve the anti-slavery movement. Like a modern writer he has to negotiate the demands of truth and of serving a good cause with a story that needs to be sold in a commercial culture. English history is rewritten in the former slave's competing versions of the black experience and thus inserted into the history of the "Black Atlantic". At the same time, Dabydeen's representation of exile is reminiscent of Walcott's celebration of new beginnings that are made possible by displacement.

3.3.3. Belonging

More recently, women writers with a Caribbean background reexamine their histories of exile blending the social realism of Riley's kind with the playful rearrangement of historical events in much postmodern fiction. Andrea Levy (born in 1956 to Caribbean parents with a Jewish grandfather on one side) and Zadie Smith (mixed-race with some Caribbean heritage, born in London in 1975) take two different approaches to displacement. In her award-winning novel *Small Island* (2004) Levy presents the entangled histories of Britain and Jamaica during and after World War II leaving it open which of the two would be the eponymous island. The novel is told in the realist mode using four narrators to balance the stories of black and white men and women. Levy's inscribed readers are not the intellectuals Dabydeen and Phillips write for but a middle-brow audience who takes an interest in its own involvement in history. In *Small Island* the representation of history is less inconclusive than in the two male writers' books and much more down to earth than in Zadie Smith's acclaimed and criticized novel *White Teeth* (2000) that was adapted by Channel 4 into a not very successful film.

Smith portrays hybridity as a normal ingredient of everyday life in London, neither to be celebrated nor to be lamented. I see her text as transposing Brathwaite's model of miscegenation to Britain. In British reality, the freely chosen intermingling of all possible races and cultures may not have produced a fully-fledged Creole society as yet but, as statistics show, it is well under way. "[F]orty percent of children in London are born to at least one non-white parent" and the city of Leicester is projected to have more than 50 % non-white inhabitants in 2011.[30] Smith's novel does not only show hybridity as something ordinary, but racism as well. Depicting an ordinary racism along with miscegenation does away with the white liberal dream of multiculturalism as an antidote to racism. While Levy still sets large sections of her novels in the Caribbean, Smith chooses her settings from around the globe but prefers London. Similar to Phillips' novels, this eventually creates a literature that is less Caribbean than transcultural in scope and British in emotional commitment.

4. Summary: Caribbean Themes and Narratives

The transition of Caribbean writers to Britain is finally on the verge of erasing Caribbean literature in the traditional sense – a fate that the region shares with many countries in Africa whose middle classes are unable to sustain a viable literary culture. But this does not mean that there will be no literature any more that is written by people of Caribbean heritage dealing with Caribbean issues. With migration to the metropolis the thematic agenda undergoes changes, too. For the earlier writers, the focus was primarily on the Caribbean. The middle generation favours a double focus of both the Caribbean and Britain. The younger writers continue to deal with their Caribbean heritage but do so from a British perspective and with the desire to redefine the conceptions of Britishness from within.

This change in focus does not eradicate the Caribbean itself, however, which remains racially, ethnically and politically divided and a source of future literary topics. We do not know as yet how transnational literature with Caribbean elements will affect the Caribbean itself. But the advantage that writers of Caribbean heritage bring to Britain is certainly valid to the Caribbean as well. Being both insiders and outsiders at the same time they may look at both societies with an equally critical eye. Belonging both to the Caribbean and to Britain they are well qualified to debate the anxieties of belonging and not belonging to both regions.

Seen against these wider developments, Caribbean themes have both undergone a considerable change over the last fifty years and remained strikingly similar indicating questions solved and unsolved in the writers' respective realities. One of the themes that have stayed with us from the beginnings of Caribbean literature is racism in its many forms, accompanied by discrimination due to class and gender. It may take different forms in the Caribbean and in Britain but its destructive effects on the individual remain the same. Racism (especially when combined with poverty) alienates and splits the self and induces an unending search for wholeness. Other themes that continue to be debated are the form of fiction itself along with the power of language to shape the individual perception of reality past and present. Hybridity and displacement, so prominent in the critics' understanding of Caribbean literature, are clearly only two themes among many. With renewed urgency writers of Caribbean descent in Britain confront the former colonial power with the misrepresentation of its own history, demanding a reassessment of the past as a precondition for the future.

Notes

1 Sarah Lawson Welsh: "The Literatures of Trinidad and Jamaica". – In James Arnold (Ed.): *A History of Literature in the Caribbean*, vol. 2: *English and Dutch Speaking Regions*, Amsterdam & Philadelphia, 2001, pp. 62-63. For a definition and description of post-colonial literature written by transnationals especially in Britain and France see Adele King: "'Postcolonial' African and Caribbean Literature". – In Abiola Irele & Simon Gikandi (Eds.): *The Cambridge History of African and Caribbean Literature*, vol. 2, Cambridge, 2004, pp. 809-823.

2 Regardless of the paradoxes mentioned at the beginning, academic writing about Caribbean literature flourishes and is produced by scholars based both in the Caribbean and outside it. The last years saw the publication of voluminous books that combine survey articles on Caribbean literature in English by genre and region with contrastive essays. Both the two-volumed *Cambridge History of African and Caribbean Literature* (2004) edited by Abiola Irele and Simon Gikandi, as well as James A. Arnold's *History of Literature in the Caribbean* (2001) in three volumes cover the non-English speaking Caribbean as well. Among the many recently published books smaller in size and scope, Louis James's *Caribbean Literature in English* (1999) approaches Caribbean literature regionally and historically which provides valuable insights for readers who are interested in the formative influence of geographical and social place as well as history on imaginative writing.

3 Two of the main proponents of this view are Hena Maes-Jelinek and Bénédicte Ledent who claim that "[s]ince all West Indians descend from forced or voluntary migrations, throughout their history, first to the Caribbean and, after World War II, to Britain and North America, in some cases completing a triangular journey back to the Caribbean, the theme of exile remains central to Caribbean fiction wherever it is written". Hena Maes-Jelinek & Bénédicte Ledent: "The Novel since 1970". – In Arnold (Ed.): *A History of Literature in the Caribbean*, vol, 2, p. 165.

4 Edward Kamau Brathwaite: *The Development of Creole Society in Jamaica 1770-1820*, Oxford, 1971, p. 310.

5 Edward Kamau Brathwaite: "English in the Caribbean". – In Leslie A. Fiedler & Houston A. Baker Jr. (Eds.): *English Literature: Opening up the Canon*, Baltimore & London, 1981, p. 21.

6 Derek Walcott: "The Antilles, Fragments of Epic Memory: The 1992 Nobel Lecture", *World Literature Today* 67:2, 1993, 262.

7 *Ibid.*

8 *Ibid.*, 265.

9 Stuart Hall: "The Local and the Global: Globalization and Ethnicity". – In Anthony D. King (Ed.). *Culture, Globalization and the World System*, London & Basingstoke & Binghampton, 1991, p. 36.

10 *Ibid.*, 38-39.

11 Homi Bhabha: "The Commitment to Theory". – In H. B.: *The Location of Culture*, London & New York, 1994, p. 37.
12 *Ibid.*, 38.
13 Elaine Savory describes three phases of Caribbean literature using two terms denoting chronology and one term containing a political stance: colonial, anti-colonial and post-colonial. Elaine Savory: "Anglophone Caribbean Literature". – In Irele & Gikandi (Eds.): *The Cambridge History*, vol. 2, p. 719. Another slightly different classification is suggested by Frank Birbalsingh who identifies four phases: before 1950, 1950-1965, 1965-1980, and the phase since 1980. Frank Birbalsingh: "Introduction". – In F. B. (Ed.): *Frontiers of Caribbean Literature in English*, London & Basingstoke, 1996, pp. ix-xxii.
14 With the country's independence in 1966 the spelling changed from "Guiana" to "Guyana" which I shall use throughout the essay.
15 J. Downing Thompson, Jr.: "The Novel before 1950". – In Arnold (Ed.): *A History of Literature in the Caribbean*, vol. 2, pp. 117, 119.
16 Louis James: *Caribbean Literature in English*, London & New York, 1999, pp. 46-47.
17 George Lamming: "Concepts of the Caribbean". – In Birbalsingh (Ed.): *Frontiers*, p. 5. Lamming spoke about "Concepts of the Caribbean" in Toronto in November 1985 and only later published the lecture in Birbalsingh's book.
18 *Ibid.*, 3.
19 *Ibid.*, 4.
20 The British Caribbean (or West Indies) Federation that gave rise to hopes for a peaceful transition from colonialism to independence and subsequent prosperity was only short-lived (1958-1962). Already in 1944, when Jamaica had been allowed to govern itself under Crown supervision this had sparked hopes of local economic and political advancement. Against this political background Vic Reid's novel *New Day* (1949) celebrates a Jamaican identity that is rooted in the local landscapes and histories by using Creole and the story-telling tradition of the island.
21 James: *Caribbean Literature in English*, p. 93.
22 "George Lamming talks to Caryl Phillips", *Wasafiri* 26, 1997, 14.
23 For further information on the subgenre see Hena Maes-Jelinek: "The Novel from 1950 to 1970". – In Arnold (Ed.): *A History of Literature in the Caribbean*, vol. 2, pp. 137-139.
24 Bruce King: *V. S. Naipaul*. Plymouth, 1999, p. 22.
25 See the seminal work in the field by Bill Ashcroft, Gareth Griffiths & Helen Tiffin: *The Empire Writes Back. Theory and Practice in Post-Colonial Literatures*, London & New York, 1989, p. 154.
26 For a more comprehensive treatment of Riley see Jana Gohrisch: *(Un)Belonging? Geschlecht, Klasse, Rasse und Ethnizität in der britischen Gegenwartsliteratur. Joan Rileys Romane*, Frankfurt am Main, 1994.
27 "George Lamming talks to Caryl Phillips", 17.
28 *Ibid.*

29 *Ibid.*

30 Laura Moss: "The Politics of Everyday Hybridity. Zadie Smith's *White Teeth*", *Wasafiri* 39, 2003, 11.

Helge Nowak (München)

Caribbean Literature I: European Poetic Genres in Caribbean Poetry

1. Cultural Legacy and Cultural Autonomy: Aversion, Appropriation and Adoption

In late colonial and early post-colonial times, the question of how to deal with cultural heritage was always a vexed one. This is particularly true for the West Indies, the multi-cultural region *par excellence*, but one in which the most ancient, indigenous cultural legacy has been replaced by other ones, all of which were imported from distant continents and from very different socio- and ethno-cultural contexts. There has been a long-running debate in Caribbean[1] circles on how to deal with this situation, and as is well-known, various positions within the debate have been prominently taken by V. S. Naipaul, by Edward Kamau Brathwaite and by Derek Walcott.

Obviously, there are two options in such a situation. The first, radical one is to proclaim the cultural hegemony of the traditions of one ethno-cultural group over others – either those of the erstwhile colonial elite of European expatriates or, in order to bring about a "decolonising of the mind",[2] those of other, hitherto subjugated groups of the population. In *The Middle Passage*, Naipaul's account of a return journey to the region into which he was born but which he had all too willingly left to settle in the colonial metropolis, Naipaul embarked on a wholesale condemnation of the past record of cultural achievement in the colonial periphery. Even if his most notorious dictum, "nothing was created in the British West Indies",[3] was reserved for the cultural hegemony of the colonial elite, several more such sweeping statements in the book castigated other groups in society, for instance in Trinidad. In both his criticism and his poetry Brathwaite argued that the hegemonic aesthetics of the colonial elite should be replaced by the adoption (and as it were, hegemony) of another, this time based upon an African cultural legacy. Brathwaite's case is clearly one of cultural Pan-Africanism, of which the influence of the blues poems of Langston Hughes on his own poetry is further evidence. However, Brathwaite acknowledged that his poetry owes much to the Modernism of other US-American poets such as T.S. Eliot, and is therefore reminiscent also of another shift in cultural and regional allegiances in the West Indies, namely one from the Old to the New World which Naipaul had observed.[4] This already gives a hint of the second, more compromising option for writers working in times of colonial dawn or after Independence, namely to provide for cultural autonomy on the basis of a multi-cultural synthesis. This position, which invokes the name of Derek Walcott, implies the general acceptability, and even approval of literary traditions from every side of the colonial divide (and from elsewhere), in order to forge a cultural synthesis which ideally allows as many people as possible to identify with and to begin together anew, without making a clean break with the history of art in the colonial past. And yet, to begin anew with more than one cultural legacy also says that even striving to excel in conventional poetic genres will not be good enough if it means conformity just to the traditions of the erstwhile colonial centre.

Within the limits of an essay, the overall aim here is to provide a broad, but fresh and undogmatic view of generic intertextuality[5] in Caribbean poetry since 1900, which however has to declare one general interest (but for the same reason), namely to counter the impression that either colonial rule automatically goes hand in hand with aesthetic conformity, or that Decolonisation and cultural autonomy mean the end of cross-cultural generic intertextuality in poetry. This article will follow the debate on cultural legacy and autonomy outlined above through the general criticism of Caribbean poetry, through the development of a limited number of poetic genres, and through a corpus of successive, representative anthologies which have circumscribed the canon at a given time. The focus will remain on poetry in the medium of print; but this should not mean that other literary kinds in general or performance poetry in particular were less relevant – far from it. However, the picture can easily be complemented by other essays in this volume (on narrative, drama, on oral and performance poetry). Suffice to say that within the field of oral poetry and narrative, conventions from African 'orature' have been taken up in the Caribbean from the beginning of slavery. This is most obvious in the use of call-and-response techniques, for instance in ring games, in work songs and other songs, or in Anansi stories.[6] In the Caribbean, there is moreover a decided interest in continuing the traditions of oral storytelling and of performance poetry in a new media context which includes the electronic media.[7] Last but not least, the combination of spoken word and song with music and dance, well-known from ritual performances the world over, turns up again in contemporary Caribbean literary culture in multi-media forms of performance art.[8]

Naipaul's condemnation of the past record may have been an additional stimulus, at least, in the concentrated effort – visible for instance in poetry anthologies from the 1960s onwards – to collect relevant texts and thereby to correct views such as Naipaul's. Three partly overlapping phases of the publication of anthologies can be discerned, which conveniently mirror a more general periodisation (as for instance the one used and discussed in RR[9]). Of course, one has to take possible aberrations into account, especially when dealing with selections from the contemporary poetry of each phase. However, when the corpus is based on a large number of anthologies from several decades, including retrospective, historical anthologies (such as PB or RR), it is possible to mirror formation and revision of the canon more accurately. The first phase of collecting Caribbean poetry sees canon formation during the dawn of the British Empire, and it takes scarcely more than the fingers of one hand to count the more comprehensive anthologies which came out up to Independence of the greater English-speaking territories in the 1960s.[10] Anthologies from this phase (that is up to and including CV I), or later, retrospective anthologies devoted to it, could be expected to produce a greater number of examples of characteristically European poetic forms such as the sonnet or the villanelle, either because the poets or their contemporary editors would be thought more likely to be tinged by a colonial set of mind. This expectation turns out to be generally true, but not necessarily always.[11] After Independence, on average one new or markedly revised anthology appeared every eighteen months. A second phase, from the late 1960s through the 1970s, is characterised by the publication of numerous teaching anthologies (from CVerse to ACWE). They document conflicting tendencies: a canon revision and then a consolidation of the post-colonial canon is clearly in evidence, but at the same time there is the persistent endeavour to avoid a clean break with the past. Anthologies prepared primarily for schoolroom use can be expected to come up at any time with a higher number particularly of sonnets, because of the didactic possibilities and purposes connected with this genre; and this is indeed in evidence after Independence.[12] Post-Independence anthologies directed to the general reader, on the other hand, are likely to be more radical in championing the new, and therefore prone to stress cultural autonomy by editing out such genres. This is particularly noticeable in a third phase (beginning with the publication of Brathwaite's *New Poets from Jamaica* in 1979), which has led to an opening-up of the post-colonial canon for poetry that was still waiting to be canonised: poetry that is post-Independence by date, oral or meant for performance in terms of media, and increasingly characterised by female authorship and outlook. Not surprisingly, when editors devoted their energy to further new talent along these lines, they were generally less interested in the historical record, and even if they did take care of that, too – as in the influential anthology *Voiceprint* – there was usually no room for sound-poems such as the *sonetto*.[13] Highly meritorious as these anthologies are – and *Voiceprint* indeed is not only concerned with another, non-European oral tradition of Caribbean verse, but moreover breaks this tradition down into distinct genres of its own – if such anthologies alone were consulted to form an opinion of twentieth-century Caribbean poetry, the picture would be distorted once again. However, there is an element of correction: if such an endeavour was partly supported, it was also partly balanced out with regard to its *aversion* to European poetic genres by those comprehensive anthologies which were looking at both the present and the past (such as PB, RR and even WIP 1989). What is even more important, autonomy from this animosity is also in evidence; European poetic conventions continue to be referred to, are taken up, or are found to be modified in contemporary Caribbean poetry.

To the debate on the aesthetic and the political implications of those literary genres associated with the colonial centre, other notable poets, critics or editors of Caribbean poetry have contributed in their own, special ways. J. E. Clare McFarlane, Jamaica's second Poet Laureate and an influential critic and editor of Jamaican poetry from the 1920s up to Independence, shared the basis of Naipaul's argument, but also undermined it by pointing out examples of the achievement and excellence which Naipaul later decried as non-existent. Positive achievement to McFarlane however meant for instance the adoption and mastering of traditionally European poetic forms such as the villanelle or the sonnet, which showed both in his own poetry and in his benevolent attitude to like-minded poets.[14] As far as the sonnet is concerned, this is also true for the younger poet John Figueroa and for the groundbreaking anthology *Caribbean Voices* he edited.

For other poets and critics since the late 1960s, such an effort was misdirected from the start. They shared an aversion to the use of conventional poetic forms such as the pentameter, the sonnet or the villanelle, because these would always indicate, at the same time, a subservient, colonial set of mind, and a deferential attitude to Europe which in their day seemed entirely out of place. In Brathwaite's view, "British literature and literary forms [are] models which had very little to do, really, with the environment and reality of non-Europe", and he pointedly added, "The hurricane does not roar in pentameters".[15] In turn, poets and critics such as Brathwaite made disparaging remarks on the 'colonial' poetry before the 1940s, and were willing to concede a 'transitional' status, at best, to the next generation of poets. Full praise was reserved only for the achievement of those poets of the 1950s and 1960s who shed conventional genres and poetic idiom (local colouring included), and tried instead to build on African-related cultural traditions, Modernist forms of verse, and 'a language really used by black people'. Here is a late, summary statement of this new critical paradigm of post-colonial cultural nationalism in a Modernist garb:

> During the first three decades of the twentieth century, the poets [...] were mainly concerned with mastering the craft of conventional poetic forms, such as the sonnet and villanelle and ode, with little attempt to creolize or extend them and with modest introduction of local subject-matter. [...] In terms of both form and content, Caribbean poetry in English took a decisive turn in the late 1930s and early 1940s [...]. The freeing of verse form, together with some experimentation, was accom-

> panied by a new elation and seriousness in addressing the possibilities of local landscape, history, and social issues. Anti-colonialism, the necessity for Caribbean self-definition, protest against social ills deriving from considerations of class, colour, and economic status, assertion of the dignity and beauty of the black person, willingness to take poetic nurture from local cultural roots – these were some of the themes that brought a new immediacy to Caribbean poetry in English and hinted at its potential to challenge and disturb rather than merely soothe or divert.[16]

The important anthologies of Caribbean verse edited by critics of this post-Independence generation must be seen as conscious efforts to bring about a revision of the canon in favour of their different aesthetic ideals, namely experiment and 'immediacy' (meaning the commitment to regionalism, 'blackness' and progressiveness, including a concern with gender issues). Critics of this leaning however face a dilemma when they have to account for the undeniable interest of progressive, otherwise uncompromising writers such as Claude McKay or Una Marson in conventional genres, as visible in both their sonnets. Post-colonial critics of the 1980s, such as the team responsible for *The Empire Writes Back*,[17] have tried to point a way out of the dilemma by coming up with concepts such as 'abrogation' or 'appropriation', which would then allow for and even approve of poems that take up literary genres pointing back to the colonial centre, as long as they do indeed point the finger back in that direction. Still, as necessary as such a step was in furthering the debate away from mere 'aversion', these concepts, too, have been biased against an 'unpolitical' 'adoption' – as contrasted to an 'appropriation' – of such poetic conventions *per se*.

In the 1990s, the critical tide was seen to turn again, when critics called for another revision, this time of the canon as had been formed under the auspices of cultural Pan-Africanism. The non-conforming poems and poets formerly branded as 'colonial' or at best as 'transitional' and relegated from this canon, began to find again a more sympathetic hearing or even advocates. This more tolerant attitude towards the adoption of genres and other conventions which hitherto had seemed 'politically not correct' is clearly not a nostalgic return to the good old times, but a critically reflected move towards a review of the aesthetics of post-colonial canon formation. Such an approach had been pursued, even before the critical tide turned, and indeed all the way through the decades when cultural nationalist critics set the agenda, by the editors of those teaching anthologies mentioned above, which for instance had always included a large number of sonnets, old and new, and therefore had provided an equally institutionalised counter-canon to the critical consensus of the day.[18]

2. Continuum 1: Variety of Form in Villanelle and Sonnet

The following observations will be restricted to a limited number of poetic genres, which however have been traced through a fairly extensive and inherently diverse corpus of literary texts canonised at any given time. As a rule, the villanelles and sonnets discussed here, and the specimens of ode and verse satire referred to later are taken from altogether 34 representative anthologies of anglophone Caribbean literature published since the 1930s, and not from poets' individual collections (with three exceptions mentioned later). In other words: examples cited are generally those poems which compilers thought worth reprinting. A good example for the vagaries of critical esteem in the Caribbean is the villanelle, a difficult poetic form which had not only fascinated poets of the *fin de siècle*, but continued to attract many British and American poets of the twentieth century, among them W. H. Auden and Dylan Thomas. In their time, one West Indian poet, Vivian Virtue, even began his career in 1938 with a sequence of six villanelles which embellished the short Biblical account of the arrival of the Queen of Sheba. But the villanelle has never since ranked as prominently as in the days of McFarlane's *Treasury of Jamaican Poetry* (1949), and later was singled out as a kind of indicator for the imitative 'colonial' poetry of the past.[19] However, the form continues to be found occasionally, for instance in the poetry of A. L. Hendriks.[20] Three of his poems have a direct bearing on our context.

The first, but also the most recent example, "Villanelle of the Year's End. To an English Lady; from a Jamaican. December 1983", remains true to the conventional form and to the conventions of love poetry, making the poem a means by which a male lover tries to overcome the distance to his beloved, separated from him by the Atlantic. But the juxtaposition of imagery in the poem points to the real obstacle this cross-cultural couple of lovers has to overcome, namely the diversity of their individual experience of life and culture.

> This is the year's end, cold winds blow.
> Your fields burn frost-white; mine blaze red.
> I have Poinsettia; you have snow.[21]

The central paradox of the poem is that, if one makes an effort, such a union will be attainable nonetheless, across oceans, across cultures, and across the former colonial divide. This is a post-colonial poem by someone who is clearly not afraid to make use of features which had been branded as 'colonial' or 'transitional' (the Poinsettia, for example, is omnipresent in twentieth-century West Indian poetry – not only in villanelles – as a means to supply local colour). By contrast, in a second, earlier instance Hendriks had shown both a more inventive use of the form and a more home-grown theme in his "Song for my Brothers and Cousins". In a similar, but more relaxed way this curious love song was built on only two, often even identical rhymes, however without having them conform to the strict pattern of a proper villanelle. This poem, too, tried to further a union of minds across diversity. Here however this implied a call for political union within the region in times of Decolonisation, even after Jamaica had brought about the end of the colonial Federation of the West Indies by seeking Independence alone, a fact which is deplored in the scarcely veiled manner of a love song.

> O what the heart has loved cannot be torn away!
> The separate path, the lonely road is anguish, O my brothers,
> for we are still in love, no matter what we say.
> [...]
> Islands of the south have much to share with us,
> And much to give, and giving they are gay;
> are we too poor to share our gifts with others?
> are we so weak, so vain, so proud, my brothers?
> and can the heart forget its promises, all in a single day?

The songs we sing will now lament this agonized delay,
but we are still in love, my brothers, no matter what we say,
and what the heart has loved, my brothers, cannot be torn away.[22]

Finally, the third poem selected here for discussion shows that Hendriks on occasion can even assume a Modernist and a more confrontational manner. "No Equal Message" for once is a poem of fourteen lines that in a very liberal fashion calls up the conventions related to the sonnet, by showing a break and 'turn' within line 10 and by being cast in the form of unrhymed, accentual verse. In other ways, too, this poem contrasts strongly to the later villanelle addressed "To an English Lady", when it unfavourably compares a (foreign?) lady's gem to the homely beauty of a plain stone found on the beach.

Your jewel
gleaming in the light of three candles,
upon your slim wrist, fair lady,
brings me no message equal
to sea-stories my dark stone will tell.[23]

The natural qualities of the dark or "black stone" (ll. 8) are set positively against the white, artificially reflected light of the "fair" lady's counterpart, which has nothing to say about the West Indies. With such a confrontation, this 'fourteen-liner', which was published in the interval between the other two poems, that is in the early years of Decolonisation, surely would have pleased critics calling for cultural autonomy much more, and they might moreover have been pleased by outright free verse such as in the poem "An Old Jamaican Woman Thinks about the Hereafter" (1965) or by poems in 'nation-language' such as "Jamaican Small Gal".[24] When seen together over the years, Hendriks's poems are always good for a surprise, and defy any easy label for the poet's attitude to genre conventions and cultural legacy. His poetry alone frustrates any notion that Decolonisation automatically entails the end of cross-cultural generic intertextuality in Caribbean poetry, and it calls into question any simple equation between conformity to European conventions of poetry and a colonial set of mind. Hendriks's poetry is no more 'transitional' than that of Walcott (who is only eight years younger and equally at home in a variety of forms and voices); Hendriks's poetry is the product of a talented craftsman, and speaks of a truly independent mind.

The example of Hendriks is also a good justification why working with a continuum is better suited to deal with such a variety of expression than either facile labels (such as 'colonial' or 'transitional' poetry) or discrete, but also fixed categories (such as villanelle or even sonnet). The well-known concept of a 'Creole continuum' is also very useful for an appraisal of Caribbean adoptions of European literary forms,[25] and even more so if there are not only one, but rather two continua applied to both the formal and the thematic levels of expression. Continuum 1 describes the form of the individual poem, and deals with the degree of imitation and variation in a generic context. For the sonnet, this means that at the one end of the continuum we find strict adherence to either the Petrarchan or the Shakespearean pattern, as the two most common species of this poetic genre. The prime example in Caribbean poetry is of course the corpus of sonnets (of both species) by Claude McKay, of which the anthologies reprint his best-known specimen, "If We Must Die" (1919),[26] which is usually read as an anti-lynching poem, and also the poems "The Harlem Dancer", "I Shall Return" and "The Castaways", which were also cast in the Shakespearean form, but are less typical of McKay's defiant stance against white supremacy.[27] Fittingly enough, the only specimen visible in *New Poets from Jamaica* (1979) which overcame Brathwaite's avowed aversion to "British literature and literary forms"[28] is the Shakespearean "Sonnet for McKay", in which the US-American poet Bob Stewart celebrates, in congenial form, McKay's discovery and true expression of his blackness. And indeed, in the light of many other sonnets (not reprinted in the corpus of anthologies here under review) which show this attitude, it is difficult to apply the 'colonial' label to McKay's poetry, even though it is formally conventional: a combination which some critics have seen as a dilemma.[29] It is moreover remarkable that from the times of Empire, scarcely more than a handful of other sonnets have been anthologised which follow the Bard just like McKay, namely W. O. MacDonald's metapoetical "Sonnet",[30] D. A. Trotman's "To a Star" and J. A. Rodway's "Telephone",[31] and three of Una Marson's sonnets, namely "Repose"[32] and the apparent double sonnet "Renunciation" and "In Vain" (1930).[33]

What has been said about the critics' dilemma with regard to McKay's sonnets is also true for Una Marson's *oeuvre*, even though her sonnets (for instance the latter pair) are more imitative and less feminist than her other work. Most of the other 'proper' sonnets found in the corpus of anthologies are Italian sonnets, a fact which again speaks less of a directly 'colonial' or even jingoist attitude to British literary forms, and more generally of the lingering influence of Romantic poetry, of the sonnets by Wordsworth, Keats or Shelley. Late-Romantic, Italian sonnets from colonial times that have been reprinted more than once are "How Shall I Sit in Dreamy Indolence?" (1924)[34] by Harold Watson, a solitary speaker's melancholy brooding, and "One" (1929)[35] by C. M. G. (Clara Maude Garrett), which speaks of a panentheistic longing to unite with the West Indian landscape. Later examples come from John Figueroa, again a Jamaican, but one of the Windrush Generation of emigrants, and from Dennis Craig, who stayed on to follow an academic career culminating in the vice-chancellorship of the University of Guyana. Figueroa's "At Home the Green Remains"[36] is significantly dated "England, 1948" and deals with that complex home/migration/exile which was so central to his generation of writers, while his sonnet "Birth Is …"[37] is concerned with the span of human life in general terms. "Flowers" by Dennis Craig (1961)[38] is Romantic in the sense of Blake's "London", in its stark contrast of natural beauty to the ugliness of slum life in the city.

These poems from the end of the colonial era are also the last pure examples of Petrarchan (and also Shakespearean) sonnets to be found in the corpus, a fact which should however be interpreted with caution, as it does not automatically signal a break with conventions on the poets' side, but first of all an unwillingness of editors to include existing specimens in post-Independence anthologies. Vivian Virtue is a good example again, as he is often mentioned to have continuously produced a corpus of sonnets of his own and in translation which, as far as numbers are concerned, must have equalled that of his father-in-law, Claude McKay, but which has been much less esteemed by critics and editors. Of all the sonnets Virtue was concerned with, only one has been found twice in the corpus, namely his translation of a poem by José-Maria de Heredia, "The Conquistadores",[39] and only two single ones besides, namely "I Have Seen March",[40] a nature poem providing

West Indian local colour, and "The Hour",[41] Virtue's sonnet on Jamaican Independence, which tells perhaps most about critical preferences.[42] But this is also a good occasion to make another, necessary point. As extensive as the corpus under review already is, there is still one good reason for an enlargement, because in their concentration on the single poem editors of anthologies can hardly avoid to misrepresent those poets like McKay or Virtue who have written single sonnets in great numbers, or perhaps sonnet sequences, which are usually not reprinted *in toto* in anthologies. This is true for "The Negro Dancers" (July 1919), McKay's short sequence which came out at the same time as "If We Must Die", which in turn was published together with a companion piece, "A Roman Holiday" – but neither this last poem nor McKay's sonnet sequence has been reprinted in anthologies.[43] From another early sequence, "Caribbean Sonnets" (1929) by Clara Maude Garrett, only two sonnets have survived in anthologies,[44] and none from Albinia Hutton's *Sonnets of Sorrow* (1939). More prominently, but again partially represented is Derek Walcott's sequence of ten (originally eleven) sonnets, "Tales of the Islands" (1958, revised 1962). Three more recent sequences, "Lilian's Songs" by Cecil Gray, and "Sonnets from Whitley Bay" and "Frail Deposits", both by Fred D'Aguiar, are not to be found in the anthologies at all.[45] This is why a limited and clearly defined number of exceptions were made from the general rule of basing the corpus on anthologies only. These exceptions will occur, first, with regard to selections of the poetry of Claude McKay, because he is arguably the best-known Caribbean sonneteer; second, with regard to the collected poetry of Derek Walcott, who is easily one of the most versatile of contemporary Caribbean poets and one who is well-known for his unabashed but also discerning view on and practice of adoption; and third, with regard to individual collections of the poetry of Fred D'Aguiar, because he is one notable poet of the Caribbean diaspora interested in the genre. The consequential enlargement of the corpus in these cases will make itself felt when we now return to the formal continuum to see various stages of deviation from the norm.

The attempt at 'mastering the form', so often given out as typical of 'colonial', imitative poetry,[46] in fact never ended with writing canonical sonnets true to either of the two best-known conventions;

nor was it laid to rest together with colonial rule. This is a longer story, and there is more variety of expression. 'Mastering the form' included mixing the forms, in a first stage by adherence to the also conventionalised variant used by John Donne in his "Holy Sonnets".[47] In the octave, this follows the Petrarchan pattern of rhyme, but is more ambiguous in the sestet, where an overlapping of Petrarchan and Shakespearean patterns occurs because this can also be read as a third quatrain followed by an end couplet. This less than clear-cut form had been in vogue with contemporaries of McKay, but thereafter seems to have lost its appeal to other poets. Alfred M. Cruickshank from Trinidad used it in "When I Am Dead" (1932),[48] where the lyrical speaker remonstrates, in a provocative manner reminiscent once more of Donne, against having a priest at his funeral; and Cruickshank used it once more in "Let Us Be Frank" (1937),[49] where the tone reminds one rather of McKay. McKay himself took up the form in the metapoem "Poetry" (1922)[50] and in "The Lynching" (1920),[51] where the ambiguity for once is not one of form but of subject matter, of how to ascertain the thematic complex of race, crime and punishment. This variant species was much in favour with fellow-Jamaican W. Adolphe Roberts, who used it in two animal poems, in "Peacocks" (1928?)[52] and in "The Cat" (c. 1944),[53] moreover in a sonnet "On a Monument to Martí", the Cuban freedom fighter (1950),[54] and in "The Maroon Girl" (1949),[55] which celebrates the beauty of a Carib Indian as a symbol of Jamaican pride. The overtones of 'Caribbean Consciousness' in the last two poems come out even sharper when they are compared with pastoral poems such as with "The Invitation" to come and see idyllic Jamaica, sent out by 'Lena Kent' (Lettice A. King),[56] or with the altogether unspecified setting of "Trees" by Harold Watson (1924).[57]

Roughly of the same, 'hybrid' nature is the creation of a synthesis showing only the bipartite structure of an Italian sonnet but the number or even pattern of rhymes in a Shakespearean one. Claude McKay is represented in the anthologies with as many sonnets of this species as with 'regular' ones, all of them showing him from his religious side rather than as a rebel with another cause.[58] Other poems of this kind found in the corpus were written by two Englishmen living in the colonial West Indies, by the Jamaican poet McFarlane, and by A. J. Seymour, who as founder-editor of the magazine *Kyk-Over-Al* assumed a similar function as one of the patrons of literature in Guyana before and after Independence. The poems by the seemingly aptly named Sir John Squire and by W. V. Tothill defeat expectations because they are examples of 'going native', of taking the point of view of the Other. Squire's "There Was an Indian"[59] addresses colonialism by having "an Indian" fearfully witness the arrival of Columbus's ships. Tothill's "Sonnet" (1932)[60] is a sort of contrary poem to Clara Maude Garrett's "London Love" (1929):[61] in her poem, the metropolis is praised by one of the "colonial we", whereas the lyrical speaker in Tothill's sonnet considers London to be a prison from which he longs to escape, "back to Africa" which he had left behind. By contrast, Seymour's two poems, which were published together in 1954 and are among those sonnets most often reprinted in anthologies, focus on nature. "There Runs a Dream" parallels McFarlane's "On National Vanity" (c. 1948)[62] and also Walcott's "Ruins of a Great House" (1962) in its general meditation on the passing of Empire, but Seymour does not attack colonialism directly, as Walcott does in his Independence poem (which, though no sonnet, nonetheless remains closely linked with 'Eng. Lit.' in other ways). With Seymour, it is not the manor-house (Man's house) which is the central symbol, not least for slavery, but the rivers and the jungle in (still colonial) "Guiana", that is forces of Nature which ultimately win back what Nature had lost in her struggle with Man's colonisation and plantation. The second poem, "Carrion Crows", is an animal poem which on first impressions might nowadays appear as a sort of metrical Ted Hughes poem before its day, but that would have Seymour appear once more as 'transitional', whereas it seems fairer to say that Seymour quite consciously took the conventional sonnet form to balance out the contrary views of carrion crows as birds of prey and as symbols of beauty and majesty (an observation which does not seem to be particularly 'transitional' when found in contrary poems by Blake).[63] – In this case, further development of this 'synthetic' species of the sonnet in Caribbean poetry has indeed taken place, but it has to be sought outside the corpus under review, namely in the poetry of Derek Walcott and of Fred D'Aguiar. Walcott's "The Harbour" (1948) is such an example which turns from the observation of fishermen at sea to an autobiographical and metapoetical reflection on the young poet's own calling. Moreover, this and the poems “Foot Print”, “Shadow Play” and “The Last Sonnet About Slavery (After Hogarth)”, all by D’Aguiar,[64] show the impact of Modernism without making a radical break with formal regularity: all four poems are examples of this admittedly ‘hybrid’ species of the sonnet; they are progressive in their use of four-stressed, accentual verse; and they go their own way in their variations of sound repetition, in their use of original patterns of rhyme, of assonance, consonance and eye-rhymes. These differences apart, D’Aguiar’s “The Last Sonnet About Slavery” obviously remains true to the thematic interests of Claude McKay.[65]

The next stage of deviation from the norm on the continuum is characterised by a more experimental, original pattern of the poet’s own making, which on the whole remains recognisably linked with the tradition of the sonnet – roughly defined as to be a poem of fourteen lines with a bipartite structure (often divided by a ‘turn’), consistently rhymed – although poetic license may be taken with regard to individual parts of the definition. Occasionally, one finds slightly shorter or somewhat longer poems which otherwise obey convention. “Revelation” by H. A. Vaughan is an often reprinted example of a shortened Italian sonnet in twelve lines, which moreover is reminiscent of Shakespeare’s sonnet no. 130 and of others on the ‘dark lady’ in the way it sets the ideal beauty of a black woman positively against wrong conceptions stemming from Classical Greece and Rome.[66] Examples of lengthened sonnets, poems in fifteen lines but on seven rhymes, are “South Quay” (1932)[67] by C. A. Thomasios, the speaker of the House of Representatives in Trinidad after Independence, and “Jasmine” (1921)[68] by Claude McKay, who wrote also a number of double sonnets.[69] Intricate and original patterns of rhyme abound at this stage, so much so that only a few examples need to be mentioned here. “A Good Life Sonnet” by E. A. Markham,[70] a member of the Windrush generation, is formally a variation upon the ‘synthetic species’ of the sonnet. Thematically, it is an ironic variant of Renaissance conventions, a conversation-piece on the happy effects of adultery, committed by a speaker of Black English (visibly so in his use of the verb “to yashmak” in l. 8) with the married woman he meets in the foggy London winter. Considerably more gloomy are the settings of the next two poems, and yet they are also examples of the vitality of the genre. Derek Walcott showed his individual craftsmanship already in his first collection, in poems such as "A City's Death by Fire" (1948).[71] This meditation on the destruction of his place of birth, Castries in St. Lucia, was cast in the form of a sonnet in six-stressed accentual verse, and with an original scheme of five rhymes. The inner destruction of a city of which the *façade* still stands can be seen in the "Sonnet to New Flowers" (1988)[72] by Mahadai Das, a poem which not only unabashedly announces its conventional genre in the title, but thereby signals also its thematic similarity to "Flowers" by the poet's Guyanese countryman Dennis Craig (mentioned above). In the decades after Independence, some things apparently have not changed: once more, desolation and violence in the city's slums are contrasted with the natural beauty of flowers, but this time the inharmonious state of affairs is mirrored also in the form of the sonnet, which begins in rhyme, only to eschew it after the first four lines.

The form of "Sonnet to New Flowers" blends into the next stages on the continuum, which gradually sheds remaining conventions and approaches free verse. Again, the list of examples is very long in both sub-corpora, in the anthologies and in the collections by McKay, Walcott and D'Aguiar. It seems fruitful to illustrate two main points only: the degree of regularity, and the attitude of represented poets towards the conventions of the genre. With regard to the degree of regularity of form, two further stages on the continuum can be made out. There are, first, those 'fourteen-liners' which have done with the conventions of metre, rhyme and bipartition which are usually associated with the sonnet, but will not break with a regularity of form altogether. Two sub-species are recognisable at this stage, one of which is characterised by the use of accentual verse, such as in "No Equal Message" by A. L. Hendriks, referred to at the beginning of this section. Derek Walcott's sequence "Tales of the Islands" is another good example, and younger poets such as Wayne Brown or Fred D'Aguiar have followed in his footsteps.[73] The other sub-species which is connected with the decision for regularity, but of another kind, varies conventional stanza structures and partition of the sonnet. Both "Solitaire" by the Jamaican poet Vivette Hendriks and the concluding stanzas to the ode to "Kaietur",[74] by Walter MacArthur Lawrence from British Guiana, are not only instances of late Romantic, local-colour poetry, but are similarly made up of two stanzas of seven lines each. For "Solitaire",[75] her poem on the song of a local bird, Vivette Hendriks chose a form that reassembled the quatrains and tercets of an Italian sonnet by having them follow one upon another in alternation. By contrast with this example of natural beauty, Lawrence's concluding stanzas of seven long lines, which address a mighty and mythic waterfall in Guyana, are a prime West Indian version of the Sublime. Another variant of the 'fourteen-liner' at this stage of the continuum sees the use of small units such as rhyming couplets or distichs. In another landscape poem from Guyana, "The River" by 'Leo' (Egbert Martin, 1883 or 1886),[76] the rhyming couplets contribute to a jingling of sounds reminiscent of the contemporary poetry of Swinburne. By contrast, the startling sound effect of a recent, satirical poem by Fyna Dowe, "De Bubble Burs",[77] is not only due to its couplets, but to the use of a Caribbean Creole as poetic diction for a poem that is still recognisably bipartite in the Italian tradition of the genre. A considerable number of other 'fourteen-liners' are printed in distichs throughout or at least in parts. An editors' favourite is "The Word Once Spoken"[78] by Barnabas J. Ramon-Fortuné from Trinidad, a poem that addresses the general theme of the brevity and inevitable decay of life in a Modernist fashion, making use of rhyme as well as half-rhyme for sound repetition, and refraining from capitalisation on the printed page. A more recent specimen is "Mama Dot" (1984/85), Fred D'Aguiar's rewriting of the well-known nursery rhyme of "Solomon Grundy" in Black English, and in terms of race and gender – perhaps the foremost example of an appropriation of the genre in the sense of 'writing back':

"Mama Dot"

Born on a Sunday
in the kindom of Ashante

Sold on Monday
into slavery

Ran away on Tuesday
cause she born free

[...][79]

There are two other instances in which 'fourteen-liners' have been cast into the form of distichs in free verse, namely in Andrew

Salkey's "The Festival of Flowers"[80] and in Brian Chan's "By Wicklight" (1983 or 1988).[81] Both poets have moved on to the Caribbean diaspora (Salkey as member of the Windrush Generation first from Jamaica to Britain and later to the USA, Chan from Guyana to Canada), and both their poems border on the next stage of the continuum where the genre connection may be kept up in the end merely by the fact that the poem in question, usually in free verse, is a 'fourteen-liner' (and perhaps part of a sequence of this kind). Still, it is very unlikely that poets themselves will not think about this all-too-easily avoidable connection, or presume the readers to be so innocent as not to see at least an allusion in the fact. This is also very unlikely when the general attitude of the poet is rather distanced towards the conventional genre, as here with Salkey, who made no secret of his animosity when editing the anthology *Breaklight*.[82] This collection was explicitly introduced as being 'committed' to the point of view of Brathwaite and others who, by their refusal to be involved in the adoption of European poetic conventions such as the sonnet, broke with one tradition completely, in order to further the cause of another. This last position has to be regarded as the ultimate opposite on the continuum to the strict adherence to conventional patterns, and it is preceded by that stage where 'fourteen-liners' in free verse may just barely acknowledge its existence. At this penultimate stage, a larger number of poems is to be found which stem from poets like Salkey or Chan who are otherwise not represented by sonnets. Examples of such irregular 'fourteen-liners' include the aptly entitled "Variation" by Samuel Selvon,[83] and also "Savannah Lands" by Wilson Harris (AGP 76), moreover Ian McDonald's variation upon the Dark Lady theme in "Decorated for a Kiss",[84] Geoffrey Drayton's attempt at ekphrasis in "Still Life",[85] or Lorna Goodison's "I Am Becoming My Mother" (1983).[86] On the other hand, at this penultimate stage one finds also poets who are represented elsewhere on the continuum with poems which deviate less from convention. The most prominent example is Derek Walcott with his poems "The Polish Rider" (1962, another instance of ekphrasis), "Homage to Edward Thomas", the Georgian Poet (1969), and "The Morning Moon", Walcott's farewell to the genre (1976).[87] Others represented both here and elsewhere are Dennis Craig, who addresses *Négritude* and Black Beauty in his prose poem "Interlude for Native Pride"

(1970);[88] then E. A. Markham with another of his love poems, "Love at No. 13";[89] and Fred D'Aguiar with "South South-East",[90] a magic incantation full of references to flora and fauna of the Caribbean Basin, but without the pastoral overtones of local-colour poetry of earlier times. This last comparison of course begs the question as to another evaluation and perhaps gradation of poems, this time not with regard to their variety of form, but with regard to a thematic level of expression, and with regard to their degree of cultural autonomy.

3. Continuum 2: The Degree of Cultural Autonomy Visible in a Variety of Genres

The second objection which was and still is often made against the adoption of European poetic conventions by non-European poets in areas that were at one time European dependencies is that 'mastering the craft' ultimately was a sign of mere mimicry, and the mark of an unbroken colonial mindset. The summary statement quoted above calls instead for a break with tradition and a fresh start characterised by 'creolisation' of both form and content, anti-colonialism of spirit and 'immediacy' of impact. What might at first appear to be a question to be answered by either 'yes, mission accomplished' or 'no, failure to take off', is in fact again a matter of degree, and thus again a case for making use of a continuum. Continuum 2 evaluates both form and content of the individual poem, and deals with the degree of imitation and variation in a cultural and political context. I should like to illustrate this in two ways: the outline of Continuum 2 will be presented first with a sketch of the history of the long poem in Caribbean literature, and this will be followed by a more detailed illustration of separate categories, again with sonnets from the corpus as examples.

Near the one end of this continuum, we find once more an unqualified adoption of and adherence to setting, political ideologies, and cultural or literary conventions of the erstwhile colonial metropolis. In the context of Caribbean poetry, such a colonial ethos can be found most fully realised in the related genres of ode and elegy. Already the beginning of Caribbean literature in writing and in print is marked in this way, by two odes – one of them originally composed in Latin – on the eighteenth-century governors of Jamaica, Sir Nicholas Lawes and George Haldane (1718 and 1774). A century later, 'Leo' (Egbert Martin) first wrote a similar "Welcome" on the arrival of the Prince of Wales (later King George V) in British Guiana (1885), and two years later 'Leo' was awarded prize-money for his additional stanzas to the British national anthem, contributed in celebration of Queen Victoria's Golden Jubilee (1887). Notable West Indian poets such as 'Tom Redcam', Walter MacArthur Lawrence, J. E. Clare McFarlane or A. J. Seymour continued to write odes and elegies on the deaths or coronations of British royalty, or on "The Empire's Flag", up to 1952, sometimes as a starting-point to their career. Even Redcam's "Jamaica's Coronation Ode" (1932) says more about loyalty to the King than to the Country.[91]

Apart from odes and elegies, there have been a variety of long poems either by Caribbean authors or with a West Indian setting, the development of which has on the whole run parallel to the general debate on cultural legacy and autonomy among critics of Caribbean poetry. When the odes and elegies mentioned are cases of an unqualified adoption of various conventions and ideologies of the colonial motherland, local colour is added by topographical poems of the eighteenth and nineteenth centuries. Their list is quite long, and if nothing else, the sheer length of these early poems is also remarkable. "Barbados" by Nathaniel Weekes (a pastoral of c. 1,000 lines, 1754) was complemented later by M. J. Chapman's "Barbadoes" (some 2,000 lines, 1833). James Grainger's "The Sugar-Cane" (some 2,500 lines, 1764) was followed by John Singleton's "A General Description of the West Indian Islands" (of the same length, 1767), and the tradition continued through abolitionist poems such as the anonymous "Jamaica: A Poem in Three Parts" (some 400 lines, 1777) and also James Montgomery's "The West Indies" (some 1,000 lines, 1809). The lasting influence of Neoclassical taste is documented in two imitations of Spenser from the 1830s, Robert Dunbar's "The Cruise; or, A Prospect of the West Indian Archipelago" (close to 100 Spenserian stanzas, 1835) and William Hosack's "The Isle of Streams; or, The Jamaica Hermit" (of the same length, 1879; a shorter version was published in 1833 under the title "Jamaica"). Hosack's poem combined the typically neoclassical vogue for imitations of Spenser with the introduction of African and of syncretic features of Black slave culture.[92] The way from adoption with local colouring to an appropriation in the sense of 'writing back', or 'writing home' – both to Britain and to the West Indies – in an otherwise unconventional, provocative way can be discerned in West Indian anti-colonial and abolitionist poems like "Hiroona: An Historical Romance in Poetic Form", by Horatio Nelson Huggins (published posthumously in 1930, but written before 1895). This long poem about the rebellion of the indigenous Carib Indians against British rule in 1795, written in somewhat heroic couplets (albeit in tetrameter), "could also be termed the first Caribbean epic poem", as Paula Burnett has said, and "is most remarkable for the originality, at the peak of British imperial history, of his lonely anti-colonial vision",[93] ending in a vengeful prophecy of imperial doom. The further history of the long poem during and immediately after Decolonisation signals first a break with conventions related to Europe: *Jamaica* by Andrew Salkey (1973) and *The Arrivants: A New World Trilogy* by Edward Kamau Brathwaite (published as it were in instalments 1967-69, and as a trilogy in 1973) are proof of a distanced attitude towards such conventions, and mirror instead the Pan-Africanism of their creators in themes, cultural references (for instance to West African deities), and in their orientation towards 'nation-language' (in Brathwaite's terminology). This was a fresh start, and the result was impressive, especially in Brathwaite's case.[94] However, multicultural autonomy – the only one which truly becomes a multi-cultural society – appears to be ultimately reached only when the lingering animosity is overcome, too, and replaced by a general acceptance and a self-confident adoption (perhaps even fusion) of a diversity of cultural legacies, regardless of place of origin. Such an approach is most prominently visible in Derek Walcott's epic *Omeros* (1990), in his successive, shorter sequence "The Bounty" (which provided also the title to a collection, 1997), or in his earlier verse satire "The Spoiler's Return".[95] In "The Bounty", Walcott interwove an elegy on his mother with a celebration of Caribbean flora, and a reference to the fate of Captain Bligh and the men of *H.M.S. Bounty* with intertextual reference to the poets Ovid, Dante and John Clare. *Omeros* ranged even further in its scope, taking off from the Caribbean Sea and taking in for instance London, Dublin and Boston, Mass. as setting, and bringing together West Indian fishermen with the personnel and stories of the Homeric epics. Both of Walcott's long poems are made up of tercets which on the one hand refer back to Dante's *Divina Commedia* and thus once more to the European epic tradition, but Walcott combined this with features of a self-restraining Modernism such as in the use of half-rhyme or of accentual (and not completely 'free') verse. In "The Spoiler's Return", on the other hand, Walcott had taken up and fused the conventions of Classical and Neoclassical verse satire with those of the Trinidad calypso. Quotations from Lord Rochester's *Satire Against Mankind*, from The Mighty Spoiler's best-known calypso "Bed Bug", and from V. S. Naipaul (who is an object of satire in the poem) were incorporated into a long poem which moreover combined rhyming couplets and the consistent use of Creole English or 'Patois' as poetic language. Here and in *Omeros* (Chapter III), variety of expression means also linguistic variety, but this is neither local colour in the sense of mere exoticism, nor is the use of 'a language really used by black men' seen as an end in itself.

After the general outline of Continuum 2 has been sketched with a few examples of long poems, separate categories can be illustrated in more detail with a greater number of shorter poems. Again, sonnets from the corpus will serve as examples. The model is not used as a means to describe stages in a historical development, but for the purpose of a systematic classification of categories. For this reason, the five categories mentioned in the preceding sketch will appear in a different order; moreover, an additional, first category will allow for sonnets with a universal theme or an exclusively personal content. In a poem like "Peacocks" by W. Adolphe Roberts, the majestic and beautiful birds serve to illustrate the time-honoured themes of *sic transit gloria mundi* and *aere perennus*, but the poem does not make any reference in that context to either party in the colonial interaction. In other instances, the genre was adopted for metapoetical purposes, such as in "Sonnet" by W. O. MacDonald[96] or in "Poetry" by Claude McKay. In McKay's double sonnet "My Mother",[97] the personal overtones are even stronger, whereas the vicissitudes of life are addressed in more general terms in poems such as "Birth Is …" by John Figueroa,[98] "Disillusionment" by 'Miss V.M. Clerk',[99] "In Absence" by H. A. Vaughan[100] or "Repose" by Una Marson.[101] Contrary to expectations, even McKay's sonnets "If We Must Die" and "The Lynching" belong to this category, because they do not specify the ethnic or national identity of aggressors and victims, and therefore lend themselves to a more general interpretation.[102]

The second category on the continuum is reserved for those poems which show an unqualified adherence to the setting, the political ideologies or the cultural or literary conventions of the erstwhile colonial motherland beyond the fact that they adopt a conventional genre. Here, the list of sonnets is much shorter than could be expected from what has been said about the ode. It is even debatable if "The Dancer"[103] by W. Adolphe Roberts or the two poems by Una Marson, "Renunciation" and "In Vain" (1930),[104] should be included here just because they refer to mythological characters such as Alcestis or Diana, respectively. The way the lyrical speaker in Marson's poems is cast as a (female?) "slave" longing for the coming of the "king of my heart" is perhaps a more convincing reason for inclusion. Proper and remaining examples of this category in the corpus are Clara Maude Garrett's encomium on the metropolis in "London Love" (1929),[105] and "How Shall I Sit in Dreamy Indolence?" by Harold Watson (1924),[106] which makes a reference to Autumn, a season which is not marked in the West Indies, while Derek Walcott's post-Independence free-verse "Homage to Edward Thomas" is again included with qualification.

The third category in the direction of multi-cultural autonomy is characterised by the adoption of a still recognisably European genre such as the sonnet, but with additional local colour provided by a Caribbean setting, flora or fauna or by the appearance of the peoples of the region. In his poem "I Have Seen March", Vivian Virtue referred to West Indian plants and fruit, but avoided any dubious reference to seasons. Other examples of this kind, which have also been mentioned before in another context, are "The River" by 'Leo' (Egbert Martin), the concluding stanzas to W. M. Lawrence's ode "Kaietur", "There Runs a Dream" by A. J. Seymour, or "Solitaire" by Vivette Hendriks. Another way of providing local colour is by having people from the region appear, either to bring in another point of view, as in "There was an Indian" by Sir John Squire, or to stress the point that 'black is beautiful', as in "To a Tudor Street Girl" by H. A. Vaughan[107] or in editors' favourites such as

“The Maroon Girl” by W. A. Roberts (1949)[108] and “Jamaican Fisherman” by Philip Sherlock (1953).[109]

The visible attempt to achieve multi-cultural autonomy in the way it was described above is placed as a fourth category, still in the centre of the continuum. Poems that fall into this category are for example those like McKay’s “Mulatto” (1925)[110] which explicitly address ‘hybridity’ in ethnic terms, and the conflicting feelings this engenders. Other poets have discussed this multiple sense of belonging in terms of the migrant experience, such as John Figueroa in his sonnet “At Home the Green Remains” (mentioned above) and Geoffrey Drayton in his ‘fourteen-liner’ “Still Life”,[111] which makes reference both to the European painter Matisse and to “the Indies” which the lyrical speaker has left. There is also the attempt (already seen in “The Spoiler’s Return”) to achieve a synthesis of literary conventions or linguistic peculiarities related to more than one region: “De Bubble Burs” by Fyna Dowe is a good example of the way both have been achieved at the same time.[112] Another distinct subgroup within this category is characterised by its reference to particular forms of music and dance as elements of Black culture, although this is not uncontroversial. “Can I in Pride Mock Sad Buffoons” by Antonio Jarvis (1935) is a poem which refers to drumming and a tribal dance for rain as elements of the African cultural heritage in the Caribbean, but does so in the form of a Shakespearean sonnet in iambic tetrameter (!) and in British English. Gordon Rohlehr, who reprinted and critically discussed this poem in his introduction to *Voiceprint*, saw it as a half-hearted attempt and found it sounding wrong when measured against his ideal of Caribbean cultural autonomy.[113] Even though this sonnet may not rank as proper ‘voiceprint’, it is however still a good example of multi-cultural ‘hybridity’, like others in this category. Examples from the poetry of Claude McKay include “The Harlem Dancer”,[114] his short sonnet sequence “The Negro Dancers” (July 1919),[115] and the Shakespearean sonnet entitled “Negro Spiritual” (1922).[116] This line continues with “Third World Blues” by the Jamaican dancer Dennis Scott,[117] and with “Black Cat (for Miles Davis)” by Faustin Charles,[118] which incidentally is a rare example of a double ‘fourteen-liner’ (in free verse, but occasionally rhymed). All the examples mentioned are based on the general acceptance and self-confident adoption, perhaps even fusion of a diversity of cultural legacies, regardless of place of origin.

A fifth category is made up of appropriations which adopt in order to provoke. This can be discerned in West Indian anti-colonial and anti-slavery poems, and particularly in the work of Claude McKay, where the examples are copious.[119] Surprisingly, none have found their way into the anthologies in the corpus, where McKay is often represented with his religious poems. But "On a Monument to Martí", W. A. Roberts's sonnet on the Cuban revolutionary, and "The Hour", Vivian Virtue's sonnet on Jamaican independence have a place here, and so does Wayne Brown's "Famine",[120] a 'fourteen-liner' which is intersected by two lines from "Land of Hope and Glory" – a provocative combination indeed. More recent examples along the same lines are Fred D'Aguiar's "Mama Dot" and "The Last Sonnet About Slavery (After Hogarth)".

A sixth and last category is again, as in Continuum 1, reserved for the stance that shows a general aversion to conventions related to Europe, and therefore also a refusal to make use of them. Once again, Edward Kamau Brathwaite is a good case in point: even when he occasionally writes a 'fourteen-liner' such as "Pebbles",[121] which can just be included in Category 5, he does his best to play down any resemblance, but generally he has tried to avoid the sonnet altogether. With Category 6, the other end of the continuum has been reached, and the time for a summing-up has come.

4. Summing Up

At the end of this survey of the ways in which European poetic genres were adopted in anglophone Caribbean poetry, I should like to present the findings of the investigation into the way the sonnet in particular travelled and prospered in statistical form and to discuss them summarily. A distinctive genre such as the sonnet is particularly well-suited to illustrate general developments. For all parties concerned in this trans-cultural literary communication, the sonnet comes with the credentials of being a genre originating from European literatures; it is a literary kind which remains recognisable across the variability of individual shapes; and it is therefore useful not only as a category in itself but also in allowing for a demarcation and exemplification of relevant subcategories and variants. To ensure the representativeness of the analysis and the meaningfulness of the findings, a corpus was established, consisting of, first, anthologies and, second, collections of individual poets. The corpus of relevant poems takes note of anglophone originals only, and excludes sonnets circulating in translation – neither "The Conquistadores" nor other renderings into English are taken into account, however frequently they may be found in anthologies such as CV. The two continua used in the analysis of the corpus are of sufficiently general nature as to lend themselves also to the description and discussion of comparable developments in the transcultural history of other genres.

The tables given in appendices 1 and 2 survey the variability of fourteen-line-long poems and the degree of cultural autonomy visible in them. Statistical representation for each phase of publication includes both the number of individual instances found in the anthologies (A, A1, A2) and the total number of their printings in this major subcorpus (B). In order to avoid an unnecessary distortion of the general picture of Phase 1, Seymour's *Anthology of Guianese Poetry* (1954), a collection which assembles an extraordinarily high proportion of relevant poems, is presented in a row of its own (A2). This applies only to poems which were not included in other anthologies published in Phase 1 (A1), and it is followed later by a row each for those poems found outside the anthologies, namely in the specified collections of poets Claude McKay (C1),[122] Derek Walcott (C2)[123] and Fred D'Aguiar (C3).[124] This subcorpus (C) adds a considerable number of relevant poems by McKay (who is represented also in anthologies with his sonnets) and by D'Aguiar (who is not). Double sonnets were counted as single instances, but three or more sonnets in sequences were counted individually. One reason for the fact that figures in row C2 are comparatively low is that Walcott's ten-part sequence "Tales of the Islands" had already been anthologised earlier, and therefore figures in Phase 2, rows A and B. In Table 1, the six stages along the continuum comprise the cases of strict adherence to either of the two most common species of the sonnet (Stage 1) or to any other conventionalised variant, such as the one found in Donne's poems (Stage 2); the 'synthetic' or 'hybrid' species which in other ways combines Petrarchan and Shakespearean patterns (Stage 3); an individual, variant pattern of the poet's own making which however remains recognisably within the generic tradition as specified (Stage 4); the case of unconventional regularity of other kinds, achieved for example by a variation of conventional stanza structure or by the use of accentual verse (Stage 5); and the case of an irregular form visible in a mere 'fourteen-liner' which only alludes to convention (Stage 6). The results are presented in absolute figures, which has not only called for critical decisions in borderline cases, but also explains why the absolute refusal by poets to adopt generic conventions in any still recognisable form does neither figure in this table nor in Table 2. Both tables are based on actual occurrences only, and therefore do not try to quantify non-realisation as one ideal end of either of the two continua (Stage 7 and Category 6, respectively). For the same reason, and also because no comparison is deemed particularly meaningful between non-realisations and actual adoptions of convention in whatever form, the total number of poems within all anthologies and collections seen is not stated, only the number of actual occurrences. The anthologies turned out 100 relevant poems, and the three poets' collections contributed a further 51 poems, adding up to a total of 151 relevant individual poems found over the whole period (A+C). As it happened, this was also the overall number of poems found printed and reprinted in anthologies alone, but when both subcorpora were put together, the total number of printings in the whole corpus amounted to 202 (B+C). This indeed was a sizeable corpus to work upon.

In Table 1, a certain development becomes visible from one phase to another. Its general nature offers no surprises, but the details are contrary to expectation. What comes as no surprise is that the highest frequency of relevant poems occurred in the phase up to Independence, and that Stage 1 was most strongly represented with regard both to anthologies published in the colonial era (A1, A2) and to the sonnets of McKay found elsewhere (C3). This stage of generically most conventional poems is also the one for which the greatest single number of printings was found in the anthologies (B: 26), and poets and editors also paid particular attention to related forms (Stages 2 and 3). High figures for printings in each case tell that editors in this and in later phases have come to regard and present all these sonnets as classics of their kind in Caribbean poetry. Conspicuous, too, is that in successive phases, a decrease in overall numbers and more particularly in the number of 'pure' sonnets is in evidence, and this is accompanied on the long run – and again with little surprise – by a shift in attention towards free verse. Stage 6 has shown most strongly in Phase 3, while frequencies which were still particularly high in Phase 2 for variants in Categories 3 and 4 have decreased significantly.

And yet, the data do not allow themselves to be interpreted simply as a confirmation of the belief that colonialism and conventionalism go hand in hand. The formally more conventional poems allocated to Stage 1 and 2 account for no more than half of both single instances and printings found in the anthologies for Phase 1, and moreover they have to be seen in the context of the continuum. Frequencies for Stages 4 and 5, which relate to more individual or less pronounced adoption of convention, are already remarkably high in Phase 1 and continue to be so in Phase 2. Poems allocated to these two stages in Phase 1 have since been printed twice, on average, in anthologies, and therefore have impressed editors to the same degree as have more conventional specimens. In particular the more original treatment defined as Stage 4 represented an alternative to mere imitation open to and sought by poets. And although it is a fact that the overall number of new occurrences fell in later years, it is also true that it remained surprisingly stable on a high level, with anthologies published in Phase 2 and 3 (A) turning out first 27 and then a further 26 individual poems which in any way referred to the conventional genre. The collections of D'Aguiar (C3) added 19 more instances, most of which fell outside the definition of Stage 6. Moreover, in what must come as a real surprise, the overall development recently has even been countered by a small but noticeable rise in the frequency of 'pure' and most immediately related sonnets (see Stages 1 and 2 in Phase 3). Clearly, there was not only aversion to European poetic conventions, but the autonomy from such an aversion was in evidence, too. Far from dying out after the end of the colonial era, the more conventional species have remained a viable alternative to other variants and could even secure renewed interest among poets and editors. The singular example of Fred D'Aguiar is significant here: although this well-known poet in the beginning certainly did not shy away from free verse, nevertheless he is seen to embrace conventional forms later, and then with a stress on both originality and regularity (see Stages 4 and 5 in row C3). And if this minor subcorpus were enlarged, D'Aguiar's case might not even be exceptional, as occasional findings show. *Bones*, the collection by Guyanese poet Mahadai Das, included not only her "Sonnet to New Flowers" addressed above, but opened with another and similar, albeit otherwise still uncollected "Sonnet To a Broom",[125] a specimen of syllabic verse which signalled both the poet's unashamed interest in the conventional genre and her willingness to take poetic licence. Since, Cecil Gray published his sonnet sequence "Lilian's Songs",[126] and a recent edition of *Wasafiri*, which appeared while this article was being written, included E. A. Markham's "Dreams, Dreams", a 'fourteen-liner' in free verse which bows to the convention by showing a bipartite structure and a 'turn' after eight lines. It is surely too early, and altogether inappropriate with regard to these figures, to speak of a renaissance of the sonnet in Caribbean literature; if anything like it occurred, however, this would have the tenets of a cultural-nationalist criticism appear in turn as a transient phenomenon in the development of a truly autonomous, multi-cultural Caribbean poetics.

When the tables for both continua are seen together, it becomes even clearer that the poets' decision for conventional form is not simply to be equated with a colonial set of mind. Of all the categories along Continuum 2, it is Category 2 (defined by the unqualified adoption of features from the world of the former colonial masters) which shows consistently low frequencies both in the colonial era and in later phases. The small rise in Phase 3 is only due to the reprint of two of Una Marson's sonnets in a historical anthology,[127] and should not be interpreted as a case of nostalgia – editorial interest in reprinting poems allocated to this category has always been rather low, anyway. The higher frequencies for the more conventional types of poetry in Continuum 1 do not translate into this other possible form of adoption or even appropriation; formal imitation clearly does not correlate significantly with cultural 'mimicry'.

The most frequently represented group of poems in Phase 1 is the one which steers clear of colonial relations and concentrates instead on either universal or personal topics. You can hardly speak of escapism here (at least not with reference to colonial rule), because poems allocated to Category 1 in this phase were often reprinted later, and because this category delivers the highest single frequency again in Phase 3, long after Independence. The second most numerously represented category before Independence is Category 3, which is characterised by an adoption of the European genre together with local colouring. The high frequency of printings again says that these poems were considered canonical. As such, this is less of a surprise; what is more apparent is that already in Phase 1, attempts to achieve multi-cultural autonomy (Category 4) are as frequently found as instances of a colonial attitude (Category 2).

And it is this attempt at a multi-cultural synthesis which is most often encountered in Phase 2, and not for instance the phenomenon of 'writing back' (Category 5), which has shown a consistently lower frequency in the anthologies. No doubt such a provocative attitude will document itself also in a poet's absolute refusal to adopt any feature which could be attributed to the conventional form of the sonnet – and such a refusal principally does not figure in these tables. But if the figures assembled here do not allow to conclude that there were general reservations against such a provocative stance shown in poetry in the years following on Independence, they do at least allow to stress the influential rôle of editors in these matters of cultural politics. Although some editors have evidently favoured unconventional 'fourteen-liners' in free verse in recent decades, there have also been editors who wanted to avoid a confrontational stance in other matters, and consciously decided to give way to specimens of multi-cultural autonomy. This can be gleaned from the selection of McKay's sonnets: while collections of his poetry show that there are a large number of sonnets which can be allocated to Category 5 (C1), editors of anthologies usually avoided them and chose to present McKay in a different light.

In Phase 3, a concern with aspects related to Category 4 is most prominently visible in the sonnets, sonnet sequences and sonnet variants written by Fred D'Aguiar. Those poems of interest which have found their way into anthologies in this phase once again were more committed to general or to personal affairs, but on the whole they were no longer involved in an engagement with matters of colonialism or with a 'decolonising of the mind'. Therefore, when both subcorpora are put together and all phases remain in view,

Categories 1 and 4 on Continuum 2 show the highest frequencies, whereas Category 2 is clearly set apart from the rest with regard to its low frequency and to editors' unwillingness to reprint poems from this category. There is really no reason to speak of a correlation between mastering of the form and a subservience to former masters. The examples of McKay, Walcott and D'Aguiar have proved, too, that a recollection of traditionally European poetic genres neither has to coincide with a conventionality of expression nor with a conformity of thinking. By contrast, such a recollection could indeed help to create something new in the West Indies and in the Caribbean diaspora, and it did not necessarily require a complete break with tradition. The hurricane may not be confined to conventional forms of poetry, but a Caribbean *furor poeticus* is generally not less powerful when it listens to a wind that blows from somewhere else.

Appendix 1: Table 1: Continuum 1. Variety of Form in the Sonnet

Phase of publication / Enlargement	**No. of anthologies and editions**		**1**	**2**	**3**	**4**	**5**	**6**	**Total**
1: up to Independence	5	**A1**	11	8	5	5	4	1	34
	1	**A2**	5	1	2	3	1	1	13
	6	**B**	26	16	13	15	9	2	81
2: late 1960s through the 1970s	10	**A**	5	1	4	9	4	4	27
	10	**B**	9	1	11	10	4	5	40
3: after about 1980	18	**A**	6	2	0	3	2	13	26
	18	**B**	6	2	0	3	3	16	30
Extension of the corpus	2	**C1**	20	3	3	2	0	0	28
	1	**C2**	0	0	0	1	0	3	4
	2	**C3**	0	0	3	6	8	2	19
Total	34	**A**	27	12	11	20	11	19	100
	39	**A+C**	47	15	17	29	19	24	151
	34	**B**	41	19	24	28	16	23	151
	39	**B+C**	61	22	30	37	24	28	202

Appendix 2: Table 2: Continuum 2. The Degree of Cultural Autonomy Visible in the Sonnet

Phase of publication / Enlargement	No. of anthologies and editions		1	2	3	4	5	Total
1: up to Independence	5	A1	18	3	8	3	2	34
	1	A2	7	1	4	1	0	13
	6	B	36	5	28	7	5	81
2: late 1960s through the 1970s	10	A	5	0	5	13	4	27
	10	B	10	0	6	20	4	40
3: after about 1980	18	A	12	2	2	8	2	26
	18	B	15	2	2	8	3	30
Extension of the corpus	2	C1	9	0	1	7	11	28
	1	C2	2	1	1	0	0	4
	2	C3	6	0	1	11	1	19
Total	34	A	42	6	19	25	8	100
	39	A+C	59	7	22	43	20	151
	34	B	61	7	36	35	12	151
	39	B+C	78	8	39	53	24	202

Abbreviations

The Corpus of Anthologies, Phase of Publication, and Abbreviations Used in the Text References will be under the abbreviation as given or, where no abbreviation has been introduced, under the name of the editor with the year of publication.

2 ACWE = John Figueroa (Ed.): *An Anthology of African and Caribbean Writing in English*, London, 1982.

1 AGP = A. J. Seymour (Ed.): *An Anthology of Guianese Poetry*, Georgetown, British Guiana, 1954.

3 CAFRA = Ramabai Espinet (Ed.): *Creation Fire. A CAFRA Anthology*, Tunapuna & Toronto, 1990.

1 CaLit = G[eorge]. R. Coulthard (Ed.): *Caribbean Literature. An Anthology*, London, 1966.

3 CPN = Stewart Brown (Ed.): *Caribbean Poetry Now*, second, revised edition, London, 1992 [1985].

1 CV I = John Figueroa (Ed.): *Caribbean Voices. An Anthology of West Indian Poetry*, Vol. 1: *Dreams and Visions*, London, 1966.

2 CV II = John Figueroa (Ed.): *Caribbean Voices. An Anthology of West Indian Poetry*, Vol. 2: *The Blue Horizons*, London, 1970.

2 CVerse = O. R. Dathorne (Ed.): *Caribbean Verse. An Anthology*, London, 1967.

3 HB = Ian McDonald & Stewart Brown (Eds.): *The Heinemann Book of Caribbean Poetry*, London, 1992.

1 IAJL = A. L. Hendriks & Cedric Lindo (Eds.): *The Independence Anthology of Jamaican Literature*, Kingston, Jamaica, 1962.

3 NB = James Berry (Ed.): *News for Babylon. The Chatto Book of Westindian-British Poetry*, London, 1984.

2 NS = Donald G. Wilson (Ed.): *New Ships. An Anthology of West Indian Poems for Secondary Schools*, Oxford, 1971.

3 PB = Paula Burnett (Ed.): *The Penguin Book of Caribbean Verse in English*, Harmondsworth, 1986.

3 RR = Alison Donnell & Sarah Lawson Welsh (Eds.): *The Routledge Reader in Caribbean Literature*, London, 1996.

1 TJP = J. E. Clare McFarlane (Ed.): *A Treasury of Jamaican Poetry*, London, 1949.

2 TT = A[lfred]. N. Forde (Ed.): *Talk of the Tamarinds. An Anthology of Poetry for Secondary Schools*, London, 1971.

2 WIP (1972) = Kenneth Ramchand & Cecil Gray (Eds.): *West Indian Poetry. An Anthology for Schools*, Harlow, 1971 [i. e. 1972].

3 WIP (1989) = Kenneth Ramchand & Cecil Gray (Eds.): *West Indian Poetry. An Anthology for Schools*, second, revised edition, Harlow, 1989.

3 James Berry (Ed.): *Bluefoot Traveller. Poetry by Westindians in Britain*, second, revised and enlarged edition, London, 1981 [1976].

3 Edward Kamau Brathwaite (Ed.): *New Poets from Jamaica. An Anthology*, Kingston, Jamaica, 1979.

3 Stewart Brown, Mervyn Morris & Gordon Rohlehr (Eds.): *Voiceprint. An Anthology of Oral and Related Poetry from the Caribbean*, Harlow, 1989.

1 Norman E. Cameron (Ed.): *Guianese Poetry. Covering the Hundred Years' Period 1831-1931*, Georgetown, British Guiana, 1931.

3 Elaine Campbell & Pierrette Frickey (Eds.): *The Whistling Bird. Women Writers of the Caribbean*, Boulder, Col. & Kingston, Jamaica, 1998.

3 Rhonda Cobham & Merle Collins (Eds.): *Watchers and Seekers*, new edition, Cambridge, 1990 [1987].

2 Lorna Cocking & Joan Goody (Eds.): *Caribbean Anthology*, London, ILEA, 1981.

3 Anthony Kellman (Ed.): *Crossing Water. Contemporary Poetry of the English-Speaking Caribbean*, New York, 1992.

3 Thomas W. Krise, (Ed.): *Caribbeana: An Anthology of English Literature of the West Indies, 1657-1777*, Chicago, 1999.

3 E. A. Markham, (Ed.): *Hinterland. Caribbean Poetry from the West Indies and Britain*. Newcastle upon Tyne, 1989.

3 Pamela Mordecai & Mervyn Morris (Eds.): *Jamaica Woman. An Anthology of Poems*, London & Kingston, Jamaica, 1980.

3 Mervyn Morris (Ed.): *Focus 1983: An Anthology of Contemporary Jamaican Writing*, Kingston, Jamaica, 1983.

2 Andrew Salkey (Ed.): *Breaklight. An Anthology of Caribbean Poetry*, London, 1971.

2 Reinhard Sander (Ed.): *From Trinidad. An Anthology of Early West Indian Writing*, London, 1978.

2 A. J. Seymour (Ed.): *New Writing in the Caribbean*, Georgetown, Guyana, 1972.

3 Ann Walmsley (Ed.): *The Sun's Eye*, second, revised edition, Harlow, 1989 [1968].

Notes

1 A note on my use of terminology: 'West Indian' refers to those anglophone societies in the region which were formerly British colonies, while 'Caribbean' is understood in a wider sense, to include the Caribbean diaspora in Britain (for example the Windrush Generation of emigrants after 1948), in the USA (for example Claude McKay) or elsewhere, and also poetic works

of a predominantly Caribbean character, even if their authors were foreigners who were resident in the West Indies only for a time (such as Grainger, Singleton, Montgomery, Hosack and Dunbar, mentioned in section 3). If no other biographical information is provided, see the notes in PB. For the corpus of poetry under review, and for the abbreviations used in the text, see the bibliography to this article.

2 See Ngugi wa Thiong'o: *Decolonising the Mind. The Politics of Language in African Literature*, London, 1986.

3 "[...] nothing was created in the British West Indies [...]. In the West Indian islands slavery and the latifundia created only grossness [...]; a society without standards, without noble aspirations, nourished by greed and cruelty [...]. The history of the islands can never be satisfactorily told. Brutality is not the only difficulty. History is built around achievement and creation; and nothing was created in the West Indies." V. S. Naipaul: *The Middle Passage. Impressions of Five Societies – British, French and Dutch – in the West Indies and South America*, London, 1962, pp. 27-29.

4 See Naipaul: *The Middle Passage*, pp. 40-47 and Edward Kamau Brathwaite: *History of the Voice. The Development of Nation Language in Anglophone Caribbean Poetry*, London, 1984 [lecture given at Harvard University in 1979]. For his estimate of the influence of Eliot and Hughes, see *ibid.*, 30-31, 41.

5 *Architextualité*, that is, in the typology of Gérard Genette: *Palimpsestes: La littérature au second degré*, corrected and enlarged edition, Paris, 1983 [1982].

6 Well-known examples of ring games and work songs are "Brown Girl in the Ring", which became a hit for the pop group Boney M. as late as 1978, and "Day-O/Banana Boat", which had been popularised before by Harry Belafonte. For an example of the fresh creative appropriation of the Anansi stories in performance poetry, see Merle Collins: "Crick Crack". – In M. C.: *Rotten Pomerack*, London, 1992, 60-63.

7 Story-tellers like Paul Keens-Douglas and dub poets or other performance poets such as Linton Kwesi Johnson or Jean "Binta" Breeze have arranged for recording and distribution of their performances via radio and television, tape cassette or video tape.

8 Caribbean 'total theatre' since 1945 has encompassed for instance the Dimanche Gras shows of the Trinidad Carnival as well as plays of Derek Walcott in which he appropriated the US-American musical, as in *The Joker of Seville* and *O Babylon!* These two plays were composed in collaboration with Galt McDermot, who had become famous for the music of *Hair*. For other examples in Walcott's *oeuvre*, see Bruce King: *Derek Walcott and West Indian Drama. 'Not only a Playwright But a Company'. The Trinidad Theatre Workshop 1959-1993*, Oxford, 1995.

9 See the list of abbreviations printed before the endnotes.

10 Jamaica as well as Trinidad and Tobago saw the end of colonial rule in 1962, after they had left the self-governing Federation of the West Indies. A few years later (in 1966), Barbados and Guyana (up to then, British Guiana) followed suit. My usage of 'Independence' refers generally to these years, even though this does not accurately reflect the situation in the 'small islands'.

11 The lack of sonnets in Krise (1999) does not surprise, as the poetry in the early centuries of colonisation mirrors Neo-Classical taste in the mother-country also in its distaste for the sonnet. A surprise indeed is the scarcity of sonnets (only two, and one 'fourteen-liner') or villanelles (none) in an early anthology of poetry from British Guiana (Cameron 1931: pp. 74, 81, 114). However, this has been redeemed later by its immediate successor (AGP's total of 110 poems included one villanelle and fifteen poems in fourteen lines, nearly all of them sonnets). Sonnets were in evidence in 1930s Trinidad (see Sander 1978: pp. 210, 215, 220), and they were prominently represented in poetry from Jamaica (see TJP; in IAJL, six out of 35 poems were sonnets). A generous selection of sonnets was still to be found in CV (1966-70), a retrospective teaching anthology edited by J. Figueroa on the basis of the scripts for the influential programme *Caribbean Voices* (which was initiated by the poet Una Marson, and had been edited by Henry Swanzy for BBC Radio, 1946-59). In his introduction to the second volume, which addressed a different audience than the first, Figueroa justified his grouping of poems under the three headings "Consolidation, Continuation and Innovation" of tradition (CV II, pp. 16-20).

12 See for instance NS and WIP.

13 Apart from Brown, Morris & Rohlehr (1989), see to the same effect the general anthologies edited by Dathorne (1967), Salkey (1971), Berry (1976/1981; 1984), Brathwaite (1979), Brown (1985/1992), McDonald & Brown (1992), Kellman (1992), and also the gender-specific collections edited by Mordecai & Morris (1981), Cobham & Collins (1987/1990), Espinet (1990), Campbell & Frickey (1998).

14 See the anthologies *Voices from Summerland*, London, 1929, and TJP, both edited by J. E. Clare McFarlane, and also his historical study *A Literature in the Making*, Kingston, Jamaica, 1956.

15 Brathwaite: *History of the Voice*, pp. 8, 10.

16 Edward Baugh: "Poetry (The Caribbean)". – In Eugene Benson & Leonard Conolly (Eds.): *Encyclopedia of Post-Colonial Literatures in English*, 2 vols., London, 1994, pp. 1241-1245, 1243. He then goes on to talk of a "crucial period of transition", exemplified for instance by the work of Frank Collymore, A. J. Seymour and particularly Una Marson. See Edward Baugh: *West Indian Poetry 1900-1970. A Study in Cultural Decolonisation*. – Extract in RR 99-104 [Kingston, Jamaica, 1971]; Brown (1984) and Brathwaite: *History of the Voice*, pp. 30-39, whose term 'nation-language' indicates the context of cultural nationalism. See also the introductions to

the anthologies edited by O. R. Dathorne: "Introduction". – In O. R. D. (Ed.): *Caribbean Verse. An Anthology*, London, 1967, pp. 1-15, by Salkey (1971), pp. xv-xix, and by Rohlehr, in Brown, Morris & Rohlehr 1989, pp. 1-12.

17 Bill Ashcroft & Gareth Griffiths & Helen Tiffin: *The Empire Writes Back. Theory and Practice in Post-Colonial Literatures*, London, 1989.

18 Representative examples of critics are Laurence A. Breiner: *An Introduction to West Indian Poetry,* Cambridge, 1998, pp. 113-114 (sympathy) and Donnell & Welsh (RR). It was especially Donnell's interest in the Jamaican poet and feminist Una Marson which provided the revisionist impetus. See RR (1996), pp. 7, 13-17, 39, 116-122, 187-193. See also E. A. Markham's answer to Brathwaite's postulate of "nation-language" as a requisite of authentic Caribbean poetry in the anthology *Hinterland*, which includes his own "A Good Life Sonnet" (see Markham 1989, pp. 192-196, 201). Anthologies edited first of all for use in the classroom, and giving ample room to the sonnet, are TJP, CV, TT, NS, WIP (1972; 1989). This is true, but to a lesser extent, also for ACWE and RR. Comprehensiveness is the declared purpose of PB, and this is borne out indeed, for instance in the generous selection of sonnets, too. The exception from the rule is Walmsley (1989), which generally conforms to the view of Dathorne (Ed.): *Caribbean Verse*, and Brathwaite: *History of the Voice*, and includes only one sonnet, namely A. J. Seymour's "There Runs a Dream".

19 As in the summary statement quoted above (Baugh: "Poetry", p. 1243). On the villanelle, see the relevant entry in Alex Preminger & T. V. F. Brogan (Eds.), *The New Princeton Encyclopedia of Poetry and Poetics*, Princeton, N.J., 1993, p. 1358. TJP included not only Virtue's "King Solomon and Queen Balkis. A Villanelle Sequence" (TJP, pp. 119-124, from his first collection *Wings of the Morning*, 1938), but also a number of other villanelles by "Tom Redcam" ("San Gloria", TJP, p. 19), by Constance Hollar ("Villanelle of the Night", TJP, p. 78), by W. Adolphe Roberts ("Villanelle of the Living Pan", TJP, p. 125), and by McFarlane himself ("Villanelle of Immortal Love", TJP, p. 142). See also Doris Haper's "Villanelle" (AGP, p. 98). For a significantly different estimate of Virtue (1911-98), see McFarlane (1956), pp. 104-109, Baugh (1971), pp. 102-103 and Baugh: "Poetry", p. 1243. The only more recent, extended and quite critical discussion of Virtue's poetry is Marian B. McLeod: "The Poetry of Vivian Virtue", *Literary Half-Yearly* 32:1, 1991, 56-71.

20 Hendriks (1922-92) was a published poet since the late 1940s (like Walcott); he came to prominence first as co-editor of IAJL in 1962 and later as director of the Jamaica Broadcasting Corporation, and continued to publish verse in the 1980s.

21 WIP 1989, p. 146, ll. 1-3.

22 CVerse, pp. 34-35, ll. 1-3, 8-15.

23 TT, p. 55, ll. 10-14.

24 The first poem is reprinted in NS, p. 83, in WIP (1972), p. 28 and in Walmsley (1989), pp. 43-44, poet's note pp. 143-144, the second appears in McDonald & Brown (1992) , pp. 94-95).

25 The concept has occasionally been adopted for a classification of oral literature, see Gordon Rohlehr: "Introduction. 'The Shape of that Hurt'". – In Brown, Morris & Rohlehr (1989), pp. 1-23, 1-2, and Carolyn Cooper: *Noises in the Blood. Orality, Gender and the 'Vulgar' Body of Jamaican Popular Culture,* Durham, N.C., 1995, pp. 4-6, 20, 117, 136.

26 Calit, p. 97, TT, p. 67.

27 Most of the latter sonnets are reprinted in the two editions of WIP (1972), pp. 73, 74, 31; 1989: 118, 12-13, but "I Shall Return" was included already in TJP, p. 16, an anthology which was published in the year after McKay's death (he died in 1948).

28 Brathwaite: *History of the Voice*, p. 8.

29 See above. For a more extended discussion than here of McKay's sonnets in a Caribbean context, and of critical response, see Helge Nowak: "Outward and Return: Migration of Poetic Genres between Europe and the Caribbean". – In Christoph Bode & Sebastian Domsch & Hans Sauer (Eds.): *Anglistentag 2003 München. Proceedings*, Trier, 2004.

30 TJP, p. 131.

31 AGP, pp. 99, 126.

32 PB, p. 162.

33 RR, p. 128.

34 TJP, p. 144, CV I, p. 54.

35 TJP, p. 32, RR, p. 62.

36 IAJL, p. 93, CV I, p. 84-85, ACWE, p. 251-252, PB, p. 184.

37 CVerse, p. 29, PB, p. 182.

38 NS, p. 55, WIP (1989), p. 28.

39 CV I, p. 70, RR, p. 102.

40 IAJL, p. 134, CV II, p. 141.

41 IAJL, p. 135, PB, pp. 163-164.

42 See McLeod: "The Poetry of Vivian Virtue", for information on Virtue's translation of *Les Trophées*, the collected poems of the Cuban-born French poet de Heredia (1842-1905), containing 118 sonnets. In addition to those sonnets mentioned, which are true to conventional form and occur at least twice in the corpus and therefore are better suited to illustrate canonical preferences, there are also a number of single occurrences, of Italian sonnets only, which should be mentioned here for the sake of completeness. Two are by Jamaican contemporaries of Harold Watson and show the same fondness for archaic poetic diction: "The Dancer" by W. Adolphe Roberts and "Disillusionment" by "Miss V. M. Clerk" (TJP, pp. 118, 106). Another two were written by H. A. Vaughan, from Barbados, who is represented by "In Absence" (WIP, pp. 1989: 45), which resembles Renaissance sonnets in theme and McKay's Harlem Renaissance sonnets in tone, and by "To a Tu-

dor Street Girl" (CV II, pp. 111-112), which brings in local colour only with one of the oldest street-names in Bridgetown, Barbados, but celebrates woman's beauty in terms which are ethnically not conspicuous. Examples from British Guiana are "Von Hoogenheim", N. E. Cameron's poem on a slave rebellion, and two poems by Cecil Clementi, "Roraima" and "Kaietuk" (AGP, pp. 65, 76, 78).

43 But see Claude McKay: *Selected Poems*, which lacks the coda, and in Claude McKay: *The Passion of Claude McKay. Selected Poetry and Prose, 1912-1948*. Ed. Wayne F. Cooper, New York, 1973, and Claude McKay: *Selected Poems*, Ed. Joan R. Sherman, Mineola, N.Y., 1999.

44 "One" and "London Love", in TJP, pp. 31-32 and RR, p. 62.

45 For a discussion of these Caribbean sonnet sequences, see Nowak: "Outward and Return"; Cecil Gray: *Lilian's Songs*, Toronto, 1996, and Fred D'Aguiar: *British Subjects*, Newcastle upon Tyne, 1993, pp. 30-36. For bibliographical information on Walcott's sequence, see Irma E. Goldstraw (Comp.): *Derek Walcott. An Annotated Bibliography of His Works*, New York, 1984; this however does not extend to anthologies. The original versions of Chapter X, "You Can't Go Home Again", which was excised in 1962, and of Chapter XI, "The Lake Isle", later re-titled "*Adieu foulard*" when becoming Chapter X, were reprinted in TT, pp. 36-37. The full sequence in revised form was included in CV II, pp. 205-210; Chapter VI, "Poopa, da' was a fête", was reprinted in Brown, Morris & Rohlehr (1989), p. 32; Chapter IX, "*Le Loupgarou*", in WIP (1972), p. 16, and the new Chapter X in NS, p. 89, in Cocking & Goody (1981), p. 22, and in WIP (1989), p. 167.

46 See Lloyd W. Brown: *West Indian Poetry*, second edition, London, 1984 [1978], pp. 19-25, Baugh: "Poetry", p. 1243, and, in a more reflected way, Laurence A. Breiner: *An Introduction to West Indian Poetry,* Cambridge, 1998, pp. 104-109.

47 Other conventionalised variants such as the Spenserian or Meredithian sonnet are not in evidence. Walcott's "The Arkansas Testament" (1987) is a sequence of 24 poems in sixteen lines, which however are certainly not proper Meredithian sonnets.

48 Sander (1978), p. 20.

49 PB, p. 138.

50 CV I, p. 49.

51 Calit, pp. 96-97.

52 TJP, p. 132, PB, p. 140.

53 TJP, p. 91, NS, p. 52, WIP (1972), p. 44.

54 PB, p. 140.

55 TJP, p. 143, IAJL, p. 121, TT, pp. 40-41, PB, p. 141.

56 TJP, p. 14.

57 TJP, p. 56, CV I, p. 30.

58 The poems in this form are "Like a Strong Tree" (1925; CV I, p. 88, ACWE, p. 262; "Truth" and "The Pagan Isms" (CV I. pp. 99, 100). A variant of the variant is "St. Isaac's Church, Petrograd" (1925; reprinted in TJP, p. 139 under the title "Russian Cathedral", which reads like a church hymn and employs alternating rhyme throughout, without end couplet.

59 NS, p. 14, TT, p. 42.

60 Sander (1978), p. 210.

61 TJP, p. 31.

62 IAJL, p. 83, PB, p. 153.

63 See note 14 above. "There Runs a Dream" (AGP, p. 64) was reprinted in WIP (1972), p. 39; WIP (1989), p. 100, in Walmsley (1989), p. 115, with author's note on p. 150, and in CPN, p. 139, with one variant found only in this edition: a blank line after l.2 as another partition. This seems to be a mistake here, perhaps reminiscent of "Carrion Crows" (AGP, p. 93, TT, p. 74; WIP (1972), p. 47, WIP (1989), p. 7), which has always been printed with such an additional partition after l.3. A few additional notes on form: the two 'synthetic' sonnets by Seymour vary the Shakespearean pattern slightly in the sestet, with "Carrion Crows" rhyming *efgegf* and "There Runs a Dream" ending on *efegfg* – sharing this form with Squire's "There Was an Indian". With regard to form, Tothill's "Sonnet" sticks out because of its early caesura, after 4½ lines.

64 Fred D'Aguiar: *An English Sampler. New and Selected Poems*, London, 2001, pp. 132, 143, 149.

65 "The Harbour" appeared in Walcott's first collection (1948) as "The Fishermen Rowing Homeward". For the poem, see Derek Walcott: *Selected Poetry*. Ed. Wayne Brown, London, 1981, p. 7; for bibliographical information, see Goldstraw (Comp.): *Derek Walcott*; for a short interpretation, see the editor's note to Walcott: *Selected Poetry*, p. 94; and for a discussion of this poem together with those by D'Aguiar, see Nowak: "Outward and Return".

66 Compared with the version given in TT, p. 41 and WIP (1989), p. 35, the earlier reprint in CV I, p. 63 shows variants in punctuation (title, l.3), spelling (l.7) and line division (ll.11-12).

67 Sander (1978), p. 215.

68 CV I, p. 83.

69 Besides the companion piece to "If We Must Die" already mentioned in the text, there is the double sonnet "One Year After" (1922; Claude McKay: *Selected Poems*, pp. 48-49), and there is "My Mother" (1920), which in full length extends to a double sonnet on the Shakespearean pattern with a coda of three quatrains in the form of the Chevy Chase ballad stanza (CV I, pp. 14-15), but is only incompletely reprinted in collections of the poet (the version in Claude McKay: *Selected Poems*, lacks the coda, and in Claude McKay: *The Passion of Claude McKay*, the poem appears only as a single sonnet).

70 Markham (1989), p. 201.
71 CV I, p. 103, ACWE, p. 233, CVerse, p. 75, Cocking & Goody (1981), p. 12.
72 CPN, p. 76.
73 See Brown's "Famine" (Salkey (1971), p. 17) and, among others, D'Aguiar's "Riddle" (Fred D'Aguiar: *An English Sampler*, p. 136), which is not only intertextually related to the sonnet, but moreover to Old English forms and to nursery rhymes in general.
74 Cameron (1931), p. 81, AGP, p. 79, CVerse, pp. 45-46.
75 CV II, p. 111.
76 Cameron (1931), p. 74.
77 Cobham & Collins (1990), p. 145.
78 CV I, p. 55 and II, p. 77, WIP (1989), p. 189.
79 In an early version, "Old Mama Dot" (1984, NB, p. 26), the fourteen-liner is still combined with another section into a poem in two parts, of which the first part was made the title-poem of D'Aguiar's first collection *Mama Dot* (1985). The quotation is from this latter version, reprinted in D'Aguiar: *An English Sampler*, p. 3, and in Markham (1989), p. 317. For additional information, see Walmsley (1989), p. 142.
80 NB, p. 162.
81 Kellman (1992), p. 21
82 Salkey 1971.
83 Salkey (1971), p. 145, NB, p. 165.
84 CPN, p. 54.
85 WIP (1989), p. 129.
86 Morris (1983), p. 52, Markham (1989), p. 242, CPN, p. 127, RR, p. 398. Less well-known, but also contributing to this category were Philip Nanton with "Aerogramme" (CPN, p. 141), or the following women poets: Rosemarie Chung with "The Saddest", Berry (1981), p. 56; Christine Craig with "Coda", Karin Ammon with "Death", and Charmaine Gill with "Dear Jones" (her eulogy on the Canadian poet Daniel Cameron Jones; all three poems collected in CAFRA, pp. 124, 161, 46).
87 Derek Walcott: *Collected Poems 1948-1984*, New York, 1986, pp. 47, 103, 338.
88 CV II, p. 172.
89 NB, p. 32.
90 D'Aguiar: *An English Sampler*, p. 144.
91 The eighteenth- and nineteenth-century poems mentioned are included at least in parts in Cameron (1931), pp. 107-108; in AGP, p. 131 and in PB, pp. 99-101, 131. For "Thou Hast Done Well (Ode on the Death of Edward VII)" (1910) and "Jamaica's Coronation Ode" (1932), both by 'Tom Redcam', and for "The Empire's Flag" (1932) by Albinia Hutton, see TJP, pp. 26-28, 100-101, and RR, pp. 47-48, 53-54. Two poems by W. M. Lawrence, "Royal Requiem" (on the death of George V, 1935) and "Coronation

Ode" (for George VI, 1937), are mentioned in Brown (1984), p. 29. Both A. J. Seymour and Vivian Virtue included similar coronation odes prominently in their first collections (1937 and 1938). For Virtue's ode and also for McFarlane's elegy "On the Death of George VI" (1952), see McLeod: "The Poetry of Vivian Virtue", pp. 60-62, 65.

92 Robert Dunbar's *The Caraguin*, another long poem (1837), introduces Afro-Caribbean belief in ritual magic by way of an *obeah woman*. All the poems cited are included, in full or in form of extracts, in PB, pp. 99-129. For further examples, see Krise (1999), and see note 1 above. For a recent and extended discussion of both Grainger's "Sugar cane poetics" and of "Epic echoes in Derek Walcott's *Omeros*", see Tobias Döring: *Caribbean-English Passages. Intertextuality in a Postcolonial Tradition*, London & New York, 2002, pp. 49-77, 169-202.

93 PB, pp. 399-400.

94 For the poetry of Salkey, see Brown (1984), pp. 73-74, 78).

95 First published 1980, and reprinted in PB, pp. 249-254 and in Brown, Morris & Rohlehr (1989), pp. 163-168.

96 TJP, p. 131.

97 See note 30 above.

98 CVerse, p. 9, PB, p. 182.

99 TJP, p. 106.

100 WIP 1989, p. 45.

101 PB, p. 162.

102 See Lee M. Jenkins: "'If We Must Die'. Winston Churchill and Claude McKay", *Notes and Queries* 50:3, 2003, 333-337.

103 TJP, p. 118.

104 RR, p. 128.

105 TJP, p. 31.

106 TJP, p. 144, CV I, p. 54.

107 CV II, pp. 111-112.

108 TJP, p. 143, IAJL, p. 121, TT, p. 40-41, PB, p. 141.

109 Calit, pp. 36-37, IAJL, p. 126, TT, p. 40, PB, p. 154.

110 McKay: *The Passion of Claude McKay*, p. 126.

111 WIP 1989, p. 129.

112 There is a marked contrast between this poem and McFarlane's "On National Vanity", see in particular the last lines. Fred D'Aguiar's "Mama D ot" could also have been named here, were it not for other reasons listed in the next category.

113 See Brown, Morris and Rohlehr (1989), pp. 3-5.

114 WIP 1972, p. 73.

115 McKay: *Selected Poems*, pp. 25-27.

116 McKay: *Selected Poems*, pp. 29.

117 NS, p. 68.

118 NB, p. 76.

119 Suffice to mention a few examples only from the period between 1919 and 1922, included either in McKay: *The Passion of Claude McKay*, or in McKay: *Selected Poems*: "To the White Fiends", "In Bondage", "Enslaved", "The White City" or "Outcast".

120 Salkey 1971, p. 17.

121 Cocking & Goody 1981, p. 6.

122 McKay: *The Passion of Claude McKay*, McKay: *Selected Poems*.

123 Derek Walcott: *Collected Poems*.

124 D'Aguiar: *British Subjects*; and D'Aguiar: *An English Sampler*. Walcott's later collections up to D. W.: *The Bounty*, London, 1997, do not add more relevant poems.

125 Mahadai Das: *Bones*, Leeds, 1988, p. 7.

126 Cecil Gray: *Lilian's Songs*, Toronto, 1996.

127 RR.

Curwen Best (St. Michael, Barbados)

Caribbean Literature IV: Literature, Orature / Orality and the Matrix of Cyberculture

Dear *mumma* uh writin yu dis letter
Wha?
Guess what! Pun a computer O
Kay?

(From Kamau Brathwaite's poem "X / Self Xth letter from the thirteenth province" from the collection *X / Self*)

1. Introduction

There are several routes that could be taken to address the issue of "Literary Departures Orality / Orature". This chapter could very well concern itself with examining aspects of oral culture expression from the 'earliest' times to the 21st century, uncovering the central function of speech, verbal performance and writing within the evolution of contemporary Caribbean culture.[1] It could alternately make a case for orality as a co-equal component which, along with literary arts, helped to fashion contemporary Caribbean cultural expression.[2] We are well aware that much of that work has already been attempted, or is currently under way, and that readers can indeed use that material. While not avoiding those debates, this chapter wants to conduct another type of critique. It wants to consider some of the ways in which new emerging technologies and media impact on how we perceive orality and its related form of expression, writing. While there are many texts that deal with Caribbean orality,[3] there is little in terms of sustained academic debate on orality, literature and digital culture.

This chapter also wants to begin to examine the use of the World Wide Web by Caribbean artists, and the representation of their work and 'voices' within that medium. It considers the impact of this facility on the artists' expression and looks at how their 'performance' in cyberspace challenges us all to reconsider such concepts as orality, writing, speech, sound and video, and performance. Throughout this work, users of the technology and spectators are also asked to contemplate the extent to which emerging mediums and technologies begin to stand in for the real artists and for more traditional mediums of dissemination. The value of this kind of critical undertaking is that, hopefully, it helps to facilitate the expansion of debates about Caribbean orality, literature and cultural expression. Elsewhere I have suggested that Caribbean cultural criticism has remained predominantly 'low-tech' in an enhanced 'high-tech' global environment.[4] This continues to be the case, even though the Caribbean region has been striving to keep abreast of evolving technologies. This chapter is especially aware of the fact that current and future students pursuing Caribbean and related studies are and will become increasingly preoccupied with 'the real' and virtual media that promote, fashion and control aspects of world culture. It therefore anticipates some of the debates that have already started to preoccupy regional and other students of Caribbean literature and culture.

2. Culture, Literature, Orality and Technology

In the first decade of the 21st century orality and orature are no longer widely regarded as secondary fields of engagement and practice within Anglophone Caribbean Literature. There are, however, still lingering tensions in discussions about oral and written literature. A general overview of the contributing role of orality and orature to Caribbean literature can illustrate the source and the nature of tensions between oral arts and the scribal tradition.[5] Discourses about orality and writing cannot avoid considering these issues that have to do with the politics of history, culture, expression, representation, media and dissemination. All in all, this chapter wants to explore the nature and guises of orality in an era of technological advancement.

The critic Walter Ong addresses the implication for writing and orality in new arenas. His work, especially his seminal book *Orality and Literacy*; published in 1982, inspired a number of critics throughout the 1980s; it also has implications for the post-1990s interface between technology and literary and oral cultural expression.[6] Some critics have worked at fleshing out his suggestion that 'secondary orality' is brought on by radio and electronic technologies.[7] The suggestion however, that societies are moving towards secondary orality, might very well be a generalization and over-simplification of the complex processes that define current new modes and media of communication. Indeed contemporary media and their tools create a varied set of practices that challenge more conventional notions of writing, speech, discourse, representation, simulation and power. John December and other critics have pointed to the Internet as gesturing to tertiary orality. He suggests that "discourse need not be based upon sound in order to have oral characteristics. Rather [...] oral characteristics grow out of computer-mediated communication which gives participants greater independence over time and space".[8]

Is it possible that the tools of our mobile wireless society further erode while also masking the distance (and difference) between actions like speech and writing? Is it possible that the capacity to simulate human activities (as via the computer) renders obsolete our prior perception of functions such as speech, and writing? Do artists who create and perform their work in multidimensional or virtual environments think any more about privileging one mode of delivery over another? Do the Internet and the microcomputer mirror our human ability to 'multitask', and do they hence allow for a virtual, seamless interplay of the voice, writing and 'total performance'? These are some of the question this chapter eventually goes on to consider. But at the outset it is helpful to locate the concern with orality / orature and literature within its more traditional critical arena.

The work of researchers and theorists like Ruth Finnegan has influenced the way that critics on Caribbean literature since the 1970s have gone about analyzing the impact of orality. The leading Caribbean critic on orality, Gordon Rohlehr, though engaging the problematic of writing and orality conceptually, has best fought the case for the valorization of orature by way of highlighting and assessing the influence of oral culture on Caribbean Literature and culture, and by foregrounding the work of oral-based writers and performers. He has therefore conducted pioneering work on authors such as Kamau Brathwaite, and Slinger 'Mighty Sparow' Francisco.[9] Mervyn Morris's work, particularly on Jamaican poets, is equally noteworthy.[10] Other critics who have also done work in this area include Keith Warner, Lloyd Brown, Carolyn Cooper, Christian Habekost, and a newer generation of critics including Kwame Dawes, Louis Regis, Norval Edwards and Curwen Best. This critical tradition reflects the importance of orality to Caribbean literary and cultural studies. Not all critics are united in their approach to and perspective on orature. The various critics have used a number of different reading and critical strategies to help in their exploration of orality. The pioneering critics on Caribbean orature have tended to focus on the relationship that orature shares with the literary tradition. They have therefore conducted close readings of works, paying special attention to their literary quality, but also emphasizing the need for other criteria. More recent work rooted in postcolonial studies has tackled the phenomenon of orality, while apparently privileging questions of race, identity, nation, hybridity and intertextuality.[11] I suggests that future debates must also discuss questions of what I would call 'technologics', as discussed in the following section.

3. Approaches to Caribbean Orality and Literature

It has been widely felt that the investigation of the development of Caribbean literature and orature can be approached from two major standpoints. First, some critics and critical texts have demonstrated the proclivity for engaging Caribbean literature through an examination of the distinctive modes of writing and of oral delivery.[12] Other approaches have touched on this subject, but had other concerns in mind, such as issues relating to genres, or even gender, and an assortment of themes.[13] In any case, the use of the scribal / oral binary as a guide to understanding the evolution of Caribbean literature and culture has afforded critics the opportunity to consider the underlying politics, realities and assumptions about Caribbean people, their history, their ambitions and the forging of identities through a range of cultural expressions. Central to the scribal-oral debate has been the underlying assumption that writing is an overt feature of Western society, and that orality has its location in non-Western societies. Of course there is some logic and substance to this way of perceiving the deeper roots and routes that feed into and connect orality and writing. But a rigid compartmentalization can oversimplify the complexity of this set of relations. The work of critics like Ruth Finnegan in such texts as *Oral Literature in Africa* and *Oral Traditions and the Verbal Arts,* Kamau Brathwaite's *History of the Voice* and Rohlehr's *My Strangled City and Other Essays*,[14] have contributed to a rethinking of the more traditional outlook on literary and oral culture studies in the Caribbean. These studies have argued for a less value-centred critique. They caution against attributing all scribal and all oral expression to Europe and Africa, respectively. But for these critics, oral literature and culture is a legitimate site of investigation, no less significant than the literary tradition that has been influenced heavily by Western models.

A general survey of oral artistic expression might suggest that many peoples of the Caribbean, like other cultures of the world, voice their ambitions through oral expression. The process of institutionalized slavery, the detaining of Africans and their export to the Caribbean, brought their (the African's) dominant modes of cultural expression into play with the practice of writing. It must be said that European cultural expression also contained significant elements of oral expression. Peter Roberts, however, argues in *From Oral to Literate Culture*[15] that slave society instituted and perpetuated the belief that writing was a gift and preserve of Whites. Extending beyond early post-emancipation society, the education system which the British brought to the region functioned to accord higher status to writing. Oral performances of the types then disseminated by way of folk songs, work songs, early calypso, spiritual song, speechifying and other expressions, though serving significant functions, were often regarded as less valubale expressions.[16]

Oral poetic forms such as calypso, and variations on folk songs were significant components of self and collective expression throughout slavery and early post-emancipation society.[17] There are many songs of the post-emancipation period whose lyrics have survived to the present. Songs such as "Lick and Lock up Dun Wid" reveal the importance of rhyme, metre and topicality to the evolution of creative oral expression. When analysed as written documents, they also reveal the presence of features often attributed to written verse. These songs often reveal logical structure and thematic development, the presence of important literary devices like metaphor, simile and rhetorical tropes, including repetition. Oral, music-based forms like mento, calypso and folk songs served the various functions of celebration, reflection, lament and protest. If 'early' Caribbean creative writing of the 20th century can be said to reflect the uncertainty but also the quiet conviction of regional creative artists, then the oral tradition in some manifestations can be said to have struggled for survival.[18] But throughout the process the verbal arts has reflected the voices of redress and revolt within Caribbean cultural expression.

4. Caribbean Literary Works and Orality

Although the literary tradition has doubtlessly influenced the oral tradition, it is perhaps easier to see how the oral tradition impinged on literary expression over the decades. Caribbean poets like the Jamaican Claude Mckay and novelists like the Guyanese Edgar Mittelholzer have reflected components of the oral tradition, whether by way of language, form or structure. The scribal tradition has always been fascinated with the material and tools of oral culture. Literary works have therefore tended to portray aspects of the oral expressive culture. Critics have discussed the acute representation of the Caribbean voice in works of selected writers of prose. Mid-twentieth century works by Roger Mais, Samuel Selvon, and short stories by V.S. Naipaul, Janice Shinebourne, Jean Rhys, and Wilson Harris have all shown the influence of oral constituents. Moreover, some authors as for instance Earl Lovelace have foregrounded folk-based oral and performance-oriented phenomena like the calypso, reggae, steelpan, carnival, and other regional festivals. Similarly, the St Lucian Derek Walcott has over the decades experimented with folk and oral indigenous art forms. His plays *Ti Jean and His Brothers* and *Pantomime*, for instance, are built upon a keen awareness of St Lucian and Caribbean folk and oral culture.[19] *Ti Jean* draws from St Lucian folklore and oral tradition and explores the wordplay and physical confrontation between competing systems of knowledge (European, African and Caribbean). It therefore uses folk and oral traditions to frame the story's theme of confrontation, compassion, creativity and liberation. The play's use and manifestation of St Lucian Creole emphasizes the debt that the playwright owes to his oral source, and the central role of the vernacular in the fashioning of Caribbean history, the present and the future. *Pantomime*, though less directly concerned with folklore and oral tradition, is also in many ways an examination of European and Caribbean oral aesthetics. The main characters are a Trinidad and Tobago servant and his boss, a European. In the play, Trewe's European music hall and Jackson's Caribbean calypso epitomize their competing agendas. It is significant that the play presents their ongoing contestation through the opposition of their respective oral-musical traditions. In the final analysis however, it is the clever wordplay and 'picong' of the actors, the use of pun, and an exposure to the guile and power of oral delivery that are the work's lingering rewards.

The dramatic work of playwrights like Rawle Gibbons is even more up-front and experimental in the employment of oral tradition. In fact, Gibbons' plays like his *Calypso Trilogy* are built upon dramatizing the life and times of legendary Trinidad and Tobago oral poets / calypsonians.[20] The performance text therefore employs the actual lyrics of calypso by the greats of the past. Stage directions require the actors to vocalize the words and apply authentic melodies. Such a demanding liberating and experimental practice highlights the potential for interface within Caribbean literary performance culture. It also shows up the complexities of mastering this process of interface. Since Gibbons' work relies on oral tradition and on accurate treatment of this material, his scribal text cannot in itself provide all the substance needed to recreate the classic oral-musical standards in Caribbean folk song. The work therefore relies on the actors' knowledge of a set of information that the dramatic script cannot totally supply. The written text is therefore at times dependant on prior knowledge of the oral tradition to supplement the assumptions and ambitions of the inscription. Experiments of this kind bring to the fore the boundless arena of Caribbean literary, dramatic and cultural discourse. Experiments of this kind are a reminder that literary works do not exist or operate within a confined space, but that they depend on wider cultural references in order to fulfil their meanings.

Female writers of prose have also located the oral tradition as an important constituent within their projects. Short stories, in particular by women, have revealed an examination of folk and traditional motifs. Olive Senior's work like "You Think I Mad Miss", Jamaica Kincaid's "My Mother" and Velma Pollard's "My Mother" all explore aspects of traditional folk culture and / or myth.[21] For these writers though, the oral tradition provides the raw material with which they interrogate society's imbalance, and patriarchal norms.

5. Facilities / Media: From Little Magazines to Cassette Culture

Caribbean society has always had to fall back upon its own fluidity and dynamism. Caribbean art forms and genres have consistently come under challenges on account of internal and external pressures. Caribbean culture has been heavily influenced by extrinsic forces. These external factors have occasionally sounded the demise of traditional forms, but they have also resulted in the forging of new and renewed practices. Caribbean artists have themselves redefined their fields of practice as a result of, or as a response to, changing conditions. In the 1970s, when the threat to vinyl recordings was posed by the Phillips cassette revolution, Caribbean artists had to reconsider their art forms in light of the mass acquiring of cassette players in homes. This development gave birth to new ways of conceptualizing, performing, constructing and packaging art. The dub / performance poetry movement of that period profited from this new revolution in sound recording and its distribution and consumption.[22]

Caribbean cultural expressions have always been preoccupied with promotion, distribution and the media of communication available to them. In the 1930s literary magazines throughout the region gave impetus to aspiring writers. Many of the canonical writers of the Caribbean came to national recognition through journals like *Kyk-over-al*, *Focus* and *Bim*. Extra-regional publishing played a major part in popularizing Caribbean writers and their works in the wider international market. Many of the leading figures of Caribbean literature were elevated to wider acclaim through migration to metropolitan centres especially in Europe, but also in North America. By the 1980s, 'new' media like the cassette or tape recorder and the 'music video' also facilitated the distribution of work by a set of Caribbean oral and music-based creators who were coming into contact with early digital technology. Performance poets who had earlier invested in vinyl recordings showed greater liking for the cassette tape. The portability and mobility afforded by the cassette revolution attracted popular dub poets and recording oral poets who placed much trust in this format and medium. The sound system and the boom box were ideally suited to the purposes of these poets of the 1980s. Linton Kwesi Johnson, Brother Resistance Winston Farrell and Gregory Rabess all created, recorded and performed their oral poetry with a sense of proximity to amplified sound and new technologies. Oral poets found a format that placed them within easy reach of a vibrant new culture, one driven by youths who were at the forefront of appropriating the technology.[23]

These oral poets were also less apologetic about their closeness to the popular music arena. An overriding feature of recorded oral performances of the late 1970 and the 1980s is the presence and power of the voice, chanting and ranting on top of heavy rhythm tracks;[24] but these recordings also reveal the processed voice. Echo and delay were also effects employed to record and reproduce music-based performers. Producers like Dennis Bovell were therefore dabbling in dedicated reggae productions as well as working closely with dub / performance poets.[25] The recording aesthetics of dub poetry privileged the word. Dub poetry's recording practices also came to influence the dedicated music production arena and in turn helped to reshape attitudes to technology. Oral poets have therefore also shared this relationship with popular culture. This applies to oral poets in particular. They have been more daring than most other performers in Caribbean literary and cultural expression, with respect to the use and reshaping of technologies

6. Caribbean Literary and Cultural Studies in Cyberspace

By the mid-1990s Caribbean literary and cultural expression underwent significant transformation. This was a time of great reflection on the part of artists, writers, academics, critics and other practitioners. The Internet society was chartered around 1989. Worldwide, as in the Caribbean, the Internet influenced the way that society encountered, consumed and thought about themselves in the context of local, regional and global culture. The expansion of the World Wide Web from an esoteric education and military-driven facility to a commercial phenomenon coincided with the expansion of terms such as 'globalization'. In the Caribbean as elsewhere, all aspects of cultural expression came under the influence of leading-edge monoliths symbolized by the computer, the Internet and mobile and interactive technologies. It is not hard to conceive of how literary / cultural expression and studies have transformed on account of these developments in the years between the mid-1990s and mid-2000s.

Whereas in the late 1980s in the Caribbean the hard-copy text ruled, and dedicated libraries provided the main source of materials about literature and oral culture, this is no longer the case today: the microcomputer and World Wide Web have become the most popular facility for accessing information about Caribbean literature, orature and culture. To discuss the role of the Internet and similar technologies in fashioning Caribbean literary and oral culture is not to create a tangential or artificial sphere of debate; rather, this focus reflects what is arguably the most significant recent moment in the evolution of Caribbean cultural expression.

Writing on "Caribbean Cultural Identity on the Internet" Aston Cook warns about the dangers of embracing this phenomenon wholesale. In his article "Technologies of the Self: Foucault and Internet Discourse" Alan Aycock is less pessimistic, as he calls attention to the World Wide Web's dangers and prospects.[26] Morris, Christain Habekost, Kwame Dawes and further abroad Dick Hebdige and Stuart Hall, have alluded to the influence of innovations and technologies on Caribbean culture. Admittedly these critics have not gone the length of more recent studies by, for instance, Paul Theberge and Julian Kucklich which focus on the finer workings of technology in the context of cultural expression.[27] Caribbean literary and cultural studies is still rooted in important debates about central issues. It does appear that criticism is unwilling to unhinge itself from a preoccupation with more traditional media. But in light of contemporary developments it seems necessary at this stage to go on to engage and foreground issues related to 'technologics'.

7. From Voice-to-Text to Page-to-Voice

Kamau Brathwaite is a pivotal artist in the context of a study like this one, which concerns itself with orature, the literary tradition and orality in cyberspace. In many respects his earlier poetic experiments anticipate the dub poets of the 1970s and 1980s. Certainly his typographical experimentation and his post modem delivery anticipate the current debate about 'cyberorality'. Kamau Brathwaite has of course posed some challenges to publishers of hard-copied dedicated texts. Oxford University Press, which published some of his earlier works did not undertake to do his later works. Beginning in *The Arrivants* his experiments with nation language and page layout were evident. In works like *Zea Mexican Diary* and the later *Barabajan Poem* his new direction and work with the computer were signaled. The latter collection was now being published under his own imprint of Savacou North. He was making full use of letter size pages for his elaborate experiments with fonts and large point sizes. The appearance of Brathwaite's speech and essay in the University of Miami's on-line multi-media publication *Anthurium* reflects the ways in which the challenges faced in more traditional domains and media also plague the realm of virtual expression. It reflects the potential for surmounting these challenges, and the possibility that there are varying degrees of success to be gained over the challenges that arise in the real and virtual worlds of cultural expression.

In the work *Roots to Popular Culture* in a section titled "Technology: voice-to-text / text-to-voice".[28] I discussed the process and practice within Kamau Brathwaite's work whereby the poet on occasion palters with the potential interface between print culture and oral culture. There I argued that a careful systematic examination of the page could begin to unravel the processes within the matrix that connects the scribal arena to the oral. For instance, I set out a few rules to show how his use of typeface, fonts, point size as well as other emotive tools associated with the computer might suggest a set of specific oral codes. This is not a novel enterprise, since modern techno culture also functions by way of associative sings, symbols and sounds that stand for a set of resultants. 'Emoticons' for instance refer to a set of keyed icons that convey emotions, especially in the Web environment. In instant messaging and chat rooms, users often use these symbols that stand as replacement for emotions. Emoticons have developed to enhance the communication process in contexts where users of technology have sought to enliven and give emotion and arguably voice and soul to the limitations of more traditional text-based communications arenas.

In a quite intriguing process, poets like Brathwaite have also sought to inscribe a 'new' set of principles within the conventional literary text. This is done through a process of association of word, layout and context, and the reinforcement of a system of associative meaning. For instance, Brathwaite like other scribes of contemporary culture shortens Standard English words to reflect their nation language pronunciation, but also to suggest the ongoing tensions between words, their sound, and visual representation. Current information culture practice also facilitates the breakage of words to mirror their oral / aural delivery. But my earlier examination of word and sound and visual play in *Roots to Popular Culture*, focused on the way that advances in technology was forging an even more intricate relationship between the page and speech, between literature proper and oral delivery. Text-to-voice and voice-to-text as well as text-to-sign language technology has facilitated the more intricate interplay between different ways (mediums) of 'voicing', while also altering our conceptualization of writing, speech, signing and communication.[29]

It is justified that the text of Brathwaite's feature address to the 22nd Annual Conference on West Indian Literature, held at the University of Miami, was posted on the Internet.[30] But it is ironic that the medium to which his work also gestures, presented the most challenges to getting his written speech on-line. The late 2003 online free access journal *Anthurium*, while celebrating the liberating potential of the Internet in its inaugural edition, wrestled with the challenges of digital technology and its implications for individual, public and practical application. The editors declared that it was easy to reproduce Brathwaite's actual text to his lead article, but declared it to be more challenging to harmonize the quotations in the other essays where they quote from Brathwaite:

> [T]he task of synchronizing the variety of fonts used to reproduce and approximate Brathwaite's work in the critical essays presented yet another challenge. After careful thought and consultation, it was decided that the journal would use only variations of its standard fonts in bold, italics, and capitals. It was argued that since all attempts to approximate Brathwaite's Sycorax video style would be a misrepresentation of the original, this approach at least gave us the advantage of uniformity and coherence.

The fact of the need to engage in this kind of explanation points to the discovery by electronic literary publications that there are attendant problems in the digital domain of cultural expression. The digital dilemma concerns the pleasurable yet frustrating process engendered by robust new technologies. Yet to some extent though, the honest declaration presented in the Editor's notes to the new on-line publication cannot hope to (as it does not set out to) engage at a deeper level with the inherent tensions and indeed politics that come into being when digital technology is employed. There are always other issues to behold in the domain of digital deployment. There are always hidden codes and always hyperlinks within, connected to, and outside the field of immediate critical navigation. For example, where the editors declare to have easily accomplished the task of representing Brathwaite's speech / essay "Namsetoura & the Companion Stranger", by simply employing Adobe Acrobat (*.pdf), this version of the Brathwaite script is a little hard on the eyes and the variation in font and point size forces the reader to tweak the programme functions from page to page to compensate for the delivery of the document in this format. This is not a critique of the publication itself, rather, it is a reminder that technology's power is still relative to the range of situations and conditions under which it is used. Technology in itself is not infallible, neither are the human subjects who enlist and employ the wonders of leading-edge creations. But perhaps the compulsion to tweak the technology, an act of getting into the machine and altering the relational matrix, anticipates the very conditions that define oral delivery and performance, where performer and audience actively interact in the performative space.

8. 'Writers' and Proximity to Technology: Digital Voicing, Digital Orality

Print culture and oral culture though often conceptualized as separate spheres, do find a common domain of production and presence within the World Wide Web. Given the computer's capacities and functionalities, it is undoubtedly an instrument and medium of multiple experiences. It gives facility to the voice, to print, to the moving image, virtual representation and simulation. The very fact of being located on the Internet places the individual in close proximity to multiple facilities. (Elsewhere I discuss more fully this notion of 'proximity to technology'.[31]) On the Net a sound clip is always just a mouse click or two away. In any case, there is always a certain anxiety and expectation that the Internet provides for the user, who always expects to experience the hypertextual and multimedia capacity of virtual culture. The Internet's hypertextual and hypermedia features make it a medium of present or near-present oral, visual and experiential material. What I mean is, that traditional media are one or two-dimensional; they do not have the unending capacity and multiple links of the Web. On the Internet if an artist appears, the voice, lyrics, streaming video, are all just a click away. It should be understood that the features of 'orality' are not bound only to purely spoken-aural environments, but can also occur in interactive communicative contexts where there is speedy processing of dialogue or material. Hypertext is much more fluid, intuitive and conversant than conventional print. Hypertext is suggestive of speech.[32] Harnad refers to "electronic skywriting" hypertext – the "fourth cognitive revolution".[33] In this revolution, writing will allow us to communicate with speeds approximating that of speech, which is much closer to the speed of thought than other communication media. Indeed, the Internet compresses the sense of distance that characterizes relations within more traditional systems of scribal expression. Instant messaging and email are some of the contemporary text-based practices that exhibit the features of this 'technorality', or 'digital orality' or 'digitaurality'. I therefore argue that Caribbean oral and cultural theory requires updating to account for the complex matrix that encapsulates the range of expressions within a new digitized society. Given the still unstable nature of the Internet, video and sound streaming are fraught with imperfections. Since streaming video and audio can turn an artist's performance into a dismembered rendition, it is possible to suggest that the new arena of digitaurality requires that viewers / hearers actively compensate for the lapses in communication between the machine and its others.

Relatively few of the region's traditional scribal-based artists host their own web page. But these authors are found on a wide range of sites. They are heavily rotated on websites of academic, publishing, learning and governmental organizations and so owe their ongoing visibility on the Internet as well as their status, image and personas to these corporations. Most established writers seem to have given over their web presence and 'digital voice' to other agencies within the complex matrix of real and virtual contestation. There are two levels at which it is possible to talk about 'voicing' in the context of Caribbean Internet discourse. On the Internet, 'voicing' is an actual functionality (in that there are facilities for audio streaming and other forms of audio / oral delivery); but on the Internet 'voicing' is also a more complex act. This is to say, in the digital domain one's presence, however marked (whether by way of a photograph, one's name, or a reference to one's self) constitutes a 'voice', or a virtual digital utterance. But this being said, virtual utterances are not always reflections of one's express intentions. Not all 'voicings' (audible or unspoken) associated with an artist on the Internet really belong to the artist. Since most Caribbean artists and oral performers do not or cannot control their virtual presence they often stand apart from the image and voice of themselves 'performing' in cyberspace. The Web has the potential therefore to act as virtual ventriloquist, serving to manipulate the moving lips of Caribbean authors. Given this situation, authors have the task of seeking to fashion, and sound their real voice through some direct involvement, control and manipulation of technology's organs of speech. It is the newer, younger and oral-based artists who have tended to be more aggressive in fashioning their voice and presence in cyberspace.

It is instructive that relatively few older canonical authors have sought to gain control of their virtual presence and its facility for digital speech. Case in point, Austin Clarke: this Barbadian / Canadian author is very present on the World Wide Web. He does not appear to want control of his web presence. Nowhere are his virtual presence and its utterances more potent than when featured through "Northwest Passages: Canadian Literature Online", the book sellers.[34] There is a strong Canadian stamp about his persona, as the Canadian flag flutters visibly at the head of selected major sites where he is found. His digital performance is therefore circumscribed by strands upon strands of promotional fare. Ultimately, his voicing is not clearly articulated from the centre of his experience in the Caribbean. But arguably, his virtual de-centred presence is also reflective of the multiple voices that inhabit his literary texts. Writers of this kind seem to care little about spatial location as they celebrate the pleasures of real and virtual exile.

Some exceptions to this process of total surrendering of voice to the technological medium, are digital-oral / digitaural artists like Caryl Philips and Colin Channer, represented at their dedicated websites. Sites of this kind reflect the possibility of some control within the frontier world of writing, speech and performance. Philips' site comes with splash page, and gives information on ‘education and publication’, ‘awards’, ‘tours’, ‘agents’. This situates him closer to Caribbean pop and performance-oriented artists than to the more conventional literary artists.[35] But perhaps this has to do with Phillips’ multidisciplinary approach to the arts. His career has developed on a number of fronts. He has written fiction and non-fiction, has written plays, but has also produced radio programmes. The extent of his diverse approach to the arts is signalled by his writing the screenplay for the Merchant Ivory production of Naipaul’s *The Mystic Masseur*. Unlike some other writers, Phillips seems very conscious of digital orality, his image, his work, and the realities of virtual marketing politics. Arguably, many writers of the generation who had been internationally known before the decade of the 1990s have in many respects resigned themselves to working through the longstanding tried and true media. Phillips’ engagement with the Internet is therefore partly a reflection of his generation, of his rising popularity at the time when the Internet was becoming a commercially exploitable medium, but it is also due to his location within the world of literature, the arts, and the media. His tag as a Caribbean writer who has spent many years abroad also supports his presence on the Internet. Caribbean critics and students have for a long time debated the meaning of the term ‘Caribbean writer’. Many individuals studied as Caribbean creators have spent several years outside the region, where they work, write, speak and earn a living. Their inhabiting the space between worlds and their umbilical relation to an archipelago called ‘home’ represents their status as transient. The birth of the Internet has helped to bridge the gap between home and away. It is an ideal facility for the virtual oral testimony of exiled souls. It allows for multiple voicing. It has proven to be an excellent facility for raising further questions about identity, community and the nation.

The hosting of and exerting of control over one’s own dedicated site does not of course represent a total seizing of control over one’s image and voice in cyberspace. Caryl Phillips, for example, is otherwise represented at numerous non-official or non-dedicated sites,[36] where he is bundled with other writers. Phillips’ site does not represent the frontier possibility of digital-speak (since many other artists and genres, especially within the entertainment industry thrive on loud digital statement), but it comes closer to high-end digital voicing than the sites of many other Caribbean artists from the ‘literary’ tradition.

Colin Channer's official site[37] is more experimental or submersed in the multiplicity of functionalities and processes of the Internet. It is generally less formal. It too is professionally done, but it is more intimate and expressive on account of carefully constructed Web architecture. It speaks in formal as well as intimate tones. Here Channer shares his delight about his children (Americans of West Indian parents) celebrating the Chinese New Year at school, where they learn English and Mandarin. He says that "In their minds the world is not divided into halves of black and white, but in halves of English and Chinese". This is the nature of post-digital discourse about exile and all its attendant virtual pleasures.

Given the fact that many of the older generation of Caribbean creative authors are not located on home pages set up or even officially sanctioned by them, there is even fiercer competition among digital surrogate institutions / entities to set up de facto 'official' homepages and to speak for many Caribbean authors. Institutions are pleased to speak on behalf of and virtually for a set of Caribbean authors. Fu Jen University's (Taiwan) website of their English Language and Literature Department provides informative materials concerning Caribbean Literature. It is happy to foreground Jean Rhys' ambivalence to being fixed in any one nationality.[38] This is further grounds for laying claim to liminal writers of this kind. The important compendium of electronic resources called Englishscholar.com prides itself as having an 'exclusive to English Scholar', that is, an open page dedicated to the Belizean writer Zee Edgell. It comes with a biography, bibliography, essays, interviews and links to her associated virtual locations at Kent State University's English Department, Butterworth-Heinemann her publishers and Amazon where her books are displayed. The race to gain preeminence, to control the iconography, virtual presence and voices of some of these writers via the Internet is therefore frought by a number of entities.

There are some authors who intervene in the process. The Grenadian author and scholar Merle Collins appears at a number of locations.[39] Given her dual role as writer and academic her 'voice' is projected on two fronts. She therefore appears through her affiliation with the University of Maryland, but she also features in web streams such as ResearchChannel.[40] ResearchChannel is a consortium of research universities and corporate research divisions dedicated to broadening the access to and appreciation of knowledge by using program content creation and manipulation processes as testing medium for analogue and digital broadcast and on-demand multimedia offerings. But Collins disrupts the process of virtual control when on the University of Maryland site she actually reads from her creative work performing via Apple's Quicktime platform.[41] By actually sounding her own voice through a video and oral rendition, the Caribbean author enters into the matrix of cultural simulation and arrests the surrogate process within the machine.

My kind of reading might suggest that web sites have some life of their own. It might also suggest that many sites are insidious. The World Wide Web has ambitions of catching up with real life and of supplementing 'the real'. Within this process, a range of intentions and sites have emerged, some genuine and others insidious. Some sites are less concerned with controlling the performances of individual artists, but are more inclined to give fuller access to the oral and visual presentation by authors themselves. One of the more progressive, pioneering initiatives involving on-line access was mounted by the University of Miami in late 2003. Their "Caribbean Writers Summer Institute Digital Archives" is a virtual database of performances and moments featuring Caribbean literary and cultural figures. This facility provides students, teachers and all other navigators access to selected Caribbean writers and critics, reading or discussing their work. Its extensive subject archive features from St Lucian Kendel Hippolyte reading "Poem in a Manger" to other streams under the heading of "Carnival", "Intimidation fiction", "AIDS Drama" and "Women authors (Guyana)". The video streams are mostly taken from the proceedings of their Summer Workshop Initiative conducted throughout the 1990s. The streams are of varying lengths. Their website also gives access to the keynote address delivered at the 2003 Conference on West Indian Literature, by Kamau Brathwaite.

9. Performance Poets and Media

If Caribbean literary and cultural expression was in the past characterized by a process of competing and negotiated relations woven between scribal and oral-based manifestation, then post-2000 Caribbean literature at the cusp of its practice reveals an even more complex set of imperatives. New literary artists and oral poets are more comfortable than their elders with switching between scribal and oral media. Caribbean oral and literary traditions have hardly been able to remain apart. This is the nature of literary and cultural expression in contemporary society. There is always endless interface, endless interconnectivity and interplay. In current practice, performance artists are also employing and interfacing actual oral expression with a varied array of media. Some leading-edge poets therefore host their own web pages and / or appear on websites along with stars within the popular music domain. Because performance poets are very concerned with their image and message they tend to provide the text of lyrics, as well as streaming audio and streaming video. This multimedia preoccupation within the Caribbean literary and cultural sphere is the major trajectory of its development. This multimedia desire also reflects the influence and impact of global technology and popular culture on traditionally conservative phenomena and practices, such as that called literature.

Within the evolution of Caribbean oral poetry, performers have always been careful to represent their work through technologised sound, but have also provided the words in the cassette jackets or CD inlay cards. Linto Kwesi Johnson's 1998 CD "A Capella-Live" is therefore strong on sound and oral delivery, but LKJ has always been careful to provide his lyrics. This is not a unique practice, since pop artistes also do this; but oral poets affiliated with the region's literary sphere have been consistent in their promotion of voice, sound and the word. With the advent of the Video CD, poets have also invested in audio and video clips as viable supplements to their work, but have remained reverent to the printed text.

The popularity of audio books rose in the late 1980s. Whereas Caribbean poets and oral-based writers have had a longer relationship with audio recording, novelists, especially more seasoned canonical writers, have not wholly embraced publication in this format. Louise Bennet has appeared on recordings over the years. The storyteller, short story writer Paul Keens Douglas has published many of his works on Cassette and CD, for instance "Tim Tim". But more traditional 'literary-literary' prose writers have preferred to represent their work in print. In any case, publishers have not always been keen to invest additional sums of money into other formats. Whereas oral-based as well as more cutting-edge writers have moved to reposition themselves in the arena of virtual experience and cultural simulation, more traditional writers have relied on their affiliation with publishing houses, universities and other institutions to cast their presence in cyberspace. E-books though growing in popularity by 2005, were not widely embraced by Caribbean readers. This had partly to do with the resistance to electronic consumption generally and the challenges of owning new technologies. As elsewhere, Caribbean people were still attached to certain ways of consuming 'the book'. These digital books came in HTML Editions which meant that they could be read using the web browser or off-line. One of the preferred formats for digital reading was the Acrobat PDF format, since most systems old or new have it installed. The newer Microsoft Reader claimed to make the reading exercise less stressful on the eyes by allowing for tweaking of the appcarance and texture and size of the text. There is a degree of fixity that characterizes these publications. Users of the net are often off put by heavy text-based formats, especially when they are not interactive. Even older innovations like the telephone and newer ones like video-on-demand provide more than a one-way traffic of dialogue. Accompanying software like Mirosoft's text-to-speech package, have promised to enhance the process of consuming electronic books. E-books are therefore bound to be fully supplemented by encoded visuals and interactive features in the future, making it a more expressive medium. When one understands that cyberspace is fast becoming the leading arena for voicing complex experience, and that its expansive matrix of representation and simulation both mirrors and anticipates literature's fascination with a varied range of tools, media and experiences, then one begins to contemplate the deeper relation between literary and cultural studies on the one hand and cyber reality on the other.

10. Within / Without the Machines: Oral Performance-based Artists

Caribbean artists who are much closer to the oral, music and performance spheres have understandably been much more active in employing and engaging the Internet creatively. Given their closer association to pop, they have found the trendy functions and facilities of the Internet much more appealing and applicable to their artistic field. But even so, not all performance based writers and oral / aural / digit-aural performers have sought enhanced presence on the

Internet. Like their colleagues in the literary tradition, some are contented to be spoken of and to be spoken for.

Websites like www.57productions.com (prior to its mid-2000 evolution), provided information on over 50 writers and performers in the UK and elsewhere. This kind of bundling arrangement is effective for some authors, but it also locks the creative artist into set arrangements and representational patterns. Each artist is reduced to a greystone (grey+ white) photo and a short bio; there are few embedded hyperlinks, although there is a link to at least one other page. Sites of this kind have served as important resource locations. Although they do not give in-depth pages on each artist, they nonetheless give a sense of community and association among artists who share at least the same virtual space. Given the pressures of Web culture and the imperative of freeing the Net from its textual hinge, 57Productions unveiled a new website in the mid-2000s. Although its individual artist pages provided little more than on the old website, the new page versions seemed more expressive and digitaural, due to a significant reworking of graphics, page layout and cleaner, crisper images. The new website also began to promote its poetry jukebox which centres audio performances by a range of older and new poets. It also invests in other media, more particularly video clips. The refurbishment of the older site and the new emphasis on sound and video clips is partly a marketing tool. This shifting dynamics might also reflect a process of granting greater autonomy and 'voice' to individual artists who can now perform for themselves and virtually uninhibited. The investment in and expansion of oral, aural, visual and multimedia facilities in cyberspace marks the expansion of the discursive field. As the machines get better and faster they allow for a quicker transaction and discourse between authors, audience and other users, hence engendering the set of conditions that define orality.

Bremen University's site map for dub poetry features fewer dub poets than 57Productions, but gives more information about the culture that has supported leading dub poets. Since it is a non-commercial site its interest in broader cultural issues is understood.[42] It therefore is concerned to give its navigators samples of the performance poems as literary text. It hosts links to what it calls the "reading room". A critical comparison of these two sites reflects subtle differences that are rooted in their particular orientation. In one sense it can be said that one is clearly more commercial, while the other has education as a prime objective. Given this general reading of their orientation, it might be suggested that more commercial sites are defined by the existence of certain features and functionalities, as mentioned above, while sites that are education-driven are defined by reverence to scribal / textual features although they also exhibit multimedia capacity. Both sites reflect the multi-layered features that define performance poetry. On the one hand performance poets have a history that connects to the literary tradition, but they also evolve and participate within the realm of popular culture. This is the point therefore at which web culture wrestles with the very facilities available in cyberspace in order to represent and produce the raw material of what is performance poetry. In the final analysis, given the web's flexibility, even web pages of different orientation cannot avoid but reproduce some similar features and information, but also similar modes of delivering their divergent visions of a single artistic practice.

Artists like LKJ, Mutabaruka, Binta Breeze, Adisa, and other Rapso poets like Brother Resistance, Kindred and 3Canal either make active use of the Net, or appear with frequency there. True, the performance poets are more aggressive in ensuring, maintaining, managing and disseminating their iconography and projecting their voices. But the impression should not be given that all oral-based poets indulge in the tools of digital performance. It might be surprising to some that Jean Binta Breeze does not have a dedicated site (as of late 2004), but falls back on references through LKJ Records and Bloodaxe books. The pioneering performer Louise Bennett appears at many sites but the one that carries her official stamp, was still under construction around the mid-2000s, when it only displayed two photographs of her. Some of the biggest names (like their cohorts in the literary tradition) remain conservative in their use of technology. The website of selected stalwarts show a reverence for the word, the written word, lyrics, message and the experience of connecting with the performance by route of these processes. Thus, Benjamin Zephaniah[43] promotes his works and ware, but also provides a space for other creative people to get up their creations through a gateway on his main page which he calls "Outernet". Like his other contemporaries, Zephaniah's site places great emphasis on text and on the word. Indeed, His site appears to sacrifice other expressive hyperlinks for solid promotional and message-oriented dialogue.

Mutabaruka[44] comes with audio and video links. Navigation is not the easiest here. The contemporary navigator might be fooled by a link that says 'Videos', which does not lead to streaming clips, but rather to a listing of his selected video and filmed appearances. On the other hand, there is much more healthy posting of his lyrics from successive albums. It is perhaps disappointing for the contemporary navigator that the site does not provide sample video clips of his performance, given the fact that most websites of leading performance-based artists come with a mixed array of multimedia facilities. But arguably, Mutabaruka has always been even more conscious of his lyrics than most. He is a message-based poet above all else. It is therefore not surprising that his use of technological resources has privileged the printed word above any other single medium. He however attempts to make up for this 'lack' by providing a substantial number of still photos, to give his presence in cyberspace some sense of vitality. But one feels he would be equally happy if there were only words. The scribal tradition therefore continues to significantly impact the oral tradition in the arena of digital display. Indeed their relationship is a tight one. Critics and observers are perhaps more responsible for conceptualizing their separation than the performers themselves. Practitioners have hardly doubted the close relationship.

By contrast, around 2002 Barbados' most visible performance poet, Adisa Andwele, was showcasing his CD "Doing It Saf". The web site[45] was constituted by a single page, its information barely sufficient; it provided four audio clips. Overall the presentation was sparse. At that time the website was clearly specifically put up to provide access to his popular work of the same name. By mid-2004 the site had been upgraded and reworked. Some tweaking had been done to it. Like the artist himself who has constantly been tweaking his image, experimenting with different genres and changing his nomenclature, the new web site revealed some editing. It contained concise information about his post-2000 releases. It carried his curt philosophizing and limited samples of his literary and performance-based work. All in all, the website was self-contained, providing no external links for this artist who has a substantial history outside the secluded virtual space of his domain name. All these sites seem to scoff at the thought that the Net can sustain itself. They seem to challenge and reject its claim to autonomy and actual existence.

They therefore point users of this technology to the authors' other sites of performance, which exist in the real world.

Not all rapso poets feature on the Internet. Brother Resistance and fellow rapso performance poets largely share a quite similar orientation to their dub based colleagues. The pioneers Karega Mandela and Lancelot Layne are found in archive-type sites, and more contemporary outfits like Kindred and Ataklan are diffuse in representation, not having a focal location. The similarities between dub and rapso poets have to do with their relationship to the scribal and popular oral and music traditions. Whereas traditional dub poets were influenced by reggae culture and contemporary performers by dancehall and post-dancehall culture, rapso poets have significant influence from calypso, soca and post-soca culture.[46] But these strands of performance poetry have impacted one another. Whereas it was easier in the 1980s to talk of these as distinct movements, by the mid-2000s they have evolved, borrowed and transformed. They have intersected in many creative ways. Their point of convergence was not always defined by the two traditions themselves, since the two traditions were also being greatly influenced by extra-regional popular entertainment culture.

An artist like Brother Resistance, who has been around since the 1970s, locates his tradition in old-time carnival talkers and figures like the 'midnite robber'.[47] But in the post-2004 period, web culture has embraced this kind of performer. In turn this type of performer has courted cyberculture so as to fashion his image and message, but all the while engaging in the task of fixing the technology so that it conveys his iconography. Like some dub poets on their home page, Brother Resistance also tries to provide selected access to his material and philosophy by way of various functions of the technology. Biography, discography, photo gallery and sales are all categories and links provided. He also provides MP3 downloads. The visual layout is defined by a collage of images from different photos. These are pasted onto and below what appears to be a motley coloured aluminium barrier with traces of graffiti. All in all this gives the website and the artist a rough edge. The measure of his acknowledgement of his tradition's link to reggae culture is symbolized in his web page's showing of a hanging medallion with the words 'RAPSO' pasted onto a background of red, yellow and green.

Even younger and newer performers have tended to be more experimental than the stalwarts. They make use of text-based pages, as well as audio and video, which are all integral features of virtual post-oral culture. These new artists consciously desire and set out to interconnect oral delivery with the tools and media of a technology-driven lifestyle. An outfit like 3canal is variously accessible through carnival and soca sites. This is one of several post-oral poetry outfits influenced by post-soca and post-dancehall styles. Their popularity also coincides with the evolution of Raggasoca, ringbang and Caribbean-North American styles. Curiously around 2004 their website 3canal.com promoted what they called the 3canal Show. It could only be accessed with a user name and password. This facility was both a barrier and a marketing tool. The website's only other function was to advertise the rapso group's T-shirt line. This site reflected the height of new commercialism, but also the realities of direct product marketing. 3canal has never seemed to conform to normative standards. They have always seemed to be 'out there' somewhere. One feels that such an outfit might be better placed within the realm of Caribbean post-rapso / Caribbean alternative performance. Since information about the group could be gleaned from elsewhere, their new dedicated site seemed clearly focused on a few limited goals. One therefore suspects that the site was intended to be a transient construction. Its objective revolved around a set of specific goals. This method sprang from the recognition that the Internet is an unstable medium. Sites are constructed and they die. The 3canal experiment seems a self consciously constructed space / moment that pays homage to this very fact of cyber-reality. Like the utterance, like the voice, cyber- presence is hardly stable, it is hardly autonomous. Virtual oral-based groups like 3canal seem to have consciously thought about the status of current and future digital culture and are prepared to operate not only within, but also outside the matrix of real and virtual experience and control.

Notes

1 See Roger D. Abrahams: *The Man of Words in the West Indies*, Baltimore, 1983; and, to a lesser extent, Peter Roberts: *From Oral to Literate Culture,* Kingston, 2000.

2 See "Introduction" to Gordon Rohlehr, *Voiceprint*, Essex, 1990.

3 See the many texts that deal with orality in the Caribbean, a sample of these including Gordon Rohlehr: *A Scuffling of Islands*, San Juan, 2004. Keith Warner: *The Trinidad Calypso,* London, 1982; Mervyn Morris: *Is English*

We Speaking, Kingston, 1999; Maureen Warner Lewis: *Notes to Masks*, Benin City, 1977.

4 See the book *Culture @ the Cutting Edge* and in particular Chapter One: "Reading Culture as Multi-tracked", Kingston, 2005, pp. 1-9.

5 See Stewart Brown (Ed.): *The Pressures of the Text*, African Studies Series 4, Birmingham, 1995, for a range of discussions about Caribbean and African orality and writing.

6 Walter Ong: *Orality and Literacy,* London, 1982.

7 See Richard Leo Enos (Ed.): *Oral and Written Communication: Historical Approaches*, California, 1990, and Ruth Finnegan: *Literacy and Orality: Studies in the Technology of Communication*, Oxford, 1988.

8 John December: "Characteristics of Oral Culture in Discourse on the Net". Paper presented at the Twelfth Annual Penn State Conference on Rhetoric and Composition, University, Park, Pa., 8 July 1993, p.1.

9 Gordon Rohlehr: *Pathfinder,* Tunapuna, 1981, and "Sparrow and the Language of Calypso", *CAM Newsletter* 2 (April/May), 1967.

10 See Mervyn Morris' early essay "On Reading Louise Bennett seriously", *Sunday Gleaner*, June 1964, 7-28 and also more recently *Making West Indian Literature*, Kingston, 2004.

11 Adu-Gyamfi Yaw's 1999 PhD Dissertation "Orality In Writing: Its Cultural and Political Function In Anglophone African, African-Caribbean, and African-Canadian Poetry", University of Saskatchewan, 1999.

12 See sections of Lloyd Brown: *West Indian Poetry,* London, 1984; Kenneth Ramchand: *Introduction to the Study of West Indian Literature,* Middlesex, 1971; Edward Chamberlain: *Come Back to Me My Language,* Kingston, 2000.

13 See sections of Bruce King: *West Indian Literature,* London, 1995.

14 Ruth Finnegan: *Oral Literature in Africa*, Oxford, 1970; Ruth Finnegan: *Oral Traditions and the Verbal Arts*, London, 1992; Edward Kamau Brathwaite: *History of the Voice. The Development of Nation Language in Anglophone Caribbean Poetry*, London, 2005; Gordon Rohlehr: *My Strangled City, and Other Essays*, Port of Spain, 1992.

15 Peter Roberts: *From Oral to Literate Culture*, Kingston, Jamaica, 1997.

16 Roger D. Abrahams gives fuller insight into the structure and practice of these various oral phenomena in his *The Man of Words*.

17 See works like Dina J Epstein: *Sinful Tunes and Spirituals*, Urbana, 1977; Trevor Marshall: *Notes on the History and Evolution of Barbadian Music*, Cave Hill, 1986.

18 See banning of songs in Rohlehr: *Calypso and* Society, Tunapuna, 1990, *passim*.

19 "Ti Jean and His Brothers" in the text *Dream on Monkey Mountain and Other Plays*, London, 1972. *Walcott's* "Pantomime" appears in the collection *Remembrance & Pantomime*: *Two Plays*, New York, 1980.

20 Rawle Gibbons, *Calypso Trilogy*, Kingston, 1999.

21 See selected works by these female authors in the collection Stewart Brown (Ed.), *Caribbean New Wave: Contemporary Short Stories*, Oxford, 1990.
22 See Dick Hebdige: *Cut N' Mix*, London, 1987 and Christian Habekost: *Verbal Riddim*, Amsterdam, 1993.
23 See a more intimate discussion of the use of technology in Caribbean culture construction in the work *Culture @ the Cutting Edge*, Kingston, 2005.
24 See Habekost: *Verbal Riddim*; especially his discussion of performance and recording.
25 Hear Bovell's exciting work with Linto Kwesi Johnson for example on the 1980 release "Bass Culture" and the 1991 "Tings and Times".
26 See Cook's article at <www.dwightday.com/yardculture0702.html>; "Technologies of the Self: Foucault and Internet Discourse" by Alan Aycock at <www.ascusc.org>, accessed 12 February 2007
27 See for example Julian Kücklich: "Literary Theory and Computer Games", <http://www.cosignconference.org/download/12>, accessed 23 February 2007.
28 In Curwen Best: *Roots to Popular Culture*, London, 2001; see the section titled "Technology: voice-to-text / text-to-voice", pp. 81-86.
29 See Shelley Popson "Voice-to-Text Technologies used for Captioning Access (and Sign Access)" at <www.fsdb.k12.fl.us/rmc/training/techtools/voice2text.html>, accessed 12 February 2007.
30 <http://scholar.library.miami.edu/anthurium/volume_1/issue_1/brathwaite-namsetoura.htm>, accessed 23 February 2007.
31 An unpublished manuscript tentatively titled "Death of the Real: Caribbean Culture in the Age of the Machines".
32 See Derrick De Kerckhove: *Connected Intelligence: The Arrival of Web Intelligence*, Toronto, 1997.
33 See Stephen Harnad: "Post-Gutenberg Galaxy: The Fourth Revolution in the Means of Production of Knowledge", *The Public-Access Computer Systems Review*, 2:1, 1991, 39-53, 42.
34 See <http://www.nwpassages.com/author_profile.asp?au_id=250>, accessed 12 February 2007.
35 See <www.carylphillips.com>, accessed 12 February 2007.
36 Examples are <www.postcolonialweb.org> and <www.contemporarywriters.com>, accessed 12 February 2007.
37 See <www.colinchanner.com>, accessed 12 February 2007.
38 See <www.eng.fju.edu.tw/worldlit/caribbean/rhys.htm>, accessed 12 February 2007.
39 See for example <www.geocities.com/merlecollins/>, accessed 12 February 2007.
40 See <www.researchchannel.org>, accessed 12 February 2007.
41 See <www.mith2.umd.edu/archive/hughes/quicktime/mcollins.html>, accessed 12 February 2007.
42 See www.fb10.uni-bremen.de/anglistik/kerkhoff/DubPoetry/index.html>, accessed 12 February 2007.

43 See <www.benjaminzephaniah.com>, accessed 12 February 2007.
44 See <www.Mutabaruka.com>, accessed 12 February 2007.
45 See <www.adisasaf.com>, accessed 12 February 2007.
46 See Curwen Best's use of these terms to define the latest evolution of these Caribbean music styles in the book *Culture @ the Cutting Edge*.
47 See <http://www.brotherresistance.com/biography.htm>, accessed 12 February 2007.

Gail Low (Dundee)

Writing the Caribbean: Caribbean Book / Media History

Debates in the history of the book have sought to encourage students and critics of literature to think of the book not simply as 'text' in the narrow sense of the word, but also as 'institution', made up of a network of social, cultural and discursive relationships. Instead, book history seeks to remind us that books are material artefacts as well as imaginative and creative works. As books make the journey from "private to public spaces",[1] metamorphosing from idea into print, the connections between publishing, cultural, educational and literary institutions – and individuals – are all crucial to understanding the process of textuality and authorship. Questions concerning the historical, social, cultural, and economic aspects of writing and publishing, including the editing, production, dissemination, the marketing and reception of books in print, all fall within the interdisciplinary domain of book history. Turning to the topic of Anglophone Caribbean literature, we might ask the following questions: Who were the important publishers of writing from and of the Caribbean before and after political independence? Who read these writers? Can we say something about their audiences? Can we also account for why some writers were published and others were not? In tracing the genealogy of Anglophone Caribbean book history, can one say something about the types of book publishers looked for and published or reviewers reviewed? Were there significant networks of social, cultural and literary relationships that helped disseminate the work of these writers? These questions are neither exhaustive nor easy to provide answers to, given the paucity of archival material or the difficulties of accessing them. In the brief and necessarily selective sketch that follows, I want to show how describing and exploring the ways in which books are produced, disseminated, and circulated constitute a valuable and necessary undertaking; criticism that does not address some of these issues is a discourse that willfully blinds itself to the ways in which books are socially and materially significant.

Early literary history yields some interesting problems in relation to some of the questions posed above. Printing presses were started in Jamaica, Barbados and Antigua, Dominica and Grenada in the eighteenth century. In his survey of early print and book trade history in the West Indies, Roderick Cave notes that these presses produced official documents, almanacs, newspapers, periodicals and other ephemera. Some playscripts of plays performed locally were published, learned writing on the subject of tropical medicine, animal care and botany were also printed.[2] Planter manuals, anti-slavery tracts, as well as some literary and historical material were published later in the eighteenth and nineteenth century. Poems and articles were included within newspaper and journalistic broadsheets; John Singleton's verse, "A General Description of the West Indian Islands" appeared in *The Barbados Mercury* in 1777 while William Sherrington's poems appeared in the *Antigua Gazette* around the same time.[3] The inclusion of literary material in newspapers, and the association of newspapers with literary ventures was to figure large in Caribbean literary history. As we shall later see, magazines and newspapers provided important publishing outlets for aspiring writers in the earlier twentieth century. Helen Tiffin asserts that the connection between "newspaper publishing and local literary production" with a "largely local readership" is also evident in this early period of literary and print history.[4] Local newspapers did not simply reproduce items in the British press; while some amount of reprinting of items appeared, these papers shaped news material for their readers. Debates that were current in the metropolitan presses, for example on the topic of slavery, were given local emphasis. There were also attempts to engage directly with issues that were current in Britain from an island perspective. Such a characteristic of Anglophone Caribbean publishing – where "what was produced in the West Indies" was "overtly or implicitly enmeshed in an imperial / colonial" web – constitute, to adopt Tiffin's phraseology, a "direct dialectical tradition". J. J. Thomas' *Froudacity* (1889) written in response to J. A. Froude's *The English in the West Indies* (1888), and appearing first in *The St George's Chronicle and Grenada Gazette* in 1888, is one such example of how local writing signifies within and without in wider colonial context. The postwar metropolitan boom in the publishing of Anglophone Caribbean writers such as George Lamming, Sam Selvon, V. S. Naipaul and Wilson Harris, their literary exile in Britain in the nineteen fifties and sixties, and their counter-discursive writing might be another example of an 'enmeshed' colonial discursive web.[5]

Journals, newspapers and magazines were produced in the West Indies, but access to these was uneven across the islands, and readership was restricted to those who were wealthy enough to purchase them. While there were circulating libraries in Jamaica in 1790s, these folded quickly through lack of custom. Similarly libraries established in Grenada and Trinidad in the 1820s and 1830s rarely lasted for more than a year or so.[6] There was no circulating library in Barbados in 1821.[7] A reading room in Trinidad asked for an annual subscription fee of eight pounds in 1826.[8] Another Reading Society in Jamaica advertised a joining fee of ten shillings and six pence; but with further annual subscription rates to pay of thirty shillings, most of the population would simply not be able to afford to borrow these books. Unsurprisingly, the few book societies that were established focused predominantly on books from Britain.[9] With the departure of the planter class, the market for literature shrunk even further and by the mid-nineteenth century, Cave notes, "West Indians were buying fewer books, and then books of a utilitarian nature, often in cheap reprints".[10]

Thomas Henry MacDermot who edited *Jamaican Times* from 1904 has been described as the first Creole literary nationalist in the West Indies.[11] He argued for the distinctiveness of Jamaican identity and for literature to reflect island concerns, urging writers to be "as native as they felt it in them to be, both in manner and matter."[12] MacDermot encouraged poets such as W. Adolphe Roberts; he also published de Lisser's early essays and McKay's dialect poems. But he is perhaps best known for his attempts at publishing the "All Jamaica Library". Books then available in the Caribbean were in the main "colonial editions". Colonial editions were editions of book already published in Britain. Produced for export to major colonial markets, they were usually (but not always) done in smaller formats and sold at significantly reduced prices when compared with metropolitan editions. The colonial relationship between Britain and her colonies is thus also mirrored in such publishing practices. Local writing was exported and re-imported for metropolitan profit. Typically, colonial editions provided British publishers with a method of recuperating the costs of publishing the first print run of new books; they also worked against local publishing because they encouraged writers to seek initial publication abroad by fostering a view that writers were 'real authors' only when their books were issued by metropolitan publishing houses.

MacDermot's "All Jamaica Library" represented an attempt to intervene in this colonial relationship. It was an ambitious attempt to encourage the writing and reading of Jamaican writing through making local writing affordable and accessible. In the foreword to the first book issued under its imprint, the press proclaimed that its aim was to issue poetry, fiction, history and essays "all dealing directly with Jamaica and Jamaicans, and written by Jamaicans".[13] The imprint was published and supported by the *Jamaica Times* printery and titles were sold for the price of one shilling, a price MacDermot argued was fair but "so small as to make each publication generally purchasable."[14] In his preface to the fourth title in the series, his own novel *One Brown Girl and –*, one can see an attempt to strike a balance between idealism and commerce. The preface juggles a number of different and conflicting impulses: the desire to foster the "growth of an island literature", a wish that nothing "faithful" in "local colour, detail and dialect" be sacrificed in order to "fit a local story for publication abroad", and the need to sell books in order to stay afloat. If the preface concedes that "the fullest possible success" at home "cannot give the reward in money that would accompany even moderate success abroad", it also contends that producing material that Jamaicans be proud of as "the work of a son of the Island" must ultimately be the primary concern. In the same forward, MacDermot remarks that the first print run of series sold one thousand copies and that two further printings had to be ordered.[15] Unfortunately, the early success of the series was not to last, and having issued four books, including two of MacDermot's own novels (published under the pseudonym "Tom Redcam"), the All Jamaica Library folded.

Not unlike MacDermot, the conjoining of journalism and literature is again repeated in the case of Herbert de Lisser, who was editor of the *Gleaner*, and A.R.F. Webber who edited the Guyanese *Daily Chronicle*. Webber's *Those That Be in Bondage – a Tale of Indian Indentures and Sunlit Western Waters* was published by the *Daily Chronicle* printing press in 1917. Webber also took an interest in history of the region, publishing a history and yearbook of

British Guiana locally in 1931. Not unlike Webber who was his colleague in the West Indian Press Association, de Lisser's newspaper associations facilitated the publication of his first novel, *Jane's Career* (1914), which was serialised in the *Gleaner*. His subsequent nine novels first appeared in the *Planter's Punch,* an annual de Lisser himself founded. De Lisser's first two novels were published in book form with the London firm of Methuen, and colonial editions were made available in Jamaica. But such a pattern metropolitan publishing was to change; in an author's note fronting his third novel *Triumphant Squalitone,* published by *The Gleaner*, de Lisser tells his readers that the local rights to the manuscript was sold to the local firm of Fred L. Myers and Son. His reasons for not selling the local rights of his book to a metropolitan publisher are framed in similar terms as MacDermot's. While not being adverse to having a London publisher issue his work, de Lisser explains that he wished to build up an audience for local writing: "The best, from the Jamaican reader's point of view, is that he thus obtains the work much more cheaply than he otherwise could." The book, funded through commercial advertisements (many of them belonging to the firm of Fred Myers and Son) sold allegedly for a full "50 percent below its cost of production [... and at] no financial profit to its publishers".[16] The audience for the book was of course a restricted one. Advertisements in the book, offering a range of products from household products to champagne and cars, indicate that the book's intended readership was Creoles or whites with a reasonable disposable. Yet if de Lisser's experiment in local publishing was to be sustained for his next book, the London firm of E. Benn published all his subsequent novels. However, de Lisser's last posthumous novel was published by the Jamaican Pioneer Press. In their desire to foster the reading of local writing, and in their wish to capture the authenticity of the lived cultures in their representations, de Lisser, Webber (and to some extent MacDermot) can be said to be precursors to the flowering of Caribbean writing preoccupied with folk cultures associated with the much later and politically left of centre New Beacon group of writers.[17]

From the mid-twenties onwards, exhortations to publish locally, and to read local writing, seemed like forgotten tracts as writers such as W. Aldophe Roberts, Claude McKay and Jean Rhys made their journey to the US and to Britain in search of a professional writing career. Migration may have had some impact on the way writers approached their subject matter. Claude McKay whose poems were published in the *Gleaner,* and whose first volume of poetry was issued in Jamaica, was praised initially for his manipulation of dialect. In contrast, his later poetry is written in Standard English, reflecting an appeal to a different kind of readership, a move that is motivated, Edward Baugh notes, "by what he saw as the slighting of the Creole poetry".[18] McKay is, of course, a key figure in the Harlem Renaissance, and his novels are viewed by some critics as "the founding texts of the black Caribbean novel".[19] Adolphe Roberts, a novelist, journalist poet and historian was also a respected and prolific writer; based in and published in the US, he kept his connections with Jamaica alive, publishing *Six Great Jamaicans* with the Pioneer Press, and returning to Jamaica to help set up a local branch of the Jamaica Progressive League, a lobby group for Jamaican self-government. Jean Rhys, as a child, was sent to school for a time in England; she returned to England as an adult to live a bohemian life, living off her wits and mixing with various artists and writers, including Ford Madox Ford who was an early mentor. All of her novels, published abroad, are said to reflect her own troubled life. After the appearance of *Good Morning Midnight,* she disappears from the literary scene until her 'rediscovery' by the critic Francis Wyndham and the Andre Deutsch editor Diana Athill, during the boom time in the metropolitan postwar publishing of Anglophone Caribbean writing in the nineteen sixties.

The career of the Jamaican poet, playwright, journalist and broadcaster, Una Marson, in many ways encapsulates growing attempts at developing the groundwork for a thriving literary culture; these, of course, are not always successful. Marson created the monthly magazine *The Cosmopolitan* for women in 1928 that, according to Delia Jarrett-Macauley, set out to air boldly "feminist views, literary and cultural topics and a range of social issues".[20] The magazine, which was Jamaican in orientation, encouraged the work of Jamaican writers, particularly that of its Poetry League members, an organisation that served to promote poetry through lectures, discussions and publications. *The Cosmopolitan* folded in 1931 after falling sales and declining advertising revenue caused by economic depression after the stock market crash in the United States.[21] Marson's publishing and literary ambitions did not stop there. She self-published three volumes of her own poetry. She also set up a "Readers and Writers Club" in Jamaica in the late thirties after a long period in Europe, a club that encouraged intellectual discussion and debate, and supported local writing. Later, she worked for the BBC "Caribbean Voices", broadcasting a range of works by Caribbean writers, and in 1949, managed to secure funding from *The Gleaner* to start up the Pioneer Press as a publishing house to publish Caribbean creative writing, natural history, biographies and autobiographies. The press issued fiction and poetry for younger readers, an autobiography by J. A. Somerville and a posthumous volume of MacDermot's poetry. It also published a volume of Louise Bennett's dialect verse. While the quality of its output was uneven, the Pioneer Press provided a much-needed publishing outlet for local writers.[22]

The drift of writers abroad, occurring most famously in the nineteen fifties, was in large measure due to the difficulties of sustaining a career as a writer. George Lamming who journeyed to London to establish himself as a writer, remarked that given the colonial forms of education, the "greater mystery" was "that there should be any West Indian writers at all." Lamming asserted that a writer "cannot function; and indeed, he has no function as a writer if those who read and teach reading in his society have started their education by questioning his very right to write."[23] There was, of course, a tradition of self-publication. Una Marson, Derek Walcott and Arthur Seymour self-published some of their work; but the lack of a sustained literary circuit of publishers, reviewers, critics, agents and readers worked towards the impoverishment of a book culture. In 1948, the editor of the forward looking English magazine, *Life and Letters* mourned the absence of Jamaican book publishers:

> There are Jamaican authors and have been for long, Constance Holler, Claude McKay and Adolphe Roberts […]. But there is no Jamaican publisher. Consequently, authors such as the last two I named go to America. If a Jamaican poet wishes to produce his slim volume he has to do so at his own expense […]. Until books can be published there can hardly be expected to be readers. A poet may write on a desert isle… but readers can't read or develop reading without books.[24]

Herring's comments concerning the lack of general publishers, as opposed to newspaper or educational publishing, generally holds true for the Anglophone Caribbean even for the two decades that was to follow.

The 1930s and 1940s also saw the rise of important little magazines and reviews such as the *Forum Quarterly*, the *Forum Magazine*, *Bim*, *The Quarterly Magazine*, *Trinidad*, *The Beacon*, *Picong*, *Callaloo, Kyk-over-al* and *Focus* that would do much for the development of Anglophone literature. They published a range of poetry, fiction, dramatic scripts, reviews and essays. They also enabled a critical forum for a range of political, social and aesthetic issues. Their contributions cannot be overestimated. Circulation figures were small, and the finances difficult to sustain, but, as Reinhard Sander records, that there was an audience for them cannot be disputed. For example, the sales figure for the *Trinidad* was put at round 1,000 copies while the *Beacon* sold between 1,500 and 5000 copies between 1931 and 1933.[25] The economic depression and labour unrest of the nineteen thirties fanned the flames of cultural nationalism and many of these magazines were informed by a desire to stimulate thinking about the nature and distinctiveness of Caribbean art in general, and distinctive regional artistic practices in particular. Sander notes that although the *Trinidad* only published two volumes, the magazine issued benchmarks for literary contributions that were to be echoed by many of the magazines that followed. Editors of *Trinidad*, Alfred Mendes and C. L. R James, were adamant that West Indian writing ought to be true to "West Indian settings, speech, characters, situations and conflicts" and not written in imitation of foreign writing.[26]

Trinidad was the product of a loose network of writers and intellectuals who met to exchange ideas, to read each other's work and to engage in political debates. Albert Gomes, recalling these meetings later in life, speaks of it as a "tiny oasis of artistic appreciation" in an otherwise indifferent Trinidadian society.[27] Gomes also felt that the group lacked social and political engagement, and with help from James, Mendes and R. A. C De Boissiere, set up *The Beacon* which succeeded the *Trinidad.* The magazine galvanised its own left-leaning circle, many of whom contributed to articles, poems or fiction to the critical and literary endeavour. Gomes remembers *The Beacon* as a radical magazine by "Trinidad's angry young men of the Thirties" that served to arouse a complacent middle class Trinidad out its "torpor", "smugness" and "hypocrisy".[28] The magazine was partly funded by advertising but its radical nature rendered it difficult to finance through these channels. As Gomes remarks, "during the magazine's brief and turbulent life, these businessmen [sponsors] were under considerable pressure from various groups in the community, who feared the rising popularity of a magazine that so unequivocally and irreverently opposed their cherished convictions".[29] *The Beacon* relied on its circle of activists, writers and intellectuals to keep it afloat; it was a wide-ranging magazine and encouraged not only literary and critical contributions but also history, politics, films and music. Like its predecessor, *The Beacon* encouraged indigenous writing that was faithful to the cultures from which it sprang, arguing that it was exceedingly "difficult to write well of persons and things beyond one's ken",[30] observing that "the average Trinidad writer must regard his fellow-countrymen as his inferiors, an uninteresting people who are not worth his while", because "he peoples them with creatures from other planets, American gangsters and English M.'s".[31] In defending James's short story, "Triumph", the magazine argued that writers should not seek to be "aping another man's culture"; a local writer should "break away as far as possible from the English tradition" as it was "incongruous" with the "West Indian scene and spirit".[32] Both *Trinidad* and *The Beacon* inspired socially conscious realist fiction which dealt with Trinidad's working class "barrack-yards", of which the novels of Mendes and James are most well known. Yet the brief but brilliant run of these magazines in Anglophone publishing history pointed to the dearth of publishing opportunities in the Caribbean, and the difficulties of making a living as a writer. James left in 1932 for London; the London publishers Secker and Warburg published his first novel, *Minty Alley*.

The nationalist impulse gathered pace with a later generation of little magazines emerging in the forties such as *Bim*, *Kyk-over-al* and *Focus,* who would between them publish many of the now established names in the Caribbean canon such as Derek Walcott, George Lamming, Sam Selvon, Wilson Harris and Martin Carter. As the editor of *Kyk-over-al* was to note, "self-definition and self-discovery" was in the air.[33] *Focus* was a Jamaican journal edited by Edna Manley whose forward to the first volume locates the magazine as part of an effort to explore within the arts, a process of decolonisation; Manley remarks more recently of the writers associated with the magazine:

> [Y]ou had on the one side people who were determined to break Jamaican poetry out of the Wordsworth tradition, then you had the people who felt there was this need to give Jamaica a new image […] all this was totally new thinking for Jamaica.[34]

With its links to the Little Theatre Movement, *Focus* also published short plays in addition to poetry and fiction. *Kyk-over-al* was based in Guyana and was started as a publication of the British Guiana Writers Association and British Guiana Union of cultural clubs. It was edited by the poet, critic and (of necessity) publisher, A. J. Seymour, who declared that the journal's aims was to be "an instrument to help forge a Guyanese people, make them conscious of their intellectual and spiritual possibilities".[35] *Kyk-over-al* helped initiate a tradition of literary theory and criticism that addressed the nature of aesthetic practices of the West Indies as a region, and Seymour himself published sixteen small volumes of poetry by West Indian writers, not including volumes of his own verse. *Bim* based in Barbados, edited by Frank Collymore, is perhaps the most important magazine of the group; it was, as Lamming remarked, "the one thing alone [that] kept us going […] a kind of oasis in that lonely desert of mass indifference, and educated middle-class treachery."[36] Lamming's remarks are upheld by many others; Edward Baugh, for example, has commented that, "[f]or the fact that we can now speak of a West Indian literature, we owe much to *Bim*."[37] *Bim* started life as a regional magazine but as it developed, it took material from across the English speaking Caribbean; Lamming observed "[t]here are not many West Indian writers today who did not use *Bim* as a kind of platform" and in interviews speaks of recruiting contributors for *Bim* from Trinidad.[38] Furthermore, *Bim*'s connections with the BBC "Caribbean Voices" resulted in a fruitful exchange of material between the two institutions where what was broadcast in the latter would appear in print in the former, and vice versa. The friendship between Collymore and Henry Swanzy who was then editor of "Caribbean Voices" meant that their respective recommendations for publication either in the magazine or on air were taken seriously. Collymore wrote frequently to Swanzy to solicit support for writers migrating to Britain to obtain work; he also sought advice about getting particular poets published, the most famous case being the young Derek Walcott.

The BBC "Caribbean Voices" has a special part to play in this literary and history sketch because it marks the emergence of Anglophone Caribbean writing in London, a period of publishing history that was to lead Ken Ramchand to observe somewhat provocatively that London during this period of postwar literary history "was indisputably the West Indian literary capital".[39] "Caribbean Voices" was part of a transnational circuit of literary and cultural exchange, and one of the reasons why many writers chose to make to journey to London in the post-war period. Started by the Jamaican poet Una Marson in 1943, but achieving a coherent corporate and literary identity under the editorship of Henry Swanzy, it consisted of weekly half-hourly broadcasts from 1943-58. The programme was a transnational institution in the modern sense of the word because (predominantly) original material was collected the BBC agent in Trinidad, edited and selected in London to be broadcast back to the West Indies. Under the editorship of Swanzy and later Naipaul, the BBC paid writers, commissioned reviews and criticism from London and the Caribbean, and employed resident West Indians to read work in its London studios. Material also came from the Anglophone Caribbean little magazines. In this way, "Caribbean Voices" functioned like a "publishing house", canvassing and paying for new material, and in doing so, generated contacts and interest among writers and contributed to the nurturing of a literary culture.[40] The programme's raison d'etre was to "build up some kind of contemporary tradition by the exchange of writings between the Islands". Swanzy cast himself as a caretaker and mentor to the region's literary output, but he was also sensitive to the contradictions of producing a metropolitan programme broadcast for an indigenous population in the West Indies. It is clear from the programme correspondence files that Swanzy was acutely sensitive to the charge that what he was doing was tantamount to the imposition of foreign standards. He defended the programme's remit and role, arguing that the relationship was to be a temporary one until a more properly indigenous enterprise emerged with, possibly, Swanzy predicted, the creation of the University of the West Indies.

Not unlike the little magazines of the same time, Swanzy championed a regional writing that had a Caribbean reference, outlook or worldview, and rejected items that lacked "local colour", a characteristic that he himself did not define except in very general terms.[41]

The injunction to write with a feeling for the local setting and scenery may also have its drawbacks in the material sent for inclusion in the broadcasts; Swanzy complained to the BBC agent, Gladys Lindo that some of the submissions seemed formulaic "written to order [because] the BBC likes local colour".[42] Swanzy's interpretation of "local colour" also extended to folk cultures, and there were complaints that the programme was including too much "low life".[43] Swanzy's task as editor and his role as gatekeeper needs further investigation, for example, in relation to the under-representation of women writers. For out of nearly four hundred contributors to the series a little less than twenty percent were women. Some evidence can be gleaned from what Swanzy's preferences, for example, he disliked the domestic and romantic biases of some of the material sent, which he described as "sweetly pretty poems by [...] spinster ladies, probably teachers".[44] Lindo also selected material according to what she saw as Swanzy's preferences; in a letter dated 29 June 1948, Lindo refers jokingly to a Mrs Hutton who represented "one of the tuneful ladies whom [he] so much abhor[ed]".[45] More archival investigation is necessary to answer Beryl Gilroy's charge that the camaraderie of male writers, publishers and their advisers in the immediate postwar period did not extend so easily to women.[46]

"Caribbean Voices" also enabled a network of connections between writers, publishers, reviewers and readers employed by publishing houses in London. Lamming, Selvon, Naipaul, Harris, Andrew Salkey, John Figueroa, Edward Kamau Brathwaite and others came in search of educational and publishing opportunities. Swanzy, and later Salkey and Brathwaite acted as mentor to the circle of exiled Caribbean writers in London. Such an informal network is important to examining the process by which manuscripts are transformed into published books, as for example Arthur Calder-Marshall and Walter Allen's role in encouraging and promoting Lamming's *In the Castle of My Skin,* or William Plomer and Alan Ross's support of Walcott's poetry which led to its publication by Jonathan Cape, or Salkey and Charles Montieth's positive responses to Wilson Harris's work which led to Faber and Faber to take the risk it did. Francis Wyndham and Diana Athill's hand in reviving Jean Rhys's status with the publication of *Wide Sargasso Sea* by Andre Deutsch can be partly reconstructed through the publication of her correspondence.[47] Sympathetic reviewers and publicshers' readers in the literary establishment of the time such as Alan Ross, the editor of the *London Magazine,* the poet and broadcaster Roy Fuller, the journalist and writer Colin MacInnes, Calder-Marshall, James Burns Singer, Dan Jones, Anthony Rhodes and Anthony Cronin, all of whom reviewed extensively with the *Times Literary Supplement* kept Caribbean writing in the literary limelight for a time. As David Dabydeen has remarked of this period of metropolitan literary history, West Indian writing was "reviewed [...] on an immediate and regular basis".[48] Such enthusiasm was to fade in the later sixties in Britain but in the fifties and throughout the mid sixties, Anglophone Caribbean writing was seen to be a literary *tour de force* in London.

The Caribbean Artists Movement (CAM), founded in London in 1966, is perhaps the single most important development in the mid to late sixties; it brought together critics, writers and artists to debate the nature of a Caribbean aesthetic, the role of the intellectual, the problems of writing and publishing in the Caribbean, and the nature of the oral and literary traditions in Caribbean writing. CAM started life in London but soon became a transnational organisation that promoted intellectual traffic particularly between London and Kingston, Port of Spain and Georgetown (in its early years). CAM's members comprise not only writers, artists and critics who were concerned with the independent islands of the Caribbean but also student activists concerned with a more assertive grassroots politics – and a black British identity in a country that had already seen the 1958-9 race-riots, the 1962 Commonwealth Immigration Act and Enoch Powell's infamous 1968 incitement to racial hatred with his 'rivers of blood' speech. From 1970, CAM produced the influential journal *Savacou* that published not only academic and critical essays, but also creative writing. Two important transnational publishers, Bogle L'Overture and New Beacon Books were formed out of these periods of intellectual and creative ferment. Motivated by a desire to reprint neglected Caribbean writing and to provide an outlet for new writing, both have made major contributions to the publication and distribution of Caribbean writing in Britain and in the Caribbean.[49]

The spread of literacy and educational opportunities also helped foster a market for local writing in the Caribbean. The University of the West Indies (UWI) was established 1948 as an external college of the University of London.[50] The founding of the college was motivated by a desire to reinforce colonial links through reproducing a British model of education for the tropics. Criticised by Lamming in *The Pleasures of Exile* for doing little to reverse the colonial legacy, the college was conservative in its early years and the curriculum in its English department followed its London college mentor. Yet changes were also afoot with the return of academics such as Sylvia Wynter, Edward Kamau Brathwaite and others. Research was undertaken on the Dictionary of the Jamaican dialect, and the local unrest in Kingston in 1959 and 1960 prompted the M. G. Smith, Roy Augier and Rex Nettleford report on the Rastafarian movement which did much to try and bridge the divide between the scholarly community and the wider populace. The University provided a forum for intellectual and cultural exchange. The West Indian Extra-Mural Programme, in particular, was an astounding success given the ambivalent place it occupied initially in the University departmental structure. It organised research into local history, gave central place to the creative arts, fostered and built a more democratic and regional expressive arts. The department published the respected journal *Caribbean Quarterly* from 1951, as well as plays; it edited anthologies – and was in many ways progenitor of programmes in Caribbean studies. Intellectuals at the University, who had a stake in the cultural life of the Caribbean, wrote poetry or plays, and promoted theatre workshops. Derek Walcott, John Figueroa, and Errol Hill were on the staff of the Extra-Mural Department.

If publishing opportunities did not significantly increase with the launch of Heinemann Educational's Caribbean Writers Series in 1970, modelled on HEB's successful African Writers Series, the series made available reprints of important works by established Caribbean writers. The creation of a local publishing firm of HEB in Jamaica headed by Ian Randle made inroads into publishing locally, but this was restricted mostly to the educational market of school textbooks, which still forms the largest sector of the book trade in the Anglophone Caribbean where a majority of the population cannot always afford to buy books for leisure purposes.[51] The University of the West Indies Press and Ian Randle Publishers are currently the two most significant Caribbean-based publishing companies, issuing both academic as well as creative writing. Multinationals in the form of Macmillan and Longmans Caribbean are still major players in the field of educational publishing. Small transnational houses like the Leeds based Peepal Tree, modelled in part on New Beacon and Bogle, have a trading presence on the islands. Peepal's size and ethos has also enabled it to occupy a niche in publishing Caribbean writing that may not be deemed commercially viable by larger multinationals. When Heinemann decided not to publish Beryl Gilroy's writing on the grounds that her work would not sell, Jeremy Poynting, coming to the opposite conclusion, published Gilroy.[52]

Caribbean Women's writing comes into prominence with the explosion into print of women writers from the nineteen seventies and continues to the present day. Some have migrated to the United States, for example Paule Marshall, Audre Lorde or Jamaica Kincaid, and have contributed to an international women's movement and marketed with this readership in mind. Elaine Savory Fido has argued that the presence of women's groups such as the Caribbean Association for Feminist Research and Action have helped to foster creative links between writers within it;[53] an anthology of women's poetry, *Creation Fire* for example, had its genesis at the launch of the organisation. But the emergence of Caribbean women's writing as a distinct category begs a number of questions that are raised in recent critical accounts of the field, notably that of Evelyn O'Callaghan, Sandra Courtman and Denise deCaires Narain and Alison Donnell.[54] Together they query: who has been identified as belonging to the canon of Caribbean writing (and why) and how have their gender impacted on their inclusion or exclusion? Has the nationalist agenda of the formative years of the Caribbean canon-making in the postwar excluded others – especially women – who may choose to write about very different concerns? Does the choice of genre – poetry as opposed to fiction, autobiography rather than poetry or fiction – affect the recognition and acknowledgement of women's writing in previous histories of Anglophone Caribbean writing? Does the writer's racial status have repercussions on her status as Caribbean? How and in what ways do anthologies of women's poetry consolidate Caribbean women's writing as a discrete category?

As can be seen by this highly selective and brief book history inquiry into Anglophone Caribbean literature, there are many more questions than answers. This is especially true where archives are not complete or where they are not always open for scrutiny.[55] Yet even in this very partial account we can see how books as material artifacts necessitate an understanding of how they have been produced and disseminated, and how literature as an institution circulates within socially significant and cultural important networks.

Notes

1 David Finkelstein & Alistair McCleery: “Introduction”. – In D. F. & A. M. (Eds.): *The Book History Reader*, London and New York, 2002, p. 3.
2 Roderick Cave: *Printing and the Book Trade in the West Indies*, London, 1987, pp. 17-24.
3 Helen Tiffin: “The Institution of Literature”. – In A James Arnold (Ed.): *A History of Literature in the Caribbean*, vol. 2: *English and Dutch-Speaking Regions*, Amsterdam and Philadelphia, 2001, p. 58.
4 *Ibid.*
5 *Ibid.*, 59.
6 Cave: *Printing*, p. 28.
7 Evelyn O’Callaghan: *Women Writing the West Indies, 1804-1939,* London & New York, 2004, p. 2.
8 Cave: *Printing*, p. 26.
9 O’Callaghan: *Women Writing the West Indies*, p. 2.
10 Cave: *Printing*, p. 27.
11 Kenneth Ramchand: *The West Indian Novel and its Background*, London, 1970, p. 52. Booker and Juraga describe him “a Jamaican nationalist”; see M. Keith Booker and Dubravka Juraga: *The Caribbean Novel in English*, Portsmouth, 2001, p. 5.
12 W. Adolphe Roberts: *Six Great Jamaicans*, Kingston, Jamaica, 1951, p. 96.
13 Cited in Mervyn Morris: “The All Jamaica Library”, *Jamaica Journal* 6, 1972, 47.
14 Tom Redcam: “The Unusual Preface”. – In *One Brown Girl and -* , Kingston, Jamaica, 1904.
15 *Ibid.*
16 Herbert de Lisser: “Author’s Note”. – In *Triumphant Squalitone*, Kingston, Jamaica, 1917.
17 Selwyn Cudjoe notes for example that “these works of the authors of this period paved the way for a Caribbean renaissance of the thirties in which one saw the flowering of the islands’ arts and culture and more self-assertive Caribbean presence”; see Selwyn Cudjoe: “Identity and Caribbean Literature”, <www.trinicenter.com/Cudjoe/2001/June/24062001b.htm>, accessed 14 February 2007. Donnell and Welsh note that if de Lisser’s and Webber’s novels are “authentic to the lived experience of the majority population, their emphasis upon hardship, poverty and struggle”, their position as middle-class Creoles is held in tension to their rendering of this

'truth'; see Alison Donnell & Sarah Lawson Welsh (Eds.): *The Routledge Reader in Caribbean Literature*, London & New York, 1996, p. 32.

18 Edward Baugh: "A History of Poetry" – In *A History of Literature in the Caribbean, Volume 2: English and Dutch-Speaking Regions*, p. 233.

19 Booker and Juraga: *The Caribbean Novel in English*, p. 6.

20 Delia Jarrett-Macauley: *The Life of Una Marson 1905-65*, Manchester, 1998.

21 *Ibid.*, 38.

22 *Ibid.*, 187-189.

23 George Lamming: *The Pleasures of Exile*, London, 1960, p. 27.

24 Cited in Ramchand: *The West Indian Novel and its Background*, p. 73. Ramchand notes that the magazine was devote two complete issues to Caribbean writing much its metropolitan popularity and acclaim.

25 Reinhard W. Sander: "Introduction". – In R. W. S.: (Ed.): *From Trinidad: An Anthology of Early West Indian Writing*, London et al., 1978, p. 2.

26 Reinhard W. Sander: "The Thirties and Forties". – In Bruce King (Ed.): *West Indian Literature*, London, 1979, p. 50.

27 Albert Gomes: "Through a Maze of Colour". – In Donnell & Welsh (Eds.): *The Routledge Reader*, p. 166.

28 *Ibid.*, 168.

29 *Ibid.*, 167.

30 Sander: "The Thirties and Forties", p. 27.

31 *Ibid.*

32 *Ibid.*, 3.

33 Cited in Mervyn Morris: "Little Magazines in the Caribbean", *Bim* 17, 1985, 4.

34 Cited in *Ibid.*, 7.

35 Cited in Arthur Seymour (Ed.): "Literature in the Making: The Contribution of *Kykoveral*", *The Golden Kykoveral: Anthology Selections from 1-28,* 33/34, April 1986, 6.

36 Lamming, *The Pleasures of Exile*, 41.

37 Cited in John Wickham: "Introduction". – In J. W. (Ed.): *Bim: Literary Magazine of Barbados 1942-73*, vol. 1, New York, 1977, p. v.

38 Reinhard Sander & Ian Munro: "The Making of a Writer – A Conversation with George Lamming". - In Donnell & Welsh (Eds.): *The Routledge Reader*, p. 269.

39 Ramchand: *The West Indian Novel and its Background*, p. 63.

40 This is Phillip Nanton's phrase taken from Phillip Nanton: "'What does Mr Swanzy Want? Shaping or Reflecting?' An Assessment of Henry Swanzy's Contribution to the Development of Caribbean Literature", *Kunapipi* 20:1, 1998, 11-20; Phillip Nanton: "'Whose Programme Was it Anyway?' Political Tensions and Caribbean Voices: the Swanzy Years", Unpublished paper presented at the Symposium "Henry Swanzy, Frank Collymore, and Caribbean Voices", hosted by University of West Indies and the University of Birmingham at Cave Hill Campus, Bridgetown, Barbados 9-10 July, 1999, and Glyne Griffith: "Deconstructing Nationalisms: Henry Swanzy, Carib-

bean Voices and the Development of West Indian Literature", *Small Axe* 10, September 2001, 1-19.

41 See for example correspondence between Swanzy to Mrs Lindo, 13th August 1946, complaining of a stream of material rejected because of their "complete absence of local colour" quoted in Gail Low: "Finding the Centre: Publishing Commonwealth Writing in London – The Case of Anglophone Caribbean Writing 1950-65", *Journal of Commonwealth Literature* 37:2, 2002, 30. Later, when asked to define more precisely the kind of material he would look for, Swanzy replied, "I do not feel that perhaps one can lay down a hard and fast rule: I think it depends on circumstances [...] a specific West Indian weltanschauung – I am sorry, it's the only word that will do – is still in the making, and therefore a general story laid in some other part of the world is so frequently indistinguishable from an ordinary [...] American or British story, that it really is not worth including in the programme." Letter to Gladys Lindo 6th August, 1947, quoted in Low: "Finding the Centre", 31.

42 Letter from Henry Swanzy to Mrs Gladys Lindo, 20th September, 1948, *Ibid.*

43 Letter from Swanzy to Lindo, 4th August 1947, quoted in *Ibid.*

44 Letter from Swanzy to Mrs Gladys Lindo, 13th August, 1946, quoted in *Ibid.*

45 Letter from Mrs Gladys Lindo to Henry Swanzy, 29th June, 1948, quoted in *Ibid.*

46 Gilroy complains that readers working for publishing firms rejected her work as too psychological, strange, way-out, difficult to categorise, for it did not fit the pattern of Anglophone Caribbean writing that was critically acclaimed at the time. For her full account see Joan Anim-Addo: *Leaves in the Wind: Collected Writings of Beryl Gilroy*, London, 1998, pp. 211-213. For an attempt at recovering women's writing in the nineteen fifties and sixties, see Sandra Courtman: "Introduction". – In Joyce Gladwell: *Brown Face, Big Master,* Oxford, 2003.

47 See Jean Rhys: *Letters 1931-1966*. Ed. Francis Wyndham & Diana Melly, London, 1984.

48 David Dabydeen: "West Indian Writers in Britain". - In Ferdinand Dennis & Naseem Khan (Eds.): *Voices of the Crossing*, London, 2000, p. 70.

49 For a discussion and comparison of these two publishers see Harry Goulbourne: *Caribbean Transnational Experience*, London, 2002, pp. 136-159. Also see Brian W. Alleyne: *Radicals against Race*, Oxford, 2002 for a more specific focus on New Beacon.

50 For a history of the University of the West Indies see Philip Sherlock & Rex Nettleford: *The University of the West Indies*, London & Basingstoke, 1990.

51 See Global Publishing Information: *Publishing Market Profile: Caribbean*, London and Manchester, 2002.

52 Jereny Poynting: "Praise God, We're Hanging On! Peepal Tree Press: 18 not out", *Moving Worlds* 3:2, 2004, 134.

53 See Carole Boyce Davies & Elaine Savory Fido: *Out of the Kumbla*. Trenton, New Jersey, 1990, p. xi.

54 O'Callaghan: *Women Writing the West Indies*, 2004, p. 2; Sandra Courtman: "Introduction". – In Gladwell, *Brown Face, Big Master*; Sandra Courtman: "Not Good Enough or Not Man Enough? Beryl Gilroy as the Anomaly in the Evolving 'Black British Canon'". - In Gail Low & Marion Wynne Davies: *A Black British Canon?* Basingstoke, 2006, pp. 50-73; Denise deCaires Narain: *Contemporary Caribbean Women's Poetry*, London, 2002; Alison Donnell: *Twentieth-Century Caribbean Literature*, London & New York, 2006.

55 Much of the editorial notes and memos from the Andre Deutsch material at the Tulsa archive in the US, for example, have not been preserved; Naipaul's personal correspondence deposited at the Tulsa archive is not open for inspection until after his death. The Faber archives, which would present a rich source of archival material for the metropolitan publishing of Anglophone Caribbean writing, are not presently open to the public.

Hubert Devonish (Kingston, Jamaica)

Speaking the Caribbean: Turning Talk Into a Language in the Anglophone Caribbean

1. Languages under Construction

Language consciousness is far from a universal phenomenon or one that remains the same for all time. Illich[1] documents the efforts of the Spanish grammarian, Nebrija, via his 1492 work, *Grammática Castellana*, to convert the common speech of the people of Spain into a standardised and formally recognised language. The work of Nebrija was to seek to impose on common speech prescribed rules patterned on Latin grammar, bearing little relationship to the rules used by speakers in the course of daily interaction. He laboured to produce an artificial linguistic construct in the form of standardised Castilian, which no one spoke and which had to be formally taught and learnt with the assistance of grammars such as the one he had written. Similar developments took place or were to take place with various other European languages, notably English, Dutch, French and Portuguese, just to take as examples the major colonial languages.

This drive towards to construction and consolidation of speech forms into artefacts came from the development of writing and its mass production in the form of the invention and widespread use of the printing press. The mass production of written language messages in print favoured standard forms of language expression capable of reaching a mass market and readership. Such standardisation could only take place through creating an abstraction that corresponded to the speech of no one in particular but which was generally accepted. However, this standard arising from necessity quickly developed into a norm whose beauty, correctness and quality was extolled above all other forms of the language, and in relation to all other languages as well.[2]

In the post-European colonisation era and in what has now come to be called rather tautologically 'the globalised world', accepted notions of what constitutes a language are a heritage of the past five centuries of European language related developments. These originally European ideas are now 'globalised', 'universal' and part of the ideological baggage of a large section of mankind. It is arguable that forms of speech which fail to be (re)constructed into the artefacts we currently refer to as languages, are inexorably being forced into extinction. It is this process of language (re)construction and its opposite, the failure to (re)construct, which we will seek to examine within the 'Anglophone Caribbean'.

1. What is the 'Anglophone Caribbean'?

Current usage in the Caribbean treats 'Anglophone', perhaps because it is less semantically transparent than 'English speaking', as the politically correct label when applied to particular countries within the region. What, however, does the term 'Anglophone Caribbean' mean? 'Anglo' is simply a derived Latinate form for 'English' and 'phone' most immediately a French derived suffix meaning 'speaking'. In the parts of the Caribbean defined as 'English speaking' or 'Anglophone', such a description is only accurate depending on the definition one has of what constitutes 'English'. Does the term 'English' only include forms of English considered as 'acceptable' for purposes of international communication? And does the label apply to a country in which the mass vernacular cannot, by any twist of the imagination, be constructed as a form of English, however deviant?

If 'Anglophone' is to have any meaning in a discussion about Caribbean language situations, it will have to be used to apply to those countries and territories in which English is the official language. Such a usage would take in all the entities that are part of the Commonwealth Caribbean. The Commonwealth Caribbean would include current colonies of Britain or those which have been its colonies up until the latter half of the 20th century. Since English is one of the official languages of the Netherlands Antilles, they, and in particular the 'English speaking' islands of Sint Maarten, Sint Eustatius and Saba, would also fall within the 'Anglophone' Caribbean. The definition would also include the United States Virgin

Islands of St. Croix and St. Thomas, but not Puerto Rico, which, although a United States possession, has Spanish as its official language.

There is, as well, that troublesome term 'Caribbean'. Custom and practice, particularly as these relate to culture and language, relaxes this strictly geographical term to include not just the islands of the Caribbean but the Central American mainland country of Belize, and the South American mainland country of Guyana. Belize, at least, has a Caribbean Sea coast but Guyana does not even qualify on such grounds, being bordered as it is by the Atlantic Ocean. Both Guyana and Belize, however, are linked linguistically and culturally to the Commonwealth Caribbean and are considered by popular consensus to be an integral part of this grouping.

Using the criteria just discussed, the countries included under the broad umbrella of the 'Anglophone' Caribbean would be Anguilla, Antigua & Barbuda, Barbados, Belize, the British Virgin Islands, the Cayman Islands, Dominica, Grenada (inclusive of the islands of Carriacou and Petite Martinique), Guyana, Jamaica, Montserrat, the Netherlands Antilles (specifically its Leeward Island territories of Sint Maarten, Sint Eustatius and Saba), St. Kitts & Nevis, St. Lucia, St. Vincent & the Grenadines, Trinidad & Tobago, the Turks & Caicos Islands and the U.S. Virgin Islands.

2. What are the Language Varieties?

Most sociolinguistic approaches to discussing these countries and territories divide the languages in use into the following categories: (i) indigenous languages, (ii) Creole languages not lexically related to English, (iii) basilectal / conservative varieties of English-lexicon Creole most deviant from English, (iv) mesolectal or intermediate varieties of Creole diverging from basilectal Creole as a result of varying degrees of influence from English, (v) those forms of English most divergent from basilectal Creole and notionally closest to 'International English'.

It is difficult to estimate the number of speakers of any particular language variety since this depends on how one defines what constitutes a speaker of a variety. Speakers generally do not have linguistic repertoires consisting only of a single language variety. Rather, repertoires may span several varieties, with varying levels of competence in each of these language varieties. In addition, the use of particular varieties may be restricted by social convention to specific contexts or domains.

Even though English lexicon Creoles are the varieties which are most widely spoken, some special attention has to be given to French-lexicon Creole in St. Lucia, Dominica, Grenada and Trinidad. Use in the last two cases tends to be restricted to isolated rural communities and older speakers. For Guyana as well, French-lexicon Creole varieties are in use, occurring in the main in communities of St. Lucian immigrants and their descendants, notably in settlements such as Mahdia, located in the interior of the country. Guyana has, in addition, Berbice Dutch Creole, which may be on the verge of becoming extinct, as well as Skepi, Essequibo Dutch Creole, which is already extinct. The two Dutch Creoles are or were not mutually intelligible, with the latter showing a great deal of similarity to Negerhollands, the Dutch Creole of what is now the U.S. Virgin Islands.[3] Negerhollands itself became extinct during the 20th century.

In the cases where both an English-lexicon Creole basilect and a mesolect exist, there is considerable difference between the extent of the usage of each of these. In countries like Guyana, Belize, Tobago and Jamaica, more basilectal forms of speech may be quite widespread, particularly in the rural areas, with use remaining vibrant. On the other hand, basilectal speech may be on its way to becoming moribund in Trinidad, where it has come to be associated with use only amongst older and less educated rural speakers.

Dominica provides an interesting contrast. It has an English-lexicon basilectal Creole, referred to as Kokoy. This variety is associated only with the Wesley-Marigot area in the north-east of the country.[4] It retains vibrancy in everyday use, particularly in its role as a de facto ethnic language, serving to culturally distinguish its speakers from other Dominicans. There is, as well, French-lexicon Creole traditionally spoken in areas of Dominica outside of the Wesley-Marigot area. In Dominica, there existed an Arawakan language, Karipuna, which became extinct in the early part of the 20th century. The related language variety, Garifuna, historically spoken in St. Vincent, and reportedly also extinct in that island, thrives in Belize in Central America. St. Vincent differs from Dominica in not having a French-lexicon Creole and in having a basilectal English-lexicon Creole which is in wide use across the country.

3.1 How Did They Originate?

Caribbean Creole languages owe their origins to European colonisation of the region. Historically, the central feature of this development is African-European contact in plantation slave societies within which speakers of European languages occupied dominant positions in relation to Africans imported as slave labour. Crudely oversimplifying, what emerged was a language contact situation involving a particular European language, be it English, French, Dutch or Spanish-Portuguese, on one hand, and speakers of a fairly heterogeneous group of West African Niger-Congo languages on the other.

Over time, language varieties emerged which derived the bulk of their vocabularies from the European language in question but which showed features of phonology, morphology and syntax highly divergent from the European language. In the case of phonological features, it is widely accepted that Caribbean Creole phonology shows influence from the West African substrate languages. In the area of morpho-syntax, however, there is great controversy. One view, typically represented by Alleyne,[5] is that these features are also a result of West African retentions in these newly formed Caribbean Creole languages. Diametrically opposed is Bickerton.[6] He posits that the linguistic heterogeneity in early Caribbean plantation society produced an unstructured pidgin which served as an early lingua franca amongst the various language groups. This meant that children born into such a community lacked the stable and structured linguistic input available to children in more normal linguistic communities. Children in early Caribbean plantation society, in the absence of a structured linguistic input from adults, had to fall back on a linguistic bioprogramme, which they used to create new languages, Creole languages, essentially from scratch.

However formed, it is generally agreed that Creole language varieties became, over time, the native language of locally born speakers, in particular those of African descent but as well those of European descent. Eventually, these forms of speech also came to serve as lingua francas across all ethnic and social groups, including the succeeding waves of imported West African slaves. Against the background of these events, the European language of the colonising power continued to function as the language of government and of public formal interaction amongst the dominant group.

3.2 What Kind of Language Situations?

> DIGLOSSIA is a relatively stable language situation in which, in addition to the primary dialects of the language, [...] there is a very divergent, highly codified [...], which is learned largely by formal education and is used for most written and formal spoken purposes but is not used by any sector of the community for ordinary conversation.[7]

Of the four defining situations which Ferguson establishes for diglossia, two, i.e. Greece and Arabic, involve classical / literary varieties of an 'internal' language as the High or H language variety. Haiti as a defining situation for diglossia is representative of one of the possible types of the diglossia, one which I here term 'conquest diglossia'. This is diglossia resulting from the imposition of the H(igh) language as a result of an act of conquest on a local population whose native language comes to function as the L(ow). This, I propose, is the form of diglossia that has typically operated in the 'Anglophone' Caribbean. In the 'Anglophone' Caribbean, what can be observed now across a range of territories is various stages in the resolution of 'conquest diglossia'. Ferguson himself envisaged such a process when he suggests that in many situations, "H fades away and becomes a learned or liturgical language studied only by scholars or specialists and not used actively in the community. Some form of L or a mixed variety becomes standard".[8] Alternatively, of course, L can die, replaced entirely by H. We would suggest that the outcome depends on the success with which L can be (re)constructed as a language in the same sense that H is considered to be a language.

4. Constructing Linguistic Abstractions

4.1 Standard Caribbean English: The 'High' Language

Forms of language approximating Internationally Acceptable English (IAE) exist in each territory, under local labels such as Standard Guyanese English, Standard Belizean English, etc. or under the regional label of Standard Caribbean English. It is these language varieties that function in the role of official languages in these societies. As is frequently the case in countries of Anglo-Saxon tradition, there tends to be no explicit legislation in these countries declaring that English is the official language. Rather, custom and practice take this fact as given.

Up until the start of the process of granting independence to British colonies in the Creole speaking Caribbean in 1962, the sole model for English language usage in the Caribbean was the abstraction which was labelled Standard British English. Standard Caribbean English, a linguistic abstraction associated with the new political class about to inherit political power, had no status. This situation was described as follows:

> As home-made, the Caribbean linguistic product has always been shame-faced, inhibited both by the dour authority of colonial administrators and their written examinations on the one hand, and by the persistence of the stigmatised Creole languages of the labouring populace on the other.[9]

The Caribbean Lexicography Project, hereafter CLP, was set up in response to the need for Caribbean varieties of English, as distinct from both British English and English-lexicon Creole, to be used for official and public-formal functions. The project was established in 1971 in the aftermath of the first four 'Anglophone' countries gaining their political independence. The CLP was based at, and was to a significant extent financed by, the University of the West Indies, an institution owned and funded by all the territories of the Commonwealth Caribbean with the exception of Guyana. In addition to university support, the project received direct financial support from the governments of Guyana, Barbados and Trinidad and Tobago. This was as close as one could get to an official transnational enterprise for codifying an officially recognised variety of Caribbean English to function in the role of official language in the respective countries.

The major objective of the project was to produce the *Dictionary of Caribbean English Usage* (DCEU):

> [T]he emergence of the obligatory self-reliance and nationhood of many English-speaking territories made its organized documentation a necessity.[10]

The dictionary had as its main aim to describe Standard Caribbean English and make prescriptions for it. Amongst the goals of the dictionary was to describe and be a prescriptive reference point for a Caribbean standard variety of English which could function as national language in each of the twelve independent states which make up the wider Commonwealth Caribbean. [11] The dictionary, however, struggled with a major underlying contradiction. The features that made Standard Caribbean English distinctive from metropolitan varieties of Internationally Acceptable English were features representing linguistic influence from the Creole languages widely spoken in these countries. The problem was one of how to so codify Standard Caribbean English that it allowed in a limited number of Creole features for purposes of local 'colour' and identification, while retaining its overall coherence as a form of English that was 'Internationally Acceptable'.

The dictionary approached this problem by claiming to cover all of what it rcfcrs to as 'Caribbean English'. It establishes a hierarchy of 'Formalness' "using four descending levels, – *Formal, Informal, Anti-formal, Erroneous*"[12] (italics in original). This was used as a basis for both describing forms and prescribing for their use. The Formal was defined:

> Accepted as educated: belonging or assignable to IAE; also any regionalism which is not replaceable by any other designation.[13]

The Informal was defined:

> Accepted as familiar; chosen as part of usually well-structured, casual, relaxed speech, but sometimes characterized by morphological and syntactic reductions of English structure and other remainder features of decreolization.[14]

As for the Anti-Formal, this was

> Deliberately rejecting Formalness; consciously familiar and intimate, part of a wide range from close and friendly through jocular to coarse and vulgar; any Creolized or Creole form or structure surviving or conveniently borrowed to suit context or situation.[15]

Erroneous was that which is "not permissible as IAE (Internationally Acceptable English), although evidently considered to be so by the user".[16] The DCEU divides speech varieties of Caribbean English into three main categories, the Formal, the Informal and the Anti-formal. The actual identification of the forms associated with each variety is based on their appropriateness for use in situations of varying levels of intimacy amongst interlocutors. Forms associated with the first category are unmarked in the dictionary and can be presumed to have been described as part of Caribbean Standard English and to have been prescribed for it. The linguistic forms associated with the remaining two levels of Formalness are so marked in the dictionary and have, according to Allsopp's definition, increasing degrees of Creole influence. The Informal variety is viewed by him as consisting of "remainder features of decreolization" and the Anti-formal as composed of, among other features, "any Creolized or Creole form or structure surviving or conveniently borrowed to suit context or occasion".[17] All of this suggests, as the speaker becomes more informal, the incorporation of increasing numbers of Creole features into what is otherwise Caribbean Standard English. How then is this constructed Caribbean Standard English distinct from those other language forms variously described in DCEU as 'basilectal' Creole, creolised language or just plain Creole?

The DCEU takes the approach of inclusion. Creole language forms are treated as falling within its definition of Caribbean English, albeit not quite 'standard', where they are treated as Creole "remainder features" as well as Creole "borrowings" and "survivals". According to the dictionary, these, when employed in Caribbean English, produce less Formal language varieties, with their heaviest presence at the Anti-formal level:

> Deliberately rejecting Formalness; consciously familiar and intimate; part of a wide range from close and friendly through jocular to coarse and vulgar; [...] When such items are used an absence or a wilful closing of social distance is signalled. Such forms survive profusely in folk-proverbs and sayings.[18]

The above explains why the forms regarded as Formal in the dictionary are left unmarked whilst those regarded as Informal and Anti-formal are marked. The last two are marked to indicate their inappropriateness for use in situations requiring the Formal variety. Prescribing for Caribbean Standard English involves him "omitting the mass of Caribbean basilectal vocabulary and idiom in favour of the mesolectal and acrolectal, and using a hierarchy of formalness in status-labelling the entries throughout, the work is being prescriptive. This is in keeping with expressed needs, and with the mandate agreed and supported by successive regional resolutions".[19] We have here the essence of the language ideology prevalent in diglossic situations in which, as Ferguson[20] states: "H alone is regarded as real and L is reported 'not to exist'." The ideal of Standard Caribbean English is being constructed to exclude Creole "remainder features", "borrowings" and "survivals" which are left to hang without the benefit of some specific, even if equally idealised language label.

4.3.1 English-Lexicon Creole Languages: The Low Language

These language varieties are known by many names, which vary from one speech community to another, e.g. 'Creole' in Belize, 'Creolese' in Guyana, 'Kokoy' in Dominica, 'Patwa' in Jamaica, etc. A popular perception shared across these communities is that these are dialects of English. As a consequence, the term '(the) dialect' is also a fairly common label.

English-lexicon Creole languages are present in public consciousness hidden amongst 'dialects' of English. Thus, Louise Bennett, noted as a pioneer 'dialect' poet in Jamaican, writes in a poem defending Jamaican 'dialect', in which she associates Jamaican Creole with British regional / non-standard dialects such as Scots, Yorkshire and Cockney. In this poem entitled "Bans o' Killing", she asks the opponents of Jamaican Creole who have vowed to destroy it:

> 'Yuh gwine kill all English dialect
> Or jus Jamaica one? '
> [Are you going to kill all the English dialects
> or just Jamaica's?]. [21]

We have already seen, with reference to the DCEU, how idealised the notion of Standard Caribbean English is. The prevailing language ideology simultaneously emphasises the internal coherence of the language forms which are closest to IAE, while minimising any such coherence in those forms of speech regarded as deviant from IAE. This shows itself in the academic work on these language situations. Thus, DeCamp criticises the work of Bailey[22] on grounds that it "is an abstract ideal type, a composite of all non-standard features, a combination which is actually spoken by few if any Jamaicans".[23] In the approach of DeCamp, Jamaican Creole has ceased to exist, watered down to increasing degrees along the 'post-Creole continuum' by influence from Standard Jamaican English. Despite her difference in perspective, this is a characterisation with which Bailey[24] seems to be in agreement when she states, "The speakers of unadulterated JC [Jamaican Creole] are rare indeed".

The cloak of invisibility has begun to slip from Caribbean English-lexicon Creoles. They are beginning to receive the trappings of 'languagehood', notably standard writing systems, technical terminology and emerging morpho-syntactic norms. The question constantly raised when sceptics challenge the 'languagehood' of Caribbean English-lexicon Creoles is that of how different they actually are from English. Given that language is a psychological construct, the extent of difference is never really an argument for 'languagehood'. Spanish and Portuguese are regarded as separate languages whereas some much more different language varieties are regarded as dialects of Chinese. Nevertheless, given the invisibility of these L language varieties as artefacts worthy of the label 'a language', we do need to consider what the differences are between these Creole languages and English.

When compared with Standard Caribbean English or other varieties of IAE, Caribbean English lexicon Creoles, hereafter ECs, have within their phonologies, (i) a smaller number of vowels, (ii) a smaller number of consonants, (iii) a less complex syllable structure, and (iv) a tonal system which allows for the distinctions in pronunciation between otherwise homophonous pairs of words, e.g. / fáada / 'biological father' vs. / fâadá / 'Roman Catholic priest'.

At the level of the lexicon, there is a small proportion of the vocabulary, probably no more than 5% of words in everyday use, which are not of English origin. Prominent among these would be words such as *nyam* 'eat' and *pikni* 'child'. For the bulk of the vocabulary of English origin, there are several peculiarities which serve to distance them from English. Often, the EC form for an English word is not predictable from the English form, e.g. EC *tek* vs. English 'take', EC *brok* vs. English 'break', EC *lef* vs. English 'leave', EC *shub* vs. English 'shove'. In addition, many items in EC have a deceptive relationship with their English equivalents. Thus, we have EC *fut* which both covers the meaning of two English words, 'foot' and 'leg' and EC *az* which means 'as soon as' rather than English 'as, i.e. simultaneous with'.

However, it is perhaps at the level of the syntactic structure that ECs show the greatest divergence from English. The systems of marking tense, i.e. the time an action is viewed as taking place, and aspect, i.e. whether an action is completed or progressive, are radically different in the two languages. At the risk of grossly oversimplifying, English signals these categories through a combination of (i) suffixes as in '-ed' in 'laughed', (ii) pre- and post-verbal combinations, involving pre-verbal forms of the verbs 'have' or 'be' and post-verbal '-ed / -en' or '-ing' as in 'I have spoken' or 'I was speaking'. The EC system, by contrast, uses exclusively pre-verbal markers, which do not change form for the number or person of the subject, with (i) the unmarked form of the verb marking completion, as in *mi taak* 'I spoke / have spoken', (ii) *a*, *da* or *de*, depending on the EC variety, signalling the progressive as in *mi a taak* 'I am speaking', (iii) *bin* / *ben* / *en* or *did* occurring in the slot preceding that for the progressive, marking an action which was occurring prior to another, as in *mi bin a taak* 'I was speaking / had been speaking'.

In marking pluralisation, EC only does so with definite nouns, e.g. those which take the definite article, *di* 'the'. This it does by placing the third person plural pronoun, *dem* 'they, them' after the noun phrase to be pluralised. Thus, a noun phrase such as *di bluu buk* 'the blue book' becomes *di bluu buk dem* 'the blue books'. In similar fashion, proper nouns such as *Bil* 'Bill', *Sita* 'Sita', etc. can be pluralised to produce *Bil dem*, *Sita dem*, etc. which can be translated as 'Bill / Sita and friends / family'. Whereas in EC, an indefinite noun phrase such as *bluu buk* cannot be pluralised by the addition of *dem* to form **bluu buk dem*, English can pluralise 'blue book' to produce 'blue books'. English also contrasts with EC in not being able to pluralise proper names like 'Bill / Sita' to produce the meaning 'Bill / Sita and friends / family'.

A common view is that EC syntax is divergent from English as a result of being a simplification of English. Let us examine the following sentences involving the use of copulas, comparing their EC forms and their English translations.

i)	Yu a di man	'You are the man'
ii)	Yu de ya	'You are here'
iii)	Yu fat	'You are fat'

The EC sentences use *a* before a noun phrase predicate such as *di man* 'the man' in (i), to signal the link between it and the subject, *yu*, i.e. to mark the equational copula. In (ii), where the predicate is a locational adverb, *ya* 'here', the linking form is *de*. In (iii), where the predicate is an attribute, *fat*, there is a requirement that there be no linking form. Creole speakers, therefore, need to be conscious of whether the predicate is a noun phrase, as in (i), a location as in (ii) or an attribute as in (iii), to select the appropriate copula or linking form. By contrast, as can be seen by the English translations, a single copula form, the appropriate form of the verb 'to be', here, 'are', is employed. In the area of copula choice, it is English actually that has the much simpler system.

The above comparison suggests vocabulary differences across EC and English which might characterise the distance between languages such as Portuguese and Spanish. Differences in phonology might be equivalent to those between Spanish and French, and morpho-syntactic differences more of the order of that between English and German. These differences have traditionally been viewed as merely as evidence of EC being a non-standard, unstructured or 'broken' version of English. However, political, social and cultural changes have occurred, starting in the 1950s, that have had a considerable effect on official and popular perceptions of ECs, though not entirely transforming these perceptions.

Perhaps the most obvious change has been at the level of the education policy. At the level of the Ministries of Education in most of the countries, there is an official acceptance that the ECs which most pupils enter the school system speaking are linguistic systems quite distinct from English. An interesting attempt to translate this awareness into practical action is the material prepared by Velma Pollard,[25] which has been in use well before the publication date, in the training of teachers of English language for the Caribbean. The very title, "From Jamaican Creole to Standard English" is suggestive of the stance that it takes on the issue of the separateness of the two languages. Pollard, with reference to the goals of the handbook, states: "The intention is to help teachers help their students move from being able to use only one language (J[amaican]C[reole]) to being able to use the two languages which we need to operate successfully in the Jamaican situation."[26]

The presence of written EC in schools has been in an English oriented orthography rather than any of the more strictly consistent writing systems being proposed. Over the years, school textbooks increasingly have come to include works of Caribbean literature, some of which is written in English-lexicon Creole. Literary Creole writing tends to employ the orthographic traditions of English 'dialect writing'. This system of orthography relies for its readability on indications to the reader of the ways in which the 'dialect' has deviated from the 'standard' form of the language, English, e.g. by the use of apostrophes to indicate sounds 'left out' of the 'standard' English original. One example of this was the above quotation from the Louise Bennett poem, "Bans o' Killing".

Public calls have been made for an official language policy that would recognise English and Jamaican (Creole) as official languages. Among the other developments has been a drive to develop and popularise standard writing systems for these languages. The 1961 Cassidy writing system for Jamaican Creole was originally developed for specialists wishing to write that language.[27] The writing system has, however, been co-opted by some language activists who see it as the basis for an efficient standard orthography for Jamaican Creole. In the Belizean Creole case, Creole language activists have agreed on a standard orthography for the language and a handbook on how to use the orthography has been produced along with a 140 page dictionary.[28] The Bible translation activities of the Summer Institute for Linguistics (SIL) in Belize have so far proceeded using this newly emergent writing system for Belizean Creole.

In the Jamaica situation, as a counter to the 'dialect writing' orthographic traditions, there have been experiments with popularising a phonemically based orthography for Jamaican Creole developed by Cassidy.[29] One such activity lasted for six years during the 1990s and involved a Jamaican Creole newspaper column written by Carolyn Cooper fortnightly in the *Jamaica Observer*, using this orthography.[30]

In the electronic mass media, Shields-Brodber[31] refers to "(t)he gradual erosion of diglossia in Jamaica, accelerated by programmes such as phone-in radio talk shows". She describes a process by which hosts of such programmes "code-switch regularly from English to Creole for a variety of pragmatic purposes, and / or acts of identity, and who thereby provide a certain legitimacy for the use of J[amaican] C[reole] in public / formal media […] and callers with demonstrably weak mastery of English, who shift to JC". Scripted programming other than drama would normally be in English. Drama, advertisements for products of mass consumption, live interviews, etc. allow for the use of English-lexicon Creole languages. This is generally the pattern throughout those parts of the 'Anglophone Caribbean' within which an EC is widely spoken.

Some relatively radical activities have been carried out aimed at breaking English-lexicon Creoles out of the roles to which they have been confined. Between 1982-1984, on Radio Central, a regional radio station broadcasting to a primarily rural audience in central Jamaica, local news in what was styled 'the local language' was employed in daily newscasts. Then, on Irie FM, a national radio station, for over a year, between 1993-4, there was a weekly news summary broadcast entitled 'Big Tingz Laas Wiik' on the programme 'The Cutting Edge' hosted by the poet, Mutabaruka. The latter experiment was quite popular and when it ceased, due to difficulties with financing the activity, there were numerous public expressions of regret. In this same period in Jamaica, the Bible Society of the West Indies produced an audio tape of portions of the New Testament translated into Jamaican Creole. These translations received some level of public exposure, particularly by being broadcast on the radio, along with what might be termed qualified public acceptance.

Recent developments threaten to have far reaching effects across the 'Anglophone' Caribbean. One such occurred in New York State in 2000. Approximately 20,000 immigrant children from the 'Anglophone' Caribbean enter the education system of the state of New York each year. The Board of Regents of the State of New York Board of Education requested technical advice from linguists as to the issue of ECs being "languages other than English". In response to technical presentations made to it in December, 2000, by the Board declared that Caribbean English lexicon Creole languages are "languages other than English". What had occurred was a declaration on the 'languagehood' of ECs. Such 'languagehood' had to be recognised before pupils in the New York State system could access educational services directed at pupils designated as being Limited English Proficient who came from backgrounds in which English was not the home language. Immigrants from the EC speaking Caribbean routinely declare English to be their home language. The New York State system, therefore, has had no choice but to treat lack of English proficiency amongst pupils from this group as indicating a need for Special Education. The need for the decision was to try and circumvent the fact that parents did not declare EC to be their home language. They had no mental construct of EC as anything other than English, albeit 'incorrect' or 'a dialect' form of English.

The effect of the decision is that, subject to certain conditions, bilingual education has to be provided to such pupils, inclusive of language arts in the native language and bilingual instruction in content subjects.[32] The decision means that speakers of Caribbean English-lexicon Creole languages have rights to English / Creole bilingual education in New York State, rights not available to them in their home countries. The developments in New York State are likely to have a profound impact on debate about language education policies and practices in the home countries. 'Languagehood' for ECs constructed or manufactured abroad is likely to have an effect on popular constructions of speech and language within the Caribbean itself.

4.3.2. French Lexicon Creole Languages: Other Low Languages

The French-lexicon Creole varieties, as spoken in St. Lucia, Dominica and in a more restricted way in Trinidad, Grenada and Guyana, are traditionally and popularly known as '(French) Patwa / Patois'. However, associated with the 1981 officially sanctioned Seminar on an Orthography for St. Lucian Creole and a similarly titled 1981 report, a more 'politically correct' label for the language, Kwéyòl, has emerged, at least amongst the conscious promoters of the language. Use of this alternative title seeks to avoid the pejorative associations of the traditional labels.

Even though no language statistics exist, it is difficult to disagree with the statement that while French-lexicon Creole remains the native language of many St. Lucians, the proportion of monolingual speakers of this language has diminished considerably. This has been a result of the emergence and increased acceptance and use of non-standard / mesolectal English-lexicon varieties showing influence from French-lexicon Creole. These, according to some analyses, constitute the mid-range on a continuum between the basilect, French-lexicon Creole, and the acrolect, English. This development has created a significant number of bilinguals and even some persons who are monolingual in the non-standard / mesolectal varieties.[33] This situation is probably even truer of those areas of Dominica in which French-lexicon Creole has been the vernacular language traditionally used.

In spite of the above, the status of French-lexicon Creole in both St. Lucia and Dominica has been steadily on the rise. The year 1981 was a turning point in the development of the French lexicon Creoles of St. Lucia and Dominica. It was in this year that a government-supported Seminar on an Orthography for St. Lucian Creole was held.[34] An orthography, based on phonemic principles, was approved for St. Lucian Creole and eventually accepted for Dominican French-lexicon Creole, as well. The seminar was the catalyst for the creation of two Creole language organisations. In St. Lucia, Mouvman Kwéyòl Sent Lisi (Mokwéyòl) was set up and in Dominica, the Komité Etid Kwéyòl (KEK). These organisations have been responsible over the years for the promotion of writing in French-lexicon Creole using the standard orthography, notably through bilingual Creole / English newspapers which have appeared intermittently, i.e. *Balata* in St. Lucia and *Konn Lanbi* in Dominica.

In the electronic media, French-lexicon Creole in St. Lucia is expanding considerably. Traditionally, the use of this language on radio targeted the rural and the uneducated, generally considered to have low levels of competence in English. However, the range of programming has expanded considerably and is being aimed at a much wider cross section of the population. Radio news broadcasts, public education documentaries and Government Information Services programmes are currently broadcast in French-lexicon Creole. In addition, there has been strong encouragement of the public to use the language during call-in programmes, resulting in it being widely used in this domain.[35] In large measure, the developments in St. Lucia in the electronic media seem to follow the pattern discussed by Shields-Brodber[36] for Jamaica.

At the symbolic level, the most significant development was the 1998 change in the Standing Orders of the St. Lucia parliament. This change formally admitted the use of St. Lucian French-lexicon Creole into parliamentary proceedings. This event marked official recognition of a practice which had emerged in the late 1990s, in which oral presentations in parliament were delivered in both French-lexicon Creole and English. The change in the Standing Orders, however, was circumscribed by an explicit statement that use of Creole was limited to oral exchanges and that the official record of proceedings would continue to be kept in English.

A 1999 'Concept Paper' on language policy commissioned by the Ministry of Education, Human Resource Development, Youth and Sports of St. Lucia on the recommendation of the Governor-General, herself a linguist and language activist, is quite significant. This paper presents proposals for an official language policy for St. Lucia which would recognise St. Lucian French-lexicon Creole as (i) a joint official language alongside English, (ii) the national language, i.e. the language of national identity associated with cultural and folk heritage, (iii) a promoted language, i.e. used by government agencies in public communication, (iv) language of literacy in adult literacy / education programmes.[37] The paper is intended to form the conceptual basis for the formation of a Commission for the Development of St. Lucian French Creole. The goals of this commission would involve both the status and corpus planning of St. Lucian French-lexicon Creole. Given the on-going tradition of co-operation between St. Lucia and Dominica on language matters, it is likely that developments in St. Lucia will trigger off similar moves in Dominica. As with ECs, the French lexicon Creole speech varieties are being (re)constructed as 'languages' complete with writing systems, official recognition and a formal role in the education system, including in the area of literacy.

4.3.3. The Indigenous Languages: More 'Low' Languages

There are just two countries in which indigenous languages remain in active use. The first is Guyana with the Cariban languages, Carib, Macushi, Akawaio, Wai-Wai and Arekuna, and the Arawakan languages, Arawak and Wapishiana, and another language, Warrau. The other country is Belize, with Garifuna, an Arawakan language, and Mayan, the latter divided into three ethno-linguistic sub-groups, Mopan, Yucatecan and Kekchi.

Indigenous languages, notably those of Belize and Guyana, generally play no open and obvious role in the formal education system or in the mass media. They continue to function in the main, as exclusively oral languages, restricted to the ethnic communities within which they have traditionally been used. They exist in some kind of societal trilingual / triglossic relationship with (i) English and (ii) an English-lexicon Creole.

In all cases of indigenous languages listed above, the number of persons identifying themselves as members of an ethnic group is significantly larger than those who speak the language of that group. Even though many of the languages appear to be transmitted to children, invariably the proportion of the children acquiring the language is falling with each passing generation. All of the languages listed above, therefore, can be considered to some degree endangered. A glaring example is that of the Arawaks, the largest indigenous ethnic group in Guyana, making up 33% of the indigenous population. No more than 10% of the group, however, are reported to be speakers of Arawak (Lokono), the historical language of the group.

The view amongst indigenous language activists is that the only way in which speech forms can survive in the face of modern languages is to be (re)constructed in the likeness and image of their linguistic competitors. These include the development of writing systems, along with the associated reverence for the written word and the development of abstract standard varieties. This seems to be the inspiration behind a series of community initiatives in the preservation of indigenous endangered languages of Guyana. These include the production of nursery and primary school primers for Makushi, and the compiling of a trilingual Makushi-English-Portuguese dictionary.[38] Similar moves have been made amongst the Wapishana, with teachers being trained to read and write the language and make teaching materials in that language, as part of a thrust towards native language literacy and bilingual education.[39] Melville[40] reports the absence of any focused activity in favour of Lokono (Arawak). He does suggest, however, that some villages have, from time to time, organised classes. He indicates, however, that the work of the group organised by the Catholic Church at Santa Rosa, a Lokono community, appeared to be developing well. All of this is against the background of the pioneering work done by Father John Bennett,[41] a Lokono Anglican priest, who has produced an Arawak-English dictionary as well as a set of ten lessons in Lokono.

Garifuna would appear to be the healthiest of the remaining languages, even though some estimates suggest that only about half of the ethnic Garinagu speak the language. Also, even though the language is being transmitted to children, this appears in the case of Belize, to be happening in only one of the five Belizean ethnic Garinagu communities.[42] To counter this language attrition, an active movement amongst the Garinagu of Central America supports the promotion of the language. A native speaker linguist, E. Roy Cayetano,[43] as part of the Garifuna Lexicography Project and under the aegis of the National Garifuna Council of Belize, has compiled an English-Garifuna / Garifuna-English dictionary aimed at use by members of the community and general public. It employs a consistent, phonemically based writing system which is being promoted as the standard orthography for representing the language. The dictionary and writing system function as part of cultural preservation and promotion activities by the Garinagu of Belize. Garifuna is used in a limited way in the electronic mass media. This is encouraged and reinforced by the widespread use of Garifuna in the music lyrics of punta rock, an extremely popular form of modern Belizean music originating amongst the Garinagu population.

A significant and bold step in the area of language policy with reference to Garifuna was taken when the Central American Black Organisation (CABO) issued a declaration in 1997, on the initiative of the National Garifuna Council of Belize, in the form of a "Language Policy of the Garifuna Nation", along with the "Garifuna National Language Preservation Plan". According to Langworthy,[44] however, the response to this quasi-legal framework at the level of individual communities seems to have been patchy. Individual communities have initiated small scale language preservation activities but this has been localised and limited in its effect.

At the level of international recognition, Garifuna stands out head and shoulders above the other Caribbean indigenous endangered languages. In 2001, UNESCO declared Garifuna to be one of the 19 masterpieces of the Oral and Intangible Cultural Heritage of Humanity.[45] Ironically, a case for this may have been easier as a result of a writing system being developed for the language, and significant enough bodies of transcription of this oral material made and analysed.

5. Conclusion

The developing situation raises a paradox. It is through orality and as a medium for reproducing traditional cultures and societies that Caribbean vernacular languages have been transmitted and survived through the centuries. The increased significance of modern communication domains which either involve writing or are dependent on writing, produce conditions which tend to marginalise unwritten languages. Moves to (re)construct Caribbean vernacular languages as written standardised languages in the image and likeness of European languages give an opportunity for these vernacular languages to be introduced into modern technological domains and functions. However, how possible will it be for this to happen while retaining the essential vibrancy and orality that has been the basis for the survival of these languages so far? What would be the purpose of converting previously unwritten vernacular languages into standardised written languages that function in new technological domains but that are uprooted from their original community-based orality? Will the short-term gains made by the ideological and scribal (re)construction of these languages in the long term remove the very basis for their continued existence as vehicles of traditional cultures and societies? Only time will tell.

Notes

1 Ivan Illich: *Shadow Work*, Salem, NH, 1981, pp. 33-51.
2 *Ibid.*, 35-51; Walter J. Ong: *Orality and Literacy: The Technologizing of the Word*, London, 1982, pp. 117-138.
3 Ian Robertson: "Berbice Dutch – A Description", Unpublished PhD dissertation, University of the West Indies, Trinidad, 1979; I. R.: "Berbice and Skepi Dutch. A lexical comparison", *Tijdschrift voor Nederlandse Taal- en Letterkunde*, 105:1, 1989, 3-21.
4 Pauline Christie: *History and Status of Creole Languages: Papers by Pauline Christie*, UWILING Working Papers in Linguistics, UWI, Jamaica, 1989, p. 65.
5 Mervyn C. Alleyne: *Comparative Afro-American*, Ann Arbor, 1980, pp. 136-180.
6 Derek Bickerton: *Roots of Language*, Ann Arbor, 1981, pp. 43-135.

7 Charles Ferguson: “Diglossia”. – In Dell Hymes (Ed.): *Language in Culture and Society*, New York, 1964, p. 435 (capitals in the original).
8 *Ibid.*, 437.
9 Richard Allsopp: *The Dictionary of Caribbean English Usage*, Oxford, 1996, p. xvii.
10 *Ibid.*
11 *Ibid.*, xix.
12 *Ibid.*, lvi.
13 *Ibid.*
14 *Ibid.*
15 *Ibid.*, lvii.
16 *Ibid.*
17 *Ibid.*, lvi-lvii.
18 *Ibid.*, lvii.
19 *Ibid.*, xxvi.
20 Ferguson: “Diglossia”, p. 431.
21 Louise Bennett: *Jamaica Labrish*, Jamaica, 1966, p. 218.
22 Beryl Loftman Bailey: *Jamaican Creole Syntax: A Transformational Approach*, Cambridge, 1966.
23 David DeCamp: “Toward a Generative Analysis of a Post-Creole Speech Continuum”. – In Dell Hymes (Ed.): *Pidginization and Creolization of Languages*, Cambridge, 1971, pp. 349-370, 350.
24 Beryl Loftman Bailey: “Jamaican Creole: Can Dialect Boundaries Be Defined?” – In Hymes (Ed.): *Pidginization and Creolization*, 1971, pp. 341-348, 342.
25 Velma Pollard: *From Jamaican Creole to Standard English: A Handbook for Teachers*, Caribbean Research Center, New York, 1993.
26 *Ibid.*, p. v.
27 Frederic Cassidy: *Jamaica Talk*, London, 1961, p. 433.
28 Belize Creole Project: *Bileez Kriol Glassary an Spellin Gide*, Belize City, 1997.
29 Cassidy: *Jamaica Talk*, p. 433.
30 Carolyn Cooper: “(W)uman Tong(ue): Writing a bilingual newspaper column in ‘post-colonial’ Jamaica”. – In *Conference Presentations*: 13th Biennial Conference of the Society for Caribbean Linguistics, Mona, Jamaica, 2000, pp. 91-96, 94.
31 Kathryn Shields-Brodber: “Hens can crow too: The female voice of authority on air in Jamaica”. – In Pauline Christie et al. (Eds.): *Studies in Caribbean Language II*, Society for Caribbean Linguistics, Trinidad, 1989, pp. 204-227.
32 Board of Regents: “Part 154: Apportionment and services for pupils with limited English proficiency”. – In *The State Education Department*, The University of the State of New York, June 1999, Part 154.2g & 4.

33 Ministry of Education, Human Resource Development, Youth & Sports: *Concept Paper on Language Use, Language Policy and Language Planning in St. Lucia etc.*, St. Lucia, 1999, p. 10.

34 Pearlette Louisy & Paule Turmel-John: *A Handbook for Writing Creole*, Research St Lucia Publications – Special Series 1, 1983, St. Lucia.

35 Ministry of Education: *Concept Paper*, p. 14.

36 Shields-Brodber: "Hens can crow too", p. 202.

37 Ministry of Education: *Concept Paper*, pp. 18-26.

38 Miranda La Rose, "Makushi Language Project Launched", *Stabroek News*, 2 April 2003, <www.landofsixpeoples.com/news301/ns3040210.htm>, accessed 12 February 2007.

39 GINA (Guyana Information Agency): "Native language seminar geared at preserving Amerindian languages", November 25, 2003, <www.gina.gov.gy/archive/daily/b031125.html#NativeLanguage>, accessed 12 February 2007.

40 Ian Melville: "Guyana Indigenous Culture, Past and Present", presented at the *Indigenous Rights in the Commonwealth Caribbean and the Americas Expert Meeting*, Georgetown, Guyana, 23-25 June 2003, <http://www.cpsu.org.uk/downloads/Ian%20Melville.pdf>, p. 3.

41 John Bennett: "An Arawak-English Dictionary with an English word list", *Archeology and Anthropology* 6, 1989, 1-2.

42 Geneva Langworthy: "Language Planning in a Trans-National Speech Community", <http://jan.ucc.nau.edu/~jar/ILAC/ILAC_5.pdf>, accessed 12 February 2007.

43 E. Roy Cayetano: *The People's Garifuna Dictionary*, National Garifuna Council, Dangriga, Belize, 1993.

44 Langworthy: "Language Planning", p. 45.

45 UNESCO: "UNESCO adopts international convention to safeguard intangible cultural heritage", <http://portal.unesco.org/en/ev.php@URL_ID=16783&URL_DO=DO_TOPIC&URL_SECTION=201.html>, accessed 14 February 2007.

Sabine Sörgel (Mainz)

Staging the Caribbean: Derek Walcott's Theatre in Performance

1. Introduction: Caribbean Theater Aesthetics in the Context of Creolization and Postcolonial Independence

> The true richness of the theatre is the complexity of the human being, and this makes us, potentially, one of the richest nations in the world.[1]

Caribbean theater aesthetics and their postcolonial politics evolve from the region's complex history of conquest, colonization and plantation slavery. Due to this voluntary and forced migration from Europe, Africa and Asia, Caribbean culture has been frequently regarded as emblematic of the contemporary discourses on cultural hybridization, globalization and transnationalism in the sense that Caribbean identity construction no longer fits into essentialist parameters of racial categorization and origin. In this respect, discourse on Caribbean creolization appears as a forerunner of the European and North American discourses on pluralism, postmodernity and the postcolonial condition. According to Jean Bernabé, Patrick Chamoiseau and Raphaël Confiant the concept of "creolité" addresses this new self-awareness of cultural diversity "[n]either European[s], nor African[s], nor Asian[s]."[2] Instead of following the colonialist bias and its divisional categories, Caribbean identity thus proudly proclaims itself Creole as a self-chosen expression of autochthonous culture and independence. However, due to the region's violent history of colonization and plantation slavery, creolization has also been contested from an Afrocentric perspective.[3] Though the African diaspora makes up for the ethnic majority of the region's population, colonial administration has paradoxically sought to disenfranchise and debase the descendants of former slaves to the margin of society throughout local history.[4]

Plantation slavery had thus elicited a deeply entrenched personality complex among African Caribbeans, which Martiniquean psychiatrist Frantz Fanon described in terms of a paradoxical identity formation process under the well-known "black skin, white masks" dichotomy. Fanon's writings addressed the absurdity of an African-Caribbean subject-constitution based on the psycho-pathological struggle towards colonialist 'whiteness', in a situation where one was never quite the same.[5] As Homi K. Bhabha's postcolonial critique has more recently pointed out though, one needs to rethink the meaning of colonialist stereotype as much as Enlightenment's underlying idea of an essentialist identity concept. If the white man's gaze 'broke up' the black man's body concept, this act of "epistemic violence" also deconstructed the white man's own frame of self-reference.[6] In this respect Bhabha does not consider the racial dichotomy as a "neat division," but rather regards it as "the disturbing distance in-between that constitutes the figure of colonial otherness – the white man's artifice inscribed on the black man's body."[7] Bhabha's re-reading of Fanon influenced his own work which has dealt extensively with the ambivalence of colonial mimicry. According to Bhabha's analysis, colonial mimicry's immanent theatricality bears a latent subversive potential, which in its imitation of the other articulates an ambivalence of ironic critique.[8]

This ironic ambivalence of the (post)colonial encounter becomes a constitutive part of Caribbean theatre aesthetics, which build on African-Creole folk traditions, Carnival and oral history from the African, Asian and European Diasporas that have historically made the Caribbean islands their new homes in the New World. Hence, Caribbean theatre aesthetics do not only write back to the colonialist western theatre practice, but inventively create a Creole aesthetic that can be seen as paradigmatic for the West Indian theatre and culture of the future.[9] While a certain similarity may be found throughout the Caribbean islands in terms of their shared African-derived aesthetics, the following historical survey will focus on the Anglophone region and there in particular on two islands: Trinidad and Jamaica. For one reason these two have been the focus of my research over the past five years, yet also they share a brief but significant time-frame of political Federation in 1958, shortly before both islands achieved national independence in 1962. Part of the independence struggle was actively furthered by the local arts and especially the national theatre and dance movement. Investigating

African-Caribbean local traditions such as Carnival, folklore, oral history and religious ritual, dramatists of the formative years have created a highly complex art form, which contemporary theatre and performance studies have described in terms of a syncretic, cross-cultural and postcolonial aesthetic. [10] Caribbean theatre aesthetics therefore present a kaleidoscopic prism of African- and Asian-derived performance practices blended with canonical forms of European drama and theatre. However, while this may speak to a certain postmodern sensibility of hybridity and pastiche, these forms are oftentimes performative in the sense that they refer to cultural memory and embodied practices of the African diaspora in the New World. One therefore needs to consider the socio-cultural context out of which these forms emerged and have then been consciously introduced onto the national theatre stage in order to grasp their full political dimension in the postcolonial independence struggle. The present article therefore begins with a brief historical survey to contextualize the emergence of Trinidad's and Jamaica's national theatre movement, before the argument turns towards an in-depth reading of three of the seminal theatre works by Derek Walcott as performed by the Trinidad Theatre Workshop's Boston tour in 1994.

2. The Emergence of the National Theatre Movement and the Development of Pre-Independence Pan-Caribbean Consciousness

The emergence of a pan-Caribbean national consciousness probably dates as far back as to the San Domingo slave revolution of 1791 after which Haiti was proudly proclaimed as the first independent black republic outside Africa.[11] Even though most of the other Caribbean islands should not achieve independence up until the 1960s, there has been a continuous struggle and revolt against colonial rule coming from grassroots opposition, slave rebellion and independent maroon communities throughout the entire region. Moreover, folk resistance has played a significant part in the struggle towards full Emancipation in 1834/38, thirty years after the abolition of the slave trade. Yet, despite this shared history of effective resistance, it has been difficult to define a Pan-Caribbean (trans)national consciousness for the entire region, because of its divided colonial policies and language barriers.[12] Beginning with

Marcus Garvey in the 1920s and furthered by the 1930s political unrest caused by the Great Depression, Caribbean politicians as well as the emergent workers' movement became increasingly engaged with the reconciliation of these divisive social and ethnic policies in an effort to build a common national denomination and affiliation.[13]

Interestingly enough, national independence politics turned towards the arts in order to achieve this unification process by establishing a series of Pan-Caribbean festivals with the first held in Puerto Rico in 1952 and the second on occasion of the West Indies Federation in Trinidad in 1958. In fact, one may claim that Jamaica and Trinidad have been the pioneers of this movement.[14] Spearheaded by the political leaders Norman Washington Manley and Eric Williams, the islands' artistic, educational and political exchange dates back to as early as at least 1955, when Caribbean dance theater pioneer Beryl McBurnie visited Jamaica on occasion of the 300-year centennial celebrations in order to inspire a sense of shared cultural heritage in the region.[15] When McBurnie returned, only a year later, she lectured as a dance tutor at the University College of the West Indies' summer school in Kingston, where she in fact gathered the future generation of the Caribbean's first league theatre and dance artists. Among them were Derek Walcott and Errol Hill as well as many of the founding members of the renowned National Dance Theatre Company of Jamaica.[16] McBurnie's role is significant in this context, because her anthropological investigations of Caribbean folk culture not only inspired a sense of rhythm, gesture and rhyme that is key to Caribbean dramatic writing and theatre practice, but also nurtured a sense of an embodied identification and meaningful way of self-expression in terms of founding an African-Caribbean performance tradition based on the Caribbean's ancestral heritage in Yoruba and Congo ritual. The pre-independence arts' movement thus connected the Caribbean's uprooted African diaspora to a somewhat imaginary and yet no less important homeland in order to reconcile this exiled community to its new nation.

In this respect Caribbean theatre practice pays tribute to the region's struggle for cultural independence and international recognition at the beginning of the 1960s. While Derek Walcott constantly lamented the lack of government support for building a national theatre in Trinidad, other musicians, dancers, painters and theatre practitioners met for a symposium called "The Artist and West Indian Society" to debate the role and significance of the artist in 1962, the year of Jamaica's and Trinidad's independence.[17] To dwell on the arts as a crucial factor in cultural self-definition at that point of Caribbean history, was hence to become one of the main tenets of the Trinidad Theatre Workshop as well as The National Dance Theatre Company of Jamaica, the two leading flagships of cultural independence in the Anglophone Caribbean. As will be shown in the following reading of selected plays by Derek Walcott, grassroots resistance, folk cultural patterns and carnivalesque role reversals still inform much of the Caribbean's theatrical appeal.

3. "Fighting the White Devil" – From Street Theater to the Modern Stage

In his 1966 retrospective article "The White Devil: A Story of Christmas" Derek Walcott describes the theatre of his childhood in St. Lucia. The Santa Claus of Walcott's memory does not have very much in common with the Santa Claus of our Western imagination: on the contrary, Papa D'jab is an ugly old man, a child-devouring beast in red underwear, with a wildly swinging lion's tail and a flour-powdered face covered by a bristly beard. Papa D'jab reeks of rum, a drunkard, who is accompanied by a band of little imps, children masked as devils in the Trinidad Carnival fashion. Christmas in St. Lucia appears rather different: instead of sweet singing angels, the white masked devil roams around. One could hardly imagine a more explicit ambivalence: God, Santa Claus or Devil – in a sense they have all become one. In his article Walcott remembers Flavier as the part-incarnate: an actor who does not even need a stage for his performance. Measuring his space with huge steps, Flavier soon builds his arena, which is surrounded by a group of people who come to watch. A street crossing is all that they need for the moment. "Give the devil a child for dinner!" hollers the starved apparition. His mime and gestures keep repeating, the whole procedure reminds one of a dark mass, a ritual, during which the devil's favorite son rebels against the father and at the end of which one of them has to be slain.

Parallels to Lucifer, the Bible's fallen angel, come to mind, and yet they do not quite fit the image. This scene bears comedy and testifies to a humor that does not match the moralizing finger cue of a middle age Anti-Christ or passion play. The mythology is blurred and Papa D'jab's litanies in a stammered mumble can no longer be understood in the traditional way. St. Lucia's theatre in the 1930s appears as a chaotic jump-up of little devils who do not respond to the law of obedience.[18] It is rather a powerful expression of anarchy and freedom that Walcott understands all too well when he describes it as follows:

> That was the only public theatre we had then. Nobody bothered with its origin, its meaning, and whether it was a savage parody or parable, or even a powerful mixture of African and Christian rites. I am still not sure. But it was malign, even when it was funny, and it was certainly more complicated, more symbolic than the jolly, foreign figure of an apple-cheeked, snow-bearded and generous old man. It was Manichaean. It reminded us of barbarism, of fetish and dark ceremonies, and it was disturbing in the season of goodwill that it should harrow us with the thought of hell and black magic, with the parable of the Son slaying the Father or the Father, more usually, slaying his own Son.[19]

Twenty years later Flavier is dead. The myth appears degenerated, a loose farce, lacking its ritual force, for the belief in God and Devil did not survive. No one, so it seemed, could fill the part.

Yet, twenty years later, Walcott is a grown man with an ambitious vision of the West Indian theatre, deeply indebted to this childhood memory, as can be seen in his first full length play *Ti-Jean and his Brothers*. In this early play Derek Walcott revives the myth of the white devil for the public stage. Following the plot-line of Jamaican Anansi tales, Walcott puts his drama into an epic frame that reshapes the theme by giving it a more secular form. According to Sherlock's *Anansi the Spider Man,* Anansi is a fable animal of the West African imagination who came to the Caribbean with the diaspora.[20] He lives in small villages and forests and is said to possess magical force, which helps him to switch shape, especially when he finds himself in great danger. Trickery and magic guile are his tools to counter the attacks of those who are in power. This Caribbean variant of the Christian David and Goliath story serves Walcott as the basic motif to develop his dramatic plot. Ti-Jean and his two older brothers Gros Jean and Mi Jean are the West Indies' rebelling sons fighting against evil. The play has been read, therefore, as an allegory of the West Indian slave revolts.[21]

Gros Jean, the family's biggest son, relies on his physical strength, whereas Mi Jean trusts in his Western book learning. Both brothers fall prey to the white devil's temptation, as they strive to become what he is and neglect their own heritage. They are merely interested to obtain 'white' power. In this respect, one might argue, that the devil's imperialist notion has already taken over, since Gros Jean's self-perception is modeled on the white image and so is that of his younger brother, whose intellect aspires nothing more than a shallow imitation of white supremacist thinking. A "poor shaving monkey" he is, indeed, whose imitation remains void of Anansi cunning and therefore does not succeed.[22] Ti-Jean, on the other hand, knows how to play devil. His cunning is based on an inborn instinct and his eloquent imitation of the imperialist discourse tricks the white devil with his own means.

In this sense, Ti-Jean's performance becomes a paradigmatic example of Bhabha's mimicry. Just as the Anansi of West African folklore, Ti-Jean also appears to be a master of ambivalence. Multiple meanings, double entendre and irony are his weapons to successfully mislead his oppressor. This kind of ambivalent imitation goes back to the subversive strategies of the slaves. Richard Burton has thus pointed out that the slaves consciously developed play strategies to trick certain conveniences from their masters.[23] Furthermore, he argues that each kind of opposition bears a moment of play as it takes place within the dominant system rather than coming from without. Step by step one tactic manoeuver leads to the next and takes advantage of the loopholes in the power net.[24] An example of this strategy in the play can be found in the scene where Ti-Jean incites the slaves to put fire to the plantation's cane fields.[25] The burning of canes has historically been closely linked to Carnival and revolutionary upheaval.[26] Commonly referred to as 'canboulay', the burning of the canes at the end of the harvest was traditionally a time for merriment and joy. As Walcott explains:

> The origins of Carnival are religious or, more strictly, Roman Catholic [...] This religious festival may have its roots in pagan rites, those of the awakening of spring, and while there is no spring in our climate our Carnival coincides with the cane crop-over or cannes-brûlées. The canes are burnt for the harvest, and like the wine festivals of early Europe, it is a time for singing and dancing. It was a respite for the slaves who harvested the canes, and they used the chance to compose impromptu, satirical lyrics on their masters, or on each other.[27]

In contrast to Walcott, however, Errol Hill traces the ritual's origins back to a different source. He states a more brutal practice, namely, that the slaves were summoned under whipping, whenever a fire broke out on one of the plantations in order to save the harvest. According to his study, the canboulay ritual was later integrated into the Creole Carnival and marked its first indigenous moment.[28] As an import from the French aristocracy, carnival was eventually appropriated by the freed slaves and turned into something of their own. Whichever variant may be true – and it appears just as likely that Hill and Walcott both have a point here – it is interesting to note that canboulay survived in the carnival tradition where it came to represent an element of oppositional play and commemorated the liberation from slavery.

Turning to the canboulay ritual in *Ti-Jean*, it obtains an even more complex meaning, since cane burning in this case becomes an inversion of slave history, as when Ti-Jean in his role as foreman shouts in a call and response exchange with the cane burners' chorus:

> TI-JEAN: You are poor damned souls working for the Devil?
> VOICES: Yes! Yes! What you want?
> TI-JEAN: Listen, I'm the new foreman! Listen to this: The Devil say you must burn everything, now. Burn the cane, burn the cotton! Burn everything now!
> VOICES: Burn everything now? Okay, boss!
> [*Drums. Cries. Caneburners' chorus*]
> TI-JEAN: The man say Burn, burn, burn de cane!
> CHORUS: Burn, burn, burn de cane!
> TI-JEAN: You tired work for de man in vain!
> CHORUS: Burn, burn, burn de cane![29]

The burning of the cane crop and the singing do not only evoke a carnival atmosphere in the theatre, but also allude to the rebelling tradition of the feast.

Carnival and folklore thus build the structural frame of Walcott's theatre aesthetic. Especially the design of the devil part which switches roles from Papa Bois to old man and white planter is highly reminiscent of the devil masquerade in the Trinidad Carnival. As Max Harris in his article on "Playing Devil" demonstrates:

> Wearing a white mask over the face and black varnish over the body was almost certainly intended to recall the offensive Carnival fantasy of

white planters playing black field hands. Since the freed slaves were now also imitating Devils imitating slavery, in a kind of "slavery is hell" equation, the layers of mimesis at work in these performances are richly suggestive. Actors simultaneously playing white planters as Devils suggest a kinship between the two. At the same time, since both black skin and chains are part of the traditional Christian iconography of demons as well as marks of slavery, there is the reminder that black humanity had to be demonized by whites in order to justify slavery.[30]

In the 1970 interview "Derek's Most West Indian Play" Walcott declared *Ti-Jean* to be his "most West Indian play", written out of "a fierce but illuminating nostalgia for the untheatrical simplicities of St. Lucia". Yet, it seems that it is exactly this "untheatrical" simplicity that bears a highly theatrical potential, when transferred to the stage.[31]

An even more elaborate example of the carnival aesthetic is Derek Walcott's musical *The Joker of Seville*, which transfers Tirso de Molina's Don Juan myth to a Caribbean setting of calypso and carnival.[32] Written as an adaptation for the Royal Shakespeare Company in 1974 the play wittily undermines the original's 17th century honor-code moralizing with satire and irony. In this respect, Walcott's *Joker* reads as persiflage of colonization, which is largely conveyed through his use of Creole folklore and an overall emphasis on the theatricalization of the piece. Walcott begins the play with a prologue that establishes the setting as a field on a Caribbean estate. The 1994 Boston production correspondingly opened with a candle procession of the chorus. The performers are masked in Carnival fashion: the women in the typical Dame Lorraine costume and the men with aristocratic top hats and white 18th century wig. In traditional carnival, the Dame Lorraine mask was a caricature of the planter woman. Originally, only men dressed up in the costume, while today it has become more and more popular with women also.[33] After the noble characters the stickfighters and market women make their entrance. Dressed in plain white cotton robes they move rhythmically forward and join the others in a circle around the stickfight arena (gayelle) in the middle of the stage.

This approximately five-minute long sequence follows Walcott's dramaturgy as he planned to direct the play as 'calinda', the Afro-Creole term for the stickfight. Walcott's Don Juan is a stickfighter and he structures his play as an episode within the frame of the traditional canboulay. Candle procession, costumes, stickfight and burroquite together with music and drumming are part of the traditional Trinidad Carnival and just as carnival begins on Jour Ouvert with the blow of the cow horn, so does the play in the Boston production.[34] J. D. Elder, musicologist and anthropologist from Trinidad, has examined the structural elements of canboulay and their remnants in the Trinidad Carnival.[35] Iconoclastic objects as the burning candles, the stick (bois), or the African drum (ka), he argues, assume a psycho-sociological function in the sense that carnival developed as an expression of cultural resistance towards white upper-class racism and discrimination. The group procession demonstrates communal strength, while the imitation of the nobility, the mock march and satirical singing ironize white behavior.[36] This socio-cultural dimension of the carnival procession becomes relevant for Walcott's play, because he employs it for further theatricalization. In his play the carnival characters assume apart from their role as such yet another one, namely, that of the play. This doubling-strategy functions on two levels and lends the portrayed character a two-sided complexity: on the one hand the meaning of the carnival character, on the other that of the role in the play. This doubling strategy becomes especially significant for the play's protagonist Don Juan who enters the stage among the crowd of the stickfighters.

Originally, the stickfight (calinda) is part of the Trinidad Carnival. Calinda, traditionally, did not only designate the fighting with sticks, but also referred to the fighter's singing, which was accompanied by African drums. According to old-star calypsonian Raymond Quevedo (Attila the Hun) the calinda developed as a liberation hymn during slavery.[37] Around 1900 the term calypso was introduced to refer to the singing only, while calinda remained the term for the fight. Trinidad stickfight and calypso are therefore both part of the Afro-Creole tradition in the Caribbean which came to the islands with the Middle Passage and developed as the slave's prime expression of fierce resistance and cultural criticism. As Peter Mason describes:

> Many of these songs clung to African traditions of call and response, to a heavy reliance on satire, ridicule, gossip and sexual innuendo, and with much emphasis on the highly prized skill of extemporising, or making up new verses and lines on the spot – all features which are preserved in some form or other as staples of the average calypsonian to this day. In slave communities where the oral tradition was paramount,

> the songs were also a way of spreading news and providing a commentary on topical events. And they also became an important means of criticising the plantation owners in an environment where open defiance could otherwise lead to death. Sometimes songs were used to flatter masters, but just as often to condemn and laugh about them behind their back, usually via oblique references in patois.[38]

In the light of Mason's analysis calypso and stickfight become the two predestined forms of the Joker's expression in Walcott's dramatic text and directing, since irony, sexual innuendo and satire appear as the character's key features in this Caribbean interpretation of the European-based myth.

Walcott's Joker is a legendary figure which dies and is reborn each carnival season. This ritual does not know forgiveness: sans humanité is the play's motto, a well known refrain from many Trinidad calypsos. In a series of articles Walcott has time and again referred to the calypso as Trinidad's "Poetry in Song".[39] Accordingly, Walcott's dramaturgy translates calypso verse into drama. As he explains:

> I felt a contemporary, provincial, and immediate enthusiasm for the play because of Trinidad. The wit and panache, the swift or boisterous élan of his [Tirso de Molina's] period, or of the people in his play, are as alive to me as the flair of Trinidad music and its public character.[40]

Trinidadian calypso is known for its social criticism and blunt satire, which both form part of the Joker's character in the play. In this respect, Walcott's Don Juan reads in line with Bhabha's theory of ambivalent colonial mimicry as he appears a hated exploiter and loved seducer at the same time. Juan is a player and joker, unreliable in his guile and trickery. Yet, it is this unreliability, his capacity to change perspective which makes him a liberator.

Not only in respect of the characters, but also in regard of the formal structure the *Joker of Seville* makes extensive use of Trinidadian folklore. The musical as a theatrical hybrid offers Walcott and the Trinidad Theatre Workshop the opportunity to dwell on the possibility of a West Indian compound of acting, singing and dance. In the Boston production there is a scene in which the Trinidad Theatre Workshop Dance Company performs a dance that is reminiscent of an evangelist revivalist meeting. Music and dance in the Caribbean have long been regarded as inseparable elements. J. D. Elder writes:

> The usual pattern of evolution, according to the cultural anthropologist, is one in which a start is made with the spontaneous, uninhibited, religious folk music which the people as a community produce, the function of which is not differentiated, since there is no specialization among singers or in the function of that music. At this level, music – and music here is defined to include dance – music at this level is tied in with work and welfare, both physical and in respect to good relationship with the gods, either benign or malevolent.[41]

According to Elder's analysis music and dance thus embody regenerative power, which in its kinaesthetic impact can still be noted on stage.

The musical appears to be an ideal form to abstract from this religious ritual, in particular its patterns of dance and music in order to create a West Indian theatre idiom. As Walcott stresses in his article "Patterns to Forget," the musical can achieve a symbolic meaning of its own as long as it does not suffice in illustrating the dramatic text, but maintains the expressive autonomy of each form.[42] Walcott outlines this aesthetic vision with reference to Beryl McBurnie's drum-and-chant ballet. He describes McBurnie's dance as based on movements closer to acting rather than classical ballet. Her specific combination of folk elements and modern dance technique, therefore, tend to be episodic and could thus easily be integrated into a musical structure. In concern of music, Walcott argues for the art of the calypsonian who could serve as a role model for a West Indian actor-singer.

Comparing these statements to the choreography of *The Joker of Seville* production in 1994, a lot of correspondences can be found. The revivalist dance stands alone. Its kinesthetic meaning remains autonomous, just as that of the following calypso, delivered by Claude Reid as Catalinion. The episodic character of the musical assumes next to its mere aesthetic form also a socio-cultural dimension. As was already stated, calypso traditionally served as a forum of social critique. Alluding to a locally well known calypso called "Sophie went in the sea to bathe", the refrain of the fisher girls in the play reads: "Tisbea went and bathe, / a swordfish take she maid. / Tisbea, oh! Oh, oh! / Fire in the water!" and then: "That rod is the rod of correction, / but it point to the Promised Land".[43] The reference to the known calypso is interesting, because it serves as a binding link to the audience as it generates a certain expectation of mock comment. The allusion works on several levels: the rod may be seen as a reference to the slave overseer's whip, for example, yet it was also a synonym of the Bible.[44] Certainly, it is also reminiscent of the stickfighter's bois. Whether whip, Bible, or stick the rod's meaning is indisputably a highly ambivalent metonym for all kinds of complex meanings. When dance and singing shall convince Tisbea to keep hold of the rod, then one might want to read this as an appeal towards cultural appropriation. In this respect, the rod is also alluding to the process of colonial mimicry as a strategy of postcolonial resistance turned upon the oppressor. As Walcott has argued in his seminal essay "The Muse of History" on behalf of the creolization of Christianity in the Caribbean:

> What was captured from the captor was his God, for the subject African had come to the New World in an elemental intimacy with nature, with a profounder terror of blasphemy than the exhausted, hypocritical Christian. He understood too quickly the Christian rituals of a whipped, tortured, and murdered redeemer [...] Good, the missionary and merchant must have thought, once we've got them swinging and clapping, all will be peace, but their own God was being taken away from merchant and missionary by a submerged force that rose and took possession and where in fact the Hebraic-European God was changing color, for the names of the sub-deities did not matter, Saint Ursula or Saint Urzulie; the Catholic pantheon adapted easily to African pantheism. Catholic mystery adapted easily to African magic.[45]

Religious practice, as manifest in dance and music, consequently became an autonomous space of self-expression for the slaves. Despite of their captured status, dance, music and religious belief embodied the slave's freedom and self-determination. The danced body experience became paramount in this, since dance, historically, was the only independent form of expression that belonged to the slaves only and was neither controlled nor understood by the white slave masters.[46]

Dance consequently becomes the central moment of liberation in the Trinidad Carnival and it is this motif that is also prevalent in the play. The "Little Red Bird"-Song, for example, elaborates on the theme with its refrain: "Every heart has the right to its freedom." In the Boston production it is sung for the first time by the Boy Actor in the Seville market scene. Don Juan enters with typical arrogance and mock attitude, asking the boy to sing a song, while disrespectfully commenting on his physical appearance. This reminds one of the slave trade, especially because of Rafael's response to Juan's possessiveness:

> You're a rich man, with possessions,
> a servant, and all: we've met men
> who believe that their positions
> entitle them to slaves, and when
> they point a finger, that's the end.[47]

The introduction of the song at this point underlines the freedom motif of the play, which is furthermore supported by the entrance of another carnival character to the scene. This character, whose performer is walking on stilts and costumed as a bird with bamboo wings and beak, is known as Moco Jumbie. The etymology derives from African Yoruba and translates 'African Spirit'. According to the legend, Moco Jumbie came all the way from the West Coast of Africa across the Atlantic Ocean to the Caribbean, where he still appears in Carnival to announce that despite of all suffered miseries he stands "tall, tall, tall".[48] Therefore, it appears to be no accident that the Moco Jumbie accompanies this scene, in which the market buffoons represent the theatrical profession in general: for the theatre traditionally serves as a free space of articulation, a latent threat to those in power as Rafael sings: "One day you [Don Juan] will butcher no more."[49]

Walcott's integration of carnival elements into his adaptation of the myth manages to combine the modern theme of freedom with the traditional folk elements of the islands. He thus creates an associative reference frame for his local audience to connect a kind of existentialist thinking of moral freedom with a West Indian cultural practice. As Ismond has commented the New World's promise breaks with the colonial burden and reinvents the oppressing traditions into innovative force.[50] Body movement and expression, whether in love, dance or theatre thus assume a central role in this development, for they appear as the central medium of self-definition to create its own idiom on and off-stage.

A similar kind of interaction also takes place during the performance of Walcott's *Joker*. At the Little Carib premiere of the play in 1974, people were asked to dress leisurely and to bring their own cushion as seat. The Trinidad Theatre Workshop had constructed an arena within the theater so that it evoked the impression of the stickfight arena. Accompanied by a creole breakfast, Parang music and the Astor Johnson Repertory Dance Company's dancing the performance became a social gathering to last from morning well into afternoon. The production was a success and played to "sell-out crowds" for several weeks.[51] With this production Walcott achieved what many Western theatre practitioners of his time were striving for in vain. The stickfight set and Carnival atmosphere integrated the audience easily into the onstage performance of the archaic myth. Through 'sameness in difference' Walcott reveals the universal impact of his Don Juan adaptation, which becomes a convincing example of cultural resistance and criticism, while at the same time adhering to modern aesthetic standards.[52] Walott's hybrid theatre idiom hence works on the margins of Western and indigenous tradition. It navigates between the two poles, not debasing either, and thus gains a new perspective on Caribbean cultural heritage as the regenerative force for a truly West Indian theatre art form.

4. Staging Cultural Consciousness: *Dream on Monkey Mountain* and the Kinaesthetics of Caribbean Self-Discovery

Walcott's theatre aesthetic has been frequently described as 'total theatre', a reference to his work with different media, which makes use of tableaux configuration, music, dance and acting. In his review "Landmark for Local Drama", John Mercer, for example, refers to the 1969 production of *Dream on Monkey Mountain* as a successful venture into the new theatrical forms of the day.[53] Dance, singing, movement, and blocking are in his opinion more constitutive of the stage action than the spoken verse. Meaning and plot derive from the visual and paralinguistic level rather than the semantic level of the dramatic text.

Derek Walcott's affinity for the visual arts becomes significant for his work on the stage. Already the very first stage direction of *Dream on Monkey Mountain* hints towards this: an African drum shall be illuminated in a way that it becomes the mirror image of the sun.[54] This iconic reference creates a powerful image of the play's basic conflict of the divided colonial self, which, furthermore, reads as a foreboding of the protagonist's psychological split: Makak, the 'ape' who lives the dichotomy of desiring whiteness while being black. West Indian mythology and dance accordingly form the basis of Walcott's emerging vision of a West Indian Theatre aesthetic. This search for a West Indian theatre aesthetic can also be traced along the lines of *Dream on Monkey Mountain*, where Walcott already at the beginning states that a production of the play will need dancers, singers and performers to meet the precision and vitality of Kabuki theatre and where he also mentions his indebtedness to McBurnie's dance *Spirit* for the healing scene.[55] McBurnie's choreography was based on a fusion of African and West Indian folklore. Renowned mythological figures as Papa Bois, Diablesse and Douen made a danced appearance. McBurnie's *Spirit* stood out, because it made use of mime, movement and dance features to translate the mythological beings into dance. Such a production certainly blurred the border between dance and theatre and especially the Diablesse, a she-devil in the shape of a beautiful woman set out to seduce men, can be seen as a direct influence on Walcott's play.[56]

Although it is of course not clear how much of the original production still survived into the 1994 revival of *Dream on Monkey Mountain* by the Trinidad Theatre Workshop at their performance at Boston University, the video still testifies to the majority of the above mentioned observations. Characteristically, the performance begins with a dance by the Trinidad Theatre Workshop Dance Company. The mythic figures of Diablesse, Baron Samedi, a character that I interpret as Papa Bois, and another one reminiscent of a Rastafarian Lion are introduced: Accompanied by rhythmic drumming, the piece thus assumes an atmosphere of what Okagbue has referred to as "ritual-dream technique".[57] Typical for this technique is a circular structure that resembles the cyclic cosmology of African myth. Just as life in African cosmology returns to its origin, dramatic action also leads back to its beginning. This pattern is affirmed by Walcott's *Dream on Monkey Mountain* which starts and ends in Makak's prison cell. Even more so, because Makak also returns to his origin in terms of character development from charcoal burner to African King and charcoal burner back again. Chronology and frame of space are easily transcended, again similar to the structure of the African cosmos, in which the living communicate with the dead, ancestor spirits and the unborn.

The ecstatic moment of the dance, consequently, can be interpreted as a symbolic link to the spiritual world. The dancers' stylized movements express a majestic, if not to say sublime notion of spiritualistic knowledge. For example, the dancer of Baron Samedi, a Haitian death symbol, paces forward with huge steps, an almost sliding movement that is supported by the use of gigantic sticks which are about two heads taller than the performer. His half black, half white masked face together with his black suit and top-hat add to the symbolic meaning. Similarly, the Diablesse appears all in white with a pair of wooden breasts, probably to associate an African goddess. The costume's iconography appears ambivalent, which of course is true to the poetry of the dramatic text. In addition to the play's characters, the Boston performance introduces the two already mentioned figures of Papa Bois and Lion. While the first wears a carnival costume like dress of green-colored fabric strips, the second's costume is red-colored and he wears a long golden dread-lock wig. At the end of the dance, both take position behind Makak on the left-side stage and Ţigre and Souris on the right side, presumably to mark the two prison cells and lend them symbolic value on an interpretive level, such as, for example, colonial subconscious next to Rastafari and Négritude.

The representation of the spiritual through the on-stage presence of the mythological figures sets up an atmosphere that alludes to Caribbean religious practice as for example Haitian Vodou or Trinidadian Shango. Cultists of these religions perform distinct dances, accompanied by drumming to pass into trance, a heightened state of perception that enables the practitioner to communicate with the spirit-force of the ancestor. These processes are culturally encoded, as Brenda Dixon Gottschild has pointed out in the sense that they are danced expressions of religious belief rather than a superstitious practice as the biased European term of 'possession' historically suggested.[58] Danced religions in the Caribbean dissolve the boundary between the secular and spiritual. The organic experience of community and gathering are brought about by the rhythmic impact of dance and drumming which are both essential to the trance experience. Traditionally, these gatherings took place in the yard to generate spiritual healing, community, survival and self-discovery. As Edward Kamau Brathwaite has described this cultural pattern in the context of Jamaican Kumina practice:

> The yard, protected by fence, gate, white markings at the gate-posts or just inside the threshold; the sacred pole or holy tree, the whitewashed stones of heaven's thunder, the pigeons (doves) in tree or cote: coo-coo-cu-ru-ing:

> the steps, the entrance to the shepherd's hall or house: reception / waiting room; a room off: healing: bed, table, floor-mat; another room: the heads down close, together, low slow incision of the voice: listen, listen, touch: secular and polyphone advice: single, groups: join, wait, alone; another door, steps, the inner courtyard: dirt, tile, cement: the 'bood' or hounfort, chapel, church or Holy Tabernacle: sticks, drums, rattles, dancing: whirl, spin, saló, damballa's bellows; and beyond, the balm-yard; and beyond that herb, bush, weed, jiggey; and beyond that heal, stream, water, spirits, ancestors, the mourning ground of gods.[59]

During this process the yard serves as the center for community gathering, healing practices and communication which is partly transferred onto the West Indian Theatre stage as it integrates certain ritualistic patterns into its aesthetics. In *Dream on Monkey Mountain*, for example, this spiritually inspired rhythm is still apparent, even though it is no longer linked to religious roots but transformed into a secular arts idiom. While *Dream on Monkey Mountain* may thus be read as a diaspora-play which addresses imaginary longings for an imaginary homeland, the dramatic development also makes clear that such a fantasy does no longer exist. Makak's mother Africa is as much an illusion as the white Diablesse. They are both romantic constructions of a devastated mind in exile which eventually turn out to be self-destructive. African essentialism is as much a dead end street as is white racism. Colonialism is no longer an answer and neither is mere imitation of it. Yet, Creoleness offers a liberating perspective and that is what Walcott's theatre stands for: a new beginning and the making of a freed mind that accepts the exiled situation to start another self-invented life.

Derek Walcott's theater appears therefore as an emblematic example of cross-cultural theatre aesthetics which owe as much to the African heritage as to the Asian and European. Hence, his Caribbean theatre aesthetic seeks to overcome binary divisions such as high and low culture, African or European in an effort to deconstruct colonialist notions of cultural difference. In this respect Caribbean theatre manages to engage its international audiences in a creative encounter that may be exotic and politically enticing at the same time. While the uninitiated may not grasp each and every single key of the Caribbean's cultural complexity, the theatre performance will still serve as an enunciative practice of voicing cultural identity and independence. The impact of Walcott's theatre aesthetic, ultimately, resides in this theatrical blend that successfully integrates African, Oriental, West Indian and Western theatre practice. In Walcott's theatrical world tradition and modernism do not exclude each other, but raise interesting questions of our cultural identity in an increasingly globalized cultural environment. As this theatre allows for the ambivalence of difference to take place, it actually manages to build on Bhabha's somewhat utopian notion of a third space to attack the still prevalent cultural binaries. Following the Trinidad Carnival's battle cry "Play Mas!" this means to actively enjoy the freedom of becoming whoever one may wish to be.

Notes

1 Derek Walcott: "The Outlook for a National Theatre", *Sunday Guardian*, 22 March 1964, 16.
2 Compare Jean Bernabé & Patrick Chamoiseau & Raphaël Confiant (Eds.): *Éloge de la Créolité*, Paris, 1989, p. 75. At the same time there is a continued contestation of the term and concept, because of its historical bias and genealogy as a racializing discourse. For further discussion of the concept compare Verene A. Shepherd & Glen L. Richards (Eds.): *Questioning Creole. Creolisation Discourses in Caribbean Culture*, Kingston, 2002, and Shalini Puri: *The Caribbean Postcolonial. Social Equality, Post-Nationalism, and Cultural Hybridity*, New York & Basingstoke, 2004.
3 Compare Mervyn C. Alleyne: *The Construction and Representation of Race and Ethnicity in the Caribbean and the World*, Kingston, 2002, as well as his *Roots of Jamaican Culture*, London, 1988.
4 Especially in the case of Jamaica colonial adherence to white elitism appeared particularly absurd, since approximately ninety percent of the population is of African ancestry. Black Power was thus a significant influence on Jamaican independence politics and the national arts movement. Compare Rex Nettleford (Ed.): *Norman Washington Manley and the New Jamaica, Selected Speeches and Writings 1938-1968*, London, 1971.
5 Frantz Fanon: *Black Skin, White Masks*, London, [1952] 1986.
6 Homi K. Bhabha's foreword to Frantz Fanon: *Black Skin, White Masks*, London, 1986, p. 12.
7 *Ibid.*, 16.
8 Homi K. Bhabha: *The Location of Culture*, London & New York, 1994, pp. 85-92.
9 For further reference see Bill Ashcroft & Gareth Griffiths & Helen Tiffin (Eds.): *The Empire Writes Back: Theory and Practice in Post-Colonial Literatures*, London & New York, 1989.

10 The term 'syncretic theater' derives from Christopher Balme's study of postcolonial theatre in which he has pointed out the difference between the European-based intercultural theatre of Peter Brook or Ariane Mnouchkine and the syncretic theatre of, for example, Wole Soyinka and Derek Walcott. While the former appropriates foreign performance practice for at times quite controversial productions, the latter confronts the recipient with much more complex semiotic references which often elude a total decoding. For further reference see Christopher Balme: *Theater im postkolonialen Zeitalter: Studien zum Theatersynkretismus im englischsprachigen Raum*, Tübingen, 1995, and *Decolonizing the Stage: Theatrical Syncretism and Postcolonial Drama*, Oxford, 1999, as well as Helen Gilbert & Joanne Tomkins (Eds.): *Post-colonial Drama. Theory, Practice, Politics*, London & New York, 1996. More recently, Jacqueline Lo and Helen Gilbert have coined the umbrella term 'cross-cultural' theatre in an effort to subsume and specify the aesthetic and political debates at stake in these performances. See Jacqueline Lo & Helen Gilbert: "Toward a Topography of Cross-Cultural Theater Praxis", *The Drama Review* 46:3, 2002, 31-53.

11 Compare C. L. R. James: *The Black Jacobins. Toussaint L'Ouverture and the San Domingo Revolution*, London, [1938] 2001.

12 Compare Norman Girvan: "Reinterpreting the Caribbean", – In Brian Meeks & Folke Lindahl (Eds.): *New Caribbean Thought. A Reader*, Kingston, 2001, pp. 3-23.

13 Compare Philip Sherlock & Hazel Bennett (Eds.): *The Story of the Jamaican People*, Kingston, 1998, pp. 346-361.

14 For further reference see Rex Nettleford: *Caribbean Cultural Identity. The Case of Jamaica. An Essay in Cultural Dynamics*, Kingston, [1978] 2003.

15 Beryl McBurnie: *Dance Trinidad Dance*, Booklet, n.d., p. 6.

16 For a more detailed discussion compare my dissertation "Dancing Postcolonialism – The National Dance Theatre Company of Jamaica", Dissertation, Johannes Gutenberg-Universität Mainz, 2005.

17 Derek Walcott was working as a theatre critic during this period and his journalistic writing testifies to the importance of a national theatre movement of the time. Also Errol Hill contributed significantly to this discourse on theatre and decolonization and postcolonial independence. Compare Derek Walcott: "The Sound and the Fury of Our Theatre", *Public Opinion*, 13 July 1957, 4; "Need for a Little Theatre in Port-of-Spain", *Sunday Guardian*, 23 February and 19 July 1960, 22; "National Theatre is the Answer", *Trinidad Guardian*, 12 August 1964, 5 and Errol Hill (Ed.): *The Artist and West Indian Society: A Symposium*, Kingston, 1963.

18 The term 'jump up' has become a synonym for taking part in the Trinidad Carnival masquerade. It refers to the part after nightfall, when the maskers and civilians join in the so-called 'jump-up' revelries.

19 Derek Walcott: "The White Devil: A Story of Christmas", *Sunday Guardian Magazine*, 25 December 1966, 20-21.

20 Philip M. Sherlock: *Anansi the Spider Man: Jamaican Folk Tales*, London & Basingstoke, 1983.

21 See Eric Roach: "This Musical Fuses Both Traditions of Folk Legend", *Sunday Guardian*, 28 June 1970, 11, and Albert Ashalou: "Allegory in Ti-Jean and His Brothers". – In Robert Hamner (Ed.): *Critical Perspectives on Derek Walcott*, Washington, D.C., 1993, pp. 118-124.

22 Derek Walcott: *Ti-Jean and His Brothers*. – In *Dream on Monkey Mountain and other Plays*, New York, [1970] 1999, p. 129.

23 Richard D. E. Burton: *Afro-Creole: Power, Opposition and Play in the Caribbean*, Ithaca & London, 1997, p. 50.

24 *Ibid.*, 62.

25 Walcott: *Dream*, p. 148.

26 Milla C. Riggio: "Resistance and Identity. Carnival in Trinidad and Tobago", *The Drama Review* 42:3, 1998, 11-14.

27 Derek Walcott: "Magnificence and Art in the Carnival Spectacle", *Trinidad Guardian*, 5 March 1962, 6.

28 Errol Hill: *The Trinidad Carnival: Mandate for a National Theatre*, Austin & London, 1972, pp. 10-11.

29 Walcott, *Dream*, p. 149.

30 Max Harris: "The Impotence of Dragons: Playing Devil in the Trinidad Carnival", *The Drama Review* 42:3, 1998, 11.

31 Derek Walcott: "Derek's Most West Indian Play: Ti-Jean and His Brothers", *Sunday Guardian Magazine*, 21 June 1970, 7.

32 Derek Walcott: *The Joker of Seville & O Babylon! Two Plays*, New York, 1978.

33 Carol Martin: "Trinidad Carnival Glossary", *The Drama Review* 42:3, 1998, 225.

34 Burroquite, from Spanish "borriquito" (little donkey), is a traditional masquerade played in the Trinidad Carnival. The costume is a hybrid of Hindu worship and the Spanish bull-fight tradition, in which the donkey acts as a "super-phallic" character. It uses the masquerader's own legs which are covered by a wired frame and cloth of papier-maché.

35 J. D. Elder: "Cannes Brûlées", *The Drama Review* 42:3, 1998, 38-43.

36 *Ibid.*, 40.

37 Errol Hill: "Calypso and War", *Black American Literature Forum* 23 1, 1989, 62-63.

38 Peter Mason: *Bacchanal! The Carnival Culture of Trinidad*, Philadelphia, 1998, p. 20.

39 Derek Walcott: "Our Poetry in Song: Kaiso, Genius of the Folk", *Sunday Guardian*, 9 February 1964, 13; "Popular Poets Are Now Severely Tested", *Sunday Guardian*, 14 February 1960, 7; "Don Juan was a Stickman!" *Trinidad Guardian*, 18 November 1973, 4.

40 Derek Walcott: "Soul Brother to the Joker of Seville", *Trinidad Guardian*, 6 November 1974, 4.

41 J. D. Elder: "The Future of Music in the West Indies". – In Hill (Ed.): *The Artist in West Indian Society*, p. 38.
42 Derek Walcott: "Patterns to Forget", *Trinidad Guardian*, 22 June 1966, 5.
43 Walcott: *The Joker of Seville*, pp. 42-43.
44 For this reading of the rod compare Burton: *Afro-Creole*, pp. 9-10.
45 Derek Walcott: "The Muse of History". – In Orde Coombs (Ed.): *Is Massa Day Dead? Black Moods in the Caribbean*, Garden City, NY, 1974, p. 12.
46 For a discussion of folk ritual, religion and dance in this context compare Rex Nettleford: *Inward Stretch Outward Reach: A Voice from the Caribbean*, London & Basingstoke, 1995, pp. 98-99.
47 Walcott: *Joker of Seville*, p. 55.
48 Martin: "Trinidad Carnival Glossary", 230-231.
49 Walcott: *Joker of Seville*, p. 55.
50 Patricia Ismond: "Breaking Myths and Maidenheads". – In Robert Hamner (Ed.): *Critical Perspectives on Derek Walcott*, Washington D.C., 1993, p. 251.
51 Therese Mills: "Sell-Out Crowd Enjoys The Joker", *Trinidad Guardian*, 1 December 1974, 3, 5.
52 Ismond: "Breaking Myths and Maidenheads", p. 251.
53 John Mercer: "Landmark for Local Drama and Triumph for Workshop", *Trinidad Guardian*, 29 January 1969, 11.
54 Walcott: *Dream*, p. 212.
55 *Ibid.*, 208.
56 Compare Molly Ahye: *Cradle of Caribbean Dance: Beryl McBurnie and the Little Carib Theatre*, Petit Valley, Trinidad and Tobago, pp. 1983, 44-45.
57 Osita Okagbue: "The Strange and the Familiar: Intercultural Exchange Between African and Caribbean Theatre", *Theatre Research International* 22:2, 1997, 125.
58 Brenda Dixon Gottschild: *Digging the Africanist Presence in American Performance: Dance and Other Contexts*, Westport, CT, 1998, p. 10.
59 Edward Kamau Brathwaite: "Kumina", *Savacou Working Paper* 4, 1982, 46-47.

Denise deCaires Narain (Sussex)

Gendering the Caribbean

O Adam
make me a poet please
and not no wo-man poet
let me be free
and gender-
less dear Ad…

At this point I stopped Eaves-droppping[1]

Most accounts of Caribbean writing designate its 'proper' beginnings with a group of writers who started publishing in the fifties and sixties while based, for the most part, in Britain. These writers – V. S. Naipaul, Samuel Selvon, George Lamming, Wilson Harris, Derek Walcott, Kamau Brathwaite, to name a few - were all male. It wasn't until the late 1980s that this gender balance began to shift and Caribbean women writers started to be published more widely. It would not be contentious to say that Caribbean women writers are now *more* visible than their male counterparts. In what follows, I will explore the ways that the Caribbean has been conceptualized, both implicitly and explicitly, as a gendered space and outline some of the factors which might account for the shift away from the male-dominated literary culture of the 1960s.

The historical context out of which Anglophone Caribbean literature and culture was produced is one of conquest and destruction. Columbus's so-called 'discovery' of the 'New World' was rapidly followed by the decimation of the native peoples he found there. As George Lamming puts it, "what we know about the modern Caribbean is that it is an area of the world that began with an almost unprecedented act of genocide".[2] Decades of buccaneering and piracy and the cavalier exchanging of 'ownership' of the islands were eventually replaced by settlement and the establishment of plantations on the islands (and on the mainland of South

America). The labour required for the plantations to be functional led to the shipping of millions of slaves from Africa. When slavery was abolished, Indians were shipped to the West Indies as indentured labourers (small numbers of Chinese and even fewer numbers of Portuguese were also deployed for a short time as indentured labour). Even this most cursory outline of Caribbean history conveys the sense of brutality and high-handed imperial machismo which created the modern Caribbean. The legacy of this volatile history continues to shape debates about literature and culture in the region in a range of ways that have significant implications for the gendered identity / identities of the region.

While the outline of the main trajectories in Caribbean history sketched above are widely accepted, it is also the case that the precise contours of this account are constantly being contested and revised in response to questions and challenges generated by sociocultural debates within the region and by ongoing research projects. The intersecting vectors of 'gender' and 'race' continue to be crucial to these revisions and these, in turn, impact upon the literary history of the Caribbean. In other words, both the 'History' and 'Literary History' of the region are unstable discourses, inflected by the cultural agendas of the day and by the kinds of research such agendas make possible. Thus, the brisk assertion at the start of this piece listing several male writers as the originators of Caribbean Literature must be read as provisional: a convenient starting point, rather than a secure foundational moment.

J.Edward Chamberlin's book-length study of West Indian poetry starts with a bald statement which conveys economically the most important historical fact in any discussion of Caribbean literature: "Slavery shaped the West Indies".[3] But, until recently, historical accounts of slavery assumed the male subject as normative, focusing on the brutalising and emasculating impact of slavery on the African man and eliding the specific experiences of women slaves. This 'male-centred' approach is perpetuated in some sociological and anthropological texts which examine Caribbean culture from a revisionist viewpoint. Peter Wilson's *Crab Antics*, for example, published in 1973,[4] suggests that the cultural spaces occupied by men and women in the Caribbean are fairly rigidly demarcated with men occupying the outside / public space, associated with reputation and women occupying the inside / domestic space, associated with respectability. Reputation and respectability represent different value systems: the indigenous and internally generated on the one hand ('nativist' / male) and the colonially-inherited, externally driven on the other ('imported'/female). Apart from the overly-neat dichotomizing of inside and outside, Wilson's model posits resistance as an exclusively male phenomenon. As Jean Besson argues:

> In particular, I challenge Wilson's thesis that Afro-Caribbean women are passive imitators of Eurocentric cultural values of respectability; that the counter-culture of reputation is male-oriented; and that cultural resistance to colonial culture is therefore confined to Afro-Caribbean males.[5]

Richard Burton's, *Afro-Creole: Power, Opposition and Play in the Caribbean*, published in 1997,[6] while offering excellent discussions of Afro-Caribbean cultural forms including religious practices, cricket and carnival, largely follows Wilson's schema and, as a result, elides the role of women in resisting colonial domination and overstates the role of African-Caribbean men as exclusive agents of resistance. This tendency is even more pronounced in Christian Habekost's discussion of the dub poet in, *Dub Poetry*, published in 1986:

> […] the poet on stage with flying dreadlocks, an angry expression on his black face, murderously kicking into the air with his motorbike-boots just as the police boots kicked him. […] Mutabaruka comes on stage half naked, chains around his bare feet and when he lets the gunshot ring out, his face distorted by pain, in "Ev'rytime Aear de Soun'" then it gets under the whitest of skins and is enough to 'blacken' the whitest soul.[7]

The hyperbolic thrust of Habekost's admiration strikes a very uneasy note, invoking an almost reverential treatment of black male anger which collapses any critical distance between performer and critic / audience, rendering the performance a spectacle of 'pure anger' to be 'simply' consumed. The idea of spectacle and display and the righteousness of male anger are features of some more recent interpretations of contemporary popular cultural forms, particularly in Jamaica, and I will return to this later.

Another strand in the revisionist work undertaken in Caribbean studies has been done by scholars who have attended to the specific ways in which slavery was experienced by women and how these women also resisted their enslavement. Barbara Bush's *Slave*

Women in Caribbean Societies 1650-1838, for example, offered a sustained discussion of the specific modes of resistance which slave women made use of, from abortion and infanticide to poisoning the planters' food and feigning illness.[8] In poetry, Grace Nichols's collection, *i is a long memoried woman*, provided one of the earliest and most sustained literary representations of slave women's culture, offering insights into infanticide, for example, in the poem "Ala":

> […] and call us out
> to see […] the rebel woman
>
> who with a pin
> stick the soft mould
> of her won child's hcad
>
> sending the little-new-born
> soul winging its way back
> to Africa – free.[9]

More recently, many sociologists and historians have charted the way that plantation slavery distorted gender roles in the colonies and postcolonies of the Caribbean. Christine Barrow argues:

> In summary, the Caribbean social-gender system has been built on an insecure and ambivalent foundation. Throughout slavery, colonialism and even today, the system imposed an ideology of masculinity and femininity while simultaneously refusing to build the socio-economic structures required to support it in practice.[10]

While much of the early work on gendering Caribbean history has been produced by feminist scholars within the general remit of 'women's studies', the emphasis has now shifted to a wider understanding of the importance of gender as constitutive of both male and female roles and, increasingly, there is a willingness to interrogate constructions of Caribbean masculinities as well as femininities. This is a welcome development, especially if it allows for the possibility of moving beyond the romanticizing tendency of some of the literature cited above with its subtext of 'men-in-crisis'. This 'men-in-crisis' line of argument gained more credibility in the wake of Caribbean feminism when arguments were made about Caribbean women themselves contributing – by their very visible presence and successes – to the further emasculation of 'the' Caribbean man. Such arguments also tended to characterise Caribbean feminism as another suspect imported ideology. It is worth noting, too, that the contributions of Caribbean feminists succeeded not only in drawing attention to women's experiences but also in unsettling orthodox views of Caribbean culture. Such interventions called into question the exclusive focus on the African male subject as the privileged focus of scholarly attention. Alongside this, the increasing willingness to make the stories of Indian indentured labourers an integral part of Caribbean history and culture has begun to transform understanding of what it means to be a Caribbean subject. Gender is again crucial to this understanding.

It has been argued that slavery 'de-gendered' both male and female slaves by violently rupturing family and kinship ties as well as forcing men and women alike to do extremely demanding physical work. Indian indentured labourers were treated differently for, although the conditions in which they worked and were accommodated were similar in many ways to those which prevailed under slavery, they were permitted to retain many of their cultural and religious practices. This ensured animosity between Africans and Indians (the familiar 'divide-and-rule' strategy of colonialism) which continue to inflect the political life of Guyana and Trinidad up to the present.[11] It is widely accepted that Indian men far outnumbered their female counterparts, particularly in the early stages of indentureship. This fact helped to consolidate the Indian woman as a 'scarce commodity' in the patriarchal symbolic system of the plantation where 'she' functioned to some extent as the prized proof of the Indian's higher status than that of the African. Already demonised for taking the black man's work on the plantations, 'the' Indian man was further demonised as 'hot-headed' and quick to use the cutlass in defence of 'his woman'. Later, as the economic wealth of some Indians increased, Indian women's participation in public life was often curtailed. Thus, when Forbes Burnham, President / dictator of Guyana and leader of the (primarily African Peoples national Congress, introduced National Service in Guyana in the late 1960s, some Indian families sent their daughters abroad to avoid any risk of them being involved in 'contaminating' sexual relations with black men. Olive Senior, in the title story of her collection, *The Snake-Woman and Other Stories*, offers a snapshot of the distorted perceptions of Indians which prevailed:

> "These coolie-woman like nayga-man", he was saying, "for the coolie-man is the wussest man in the whole world. If they have a wife and she just say 'kemps' – he quick fe chop off her head. So plenty of the coolie-woman fraid of the coolie-man and want the nayga-man working in the cane to take them back to the hill with them so they can get far away from the wicked coolie-man and furtherer away from the sea which they hate like pisen for is the sea that carry them away from India."[12]

Colonial history, then, resulted in highly racialised gender roles with white women occupying the most privileged position. Hilary Beckles cites Lucille Mair's succinct summary of this typology, "in Caribbean slave societies the black woman produced, the brown woman served, and the white woman consumed".[13] It is hardly surprising, given this context, that it was 'race' rather than 'gender' that would drive literary debates in the region, at least initially. But, while gender may not have been explicitly on the cultural agenda, I would argue that it did inform the contexts of production and reception of literary works and it was implicit in definitions of what was considered a suitably anti-colonial literary voice.

So, in *West Indian Poetry*, published in 1984, Lloyd Brown dismisses West Indian poetry from 1760 – 1940 as "uneven at best, and in some respects [...] downright unpromising"[14] because it remains enslaved to English culture and tradition. Following on from this period, the works that *are* recognised as articulating the beginnings of a suitably resisting Caribbean voice are those which deploy what I have called elsewhere a "muscular morality".[15] Walter M. Lawrence's poem "Guiana", for example concludes: "For the cry goes up from the deepest despair; God give us a chance to be men!" while, more famously, Claude McKay's "If We Must Die" represents another example of the poet as a brave and heroic figure in the face of oppression (in McKay's poem, the immediate context is that of a violently segregated deep South of America):

> What though before us lies the open grave?
> Like men we'll fight the murderous, cowardly pack,
> Pressed to the wall, dying, but fighting back![16]

This emphasis follows on, quite 'naturally', from colonial discourses in which discussions about slavery, emancipation and (eventually) self-rule were all conducted in terms of what it was to be 'a man'. Where women feature in this poetry at all, they are often represented as the land, rather than as active agents defending 'the land'. If the colonizers depicted the New World as virginal territory to be penetrated and conquered, nationalists conflated the woman with the land as the symbol of what was being fought for. The black woman in these poems is often presented as 'natural' and grounded in the earth, the symbol of everything that the white woman is not. When women themselves wrote, they were generally perceived as writing in an altogether different register, covering themes which were peripheral to the task of challenging colonial culture. So, a figure like Una Marson, publishing in the 1930s and 40s has only recently received critical attention from feminist critics whose understanding of 'resistance' is more expansive than that which obtained in Marson's time – or, indeed, Lloyd Brown's.[17] Marson's poem, "Kinky Hair Blues", for example, offers an altogether more playfully low-key register of resistance than that evident in McKay's poem above:

> I hate dat ironed hair
> And dat bleaching skin.
> Hate dat ironed hair
> And dat bleaching skin.
> But I'll be all alone
> If I don't fall in.[18]

The speaker concludes that she will have to straighten her hair and bleach her skin if she wants "some kind of man to win" and this pragmatic complicity and playful dramatising of ambivalence is a register which becomes increasingly unacceptable in the 1960s and 1970s when the demand for an unequivocally challenging nationalist voice is more urgently focused. The following extract from a well-known poem by Bongo Jerry, "Mabrak", is indicative of the robust register required:

> BLACK ELECTRIC STORM
> IS HERE
> How long you feel "fair to fine"
> (WHITE) would last?
>
> How long in darkness
> when out of BLACK
> come forth LIGHT?
> MABRAK is righting the wrongs and brain-whitening ...
> Not just by washing out the straightening and wearing
> dashiki t'ing:

MOSTOFTHESTRAIGHTENINGISINTHETONGUE -
so ...
Save the YOUNG
from the language that MEN teach,
the doctrine Pope preach
skin bleach...
        MAN must use MEN language
            to carry dis message:

SILENCE BABEL TONGUES; recall and
recollect BLACK SPEECH.[19]

The poem first appeared in a special edition of the West Indian journal, *Savacou* in 1971, titled, *New Writing*, a collection of poems which generated a heated debate, later characterised as "Afro-Saxons versus the Tribe Boys", about the relative value of African rather than European cultural models. Laurence Breiner, in an unpublished paper entitled, "How To Behave On Paper: The *Savacou* Debate" gives a good summary of the issues involved:

> Above all, the *Savacou* debate was about what amounts to the decorum of poetry – a matter of values, standards, the rules of the game [...] the critical furore over the *Savacou* anthology was most particularly about what should be printed, and about how a poem should look on paper.[20]

This debate about the decorum of poetry clearly implies a robustly masculine, black African aesthetic positioned in direct opposition to a European aesthetic, and a politics initially determined to overturn this binary, rather than to deconstruct it. That the region's two most influential poets, Derek Walcott and Edward Kamau Brathwaite, became associated with 'opposite' poles in this dichotomy (the former being perceived as more oriented to conventional European poetic models and the latter associated with a 'folk-centred' poetics) only consolidated this binary. Discussions of poetry have been so intensely focused on the roles of Walcott and Brathwaite in the formation of an appropriately authentic and muscular 'indigenous' poetic identity that both poetry and the figure of the poet have tended to be perceived as normatively male.

And both Walcott and Brathwaite, in different ways, do place the male subject at the centre of their respective oeuvres. For example, Walcott's castaway poems construct the figure of the shipwrecked castaway as an Adamic name-giver who names (and claims) the

'New World' while *Another Life* paints a picture of the artist as an embattled young man. Shabine, in "The Schooner Flight" is a "red nigger" who defends his poetry from the sneers of his fellow seamen robustly:

> Had an exercise book,
> this same one here, that I using to write
> my poetry, so one day this man snatch it
> from my hand, and start throwing it left and right
> to the rest of the crew, bawling out, "Catch it",
> and start mincing me like I was some hen
> because of the poems.
> […]
> There wasn't much pain,
> Just plenty blood, and Vincie and me best friend,
> But none of them go fuck with my poetry again.[21]

Brathwaite's *The Arrivants*, focuses on the travels and travails of the black man in the New World, whether it is the figure of 'Uncle Tom' on the plantation, 'Brotherman-the-Rasataman' or, as in the extract below, the "poor harbourless spade":

> I am a fuck-
> in' negro,
> man, hole
> in my head,
> brains in
> my belly;
> black skin
> red eyes
> broad back
> big you know
> what: not very quick
>
> to take offence
> but once
> offended, watch
> that house
> you livin' in
> an' watch that lit-
> le sister.[22]

In both poems the aggressive rhetoric used requires a male speaker for the poem to work.That poetry was the genre in which the challenge to 'English Literature' was most dramatically staged is perhaps not surprising, given the elaborate conventions and complex structures of the form and the desire of many Caribbean poets to refute these 'effete' conventions. The emphasis on challenging the conventional decorum of poetry became focused on the issue of voice – and on an authentically West Indian voice. This emphasis (evident in both extracts above) required poets to look to a range of 'everyday' folk traditions and to the vernacular Creole language for inspiration. In the process, there was a tendency for women to be acknowledged in their role as providers of 'the mother tongue' but it was the male performance of Creole speech in public spaces that came to be associated with a distinct form of cultural resistance.

In fiction, Sam Selvon's *The Lonely Londoners*, published in 1956,[23] was championed as an exemplary text because of its sustained use of a stylised Creole for the narrative voice throughout, rather than reserving Creole speech for dialogue, as was the norm. The novel focuses on a group of West Indian men who have migrated to London and who spend their time 'liming' round the city, looking for work and hustling white women (variously referred to as 'pieces of meat', 'ting', 'pussy' etc). West Indian women make only fleeting appearances as the novel charts the increasingly desperate ways that the politically impotent 'boys' seek to assert their manhood and consolidate their reputations via sexual conquest. Selvon's text, while recycling images of (white) women which define them entirely in terms of their sexuality, is primarily concerned with exposing the futility and vulnerability of the West Indian men in a racist and hostile London. Due to this focus, the casual and relentless sexism of 'the boys' did not really become an obstacle to readings of the text until well into the 1980s. In other words, Selvon's construction of an authentically West Indian voice, hailed as the major achievement of *The Lonely Londoners*, rendered the sexual politics of the text inaudible.

Another early text, V. S. Naipaul's *Miguel Street*, published in 1959, is similarly focused on 'what it means to be a man'. In these linked short stories, Naipaul describes the way a young Trinidadian boy navigates his way to manhood in a street where the men must publicly display their 'maleness' by verbal or physical conquest of other men or, more often, of women. Apart from one story, "The Maternal Instinct", which describes a (stereotyped) black woman who takes pride in the fact that her eight children are conceived by eight different men, all the stories focus on male characters who have a precarious existence in one way or another but whose stories and repartee about their exploits help to bolster their reputation on the street. The ritualised beating of women punctuates the text, defining the worlds of men and women as rigidly separate. When Bogart[24] leaves his second wife, one of the narrator's friends asks why and is told that he did so: "To be a man, among we men".[25] In another story, the carpenter, Popo, tells the boy: "Women and them like work. Man not make for work."[26] In these stories, Naipaul describes, in typically sardonic manner, the gender relations that prevail in the street and, despite the playfulness of his treatment, he exposes the lack of ambition and vulnerability of the men. In the process of this exposition of the Trinidadian man's precarious hold on masculinity, the text also hints at a deep mistrust of women; a mistrust which is prominent in many of Naipaul's other texts. Bhakcu, in "The Mechanical Genius", for example, is furious with his wife for pressurising him to buy a lorry to generate more income, because he then 'tinkers' with it and breaks it. Not only is the (Indian) woman here presented as a 'money-grabber' but she is complicit with her own mistreatment (she oils the cricket bat that her husband beats her with) and, Naipaul's young narrator suggests, the 'tongue-lashing' she gives her husband is worse than his physical abuse of her:

> All the time he had the lorry, he hated his wife, and he beat her regularly with the cricket bat. But she was beating him too, with her tongue, and I think Bhakcu was really the loser in these quarrels.[27]

Space permits me only to gesture towards the works of some of the other writers mentioned at the start of this piece. George Lamming's seminal text, *In the Castle of My Skin*, also follows the development of a young boy growing up (in pre-independence Barbados) and gradually apprehending the way that both 'race' and class unfairly curtail his ambitions. Women / girls are present in the novel as mothers and lovers but not as part of the group of boys whose consciousness the narrative privileges. Towards the end of the novel, as G prepares to leave the island for Trinidad, his mother makes him a farewell supper of cou-cou (a favourite Bajan dish). The detailed, loving description of her movements as she cooks consolidates her in the role of revered and celebrated 'Mother', a role that is the most conspicuous female role in early Caribbean texts. The exception to this would be the novels of Wilson Harris in which realism is rejected in favour of a more intuitive and suggestive discourse characterised by fluidity, circularity and excess, characteristics often loosely aligned with 'feminine principles'.[28]

More recently-published male writers are generally more alert to a wider range of possibilities than the rather limited definitions of 'woman' that characterise the earlier writing and which generally fit into the familiar Madonna / whore dichotomy. David Dabydeen, in *Coolie Odyssey* and *Slave Song*, frequently deploys what he describes as "the erotic energies of the colonial experience".[29] Dabydeen configures this as a fraught encounter between the black man (in Dabydeen's poetry 'black' encompasses both 'Indian' and 'African') and a Miranda figure who functions as the 'forbidden fruit' or prized possession of the white man. So, in "Slave Song", the speaker fantasizes or boasts:

> Is so when yu dun dream she pink tit,
> Totempole she puss,
> Leff yu teetmark like a tattoo in she troat![30]

The violence of this image strikes an uneasy cord, however much the violence can be rationalised as being integral to the poetics of the persona of the poem. Clearly, Dabydeen is deliberately overdoing the 'savage' stereotype in a manouever which seeks to deconstruct it but there is, perhaps, too much sheer delight and rhetorical swagger in lines such as, "Bu yu caan stap me cack dippin in de honeypot / Drippin at de tip an happy as a hottentot!"[31] for this reader to be convinced that it is offered 'in good faith'. Robert Antoni offers a more successful exploration of the "erotic energies of the colonial experience" in his novel, *Blessed is the Fruit*, which alternates between the first-person narratives of a white woman and a black woman in what is an innovative rewriting of Jean Rhys' *Wide Sargasso Sea*.[32]

It is not really till the 1980s when Caribbean women writers start to be published and read in significant numbers that gender is placed firmly on the region's literary agenda and the limited definitions of 'woman' circulating in male-authored texts begin to be challenged. The disillusionment which followed independence in most parts of the Caribbean compromised the dominant anti-colonial trajectory of Caribbean writing and this, coupled with the powerful influence of African American women writers (Maya Angelou, Toni Morrison, Alice Walker) and the global attention being paid to 'women's issues' during the United Nations Decade for Women (1975-1985), provided the impetus for a flurry of publications by Caribbean women. Pamela Mordecai and Mervyn Morris edited the first anthology of Caribbean women's poetry in 1980, *Jamaica Woman*.[33] The title recalls the poem, "Jamaica Oman", by Louise Bennett, a poet widely acknowledged as one of the major literary forbears of Caribbean writing. The poem opens:

> Jamaica oman cunny, sah!
> Is how dem jinnal so?
> Look how long dem liberated
> An de man dem never know![34]

The poem goes on to praise the clever ('jinnal') way in which Jamaican women exercise their strength and power without arousing suspicion in their men. The covert exercise of women's power which the poem celebrates is indicative of the cautious attitude taken by the editors of this collection in the short preface to the collection which displays a somewhat ambiguous stance to feminism:

> Because these poets are all women, one may be tempted to raise the issue of whether they are "poets who happen to be women", or something called 'woman poet'. But that is not the point. The poems are various. […] there is nothing limp in the responses of the poets here, nor is there any aggressive feminism in their work.[35]

The preface simultaneously acknowledges and denies the relevance of gender to poetic output, a caginess that perhaps suggests a suspicion about 'feminism' as an 'imported' ideology and a reluctance to risk alienating a readership for whom a nationalist, rather than feminist, agenda was paramount. However, a poem, such as Pamela Mordecai's "Protest Poem: *for all the brothers*", offers a sharp and unapologetic critique of the politics associated with 'the brotherhood'. The poem parodies the ideologically charged discourse of resistance of the brothers by placing it in dialogue with the wry, straight-talking of an 'ordinary Jamaican woman':

> 2. Blessed be the proletariat whom
>   we must mobilize
> we must motivate
> we must liberate
> we must educate
> to a new political awareness.
>
> 3. Is di ole chattle ting again: di same
> slavery bizness, but dis time di boss
> look more like we an im does be smarter.
> Not a dam soul goin' mobilize my ass
> to rass – dem jokin. Any fool can read
> *Das Kapital*: what is dat to dc poor?[36]

Jamaica Woman was an important publication, signalling both the presence of several relatively unknown women poets and the need to introduce gender to discussions about literature in the region. In the decade or so that followed, writers such as Olive Senior, Erna Brodber, Jamaica Kincaid, Grace Nichols, Merle Hodge, Michelle Cliff, Zee Edgell, Velma Pollard, Janice Shinebourne, Beryl Gilroy, Joan Riley (amongst others) published first novels or collections of short stories. And poets such as Lorna Goodison, Dionne Brand, Marlene Nourbese Philip, Olive Senior, Grace Nichols, Mahadai Das, Jean 'Binta' Breeze, Merle Collins, Valerie Bloom, Amryl Johnson (amongst others) published collections of poetry. By the early 1990s, with the publication of anthologies of Caribbean women's fiction as well as collections of critical essays about this writing and a range of international conferences focused on these writers and texts, the category 'Caribbean women's writing', became relatively well-known as a distinct field of scholarship.

The emphasis in much of this critical writing was on challenging the male-centredness of Caribbean Literature and 'giving voice' to women. In their jointly written introduction to the critical anthology, *Out of the Kumbla: Caribbean Women and Literature*, Carole Boyce Davies and Elaine Savory Fido argue:

> [T]he most urgent and central concern we must have in the sphere of women's writing is to encourage writing. The first essential is to find all the lost writers – those many, many women all over the region who

have poems in drawers and inside books, pieces of fiction unpublished and confined to obscurity.[37]

This recuperative project is one shared by many other constituencies of feminist scholars and activists in their various challenges to complacently 'male' literary traditions. But, as with other constituencies of women writers, the apparently straightforward task of 'finding' and 'hearing' those female voices eclipsed in conventional literary accounts proved more complicated than might have been expected. So, while, the editors of *Out of the Kumbla* can point to the distinctly female themes which Caribbean women write about (motherhood, sexuality, subjectivity, anxieties about identity, the relationship to nation and colonial history), distinguishing a shared ideological position on women's oppression proved more difficult. This difficulty is present in the preface to the collection in which Savory Fido and Boyce Davies discuss the relative merits of the terms 'feminism' and 'womanism'; the former favouring womanism, with its emphasis on "women's talk, customs, lore", as a "softer, more flexible option than feminism" while the latter opts for feminism as a term with more political bite.[38] In Sylvia Wynter's "Afterword", this issue is complicated further in her argument for a "demonic model of cognition" outside the discourses of both patriarchy and feminism.[39]

Evelyn O'Callaghan's *Woman Version: Theoretical Approaches to West Indian Fiction by Women*, published in 1993, though more unapologetically feminist in orientation, interrogates Caribbean women's texts in the broader context of postcolonial discourse. In doing so, O'Callaghan's work initiates an (ongoing) process of contesting and broadening the parameters of the category, 'Caribbean women's writing'. As O'Callaghan acknowledges at the start of her book, the category is a recent and contested one:

> When I first began to study West Indian fiction in the 1970s, I was under the impression that there were no women writers from the region apart from Jean Rhys, and there was some reservation about her.[40]

Doubts about Jean Rhys's place in West Indian literature revolve around the fact that she was a white West Indian whose ancestry included members of the plantocracy. Kamau Brathwaite states his views on this matter bluntly:

> White creoles in the English and French West Indies have separated themselves by too wide a gulf, and have contributed too little culturally, as a *group*, to give credence to the notion that they can, given the present structure, meaningfully identify or be identified with the spiritual world on this side of the Sargasso sea.[41]

The debate surrounding her place continues to resonate and has been documented in numerous places.[42] But, for my purposes here, I want to stress that, despite such reservations, Rhys is invariably cited as a literary mother (along with the Jamaican poet and folklorist, Louise Bennett) in most accounts of Caribbean women's writing and several Caribbean women writers have emphasised the importance of Rhys's work in their own development as writers. A brief extract from Olive Senior's poem in memory of Jean Rhys, "Meditation on Red", conveys this sense of Rhys's writing as an enabling force for contemporary Caribbean women writers:

> Right now
> I'm as divided
> as you were
> by that sea.
>
> but I'll
> be able to
> find my way
> home again
>
> for that craft
> you launched
> is so seaworthy
> tighter
> than you'd ever been
>
> dark voyagers
> like me
> can feel free
> to sail.[43]

O'Callaghan's study of Caribbean women's writing includes an early chapter, "Early versions: outsiders' voices / silenced voices" in which she discusses Rhys's *Wide Sargasso Sea* but she also, more importantly, looks at a range of other early white West Indian writers (including Phyllis Allfrey) and argues that crucial insights into West Indian women's culture can be gained from such writers.[44]

In line with this, I would argue that the very polarised representations of the white creole woman, Antoinette, and the black woman, Christophine, in Rhys's *Wide Sargasso Sea*, while indicative of Rhys's ambivalent and conflicted feelings about 'race' in the West Indies of her generation,[45] should not be replicated in debates about contemporary Caribbean women's positions. In the novel, Christophine is presented as strong and earthy with a formidable presence and vocal power while Antoinette is presented as vulnerable, uncertain of her place and tentative in her speech. Where Christophine speaks forcefully, ("Woman must have spunks to live in this world", she tells Antoinette),[46] Antoinette speaks in half sentences, muttered asides and internal monologues. Rhys's white (and white creole) women are all fragile drifting creatures whose lack of agency has made them of questionable value to some feminist critics. Christophine, on the other hand, uses forceful language to challenge colonialist patriarchy in the figure of Antoinette's husband, and may appear, therefore, to be a more positive model of female agency.

This highly vocal, strong, black West Indian woman features frequently in Louise Bennett's work in poems which articulate powerfully the oppressions which the 'ordinary Jamaican woman' faces and the feisty way in which she survives and resists these challenging circumstances. As a result, her work has been consistently praised for being grounded firmly in a Jamaican context and, in her exclusive use of Creole, her work is seen as redefining, and indigenizing, the contours of 'the poetic'. Chamberlin, for example, argues: "More than any other single writer, Louise Bennett brought local language into the foreground of West Indian cultural life."[47] Another critical text, published in 1993, the same year as *Woman Version*, is Carolyn Cooper's *Noises in the Blood: Orality, Gender and the 'Vulgar' Body of Jamaican Popular Culture*.[48] But, unlike O'Callaghan's critical quest to broaden Caribbean discourse to include an earlier group of white writers whose 'race' had tended to preclude discussion of their work as part of a West Indian canon, Cooper's project is firmly located in the contemporary moment and is focused exclusively on African Jamaican popular culture.

Louise Bennett's texts are a central part of Cooper's argument and are described as "the quintessential Jamaican example of the sensitive and competent Caribbean artist consciously incorporating features of traditional oral art into the written literature"[49] and, as such, are disruptive subversions of patriarchal, scribal discourses. In Cooper's account, the polyphonic, 'slack' oral text is set against the tightly sealed and closed scribal text: "These vulgar products of illicit procreation may be conceived – in poor taste – as perverse invasions of the tightly-closed orifices of the Great Tradition."[50] The connection is then established between woman and the oral: "Transgressive Woman is Slackness personified, embodying the porous openings in the oral text",[51] and 'slackness' is defined as follows:

> Slackness is not mere sexual looseness – though it is certainly that. Slackness is a metaphorical revolt against law and order; an undermining of consensual standards of decency.[52]

Despite the seductive slackness of Cooper's own discourse, the conflation of "slack woman" with the "promiscuous oral text" results in some problematic formulations. It hinges on a questionable binary opposition between the oral and the scribal in which all oral texts are essentially subversive and all scribal texts are inherently conservative. As such, it elides the very conservative values evident in a great many of Bennett's poems and ignores the complete absence of any explicit assertion of female sexuality in Bennett's oeuvre.[53] Further, the reliance on biologistic tropes indicated in the title itself, *Noises in the Blood*, and in references to 'bloodline', 'heritage' and so on, to describe the *embodiment* of Jamaican popular culture, does suggest a problematically essentialist and exclusivist approach to 'national' culture.[54] The kind of fancy footwork which Cooper has to engage in to keep the 'slack woman' / 'slack oral text' parallel in play is under most pressure in the chapter on ragga culture, "Slackness hiding from culture: erotic play in the dancehall" in which the infamously misogynistic and homophobic lyrics of ragga – and its accompanying body language – are interpreted as evidence of black, working-class masculinity in crisis:

> Disempowered working-class men cannot be simply stigmatised and dismissed as unqualified 'oppressors' of women. Their own oppression by gender-blind classism and notions of matriarchy itself motivates their attempted oppression of women. [...] a chain of disempowerment. The raw sexism of some DJs can thus be seen as an expression of a diminished

masculinity seeking to assert itself at the most basic, and often the only level where it is allowed free play.[55]

Cooper does acknowledge that "it is the sexuality of women, much more so than that of men, which is both celebrated and devalued in the culture of the dancehall", but she explains this double take on female sexuality by arguing that the flamboyant way in which women display their bodies in the dancehall is indicative of their power:

> The dancehall is the social space in which the smell of female power is exuded in the extravagant display of flashy jewellery, expensive clothes, elaborate hairstyles and rigidly attendant men that altogether represent substantial wealth.[56]

I would argue, however, that the violent homophobia and misogyny of ragga culture cannot be satisfactorily explained away by invoking black working-class men's oppressed status. Neither can the display of women's bodies in dancehall culture be read as simply celebrating female sexuality. Cooper is right in saying that the spectacular and famously revealing clothing worn by dancehall women challenges colonially-inherited, middle-class definitions of femininity, but this is not necessarily the primary audience for such display. When this erotic display is read in the immediate arena of the dance hall itself, it is much more difficult to interpret this display of the female body as a display of female power. The documented reality suggests that it is ragga men who control what women are actually allowed to do with their bodies. The display by ragga queens of sexual power dramatized in the dance hall remains, precisely, a display of power for as long as men control the spaces and circumstances in which that power can be acted out.

In providing sustained critical attention to popular cultural forms, Cooper's pioneering work marks an important intervention in discussions about Caribbean culture. However, in generating a plethora of articles which discuss dance hall and ragga culture, and other popular cultural forms in which men are the dominant agents, her work risks skewing Caribbean discourse back to the 'men-in-crisis' paradigm of an earlier critical moment.[57] It also implies a turn away from the literary which I believe to be counterproductive. By way of contesting this, and indicating what may be lost in such arguments I would prefer that the literary possibilities suggested in the work of both Louise Bennett and Jean Rhys be kept in play. In other words, while the robust certainties and vocal power of Bennett's women personas provide inspirational models of resistance, the anxious and uncertain register of Rhys's work may also enable other literary possibilities which both affirm the power of literary discourse itself and allow for an understanding of Caribbean literary work which shifts the focus away from an exclusive emphasis on a model of 'resistance' defined in terms of a rather static and (heterosexual) male-centred understanding of 'the' anti-colonial project.

But, in addition to refusing the pressure to choose between the cultures represented by Louise Bennett and Jean Rhys, it is also important to register the women's cultures which remain invisible and inaudible as a result of these problematically opposed 'literary mothers'. These would include the specific cultures of those underrepresented ethnicities of the region: Amerindian, Indian, Chinese, Portuguese, Lebanese and so on. As Brinda Mehta argues in her recent study of Indian women writers:

> The ideological fixity of blackness has been most evident in the field of Caribbean feminism, which remained Afrocentric in its articulation and preoccupations until the mid-1980s. With some exceptions, the dominant framework of reference for feminist issues until that time continued to emphasize the experiences of black women.[58]

A more progressive definition of Caribbean women's writing would also include lesbian women's writing and culture which, until recently, has tended to be elided in the constituency, 'Caribbean women writers'. Dionne Brand, for example, in her essay, "This Body For Itself", argues that Caribbean women have focused so exclusively on the black *maternal* body that the sexual body, including the lesbian sexual body, is absent.[59]

In this regard, the work of several writers published in the last ten or so years have suggested more diverse and accommodating trajectories for Caribbean culture and writing than have so far prevailed. Several of these writers have explored the limitations of heterosexual definitions of gender roles; Shani Mootoo's, *Cereus Blooms at Night*,[60] for example, suggests that gender roles are socially constructed, and can, therefore, be deconstructed and reconstructed in creative and enabling ways. Other texts have focused on the impact of the AIDS crisis on Caribbean subjects at home and in the diaspora; for example, Patricia Powell's, *A Small Gathering of Bones*, Jamaica Kincaid's memoir, *My Brother*, and Ramabai Espinet's *The Swinging Bridge*, amongst others.[61] There is also a growing body of critical commentary supporting this writing[62] while other critics are extending the parameters of the discourse on male sexuality in provocative ways.[63] I would also suggest that it may now be timely to revisit familiar texts within the Caribbean literary canon, by both male and female writers, so that orthodox perspectives on the 'making' of Caribbean subjects can be revised and the normatively male focus of earlier commentary can be more thoroughly challenged. In the process, more flexible and enabling gender roles may be identified and a critical discourse may be generated which is as at ease with the fluid constructions of masculinities and femininities as some of the recent prose and poetry by Caribbean writers.

Notes

1 Velma Pollard: "Version": *Considering Woman*, London, 1989, n.p.
2 George Lamming: "Concepts of the Caribbean". – In Frank Birbalsingh (Ed.), *Frontiers of Caribbean Literature in English*, London, 1996, p. 2.
3 John Edward Chamberlin: *Come Back to Me My Language: Poetry and the West Indies*, Urbana, 1993, p. 1.
4 Peter Wilson: *Crab Antics: The Social Anthropology of English-Speaking Negro Societies in the Caribbean*, New Haven, 1973.
5 Jean Besson: "Reputation and Respectability Reconsidered: A New Perspective on Afro-Caribbean Women". – In Janet H. Momsen (Ed.): *Women and Change in the Caribbean*, London, 1992, p. 30.
6 Richard D. E. Burton: *Afro-Creole: Power, Opposition and Play in the Caribbean*, New York, 1997.
7 Christian Habekost: *Dub Poetry: 19 Poets From England and Jamaica*, Neustadt, 1986, p. 36.
8 Barbara Bush: *Slave Women in Caribbean Societies 1650 – 1838*, Bloomington, 1990.
9 Grace Nichols: *i is a long memoried woman*, London, 1983, p. 23.
10 Christine Barrow (Ed.): *Caribbean Portraits: Essays on Gender Ideologies and Identities*, Kingston, Jamaica, 1998, p. xvii.
11 By far the largest numbers of indentured labourers were taken to Guyana and Trinidad.
12 Olive Senior: *The Snake-Woman and Other Stories*, London, 1989, p. 3.

13 Hilary Beckles: "Sex and Gender in the Historiography of Caribbean Slavery". – In V. Shepherd & B. Brereton & B. Bailey (Eds.): *Engendering History*, Kingston & London, 1995, p. 127.
14 Lloyd Brown: *West Indian Poetry*, p. 1.
15 Denise deCaires Narain: *Caribbean Women's Poetry: Making Style*, London, 2002, p. 5.
16 Claude McKay: "If We Must Die". – In Paula Burnett (Ed.): *The Penguin Book of Caribbean Verse in English*, London, 1986, p. 144.
17 See Alison Donnell: "Sentimental Subversion: The Poetry and Politics of Devotion in the Work of Una Marson". – In V. Bertram (Ed.): *Kicking Daffodils: Twentieth-Century Women Poets*, Edinburgh, 1997, pp. 113-124; and Denise deCaires Narain, *Caribbean Women's Poetry*, Chapter 1.
18 Paula Burnett (Ed.): *The Penguin Book of Caribbean Verse in English*, London, 1986, p. 158.
19 Bongo Jerry: "Mabrak". Reprinted in Burnett (Ed.): *The Penguin Book of Caribbean Verse*, p. 70.
20 Laurence Breiner: "How to Behave on Paper: The *Savacou* Debate", *Journal of West Indian Literature* 6:1, 1993, 1-10.
21 Derek Walcott: "The Schooner Flight". – In D. W.: *Collected Poems 1948 - 1984*, New York, 1986, pp. 345-361.
22 Edward Kamau Brathwaite: *The Arrivants: A New World Trilogy*, London, 1978 [1967], p. 30.
23 Sam Selvon: *The Lonely Londoners*, London, 1956.
24 Most of the men in the street have nicknames which signal their aspirations to transcend their 'real' identities and become 'heroes'.
25 V. S. Naipaul: *Miguel Street*, London, 1971, p. 14.
26 *Ibid.*, 17.
27 *Ibid.*, 123.
28 Wilson Harris's essay, "The Womb of Space" explicitly develops ideas related to 'the feminine principle'.
29 Burnett: *The Penguin Book of Caribbean Verse*, p. 430.
30 David Dabydeen: "Slave Song". – In D. D.: *Turner: New and Selected Poems*, London, 1994 [originally published in *Slave Song*, 1984], p. 46.
31 *Ibid.*, 47.
32 Robert Antoni: *Blessed is the Fruit*, London, 1998.
33 Pamela Mordecai & Mervyn Morris (Eds.): *Jamaica Woman: An Anthology of Poems*, London, 1980.
34 Louise Bennett: *Selected Poems*. Ed. Mervy Morris, Kingston, Jamaica, 1982, p. 23.
35 *Ibid.*, 11.
36 Mordecai & Morris (Eds.): *Jamaica Woman*, p. 101.
37 Carole Boyce Davies & Elaine Savory Fido (Eds.): *Out of the Kumbla: Caribbean Women and Literature*, New Jersey, 1990, p. 17.
38 *Ibid.*, "Talking It Over: Womanism, Writing and Feminism", pp. ix-xx.

39 "'Beyond Miranda's Meanings': Un/silencing the 'Demonic Ground' of Caliban's 'Woman'". – In *ibid.*, 355-372. Sylvia Wynter is well-known as a cultural commentator but she is also one of the few women to have published a novel in the 1960s: *The Hills of Hebron*, New York, 1962.

40 Evelyn O'Callaghan: *Woman Version: Theoretical Approaches to West Indian Fiction by Women*, London, 1993, p. 1.

41 Edward Kamau Brathwaite: *Contradictory Omens*, Kingston, 1974, p. 38.

42 For a succinct overview of these debates by Peter Hulme, followed by Brathwaite's response, and a further commentary by Elaine Savory Fido, Evelyn O'Callaghan & Denise deCaires Narain, see *Wasafiri*, 20, Autumn 1994, 5-11; *Wasafiri*, 21, Spring 1995, 69-78; *Wasafiri*, 28, Autumn 1998, 33-38.

43 Olive Senior: *Gardening in the Tropics*, Toronto, 1994, pp. 51-52.

44 See E. O'Callaghan: *A Hot Place, Belonging to Us*, London, 2004 for a book-length discussion of the work of early white West Indian women's writing.

45 See Veronica Gregg's excellent study of Rhys: *Jean Rhys's Historical Imagination: Reading and Writing the Creole*, Chapel Hill & London, 1995.

46 Jean Rhys: *Wide Sargasso Sea*, Harmondsworth, 1968 [1966], p. 84.

47 J. Edward Chamberlin: *Come Back To Me My Language*, Toronto, 1993, p. 95.

48 Carolyn Cooper: *Noises in the Blood: Orality, Gender and the 'Vulgar' Body of Jamaican Popular Culture*, London, 1993.

49 *Ibid.*, 39.

50 *Ibid.*, 9.

51 *Ibid.*, 11.

52 *Ibid.*, 141.

53 See Louise Bennett: *Jamaica Labrish: Jamaica Dialect Poems*. Ed. Rex Nettleford, Kingston, 1966; and *Selected Poems*. Ed. Mervyn Morris, Kingston, 1982.

54 To be fair, Cooper does acknowledge this issue of essentialism, Cooper: *Noises in the Blood*, p. 4: "The emotive trope of blood and bone connotes what may be constructed as 'racist' assumptions about biologically-determined culture, if the label is applied by the alienating Other. Assumed by the in-group, this figure of speech denotes a genealogy of ideas, a blood-line of beliefs and practices that are transmitted in the body, in oral discourse. However, invoking notions of an 'in-group' which revolves around a 'blood-line' does appear to fix the boundaries of the 'in-group' in relation to a black, nationalist Jamaican identification; a paradigm which is limited in both sociopolitical and aesthetic terms, given the diverse ethnicities encompassed in the region."

55 *Ibid.*, 164-165.

56 *Ibid.*, 5.

57 See several contributions to a 'Special Topic on Jamaican popular Culture'. – In Carolyn Cooper & Alison Donnell (Eds.): *Interventions* 16:1, 2004 and

the special issue on "Genders and Sexualities". Ed. Faith Smith, *Small Axe*, 7, March 2000 for further discussions and, recently, Carolyn Cooper: *Sound Clash. Jamaican Dance Culture at Large*, New York, 2004.

58 Brinda Mehta: *Diasporic (Dis)Locations: Inoi-Caribbean Women Writers Negotiate the Kala Pani*, Kingston, 2005, p. 13.

59 Dionne Brand: *Bread Out Of Stone: Recollections, Sex, Recognitions, Race, Dreaming Politics*, Toronto, 1994, pp. 9-49.

60 Shani Mootoo: *Cereus Blooms at Night*, London, 1999.

61 Patricia Powell: *A Small Gathering of Bones*, Oxford, 1994; Jamaica Kincaid: *My Brother*, New York, 1997; Ramabai Espinet: *The Swinging Bridge*, Toronto, 2003.

62 See also: the issues of *Interventions* and *Small Axe*, cited above; see also, Evelyn O'Callaghan's "Heterosexuality and Sexual / Textual Alternatives". – In C. Barrow (Ed.): *Caribbean Portraits: Essays on Gender Ideologies and Identities*, pp. 294-319; and Alison Donnell: *Twentieth-Century Caribbean Literature: Critical Moments in Anglophone Literary History*. London, 2005, pp. 181-249.

63 See for example, Jahaji Bhai: "Notes on the Masculine Subject and Homoerotic Subtext of Indo-Caribbean Identity", *Small Axe*, 7, March 2000, 77-92, and Wesley Crichlow: *Buller Men & Batty Bwoys. Hidden Men in Toronto and Halifax Black Communities*, Toronto, 2004, amongst others.

Keith Sandiford (Baton Rouge, LA)

Mapping the Caribbean: Ligon's Map and *History* – Cartographies of Emergent Knowledge in Early Barbados

Illustration 1: Richard Ligon, *A Topographical Description and Admeasurement of the Island of Barbados in the West Indies* (c. 1651); courtesy of the Bryn Mawr College Library, Gift of Louise Bulkley Dillingham, 1916.

1. Introduction

Viewed in a common relationship of map to text, Richard Ligon's *A Topographical Description and Admeasurement of the Island of Barbados in the West Indies* (c. 1651; see illustration 1) appears on its face to serve the conventional purposes of providing cartographic visualization, illustration and complement to his *True and Exact History of the Island of Barbados* (1657).[1] The one contained within the other, map prefigures text in mimetic images that depict the face and state of colonization on the island in literal, living and lively terms. A painter by training and practice, Ligon uses his artistic skill to shape the viewer's perceptions of 'settlement' by rendering Barbados in scenes of dramatic human movement and purposeful activity, both cooperating to produce an overall effect of complex spatial relations. The artistic practices so deployed invest the map with a stark mimeticism which provides the starting point for the ensuing discussion on different ways of seeing the map-text reciprocity in Ligon's work. This essay aims to explore the reciprocal relations between map and text to recover the discursive possibilities that lie beyond its merely illustrative and complementary uses.

Preceding the *History* by about seven years, the map supplies a richly suggestive pretext to the historical narrative. On a formal level, the map pretextualizes certain organic themes and structures to be figured more fully in the discursive production of Barbados for an English audience. In another sense of pretext, the map proffers its narrative of race, work, slavery, and ecological relationships in terms that are naturalized, prescriptive, and consistent with the ethics of originating new cultural forms and values on a colonial frontier. In this sense the map appears to conform to its primary functional expectations as a juridical, normative, objectively precise document. The *History* in its turn, as the earliest documentary source for knowledge about the island, appropriates a variety of metaphors of mapping which ironize specific relations of the map itself, even as it maps out discrete spaces from the cartographic imaging on the map to produce colonizing as a process that is decidedly more subject to the agencies of dynamic history than the map might disclose. Those terms define a tension between the map as a framed object and framing agent on the one hand, and the figural maps and mapping practices recoverable within a discursive text on the other.[2]

To produce some deeper understanding of these new definitions and relationships, I will adopt in this essay a methodology that pushes the terms 'map' and 'mapping' beyond their commonplace references to physical relationships, beyond delineating or plotting objects or processes within and across space. I will call my method 'cultural mapping' and will situate it at the intersection of cartography, historiography and cultural discourse. So defined cultural mapping will specify critical practices and theoretical frameworks that will elucidate the dynamics of the relationship between map and text. It will transgress the normative presumptions of both those ways of inscribing. It will prefer instead suggestive permutations that disclose relationships elided by the map but included or implied in the text. Cultural mapping reveals how the disciplinary desires of the map are crossed by the expanding materialist impulses of those very elites whose will to power are inscribed in the pursuit of enforcing those disciplines. The unfolding of the implications of that crossing can only be fully laid out by practices (narrative and critical) that recover the deeper meanings of the map in the exploration of the text. Cartographic discourse in the historical text utilizes for content the excess of the map's essence. Since the essence of the map is always already contestable, the historical discourse assimilates from the map that which is unstable, irrepressible, and incommensurable – the unrepresentable of the objective world the map seeks to represent.

In my closest alignment to their common geographical sense, I shall use the terms 'mapping' and 'cultural mapping' as conceptual strategies to disclose forms, features and functions of the linear historical narrative within the text. More to the point of establishing their utility in qualifying the *History* as discourse, throughout this essay I shall differentiate between the work of traditional map production and the ensemble of cartographic practices embedded in the text. In this application, the terms 'mapping' and 'cultural mapping' will refer to figurally differentiated processes operating within the *History,* and will code the critical and theoretically informed methodologies adopted in this essay. This definitional distinction should be understood to designate the ways in which Ligon's text both departs from the constrictions of the map and deconstructs the map's temporally marked subjectivities, In addition, cultural mapping will trace the value sets distinguishing Ligon's historiographical ethic by illustrating the biases which the *History* critiques, those it accommodates, and the new ones it invents, even as it adapts all these to meet rapidly changing conditions. This appropriating of the dual theorizing potential of mapping will serve at once to reveal the designs of the *History* and the historian, and my critical interest in both. For Ligon's *History* it will extend the theoretical possibilities of approaching the text as a historiographical narrative with undisguised colonialist objectives. For my concurrent critical purposes, it will rethink those colonialist objectives so as to align them more closely within the invention of a specific class-based subjectivity, one less subservient to traditional notions of subjecthood

What follows in the next section is an attempt to contextualize the map-text tension and to map out the broader conceptual and theoretical bases for the critique of cultural mapping I apply to Ligon's *History*. I shall draw mainly on scholarship from the history of cartography, from cultural and post-colonial theory practitioners whose growing interest in cartographic models over the last decade have made mapping an attractive model for exploring power and knowledge in colonial texts, among others.

From their origins in antiquity until the present, maps have served the important functions of marking territory, recording graphic inventories of natural and artificial features in a given territorial space and imaging the tendency of human agents to reshape that space according to their will and desire. Mapmakers like Ligon, therefore, had to respond to multiple layers of complexity engendered by the physical territory they represented and the needs of the vested interests they served. In the service of such complexity they had over time to reduce nature and culture to codifiable imaging on a flat surface, to evolve a taxonomy for diverse geographic and political formations. For powerful vested interests and knowledge workers alike both of those demands excited and answered the need to bring the unknown into consciousness. Cartography thus offered these interests and their affiliated elites knowledge; knowledge vested power; power afforded control.[3] Right through the growth of New World colonization in the seventeenth century that nexus of knowledge, power and control restricted to exclusive elites the access and the effective ability to translate them into political, economic and ultimately imperial advantages. In an illuminating statement about this nexus and its restrictive ambit, J. B. Harley points out that the map came to reify its own value, to legitimize the status quo and to freeze the reality it depicted.[4] These last three effects place in sharp relief the tension between the categorical and geometrically inscribed frames of the Ligon map and the more fluid dynamism of the historical text.

If the referenced practices and uses of cartography validate the axiom that the power to map conferred the power to control , an equally powerful deduction especially compelling for this map-text relationship is Harley's sobering assessment that maps are subjective, subject to bias, value-laden and quite liable to suppress and exclude.[5]

This distinction intimates the nature of discourse constituted in the *History*, and positions the author's related preoccupations with discipline, knowledge and power in a counter-discursive relationship with traditional subjecthood. In so far as the *History* gathers into one the pursuit of new knowledge, the norms of relations within specific systems of power and the ethics of a class-interested disciplinary order, the text in itself constitutes the definition of discourse as Foucault has formulated that concept. For Foucault, discourse produces power and knowledge even as it is created, projected and circulated within a given social field by those (more systems and anonymous structures than indviduals) best positioned to exert dominance and control.[6]

In the *History*, Ligon persistently ascribes the effects of positive production in early colonial Barbados to the knowledge, power and discipline of a specific class. This legitimating of social identities from new marginal sources rather than from central norms attenuates the links that held emergent colonial classes bound to a subjecthood under a monarchical system and a rigid aristocratic order. This largely covert design at once reproduces and transmutes the term discourse. My objective will be to read the *History*, in Foucauldian terms, as a discourse produced within the prevailing political and cultural orders of seventeenth century English colonialism but also, because so situated, capable of definition analytically as a counterdiscourse, a source of alternative resistance, producing new knowledge, new sources of power, new orders of discipline. In particular in this essay I shall be most interested in those ways in which the discourse governs the individual subjects of the *History*. I shall be interested in how counterdiscourse reinscribes them as agents of emergent forms of new cultural power. This convergence of methodologies will permit us to trace in the *History* the discursive maps of agency and subjectivity, and to (re)construct the power / knowledge nexus in which those subjects are linked and controlled.[7] With respect to discipline, the cultural cartography of the *History* maps an ethics of disciplinary order consistent with the Foucaultian norms that define discipline as a strategy for governing bodies and instituting domination in a specific social field. An important expression of discursive power, this discipline in the *History* is understood to be both conscious and unconscious.[8] In its conscious presentations, this discipline is expressed as the irrefragable criterion for the order of life and the predicates of wealth-creation in a nascent colony. In its unconscious forms, it is apprehended, in Foucault' terms, "circulating in the social field", attached to strategies of domination and resistance.[9] Of these dualistic functions in discourse, Foucault emphasized that "we must make allowance for the complex and unstable process whereby discourse can be both an instrument and an effect of power [...] Discourse transmits and produces power; it reinforces it, but it also undermines and exposes it, renders it fragile and makes it possible to thwart it [...] there can exist different and even contradictory discourses within the same strategy".[10]

It is this dialectical or self-destabilizing structure that I am especially concerned with in Ligon's *History.* In terms specifically articulated to cartography, Harley offers a view that repeats the points of subtlety and invisible agency intrinsic to Foucault's conception: Harley emphasizes that maps are capable of producing 'hidden rules' in cartographic discourse whose contours can be traced in the subliminal geometries, in the silences and the representational hierarchies of maps.[11] As this essay theorizes the *History* as a map of culture, it discloses the operation of those "hidden rules" in the process of implanting Old World social entities in a New World spatial order. Here the 'subliminal geometries' may be realized by pursuing the significance of spatialization in the constitution of identities for the disparate groups involved in colonial production. In *Out of Place,* Ian Baucom treats spatialization as a central determining figure in the ordering and control of nineteenth and twentieth century colonial spaces, and he has identified the role early colonial histories play in enacting a "cartography of culture and discipline".[12] I find his work valuable for these connections, but for my present purposes I want to push its implications much farther back to support my concern here with the formation of British identities in colonial Barbados. Both terms, culture and discipline, become inscribed as contested sites very early in colonial discourse. As Koch has shown, that contestation grew all the more intense as the development of cartographic mapping led to the increasing legitimation of private and class claims to power on the basis of individual property rights and a corresponding erosion of monarchical power.[13] This tension produces a specific critique about the formation of British identities in colonial Barbados. A peculiar ethic of consensus and apolitical coexistence kept the old Royalist-Parliamentarian partisanship in remission, and spurred instead an impetus towards independence and self-rule.[14] This identity question has certain implications for my present theoretical reading of Ligon. The *History* has to take account of a greater variety and complexity of spatial contents than the map, and thus must widen its scope to include a view of social and moral relations between diverse human agents. As deployed in this essay, cultural mapping will allow us to chart these relations by doing what Melba Cuddy Keane defines as "tracking multiple coordinates, [and] tracing multiple encounters." A cultural mapping of the text will include a definition of spatialization which situates the colonial self in relation to other identities and other spaces, and computes the difference all that makes.[15] Reading cartography 'out of' Ligon's *History* disrupts the fixed presumptive authority of Ligon's map. Applying a critique of cultural mapping to the discursive content of the *History* reveals larger multiple disciplinary spheres and the spatialization of identities and interests within those spheres. What is being proposed, then, is to bring the *History* within the readable scope and purview of contemporary theoretical and interpretive practices so selected as to deepen and expand our understanding of its significant cultural politics.

2. Desiring the Land, Mapping the Desire for Land

In keeping with some standard definitions offered for the basic nature and functions of maps, Ligon's map of Barbados may be reduced to three key functions: it is geographical, it is cadastral and it is proprietary. The geographical identity is discerned from its positioning within an ocean space which it shares with sailing vessels and large deep sea fish. That rubric would therefore include and subsume the label 'topographical' which Ligon himself used in categorizing the map. As such, the map fixes the location of and assigns names to particular places, shows significant landforms, and documents the incidence and distribution of flora and fauna. The cadastral functions of the map are notional and rudimentary. Though individual plantation holdings are only indicated by a notional building image, the deliberate labelling of each building with the owner's name, the indices of land use and the dimensions of holdings, in particular a large expanse in the middle of the map ("ten thousand acres belonging to the Merchants of London"), furnish the early references for later more detailed survey mapping of ownership and revenue activities. Similarly, the narrowly defined proprietary nature of the map lacks high resolution as to distinct boundary marks and measurements, but the location of plantation holdings by simple denomination performed the legitimating and validating functions necessary to establish ownership claims. In this respect the regular layout of the earlier mentioned plantation structures points to the density of settlement along the leeward coastal lands stretching from Macock (Maycocks in present day St Lucy) to Austin's Bay (Oistins in present day Christ Church). Such advertisement served the dual purpose of staking English claims against the designs of colonial rivals, and directing the gaze of prospective settlers towards areas of the map, especially in the extreme southern and central parts of the island, that remained unsettled or only sparsely inhabited.

Besides these mainly physical functions, images appearing on the map inscribe larger social, economic and strategic themes. Five themes concern us here: work, slavery, hunting, seaborne access and food supply. For the frequency of its occurrence, work outranks all the others in the images that render its objective performance and in those that suggest it. The extent of plantation activity suggested only by architectural form and spatial density elides the nature of the economies of labour and power that defined early colonial production in the island. Where work is given an animate face, it is represented as an activity shared between man and beast (men and camels, men and burros). Human figures depicted in the motions of work are shown driving beasts of burden or loading pack animals. Noteworthy in these images is the clear race- and class-based division of the labour so performed. White men are distinguished from other races shown elsewhere on the map. They are shown with bodies properly covered by clothes of a plain utilitarian quality as exemplified by the white men driving camels or loading burros (note: at this point in Barbados history, these were likely to be white indentured servants.[16] Black slave figures are mapped with bodies bare except for loin cloths. As a theme, slavery establishes its presence by an arresting image depicted in the northeast corner of the map. Coded with the signs of race, power and disputed liberty, the image shows a white man mounted on a charging horse in full pursuit of two black slaves in flight. The white man figures dominance and authority by the distinction of his dress, by the power exuding from the horse's charge and by the instrument he wields in his right hand. That instrument represents the dual values of interdiction and discipline mapped into the European consciousness at least from feudal times through to this emergent moment of plantation slavery in the New World. The black slaves are clearly exhilarated in their bid for freedom but their strides are drawn to look almost stylized and theatrical. Thus by a trick of aesthetic ambivalence they are rendered effete and liable to apprehension within the next gallop. The third theme repeats the hunting motif just as it reproduces similar relations of dominance, class and predation. These relations clearly evoke Foucault's "subliminal geographies". Mapped at the other end of an imaginary straight line from the preceding image, a mirror image drawn in the southeast corner shows two white men mounted on galloping horses hunting wild hogs. Just as they are collinear in geometric relation, so these two images figure equal ratios in the moral cartography of the value system the map fixes and perpetuates. A line drawn to run westward from the point where the hogs are cornered passes through other food sources (sheep). A further line drawn from the sheep to run in a southerly direction will touch a yoke of oxen. A third line pushes the trajectory back to the eastern end. Those lines together triangulate an advertisement for the sources of the colony's food supply and its technology of work (oxen); the cartographic sign of hunting advertises ownership as the preserve of the colony's early proprietary elites and the prerogative of an English monarch.[17]

The fourth theme gathers into one the map's propagandistic desires to project political power and to advertise social and economic opportunity. On the coastal margins of the map the strategic placement of naval and mercantile vessels impress upon the observer's eye not only the accessibility of the island location but, more to the point of the political propaganda function of the map, the readiness and capability of the colonial power to defend it. Accessibility advertises the interest of common landholders in attracting indentured labour to the plantations, and of more powerful economic elites in luring prospective investors to the commerce and trade that would flow from the colony's productive and consumptive economies.

Among the conventional signs found on typical early modern maps, ships in ports were understood to be signifiers of commercial power.[18]

That survey of the map's properties may be synthesized into the following points. The cartographic methods that produced the map make it a geometrical construct: Drawn to scale, the map partly attains and partly assumes certain values of linearity and regularity. In its social dimensions, the map paints a highly separable world, its human constituents differentiated by their roles and positionings in discrete spheres of action. Driven by these practices and presuppositions the map figures a closed system, its spheres of action fixed and determined; its nascent and inherent politics exclusive and hierarchical. In its turn, the *History*, as text, inaugurates a discourse that modulates and revises the authority of the map because the text by its very definition and functions must take aim at a moving target, an unfolding dynamic of forces of such diversity and novelty as to outstrip the knowledge and objectives of the map. The text inscribes but also revises the values and functions of discourse. By assuming the character of discourse, the text spatializes the map's restrictive semiosis as the map's images enter the text's field of consciousness defined as historical discourse. By this analytical light the map is reduced to its function as a frame. An artefact of time and subjectivity, the map is itself relative to the moment of its production. As such, it may accommodate but not absolutely contain the encounters and productions it seems to freeze in place. Notwithstanding the compartmentalizing tendencies of its aesthetics or its social ideology, its contents may spill over or extrude those boundaries. As the colonial body grows, its spatial arrangements must shift and redress to accommodate its growth. The shift from the map as absolute bearer of cartographic truth to the text as a site for production of cartographic discourse discloses the fluidity of the colonial body and the map's incapability to contain it within its original limits.

3. Cartographies of History: Cultural Mapping as Critique

Where figures on the map are locked in place by ideologies of race and class, cartographic discourse in the text transforms those fixed zones of exclusion and control into spaces of production. This transformation works in complex ways. One of these may be illustrated by the apparent stable fixity of the map's imagery. In the centre of the map a single indigenous figure stands guard with a bow. Assisted by the critical practices of cultural mapping, we experience that figure not merely as a native insider now become estranged outsider, but in a more striking revelation as a vanishing entity soon to be categorically displaced by inflows of African slaves. As slave numbers increased, their presence and impact in the emerging colonial society could no longer be contained within the prescribed limits represented by the map's topographical walls. As representation, the map's figure of the black slave carrying a pointed staff, hemmed in by a range of hills on one side and the roaring Atlantic on the other, will be both illuminated and ironized by its textualization in the history.

The passage from map to history alters the value of the slave from an isolated circumscribed quantity to a necessary, central, constitutive body distributed across the landscape of the emergent colony. The terms necessary and constitutive are not meant to distort or misrepresent the privilege or power of slaves in early Barbados. They are meant to reemphasize the slaves' social visibility and economic significance within the limits placed on their freedom and autonomy. Remapped within the discursive space of the *History*, these revised values and functions may be appraised through the explanatory force of spatialization. Theorized to open up a closed system and to stretch definitions of identity, spatialization illuminates one of those transdisciplinary intersections referred to above.[19] As Ligon's narrative would chart with eyewitness authority, sugar production in Barbados would decidedly redraw the cultural map of the colony. While on the 1650 map, sugar's presence and future promise are understated by the neat symbolic containment in regularly spaced buildings and sparse distribution of windmills and factories, the *History* would map the sugar narrative in a form of discursive cartography that images a geography of breached cultural frontiers. The peculiar labour requirements of the crop would be used as an argument for the necessity to deracinate and commodify Africans for slave functions in colonial domains. The need for a middle tier of managers and overseers would drive the demand for white indentured labour.

An already dwindling indigenous population would be entirely displaced in Barbados by these white and black racial transplants. In due course the personal and social relationships forged among these diverse groups would transgress age-old lines of race and class. Their original identities would gradually be spatialized: transmuted by the daily performance of their individual selves, their multiplicitous encounters with others, and by the relationship of those performances and encounters to colonized space.[20] The subjective voice of the historian would persist in ascribing the flourishing growth of the colony to an intrinsic essence and ethical virtue to be found in its English inhabitants. That voice would imagine the measure of the colony's Englishness to be found in those "men of piercing sights and profound judgments" (96) like his employer Thomas Modyford, his employer's partner, William Hilliard, and another powerful landowner, James Drax, credited as the founder of Barbados' sugar industry. But even in a narrative of growth and leadership that emphasises the distinctions claimed for this moment and these men, the effects of spatialization reshape a cultural map in which original English identity is crossed into so many new permutations, neither the objective cartography of the map nor the more fluid cartography of historical discourse can confidently or stably locate or institute them. The *History*'s account of specific colonial relationships negotiated by Ligon's patron Modyford sketch a cultural map that illustrates how the space traditionally marked for English social and cultural identity was being reshaped by crossings revealed by the shift from the representations of the map to the discourse of history.

Modiford's story strikingly illustrates the concept of identity spatialization defined through social and political negotiation. A refugee from the losing Royalist cause, once landed in Barbados, Modyford demonstrated certifiable frontier enterprise in his business dealings and political manoeuvres. By a shrewd purchase agreement, Modyford negotiated a fifty per cent partnership in a five hundred acre plantation that made him one of the wealthiest men in the colony. By astute manipulations of his location at the margins, he traded his political sympathies back and forth between Royalist and Cromwellian lines. He exploited his remoteness from the visible gaze of power brokers in the Protectorate (and later the restored monarchy) to advance his political ambitions to the highest offices in the colony, first councillor (1651), then Speaker of the Assembly (1652), then Governor of the island (1660).[21] That story repeats the *History*'s larger project of culturally mapping Englishness beyond its native boundaries. Within the pages of a cartographic text, this account of an evolving identity mirrors changes that were taking shape in mapping practices starting in the sixteenth century. As Richard Helgerson has shown, these changes had the effect of "strengthening local and national identity at the expense of an identity based on dynastic loyalty."[22] Contracted to the particular conditions emerging around Modiford and fellow colonists, Ligon's historical account shows that they manoeuvred themselves to demand increasing degrees of self-determination and political autonomy as their ownership of land brought them power and that power diminished the sway of the sovereign authority (Parliament / King) in England.

Thus recovered in the discursive formations of the *History*, spatialization helps to invent history as a different kind of cultural map. Ligon intimates the constitutive power of spatialization in his willingness to mark crossing and diversity as the sources of the colony's strength and progress. It is a spatializing dynamic that drives his impulse to rationalize the inequalities that were naturalized on the map. In the case of his patron, Ligon remaps the sources and traditions of leadership by a mode of spatialization that figures performances within and across space by crossing energy with imagination, political risk with opportunity, metropolitan identity with colonial experience.

4. The Counterdiscursive Turn

This conception of the shape and constitution of colonial cultural space positions the *History* in a counterdiscursive relationship to the map. As counterdiscourse, the *History* re-theorizes, critiques, and remaps the original geographical construction of Barbados into a complex signifying ideological system, a cultural sign constituted by the transforming identities of its local vested interests. In this part of my essay, cultural mapping will serve to recover the ways of thinking and meaning, and the shape of the conscious and unconscious mind that validate the text's identity as counterdiscourse. Before outlining those distinctive values, it must be emphasized that discourses themselves are not internally consistent, nor inherently impenetrable, nor immune to disruption or contestation. If, with respect to the relations of Ligon's writing, we can see the historiographical practices and the class ideology that existed around it as discursive fields, then both the process and effects of elaborating the *History* would in Foucault's terms, contain "a number of competing and contradictory discourses with varying degrees of power to give meaning to and organize social institutions and processes."[23] It is this competing and contradictory resistance that brings about change, and that change initiates counterdiscourse

We can now therefore outline from the *History* those subversive or contradictory practices that unfix or render unstable the dominant forces that set in motion and circumscribe the originating discourse. These main points mark the dimensions of counterdiscourse in the *History.* (1) A specific selection and emphasis of new knowledges and narrative details marks its impulse to theorize new social forms and legitimize cultural difference. (2) In its discursive practices it displays a willingness to critique pre-established hierarchies and to dissent from the moral and ethical codes that sustain them. (3) As a primordially important founding document for bringing Barbados into Western consciousness, it shifts the sources of knowledge and, indivisibly, the bases of power. (4) As counterdiscourse, it celebratorily represents colonial reality as marked by material multiplicity, racial and social diversity, and the innovative enterprising ethics that would prefigure a world system of empire. (5) The *History* identifies itself with an economy of circulation which places it at sharp variance with specific ideologies of its day.

This resistance to ideology may be contextualized by reference to two postcolonial theoretical interpretations of cartographic tropes in Caribbean writing and one specific applied example drawn from Ligon's text. Wilson Harris formulates a relation between colonial maps and colonial histories that at once illuminates and lends validity to the thesis I have undertaken here. He treats both cartographic maps and cartographic histories with equal scepticism about their pretensions to truth, exactitude and 'synchronic essentialism', preferring instead to locate their value and meaning in interstices and structures of transformation and revision such as I have defined for Ligon's map and *History* respectively.[24] In his book *Caribbean English Passages*, Tobias Doering acknowledges the value of Harris' ideas in shaping his methodology, one that contests the "homogenizing, unitary power of colonial representation"[25] and places colonial cartographies in a 'third space', an interstitial category between the pre-colonial and the postcolonial.[26] It is in such a space that my method of cultural mapping locates the cartographic structures and functions of Ligon's text, and from there that its authority as counterdiscourse derives. For writers like Ligon, the third space may be shown to precede the postcolonial: in the *History* the Barbadian colonists are so situated as to alienate the land both from its indigenous inhabitants as well as from the colonists' overlords, the early modern political authority at the power centre back in imperial London.

Selection and emphasis of new knowledges and narrative details within the *History* serve to produce counterdiscourse in the way those contents dispose the text to function as a speculative and projective instrument. This speculative and projective dimension constitutes a cultural map and may be measured in the *History*'s disposition to theorize the possibilities of engineering the social form of Barbados' nascent colonial culture. This disposition exceeds the limits of the map but maps out in the text some very well defined physical, physiological and temperamental attributes for prospective settlers.[27] For the exacting demands of sugar cultivation in Barbados, Ligon maps out of Africa male bodies that meet the colony's needs for sturdy, well built physiques, and vigorous constitutions. He produces those bodies to add an even higher cultural value by directly associating them with the idealized bodily specimens drawn from the canvases of the European painters Dürer and Titian. Though he does not set the physical standard quite so high for white male bodies, he does insist on some very strict rules of moral and ethical conduct. A stern admonition was enjoined on sybarites and mere pleasure seekers:

> These are of sluggish humour and are altogether unfit for so noble an undertaking; but if any such shall happen to come there, he shall be transmitted to the innumerable army of Pismires, and Ants, to sting him with such a reproof, as he shall wish himselfe anywhere rather than amongst them so much is a sluggard destested in that countrey, where Industry and Activity is to be exercised. (p. 108).

These criteria for screening the temperaments of colonists would ensure their fitness for work and survival on an emerging colonial frontier. This process constructs a founding historical discourse for Barbados that emphasizes the types the early vested interests in the colony were anxious to exclude. Beyond the somatic and the temperamental, the discourse prescribes and proscribes the kinds of sports and recreations judged appropriate for the colony. Ligon expressly names hunting, coursing and hawking as sports categorically unsuited to colonial Barbados. And he makes favourable and specific mention of leaping, wrestling and fencing as desirable sports and pastimes.[28] The list of exclusions sets its face firmly against upper class entitlement and privilege. If the map and the text give proof enough of race and class inequalities, the work of mapping out the foundations of cultural history spatializes the traditional social order of Englishness by tipping the normal balance of privilege away from hereditary and titled aristocracy towards white men of middling to modest means, with certifiable enterprising spirit in matters of politics and economics.

This conception of the shape and constitution of colonial cultural space positions the *History* as a counterdiscursive critique of the map. As counterdiscourse, the *History* critiques, remaps and retheorizes the geographical construct of Barbados in sharp political opposition to the limited policies and purposes of King (Charles I) and Protector (Cromwell). In concert with other early colonial commentators, Ligon pointedly notes that the early progress and political reputation of Barbados suffered from the king's imprudent grant of the proprietorship to an inept favourite, the earl of Carlisle, and from Cromwell's moral cartographic depiction of the place as a dunghill on which to dump vagabonds, convicts and political exiles. The *History* critiques these policies directly by calling attention to the presence of their moral opposites in the investor and landowning classes (men of piercing sights etc) already *in situ*, and indirectly by proscribing the slothful, the feckless, and those least amenable to an ethic of labour and industry. With this production of moral and physical constitutions, the text remaps the cartographic design of the 1650 map. Those largely unsettled spaces in the southern, eastern and central parts of the island can be re-imagined in a cartographic gesture that settles them with bodies best suited to meet the demands of such labour. Such manifest privileging of an entrepreneurial ethos at the level of the daily lived reality of colonial life finds its discursive expression in a distinct turn of the text toward a speculative and projective re-theorizing of the colony's economic geography.

The conditions of production that impinged on Ligon's writing (eyewitness, New World colonialism, emergent capitalism) marked a radical departure from prior traditions of writing. That departure shifts the bases of knowledge and distributes the sources of power with crucial consequences for interests at both centre and margins. These shifts were to radically transform the concepts of empire and its contingent relations with the colony, especially as that transformation was reflected in seventeenth century political economy and colonial Barbados.[29] Map and text reflect these shifts in the illustrations that follow. A distinctly sharper lens, powered by a progressive image of the productive linkages between colony and metropole, reveals some significant revisions in those resource and supply lines traced earlier on the map. Where those triangular spaces on the map suggest a cartography of containment and isolation based on a fiction of internal sufficiency the text's turn towards an economic exposition engages a counterdiscourse which opens up those lines and extends them outwards to England. As the imperial centre, England would be the source of investment capital, the recruiting ground for settlers and indentures, and the market source for a whole range of supplies for sustaining life and productive activities within the colony. In Foucaultian terms, the *History* reveals its nature as counterdiscourse in the contrast to be observed between the old definitions of sovereign power (King and Protector) and in the new relations and practices to be negotiated and instituted between this new emergent economy of production carried on among entrepreneurs, landowning classes, indentureds, slave owners and slaves.

Where on the map individual structures historicize a phase of small freehold economy, the text demonstrates the considerable extent to which the spatial relations implied by that density were being transformed with the advent of men like Modyford, Hilliard and Drax. Density, multiplicity and diversity would become displaced by rationalization and contraction which in their turn would constitute a new economic geography. Barbados' image would be remapped to emphasize its potential to yield lucrative opportunities for trade and commerce. The map reflects an earlier small-holding economy taken up mainly by producers of cotton and tobacco. The *History* assigns a decidedly higher value to the successor economy of large landholdings and intensive sugar cultivation. As a commodity, sugar aggregates within itself both the definition of a discursive field and the category of a very powerful agency of spatialization. As an agent of spatial transformation, the crop demanded larger expanses of arable land to yield economic profitability, and its labour requirements spatialized the relations of those racial types as yet only engaged in very narrowly imagined relations of production on the map.

In the new cartography of colonial history for which Ligon's Barbados functions as a metaphor, the discursive field is mapped by a multiplicity of human and material inputs. In addition to the metropolitan sources of capital and indentured labour, and the African sources of slave labour already outlined, sugar production spatialized the shape and identities of the chief factors in its production. Its cultivation wrought decided transformations on erstwhile edenic landscapes. The introduction of agricultural methods and innovations necessary to improve economic yields and promote imperialist objectives transformed not only the shape of the landscape, but also the processes of capitalist industrial production itself.

Beyond growing and harvesting, the depth of the *History*'s counterdiscursive field is further extended in the next important stage – sugar manufacture. There the textual cartography assumes a palpably more mechanistic form of inscription that similarly establishes the commodity as a figure of discourse and as a spatializing agent on the landscape. The proto-industrial structures of the equipment used for grinding (known collectively as the *ingenio*), boiling and crystallization loom in massive pre-eminence above the other (mainly human and animal) agencies outlined earlier. By its sheer size and power the whole mechanistic complex of boiling house, copper vats, furnaces, filling room, still house and curing house so constructs and privileges its own fantasy as to mute Ligon's candid but horrific epistemology that "in all these [mechanical structures] there are great casualties", a reference to the very common accidents in which slaves lost their limbs in the sugar mill rollers, or were burnt in the furnace fires, or scalded by hot water from the huge cauldrons. The collusion of muted moral knowledge and emergent industrial technology is produced in the service of an even greater cultural power.

The sources from which that greater cultural power derives are to be found in the discursive / counterdiscursive power of sugar itself. Sugar produces meaning in both orders of discourse by its power to argue its value on the basis of both the metropolitan and colonial inputs that went into its production and of the same two linkages constituting its consumer relations. The raw materials and industrial machinery, the investment and management assets necessary to establish an *ingenio* were sourced in the metropole. But the displacement of these and other assets in a remote spatial order would increasingly argue the value of the colony to the metropole. Through these linkages the text inscribes new economic cartographies mapping the flows of desire between the two locations. Through richly imagined formulations of risk and reward, the *History* magnetizes producers and consumers in England into an evolving discourse of knowledge and power. That nexus is concretely reflected in the opportunities and advantages available to elites at the centre and margins which will be advertised in the forthcoming excerpts.[30]

I have chosen two excerpts to illustrate how in its character as counterdiscourse Ligon's *History* remaps the terms of older production methods (centrally represented by pack animals on the map) by expanding the narrative of production with new knowledges and new relations of power. The first is taken from a larger context that focuses on the thematics of production, and maps in extensive detail the rigours of unremitting toil necessary to prepare a field for planting and the subsequent application of intensive methods to produce sugar:

> The manner of cutting them is with little hand bills, about sixe inches from the ground; at which time they divide the tops, from the Canes, which they do with the same bills, at one stroake, and then holding the Canes by the upper ende: they strip off all the blades that grow by the sides of the Canes, which tops and blades, are bound up in faggots, and put into Carts, to carry home; for without these, our Horses and Cattle are not able to work, the pasture being so extreame harsh and sapless, but with these they are very well nourisht and kept in heart. The Canes we likewise binde up in faggots, at the same time, and those are commonly brought home upon the backs of Assinigoes, and we use the fashion of Devonshire, in that kind of Husbandry (for there we learnt it) which is small pack saddles, and crookes, which serve our purposes very fitly, laying upon each Crook a faggot and one a top, so that each Assinigo carries his three faggots. (p. 89)

In this passage the *History* maps an important emergent area of knowledge and power with recognizable economic and ontological signs. Unambiguously deterministic, the terms of this map were prefigured in a tight declarative axiom more than thirty pages earlier: "Canes [must] be planted at all times that they may come in, one field after another; other wise the work will stand still" (p. 55). To serve this demanding regime of production, the cartographic terrain of the historical text is considerably expanded; the potentials for knowledge and the engines of power are similarly amplified to subsume pack animals in a deeper field, a field itself now widened to reflect the presence of greater numbers of slaves, reaping implements, draught animals and carts. Cultural mapping of this passage recovers significant sources that illustrate how identities become spatialized by economic process. The passage maps identities against a ground staked out mainly with explicitly named markers but also overlaid by the historical origins of the activity represented. Factors of labour, relations of objects to origin, use and exchange values all are contextualized here at a meeting point of colonial and metropolitan desires. African slaves were procured in the exotically named markets of Guinny, Binny Cutchew and Gambia. They were transported in ships supplied by Dutch merchants, and they worked in *ingenios* paid for with credit also extended by Dutch financiers.[31] Those draught horses and cattle appearing in the excerpt were the objects of trade between the British plantations in the West Indies, the North American colonies and the Portuguese Cape Verde islands.[32] Methods of production identified with Devonshire, together with the miscellany of handbills and pack saddles, exemplify the nexus of producers and suppliers diffused around proto-industrial England. Unstated here but documented earlier in the text, the Brazilian-Dutch origins of sugar production in Barbados add a further dimension of heterogeneity to this spatializing narrative of knowledge and identity.

The second excerpt thematizes trade and consumption. It cries up the plantation colonies as markets poised to reward the trading and investment classes in England. It matches key consumer needs in the one with key commodity merchants in the other. Assuming an initial outlay of one thousand pounds, Ligon provides some guidelines to prospective settlers as to how that investment might be distributed, and how the disparate roster of merchants, traders, artisans, suppliers, ports and industrial centres stood to benefit therefrom:

> This £1000 I would have thus laid out: £100 in Linnen Cloth, as Canvas and Kentings, wich you may buy here in London, of French Merchants, at reasonable rates, and you may hire poor Journy-men Taylers, here in the Citty, that will for very small wages, make that Canvas into Drawers, and Petticoats, for men and women Negres. And part of the Canvas, and the whole of the Kentings, for Shirts and Drawers for the Christian

> men Servants, and smocks and peticoates for the women. Some other sorts of Linnen, as Holland or Dowlace, will be there very useful, for shirts and Smocks for the Planters themselves, with their Wives and Children. One Hundred pounds more, I would have bestowed, part on wollen cloath, both fine and coorse, part on Devonshire Carsies and other fashionable Stuffes, such as will well endure wearing. Upon Monmouth Capps I would have bestowed £25, you may bespeak them there in Wales, and have them sent up to London, by the waynes at easie rates. (p. 109)

Those dense plantation settlements on the map now figure as a different economic value in the new cartography of the text. They are remapped as a large market of consumers with material needs ripe for fulfilment by producers in England.[33] The nature of the cartography here is of an unabashed, hardheaded economic order. Among other things, the passage reflects a compulsive emphasis on mensuration which extends for some eight consecutive pages in the text. That emphasis and that extension suggest a search for authority that has dual ends: mathematics yields the author a self-evident kind of credibility, even as it elides what Jess Edwards calls the "buried histories of encounters, some violent and exploitative, some more cooperative and transactional".[34]

Ligon's text supports economic practices that set it at odds with mercantilism, a prevailing economic ideology of the period. Thus it projects its power as counterdiscourse into a very vexed arena of public policy and proffers there a new economy of circulation. In their joint and separate relations, the thematic factors delineated in the foregoing excerpts image distinctly globalizing tendencies in production relations, trade, manufacture and consumption patterns which invoke the trope of circulation. A staple of seventeenth century economic ideology, circulation includes the spatial and the counterdiscursive, and advances the argument for the two in the construction of identity. The mercantilist philosophy that so dominated the debates on trade policy during the period increasingly redefined free trade (circulation) as the virtually exclusive right of English shipowners, English captains and English ships (subjects of English identity). Sir Edwin Sandys' report from the Committee on Free Trade (1604) and the two major pieces of legislation instituting mercantilist policy, the Navigation Acts of 1651 and 1660, illustrate the persistence of this issue throughout the century.[35] The Sandys report urged breaking the control of monopolies on English trade, so to expand the opportunities for circulating capital goods, and the profits to accrue from them. The Navigation Acts sought to restrict the participation of other European interests chiefly in the lucrative colonial trade.

Postdating Ligon's *History*, but pertinent for his centrality in the period's literary and economic discourse, Defoe figures as a key exponent of the circulation and free trade philosophies. Reading *Robinson Crusoe* as his illustrative text, Wolfram Schmidgen underscores the role of circulation in seventeenth- and eighteenth-century cultural formation. Schmidgen's expressed motive in focusing on *Robinson Crusoe* and specific economic writings of Defoe is to show "that the early modern circulation of goods and the forms of objectification it promotes are dynamically affected by a heterogeneous mercantile trading space" (p. 21).[36] The case of Robinson Crusoe raises two important issues. Paradoxically, Crusoe's behaviour straddles the incompatible worlds of circulation and monopoly, yet he enjoys the benefits of both. In addition, for my analysis here, it is necessary to observe that Crusoe's condition of radical isolation makes his relation to his island different in key respects from Ligon's colonists' relation to Barbados. However, the two preceding excerpts from the *History* emphasize that the colonists' preoccupation with "forms of objectification" and heterogeneity in the "mercantile trading space" were as critical in the discursive production of their economic interests and social identities as they were for Crusoe in the invention of his radical individualism. Thinking of the *History* as a system of cartographic discourse reveals the ways in which such a methodology can disclose the subtle geographies of human will, desire and action not only within the text itself but also in the connective tissues that relate that text to other parts of the ideological system.

Ligon's primary interests were, of course, vested with elites at the margins. Thus he combined within his single subjective position the roles of historian and publicist. The historian pursues the task of observing and recording. The publicist vigorously promotes the Barbados export economy. With sustained rhetorical energy and persuasive impetus, he demonstrates how sugar in particular and other colonial productions in general would add value to digestibles already familiar or highly desirable to English consumers. The effect is to play up the positive contributions of cultural production at the margins on the advancement and well-being of metropolitan culture. This is especially manifest in the loud vaunting about sugar's universal utility for preserving, in Ligon's words, "an abundance of excellent fruits of the growth of the Island, as Oranges, Lemons, Citrons, and Others, especially Ginger" (p. 85). Like other sugar panegyrists, Ligon extended this value-adding distinction to imagine the product as a rarefied (even sublime) essence, a bearer of unitary value, and thus an antidote against all kinds of natural putrescence and moral corrosion: "Sugar cane has but one single taste but of such a benign faculty as to preserve all the rest from corruption; which, without it, would taint and become rotten" (p. 85). These signs of economic relations, mystified to promise an undergirding metaphysic to the body politic itself, further define the terms of discourse operating within the text of the history. They return us resistlessly to consider the ways in which the map only intimates its unrealized power while the text advances and imagines the fullness of that power by reproducing the economies of knowledge and consumption.

5. Conclusion

Cartographic and historiographical practices have been firmly established as integral parts of the larger process by which colonialism produced its symbolic meanings and pursued its material designs. Maps figured the most powerful visualization of territorial acquisition in foreign parts as was possible to impress rhetorical and legalistic claims on the minds of imperial rivals by means of a single object. Histories could work hand in hand to offer discursive complement and extension to these claims, while using the advantages of factual observation regularly infused with critical, theoretical, speculative and reflective modes. Couched in these terms, that distinction would emphasize a kind of disciplinary divide that would associate maps with a politics of spatiality while restricting histories to a rhetoric of temporality.[37] The terms of this essay have affirmed the capacity of Ligon's map to document the physical shape and features of early Barbados, to render objects in significant social and political relationships, to suggest the kinds of 'hidden geometries' that framed the state of culture in that island at the time the map was drawn. Still, finally, the map, remains static, reified. By contrast, the *History*, as text, contrives an unfolding, dynamic narrative more fitted to document the flux and complexity of those political and economic relationships, and renders them in depth and subtlety in consistency with the new emerging colonial identities of the historian and of those interests he represented. This recognition of the emergent nature of identity within the *History*'s conceptual and ideological pattern furnished the rationale for the critique of cultural mapping developed in this essay. Mapping was assigned exclusive correspondence to the practices of physical visualization fixed in a specific moment of observation and constrained by analogous limits of knowledge. Cultural mapping charts continuous changing process and growing materialist preoccupations; it theorizes the ideologies of race and class, and publicizes the workings of desire and excess, textualizing all into a paradigm of multiplying knowledges. Applied to both Ligon's map and his *History*, terms like "hidden rules" and "subliminal geometries" point to underlying structures, meanings and knowledges that persist or circulate around or within the documents. The trope of circulation suggests that map and text, and different dimensions of cartography within the text itself, might function in a relationship of discourse to counterdiscourse. The *History* proved to be the most productive source for understanding the forms of discourse by which the founding acts of domination and the ideology that sustained them served to define and organize colonial culture in early Barbados. And, inevitably, dynamic tensions that define themselves in formal terms as counterdiscourse began to appear from the outset. Counterdiscursive elements manifest themselves in the image of escaping slaves and in the narrative of competition, emulation and threat that would define reciprocal relations and perceptions of colonists at the margins and citizens at the metropolitan centre.

Ligon's map fixes a temporal visualization of Barbados' shape and contents limited to the moment of its production; its only gestures to relationality being the defensive kinetics circumscribed in angular forms and closed tableaux. The *History,* by negotiating a more liberal exercise of its disciplinary norms appropriates the cartographic practices of geography into a more fluid image of culture. It thus produces not a single map but a system of maps. It reveals and illuminates the routes of circulation of that knowledge and power which we recognize as the formations in which discourse is constituted. Thus the discourse of truth and exactitude advertised in the eponymous terms of Ligon's title quickly pluralizes knowledge on two counts: In the first case, the sheer force of difference and diversity represented by colonial nature and culture transformed the knowledge base and consciousness of admittedly sceptical and resistant metropolitan elites. In the second the widely dispersed geographical and cultural origins of the colonists, their slaves, servants and disparate commercial relations become the powerful agents of a spatializing colonial discourse. In that transformation and spatialization lay the very seeds of a counterdiscursive reflex. The visible power wielded by colonial elites would translate into linkages of common interest with power elites in politics and commerce in England. However, a less visible but nonetheless irresistible creolizing power would insinuate itself into the national identity and farther afield along the circulating currents of empire in ways that would mark texts like Ligon's *History* as prime agents in a world-making (gobalizing) discourse.

Notes

1 Richard Ligon: *A True and Exact History of the Island of Barbados*, London, 1657. All subsequent references to this work will be abbreviated in the text of this essay as the *History*. Quotations follow the text of the second edition (London, 1673) and appear in-text followed by a page number in parentheses.

2 My thinking about possibilities for applying cartographic models to literary and cultural study has been considerably shaped by a selection of highly regarded books released within this decade. For its chronological focus on the practices of mapping at the dawn of empire in England, Richard Helgerson's *Forms of Nationhood. The Elizabethan Writing of England,* Chicago & London, 1992 was particularly instructive in stressing the role of mapping in eroding monarchical power while increasing the power of landowners. Denis Cosgrove (Ed.): *Mappings*, London, 1999 gathers scholarship from the wide ranging fields of art, history, literature, cartography itself, science, design and technology. Each essay illustrates how the "spatial turn" in most of these disciplines has had the effect of suggesting new approaches, which in turn have disrupted stable assumptions about knowledge, social and cognitive processes. The essays in Andrew Gordon & Bernhard Klein (Eds.): *Literature, Mapping and the Politics of Space in Early Modern Britain*, Cambridge & New York, 2001, focus likewise on many areas of cultural experience affected by new mapping techniques, "indicating new possibilities for thinking about gender, the body, politics

and empire within a single conceptual framework". In periodical literature the online journal *Early Modern Literary Studies* (*EMLS*) has made an important contribution to this area of study, with a special issue (September 1998) devoted to the subject and includes articles by J. Edwards and M Koch cited elsewhere in this essay.

3 Nathan White: "Geography and Mapping", <www.english.emory.edu/Bahri/Mapping.html>, accessed 15 February 2007.

4 J. Brian Harley: "Maps, Knowledge and Power". – In Denis Cosgrove & Stephen Daniels (Eds.): *The Iconography of Landscape. Essays on the Symbolic Representation, Design and Use of Past Environments*, New York, 1988, p. 303.

5 *Ibid.*, 278.

6 See Michel Foucault: *The Order of Things: An Archaeology of the Human Science,* New York, 1971, chap. 1.

7 See Michel Foucault: *The History of Sexuality*, vol. 1*: An Introduction.* Trans. Robert Hurley, New York, 1980, pp. 52, 151.

8 Michel Foucault: "The Order of Discourse". – In M. F.: *The Archaeology of Knowledge.* Trans. A. M. Sheridan Smith, London, 1972, p. 152.

9 Michel Foucault: *Power / Knowledge. Selected Interviews and Other Writings 1972-1977*, Ed. Colin Gordon, trans. Colin Gordon et al., Sussex, 1980, pp. 98, 85.

10 Foucault: *The History of Sexuality,* vol. 1, p. 101.

11 Harley: "Maps, Knowledge and Power", p. 303. This article stands high among the sources I have benefited from in my research for this essay. A respected authority in the field of cartography, Harley presents a succinct primer with which to understand the "ideological contours" of maps, and their implication in personal, elitist and nationalist aims throughout history.

12 Ian Baucom: *Out of Place. Englishness, Empire, and the Locations of Identity,* Princeton, 1999, p. 177.

13 Mark Koch: "Ruling the World. The Cartographic Gaze in Elizabethan Accounts of the New World", *Early Modern Studies* 4:2, Special Issue 3, 1988, 1-39, 10-11.

14 Hilary Beckles: *A History of Barbados from Amerindian Settlement to Nation State*, Cambridge, 1990, p. 13.

15 Melba Cuddy-Keane: "Imaging / Imagining Globalization: Maps and Models", <www.chass.utoronto.ca/~mcuddy/mapping.htm>, accessed 16 February 2007, p. 7.

16 Beckles: *A History of Barbados*, pp. 15-18.

17 Harley: "Maps, Knowledge and Power", p. 298.

18 Koch: "Ruling the World", 9.

19 I am adopting here Michel de Certeau's definition of space in relation to practice and performance. That relation offers explanatory force for the dynamics of social relations that may be recovered from emphasizing the movement, action and practices which are given greater scope in Ligon's *History* than was possible on his map. See M. C.: *The Practice of Everyday Life*. Trans. Steven Rendall, Berkeley, 1986, p. 117.

20 Baucom: *Out of Place*, p. 70, and Koch: "Ruling the World", 10. While my theorizing of the effects of English identities performed in the Barbados colonial space concurs with the positions already identified with Baucom and Koch for these identities, I depart from and push their notions farther by exploiting the resources of a trope of crossing derived both from travelling and genetics. The full definition of this kind of identity-crossing is now comprehended under the ontological: in the light of the cultural mapping systems recovered in Ligon, identity itself defines a space fashioned jointly by material and subjective elements.

21 Richard Dunn: *Sugar and Slaves. The Rise of the Planter Class in the English West Indies, 1624-1713*, Chapel Hill, 1972, pp. 81-82.

22 Helgerson: *Forms of Nationhood*, 114.

23 Foucault: *Power / Knowledge*, p. 142.

24 Quoted in Graham Huggan: "Decolonizing the Map". – In Bill Ashcroft & Gareth Griffiths & Helen Tiffin (Eds.): *The Postcolonial Studies Reader,* London, 1995, p. 407.

25 Tobias Doering: *Caribbean-English Passages. Intertextuality in a Postcolonial Tradition,* Research in Postcolonial Literatures, London & New York, 2002, p. 102.

26 *Ibid*., 18.

27 For more extended treatments of this selection, cultural mapping and the idealization of bodies in Ligon, see my "Sugar, Slaves and Machines: An Economy of Bodies in Colonizing Narratives", *Synthesis: An Interdisciplinary Journal* 2:2, 1997, 67-85; and *The Cultural Politics of Sugar*: *Caribbean Slavery and Narratives of Colonialism*, Cambridge, 2000, pp. 31-35.

28 Two sources were helpful to me in evaluating the meaning of these inclusions and exclusions: J. H. Plumb: *The Commercialisation of Leisure in Eighteenth Century England:* The Stenton Lecture, Reading, 1973, pp. 1-13, and David Cannadine: "The Theory and Practice of the English Leisure Classes", *Historical Journal* 21, 1978, 445-67.

29 What I am attempting here is to trace a shift from the episteme of the map to the episteme of the text. This paradigm accommodates the shifting bases of knowledge and sources of power at Ligon's time in the seventeenth century. Foucault's epistemes are abitrary, a priori historical mentalities that construct the world for us. By definition such constructs do not concede much freedom or autonomy to individuals to make rational creative decisions. I do not mean to coerce Ligon's colonists into that kind of rigid social structure but to see the map and *History* as abstract sign systems susceptible of a similar relational critique. See Foucault: *The Order of Things*, p. 168.

30 In a discussion on the staging of map scenes in Shakespeare plays, John Gillies makes the point that in three of four plays concerned "the division of the kingdom on the map signals a denaturing transition from a transcendental order of value (the mystique of kingdom or nation) to a mercenary 'property' relation". See Gordon & Klein (Eds.): *Literature, Mapping and the Politics of* Space, p. 110. This set me thinking about the ways in which

colonialism and empire divided the nation, (here / over there; civilized / savage) and the fears of enervation and pollution (of denaturing) these divisions engendered. The cartographic analyses applied to Ligon's documents reveal that those mercenary property relations would become spatialized to the colony and then return to transform the internal nation in such activities as conventional trade and commerce, the slave trade and bourgeois creole consumption. See also Doering: *Caribbean-English Passages*, p. 81.

31 Beckles: *A History of Barbados*, p. 20.

32 Carl & Roberta Bridenbaugh: *No Peace Beyond the Line. The English in the Caribbean, 1624-1690,* New York, 1972, pp. 94-95.

33 Thomas Tryon: "On the Making of Sugar". – In *Tryon's Letters Upon Several Occasions for the Merchant, Citizen, and Countryman's Instructor*, London, 1700, p. 219.

34 Jess Edwards: "How to Read an Early Modern Map. Between the Particular and the General, the Material and the Abstract, Words and Mathematics", *Early Modern Literary Studies* 9:1, 2003, 1-58, 18.

35 For full texts of the related documents, see Joan Thirsk & J. D. Cooper (Eds.): *Seventeenth Century Economic Documents*, Oxford, 1972; The Sandys Report is on pp. 436–444; The Navigation Act 1651 on pp. 502-505; and the Navigation Act 1660 is on pp. 520-524.

36 Following Schmidgen's argument, it is clear that Defoe's writing of Crusoe's experiences on the island and Ligon's writing of his fellow colonists' bring into being the symbolic meaning of such remote spaces as "separate economic enclaves connected by a precarious and exclusive network of travel routes." Wolfgang Schmidgen: "Robinson Crusoe, Enumeration and the Mercantile Fetish", *Eighteenth-Century Studies* 35:1, 2001, 29.

37 The categories I invoke here are taken from Gilles Deleuze & Felix Guattari: *A Thousand Plateaus. Capitalism and Schizophrenia*, Minneapolis, 1987, p. 7. Maps would fall under their arbolic (linear, hierarchic, territorialized) category; histories and cultural mapping would more closely resemble their rhizomatic system (non-linear, multiplicitous, deteritorialized).

Miki Flockemann (Cape Town)

Connecting the Caribbean: Cross-currents – the Caribbean and South Africa

> Her words move me; they are connected at base with how I have felt about language and writing. […] She speaks for me, another 'coloured' from another end of empire.[1]

In the decade following South Africa's transition to a democratic state, several multi-million building contracts in the heart of Cape Town have been brought to an abrupt halt following the discovery of mass burial sites. These discoveries can be seen in terms of the return of a repressed memory, since the remains (some of which are located in Cape Town's famous Waterfront tourist destination), do not date from the much publicised apartheid atrocities, but from an often overlooked, older slave past. This literal unearthing of the remains of the legacy of slavery with its associations of violent dislocation and social alienation, has been seen by some commentators as illustrative of the way this often forgotten history underlies the new democracy. Commenting on the finds in relation to the 'murky' history of slavery in South Africa, Anthony Holiday notes that while the first slaves arrived shortly after the colonisation of the Cape in the mid-seventeenth century, by 1717 slaves outnumbered settlers: "But murky or not, this picture of the ties, sometimes tormented, sometimes tender, that bound slaves and slave owners to one another by myriad subtle threads, is at the origins of the modern history of South Africa".[2]

These references to the complex legacies of slavery and colonisation provide a useful point of departure for exploring some of the cross-currents resulting from the similar slave legacies of the Caribbean, which has also been subjected to successive waves of colonialism as slave ships criss-crossed the Atlantic en route to the American plantations. In South Africa this involved first the Portuguese, followed by the Dutch East India Company and then the

British, with the concomitant establishment at the Cape (as in the Caribbean) of a highly diverse slave population, mainly from Indonesia, West and Central Africa and India.[3] The similarity with the Caribbean is striking in view of the scant attention that has been paid to such cross-currents, particularly in literary studies; instead, South Africa has generally been seen in relation to either Africa and / or Europe, neglecting a wider diasporean framework such as associated with the Caribbean. It is only in the last decade or so that sustained attention has been paid to the Asian connections, since these were largely subsumed within the prevailing Black / White oppositional paradigm. Such a transnational shift is evident in South African president Thabo Mbeki's controversial visit to Haiti in the dying days of Aristide's rule to celebrate the 200th anniversary of Haiti's liberation from slavery. According to Mbeki the aim was to foreground historical and cultural links between South Africa's first decade of democracy, and Haiti's slave revolt which resulted in independence from French colonial rule.[4] My concern here, however, is to identify reciprocities and to look at the ways these legacies have been translated into a variety of cultural forms, with a particular focus on contemporary fictions produced by Caribbean and primarily, but not exclusively, black South African women writers.[5]

The aim is not to offer a reductive comparative scheme that attempts to categorise common trends at the expense of the nuances of local historical and cultural specificity; instead, such an approach can offer potentially enriched perspectives by teasing out reciprocities, or even perhaps de-familiarising accepted readings by situating these within a broader diasporic context. Given the diversity of cultural heritages characterising both the Caribbean and South Africa, particularly at the Cape where the first colonial and slave settlements were established, one would expect to identify similar concerns with negotiating identities and with establishing a 'voice' – often in an imposed tongue. As indicated above, Michelle Cliff establishes a link between herself as a Jamaican creole living in the US, and South African author Zoë Wicomb, who refers to the difficulty she initially experienced in finding her voice as a black woman writer living in exile in the UK. Cliff says: "She speaks for me, another 'coloured' from another end of empire."[6] This preoccupation with being simultaneously insider and outsider, and with what Homi Bhabha and Paul Gilroy call "in-betweenness", and the "interstitial spaces" which are opened up as a result of the contemporary diasporic and postcolonial condition, not surprisingly shapes much of the work to be discussed here.[7] The diasporic experience, they claim, can provide scope for 'new' ways of being in the world. In conjunction with this is the concern with both real and imagined homes and with the concept of (un)belonging, which in turn often provides an uneasy background for redefining concepts of community in the developing nation.

This comparative approach draws on Francoise Lionnet's claim that in dealing with cross-cultural comparisons, it is possible to bypass the trap of essentialism and false universalism. Through a comparative focus, says Lionnet, readers can experience "a shock of recognition", which results in a new way of reading familiar and less familiar works.[8] While the focus here is on the way certain fictional conventions are appropriated, subverted and translated, the "relational readings" employed will show how textual meaning is located within cultural material.[9]

Apart from exploring the way interactions between peoples of African, European and Asian descent in South Africa and the Caribbean affect cultural and linguistic affinities and identities, one can identify in the works discussed below a common emphasis on various modes of transgression. These transgressions encompass the creative play with cultural forms and language, but are also embodied in a thematic focus on sexuality and the replication of familial and colonial relationships – a legacy of those "tormented and tender ties" referred to by Holiday[10] – particularly as manifested in the trope of miscegenation. Significantly, one of the most notable features of recent South Africa writing is the focus on the way 'coloured' subjectivity has somehow (and problematically) become emblematic of the establishment of a new South African nation, often as the product of rape.[11] On the other hand, the current emphasis on the performativity of identity and the way this can be linked to creative forms of negotiating a space for oneself beyond or within given identities, or as a way of surviving under repressive conditions, is also evident in a number of South African works such as Achmat Dangor's *Kafka's Curse (*1997), and Zakes Mda's *The Madonna of Excelsior* (2002).

Before looking in a more sustained way at specific examples of textual reciprocities, it is useful first to highlight some of the prevailing concerns that will inform such a comparative discussion of individual Caribbean and South African texts. The notion that there seems to be a shift from a binary focus on Africa and / or Europe to a more comprehensive, comparative perspective in relation to South African works is supported by the fact that issues that have long been the subject of studies of Caribbean writing have now also surfaced as the primary focus of debate in a number of recently published local journals as well. These include, most topically, the transformative (but for some even potentially regressive) potential of "creolite" which is not simply an "*inevitable* effect" of the particular colonisation processes, but an agent for resistance and transformation, social as well as aesthetic.[12] Secondly, coming of age stories are used by writers from across the (en)gendered race and class spectrum to represent, often retrospectively, the construction of identities during times of social transformation.[13] This equation between the child's personal development and that of the developing nation is a central focus in a number of works by differently situated black South African women and invites comparison with a number of Caribbean texts, such as Zee Edgell's *Beka Lamb* (1982). These Caribbean texts commonly use a child as narrating consciousness and this is also seen in works by South African women.[14] There have also been a significant number of novels focusing on white boyhood which attempt to reconstruct the shaping of white Afrikaner identity during apartheid, such as Mark Behr's *Smell of Apples* (1995) and *Embrace (*2000), and Michiel Heyns' *The Children's Day* (2002).

Thirdly, in the wake of the Truth and Reconciliation Hearings, there has been a renewed interest in South African narratives which attempt to "speak the unspeakable", and articulate memories of interlocked personal and public pasts. This highlights the problematic relationship between fiction and memory. Haitian writer Edwidge Danticat refers to the "testimonial" aspect of storytelling and the difficulty of finding a voice to articulate personal and historical trauma in ways that do justice to the events, and avoid sensationalising or trivialising the experiences of others. Danticat's *The Farming of Bones* (1998) deals with the 1937 massacre of Haitians by Dominican neighbours and draws on accounts of various witnesses which are then transcribed and translated into text: as one of the characters observes: "you tell the story and then it is retold as they wish, written in words you do not understand in a language that is theirs and not yours".[15] Similarly, there have been a number of South African texts which move beyond the realist forms associated with writing against and within apartheid. These offer testimonial or self-consciously fictional accounts of suppressed pasts or traumatic presents.[16] Some are also powerfully transformative texts, such as Zakes Mda's *Ways of Dying* (1995), which employs an aesthetic of transformation, and is characterised, like much Caribbean literature, by an emphasis on local knowledges, and employs popular or oral cultural forms as a strategy of resistance to dominant hegemonies. In effect creating a 'world of their own' through imaginative translation.

There are of course also significant differences between the Caribbean and the South African contexts. In terms of the colonial encounters, for instance, there was from the outset the establishment of a very strong settler community in South Africa, and the early period of close social interaction between settlers, slaves and indigenous Khoikhoi communities cannot be overlooked in terms of future cultural production. In fact, the development of Afrikaans as a local creole which was originally associated with the slave and Malay communities of Cape Town is evidence of the cultural exchange between these groups, despite the fact that the Apartheid regime later attempted to ensure the 'purity' of Afrikaans as the language of a dominant white minority.[17] One should recall that the imposition of Afrikaans as medium of instruction in black schools was one of the sparks that ignited the 1976 student uprising in Soweto, and clearly comparisons can be drawn between the role of Caribbean linguistic creoles as resistant people's or 'nation' language, and attempts by coloured people (who are demographically the majority in the Western Cape region) to reclaim Afrikaans. The enforcement in 1950 of the Population Registration Act introduced a rigid racial classification system which was legislated on the dubious basis of physical appearance, as well as of 'community acceptance'. This has resulted in a rather different history to the concept of creolisation formulated by Caribbean theorists, one which needs to be explored in more detail here. In fact, there have been concerns expressed recently that an emphasis on creolisation and the "valorizing of the diaspora experience" within the South African context obscures ongoing racial inequities which extend into the new millennium.[18] It must also be remembered that, unlike the Caribbean, South African writing has traditionally (with some exceptions of course) been grounded in a testimonial or realist tradition, and has only recently moved into more stylistically transgressive modes, in keeping with the fluidity of the social terrain after the collapse of apartheid legislation. Despite these differences there are nevertheless important advantages for comparative or 'relational' readings which explore cross-cultural reciprocities. One of the reasons for focusing primarily on the novel as emergent and even radical form is that, as Caribbean novelist and cultural commentator Wilson Harris points out, it can serve as a "medium of consciousness" in diverse contexts.[19] (The potential for such innovative appropriations and transformations of a traditionally western cultural form is evident in the number of non-metropolitan-based recipients of the Nobel prize for literature over the last decade, including two South Africans, Nadine Gordimer and J. M. Coetzee.) Zimbabwean writer, Tstisti Dangarembga, points out that the novel will become increasingly important for the African writer "in choosing as its subject the crucial interface between individuals and alienating society".[20] Moreover, if novels are read as revisionary texts, they can be a useful vehicle for both reconstruction and invention. In an interview Dangarembga comments on the role of storytelling in situations where people (like herself) "do not have a tangible history we can relate to". For this reason fiction becomes a way of exploring the processes of both forgetting and remembering.[21] Here the 'defamiliarising' effect of non-standard language use associated with Caribbean writing can act as an important vehicle for expressing cross-cultural experiences.[22]

In commenting on the similarities between Afro-Caribbean and Afro-Brazilian cultural forms, ranging from music, carnival, food and dance to religion, Caribbean critic Carole Boyce Davies notes that despite barriers of geography and language, in this case English and Portuguese, it is also "our own lack of knowledge [which continues to] keep us separate". She nevertheless claims: "[L]ooking at the Caribbean from Brazil offers a completely different reading of the Caribbean in relation to the Americas, outside of the north-south axis".[23] Similarly, I hope to show how looking at the Caribbean through the lens of selected South African texts can offer alternative and (one hopes) even fresh readings, of both Caribbean and South African works, by exploring some of these neglected cross-currents.

A number of the thematic concerns and cross-currents referred to above are interwoven in individual Caribbean texts. For instance, the strategic value of the 'in-betweenness' of the diasporic condition informs a number of coming of age stories. As Helena Lima points out, it is striking how the revisioning of this classic European form has become so often employed by writers from developing countries describing minority experience.[24] Of interest here is the use of narrative perspective to represent an emerging female subjecthood. One can compare works which are located within the Caribbean, such as Jamaica Kincaid's *Annie John* 1986, Merle Hodge's *Crick Crack, Monkey (*1981) and *For the Life of Laeticia* (1991), Michelle Cliff's *Abeng* (1984), Jan Shinebourne's *The Last Plantation* (1988) and Zee Edgell's *Beka Lamb* (1982), with those that incorporate the diasporic experience of travel as integral to a gendered rite of passage to a 'new' subjecthood. Texts here include Marlene Nourbese Philip's young adult novel, *Harriet's Daughter* (1988), Edwidge Danitcat's *Breath, Eyes, Memory (*1994), Michelle Cliff's *No Telephone to Heaven* (1987) and Jamaica Kincaid's *Lucy* (1991), to mention a few.

Several contributors to anthologies dealing with the formulation of a black and feminist aesthetic stress the dialectic that is established between insider and outsider in writing by black women. For instance, Mae Gwendolyn Henderson's emphasis on the "simultaneity of discourses", and a "plurality of voices" as a characteristic feature of black women's writing is useful for looking at texts dealing with the processes of entry into young adulthood.[25] Similarly, Cheryl Wall argues that one result of the "unmistakably polyvalent experience" of such women, is that the appeal to self in their writings is not necessarily ahistorical or essentialist.[26] By focusing on the 'genesis of identity', texts that construct apparently naïve child / woman writing subjects, negotiate the interaction between the textual and extratextual, and in the process open up questions of origin and identity in ways that can be seen as part of larger processes of decolonisation.

Common to the development of the young protagonists is her awareness of her dual position, "both outside the dominant values and inside the society that lives by them".[27] For instance reading Zee Edgell's *Beka Lamb* in relation to a South African work like Farida Karodia's *Daughters of the Twilight* (1986), offers a number of interesting reciprocities.[28] First, in the representation of the familial, religious and educational systems which the adolescent is constrained by, there is a focus on a potentially interactive, rather than dichotomised relationship between colonial or apartheid institutions, and colonial subjects. Both are set in the nineteen fifties, *Beka Lamb* describes British colonial Belize during the political turmoil prior to independence, while Farida Karodia's *Daughters of the Twilight* (1986) is set in pre-Sharpeville South Africa. However, as suggested earlier while Beka in Edgell's novel draws a conscious analogy between her own psycho-social development and her country's struggle for political independence, Meena, the narrator in Karodia's novel points to the contradictions involved in the young female subject's coming to consciousness during times of political turmoil.

Secondly, these texts establish a dual narrative focus via the close relationship between the protagonist and a slightly older friend or relative, who is situated as "not-quite the same, not-quite Other".[29] In offering a dual focus, there is a suggestion of what Daniel Ross describes as an almost "narcissistic" relationship between the two girls who see themselves reflected in each other; in this case the one who has the stronger connection to both country of origin and familial and communal history is strangely attracted to, but also fearful for – rather than of – the more alienated friend or sister.[30] Beka Lamb's relationship with her friend Toycie Qualo, who is two years older, plays a significant role in Beka's own development. Beka admires the academically gifted and attractive Toycie, and is devastated when Toycie falls pregnant, has a nervous breakdown triggered by her expulsion from the convent school, and ultimately dies during a hurricane. Her death is both a result of social alienation and the fact that she does not have a sense of communal history to draw on. Beka, on the other hand, has a nurturing community of older women who expose Beka to a sense of her own family history, the history of Belize, and the political possibilities for independence. This is demonstrated in the way the narrative, focalised through Beka, takes the form of a wake, privately held by Beka for Toycie, in which she relives, in a series of flashbacks, significant moments in her growth towards womanhood and political awareness.

In *Daughters of the Twilight*, the close relationship between Meena, the narrator, and her older sister Yasmin is suggested when Meena peers at herself in the mirror and is reassured by Jasmin, considered "the beauty of the family", that "some day you'll emerge from your chrysalis. [...] Believe me, little sister, you'll unfold just like a butterfly".[31] However, Meena makes a conscious decision to avoid becoming a replica of Yasmin. Like Toycie, Yasmin has a breakdown following the birth of her child, the product of a rape by a white man. Unlike Toycie though, Yasmin does not die but flees the country. – Karodia has subsequently reworked the novel as *Other Secrets* (2000), developing the relationship between Yasmin's daughter, her mother and aunt Meena in later years.

It is significant that Beka and Meena, through their own educational projects, self-consciously attempt to turn the colonialist and apartheid education system to practical, even counter-colonialist use. In the process they resist or subvert the effects of education as a "technology of colonialist subjectification".[32] Instead, this very 'colonialist technology' presents the space in which they can attempt to articulate 'new' subjectivities. This has some bearing on the way Meena, who is registered as Indian by birth with an Indian father and coloured mother, has herself 'reclassified' (without her father's knowledge) as coloured so that she can attend a coloured high school of her choice; in other words, she subversively annexes the power of racial classification – though she is of course still subject to it. The same can be said for the prize-winning essay that Beka writes after Toycie's death which for Beka becomes a way of revising and reconstructing social and familial histories.

The way Beka deliberately adopts different social dialects also points to her conscious affirmation of a creole identity as part of elaborating a 'strategy of selfhood'.[33] In consciously mimicking the received British pronunciation of the BBC broadcaster in describing the natural beauty of the island, she challenges the public construction of Belize as tourist commodity which masks the poverty of the majority of its inhabitants. On the other hand, when Sister Gabriela comes to collect the work Beka was to enter for the essay competition, Beka at first feels embarrassed because of the uncharacteristic untidiness of the house, itself symptomatic of the family's disorientation and distress after Toycie's death and the devastating hurricane. However, the moment Beka detects a hint of 'disrespect' in Sister Gabriela's eyes at the state of the family and their home, she adopts "her best creole drawl", and by doing so offers an unspoken challenge to the nun: "If you think all Belize people break down so easily you are mistaken".[34] This is a reference to the disintegration of Belizean social structures in the political upheaval prior to independence, but also refers to Toycie's "breakdown": here Beka is refusing to accept this apparently over-determined perception of her own development.

In *Daughters of the Twilight*, it is clear that the elocution lessons received by Jasmin are intended to groom her for a suitable position in white South African society. Meena, however, remains at home hearing the Indian-English of her father, and the robust Afrikaans-inflected vernacular of her grandmother. Her brief encounter with the highly politicised young men in Johannesburg's racially heterogeneous suburbs of Fordsburg and Vrededorp introduces her to a discourse far removed from Jasmin's affected English schoolgirl slang, and this exposure to a 'multiplicity of discourses' prepares her for potential political involvement.

Beka and Meena can be described as "historic witness[es]" to their changing society, as well as to their changing selves.[35] When Beka decides to hold her own wake for Toycie she is not only coming to terms with her childhood and emerging womanhood and independence, but expressing her connection to a broad Caribbean culture, where wakes are seen as part of a continuing African tradition, a tribute to the life force, and frowned upon by the colonial Church. Beka's ability to accommodate the cultural influences she is exposed to are a testimony to the potential for her independence. While integration of some kind is held out as a utopian possibility for her and her country (as her Granny Ivy says, "things can change fi true"),[36] in *Daughters of the Twilight* the race / class and gender polarities are represented as still so powerfully entrenched at a variety of levels that integration in the South African post-apartheid contexts appears to be much longer in coming. This points to the relationship between personal and social fragmentation during periods of transition, and draws attention to the creative possibilities for, and political implications of, the concept of cultural creolisation.

The focus on colonial subjectivity and sexuality, as well as the relationship between mother and motherland is explored in Jamaica Kincaid's *Lucy,* also described as a novel of development in which the nineteen-year-old Lucy leaves Antigua to work as an au pair in the US. However, unlike Edgell's *Beka Lamb,* Kincaid's *Lucy* explores identity in relation to leaving home and the development of a diaspora consciousness. Issues of identity are of course complicated by cultural affiliations in a diasporic context, particularly in terms of the language available in which to define oneself and one's world. As Kristen Mahlis puts it: "To lose one's tongue is to experience a permanent exile."[37] However, while "tongue" here indicates cultural alienation, Lucy also uses her tongue and "the sharpness of language" to "articulate a connection that creates distance". [38] Tongue here is both a linguistic tool, and a form of sexual expression: Lucy's celebration of her own sexuality is part of the process of liberating herself from a colonised subjectivity represented by her mother's apparently internalised obsession with the colonial ethos of social respectability. But Beka, who is younger than Lucy at this stage, has no intention of leaving Belize; instead, the cautionary lesson she learns from Toycie's pregnancy becomes associated with the development of her own independence. This points to interesting differences in the way sexuality is represented in these narratives of becoming, and underlines the emphasis on communal history in Edgell's work, whereas Kincaid in *Lucy* stresses the importance of an 'independent' or 'self-invented' subjectivity.

The association between the diasporic experience of travel and the re-definition of subjectivity is also evident in a number of short fictions by Caribbean writers, such as Michelle Cliff's "A Woman Who Plays Trumpet is Deported" (1991) and Pauline Melville's "A Disguised Land"(1990). Again reciprocities can be explored with Zoë Wicomb's story, "A Trip to the Gifberge" from *You Can't Get Lost in Cape Town* (1987) in that all explore the diaspora effects of criss-crossing the Atlantic. Moreover, the generational conflict between mothers, daughters and granddaughters described here replicates a historical dialectic between received tradition and the pressures of modernity, and in turn this is articulated with the colour-coded class hierarchy that the protagonists have to negotiate.

As mentioned earlier, Michelle Cliff is a Jamaican creole living in the US, while Pauline Melville is of mixed Guyanese / British descent; both draw on experiences not dissimilar to those Wicomb attributes to Frieda Shenton as coloured South African growing up in the apartheid racial dichotomy. As I have argued elsewhere, this affirms the need for a broader re-contextualisation of Wicomb's work than has generally been the case with much recent South African criticism.[39] Cliff's "A Woman Who Plays Trumpet Is Deported" explores a "reverse middle passage"[40] when the woman trumpet player goes into voluntary exile to Europe during the nineteen-thirties as she feels this will give greater scope to her musical expression. On the other hand, Pauline Melville's "A Disguised

Land" re-writes the severing of natal ties between mothers and children that occurs when women became the sites of reproduction necessary to maintain the labour force of the slavery enterprise (a concern also explored in Toni Morrison's *Beloved*). Melville's story is a 're-writing' in the sense that it re-situates the legacy of the commodification of black women in the contemporary British rather than American setting. In both cases their journey triggers a recognition that the legacy of slavery runs deep, in many guises, throughout history.

Cliff's "A Woman Who Plays Trumpet is Deported" (from *Bodies of Water)*, is dedicated to the memory of Valaida Snow, a trumpet player who was liberated – or escaped – from a concentration camp. Cliff connects the trumpet player's situation as woman, black, artist and exile with a combination of perceived transgressions from which she attempts to escape but which nevertheless place her in a European concentration camp. Standing in line in Copenhagen waiting to be processed for deportation with other women and children whose language she does not understand and "from whom she is apart, yet of", she has an epiphany, connecting her own experience with other unspeakable past and future histories and holocausts.[41] In Wicomb's "A Trip to the Gifberge", Frieda undergoes a journey within a journey as it were, from Britain back to Cape Town, and from Cape Town to her mother's home in Namaqualand, and then deeper inland to the Gifberge, the place of her mother's Griqua ancestors.[42] According to Wicomb, the last story breaks the silence that has existed between mother and daughter, and by implication between Frieda and her motherland. Separation is still there, represented by the fenced-off section of the mountain that prevents Frieda and her mother from having a free view of their home from the top of the Gifberge. However, referring to Frieda's return, Wicomb says that there is "also somehow a space that has been created *through her absence*",[43] and it is this in-betweenness, this "space created through absence" that can be seen as emancipatory, as Frieda is forced to recognise the position from which her mother speaks, even if she cannot agree with what she says. While one needs to be sensitive to the differences in situation along the creole continuum, a comparative exploration of the 'recognitions' and contradictions resulting from intersecting systems of knowledge and values across generations and locations shows how these become sites for the construction of potentially 'alternative' subjectivities.

As mentioned earlier, the concept of creolisation has a different genesis within the Caribbean and South African contexts. However, it is clear that there is a common focus on the way an interaction between diaspora experiences can result in what Caroline Rooney refers to as "new configurations" in the future;[44] in this case, through destablising given knowledges and identities, and through the processes of creolisation which should be seen in relation to concepts like *métissage*, syncretism, hybridity and creolity. Syncretism, for instance, refers to the amalgamation of diverse cultural forms, whereas hybridity is a contested term and has been associated with a potentially weakened cultural product,[45] or with a privileged cosmopolitanism, as well as with 'new' generic forms.[46] Caribbean writers and cultural critics like Eduard Glissant, Wilson Harris and Edward Brathwaite distinguish between *métissage*, creolisation and creolity. According to Glissant, creolity is a more reductive model than creolisation: creolity "is the interactional and transactional aggregate of cultural elements of Carib, European, African, Asian, and Levantine, that the yoke of history has put together on the same soil".[47] Creolisation, however, is an "infinite and unceasing process (*métissage sans limites*) involving cultural transformation".[48] And it is this latter definition that is of interest here, for it suggests that creolisation is a process, rather than a product. As Graham Huggan puts it, creolisation is a dialectical interaction between cultures within a wider interculturative process.[49]

For example, creolisation can be associated with representations of 'Asian-ness' as exotic or other in title stories from Olive Senior's *Arrival of the Snake-Woman and Other Stories* (1989) and Agnes Sam's *Jesus is Indian and Other Stories* (1989); this is seen in the way Senior and Sam, despite their different geopolitical contexts, destabilize dominant discourses of identity. Senior has suggested that the fact that her childhood in Jamaica was spent moving between impoverished rural and more affluent urban households goes some way towards explaining her ability to imagine the interactions along the creole continuum, and this can be extended to the interactions between African and Asian diasporas that are the focus of "Arrival of the Snake-Woman". Agnes Sam, a South African of Indian descent, wrote "Jesus is Indian" while she was in exile in the UK. The narration is situated within the child Angelina's consciousness as she negotiates her way between the constraints of growing up as a South African Indian girlchild, while having to manage the stern surveillance of Sister Bonaventura at her Catholic school who tries to force Angelina to excise Hindu words from the story she is writing about her sister and family.

In Senior's story, the recollections of the boy Ishmael are used todescribe the impact of the arrival of an outsider, Miss Coolie, on a Jamaican village at the end of last century. Even before her arrival Ishmael is half in love with and half terrified of the "Heathen" woman from India with "snake-like hips" who has chosen to cross the mountains to be SonSon's new wife and who, in the process, becomes the catalyst for changes that transform the rural community.[50] While for Olive Senior "Miss Coolie" represents the cultural outsider as catalyst, Agnes Sam's work is concerned with the Asian woman as 'cultural insider'. What they have in common, however, is the way Asian-ness, rather than representing an excluded minority, appears instead to destabilise dominant values and identities.

While Senior's "Arrival of the Snake-Woman", should be read in terms of a pragmatic cultural creolisation, in the South African context, the processes of creolisation are more difficult given that the Population Registration Act catered for a separate 'Indian' racial classification as distinct from 'Cape' and 'Other Coloureds', as well as 'White' and 'Bantu'. It is significant how creolisation has recently become a contentious issue in South African cultural debates. For example, Gugu Hlongwane discusses the criticism levelled at Paul Gilroy's *Black Atlantic* (1993) for "marginalizing Africa in his emphasis on diasporic cultural relationships and a concomitant suspicion of nation-based traditions".[51] Hlongwane, together with a number of other cultural theorists, calls for a renewed focus on the intersections of race and nation: "This insistence is pertinent to a country where black identities are asked to disappear in the currently fashionable theorisations of creolisation and hybridity".[52] Put simply, Hlongwane's concern is that concepts like creolisation are being co-opted in ways that mask the continuing racial inequities that prevail even after ten years of democracy. This has resulted in calls for a 'transitory' racial awareness, not as an absolute, but as a strategy to counter what Hlongwane describes as notions of creolisation that "clearly elide the felt racial alienation and insecurities of some members of the nation".[53] However, my own feeling is that while it is true that racism is very much alive and well in the "new South Africa" (one only has to tune in to local talk shows for a sense of the prevalence of startlingly unreconstructed racially-based views, particularly from white callers), it is nevertheless also true that there are simultaneously some remarkable examples of cultural creolisation and other interactions which point to negotiated, or transformative ways of being in the world: it seems important that the one should not negate the other, thus continuing the legacy of binaries so common to South African discourses.

Unlike "Jesus is Indian", in which Angelina's story-writing offers imagined choices and anticipates 'new configurations' in the future, in Olive Senior's "Arrival of the Snake-Woman", Ishmael uses his story to make sense of his past and of a changing, modern Jamaica: "And this is why I sometimes sit and write down the things that happened in the old days, so that my children will be able to see clearly where we are coming from, should they ever need signposts".[54] In the two stories by Senior and Sam, 'Asian-ess' is shown as destabilising both the dominant and the traditional social structures. The position of the migrant woman, far from resulting in marginalisaton within her community, is seen as a force for introducing changes. Miss Coolie converts to Christianity as this is the only way to ensure that her son will have access to education, but once the government school has been established, she returns to her Hindu faith.

This pragmatism identifies Miss Coolie as "the embodiment of the spirit of the new age";[55] her rupture from her country of birth provides her from the start "with an understanding of the world that the rest of us lacked".[56] The anticipation of 'new configurations' in the future for Angelina and the "new age" of a modern creole society for Ishmael and Miss Coolie, comes as the result of an encounter between Asian-ness and dominant and / or traditional values. However, this also entails loss, and for Ishmael, Miss Coolie always remains "a mystery". He wonders whether she has accepted her new life without regret: "I can never be sure, for there is the evidence of the saris, the red dot, the Indian names. And sometimes, when I look into her eyes, I can still see the Ganges."[57]

Reading South African works through the lens of Caribbean texts can thus offer additional perspectives. For instance, a comparison of creolisation and 'cultural convergence' described by

Senior and Sam suggests the possibility for similar pragmatic cultural creolisations in the South African context as we move away from discourses of identity based on apartheid oppositions and engage with the tricky discourses of an apparently 'new' nationhood. At the same time, this also suggests potential areas for future comparative studies. As mentioned earlier, the creative appropriation of spoken dialects by Caribbean writers can fruitfully be looked at in relation to similar concerns with voice in the South African context. While the Caribbean has established a strong tradition of incorporating vernacular voices and local knowledges in literary works, South African writers are at last increasingly beginning to experiment in a more sustained way. Interestingly, for the last decade this has in fact become a focal point of local performance trends: but perhaps this should be the subject of another comparative study.

Notes

This chapter draws on arguments presented in my unpublished doctoral dissertation, "Aesthetics of Transformation: A Comparative Study of Selected Writings by Women from South Africa and the Caribbean", University of Natal, Pietermaritzburg, 1998.

Discussion of selected texts draws from my following publications: "Not-Quite Insiders and Not-Quite Outsiders: The Process of Womanhood in Beka Lamb, *Nervous Conditions* and *Daughters of the Twilight*", *Journal of Commonwealth Literature* 27:1, 1992, 37-47; "Negotiated Readings: from Fanon's Colourless Literature to Colourful Stories by Women Criss-Crossing the Atlantic", *English Academy Review* 11, 1994, 51-62; "Asian Diasporas, Contending Identities and New Configurations: Stories by Agnes Sam and Olive Senior", *English in Africa* 25:1, 1998, 71-86; "'If I were her': Frictions of Development from Cape Town, Canada and the Caribbean: A Relational Reading", *Journal of Literary Studies* 15:1&2, 1999, 1-19; "Fictions of Home and (Un)belonging: Diasporan Frameworks in Michelle Cliff's *Abeng* and Zoë Wicomb's "Journey to the Gifberge", *Alternation*, 2001, 16-133.

1 Michelle Cliff: "A Woman Who Plays Trumpet is Deported". – In M. C.: *Bodies of Water*, London, 1991, p. 66.
2 Significantly, in August 2006 the building of a heritage centre to house the human remains led to the discovery of more remains, and work on the

heritage centre itself had to be halted. The intention is to use the centre for re-interment of the remains which have been discovered recently.

3 Between 1652-1808 the slave community was extremely diverse: "26 .4 per cent from Africa, (mostly Mozambique, but also West and central Africa), 25.9 per cent from India (Bengal, Malabar, Coromandel) and from Ceylon. 25.1 per cent from Madagascar; and 22.7 per cent from areas included in today's Indonesia." Significantly, slaves were taken from elsewhere because it was initially not Company policy to enslave "aboriginal people living there, the Khoikhoi pastoralists and Bushman hunter gatherers". See Denis-Constant Martin: *Coon Carnival. New Year in Cape Town, Past and Present,* Cape Town, 1999, p. 51.

4 There was sharp criticism of the visit locally given the fact that Haitians under Aristide were still mired in poverty. Nevertheless, in keeping with Mbeki's call for an African Renaissance, and in an attempt to redress the severing of Africans from their history, Mbeki insisted on the historical significance of the 1804 Haiti Revolution largely ignored by the school textbooks, which focus instead on the American Revolution of 1776 and the French Revolution of 1789; see Peter Fabricus: "Mbeki's historical justification for attending Haiti's celebration smacks more of voodoo than veracity", *Cape Times*, Monday 29 December, 2003, 9. What this debate also illustrates is the failure by some sectors to acknowledge links between slavery and the histories of Africa and South Africa. (Subsequently Aristide was forced to flee Haiti and is currently living in exile in South Africa).

5 As terms such as 'black', 'creole', 'coloured' and even 'white' are of course not fixed categories and may have different meanings within local South African and Caribbean contexts, I have opted not to use capitals, and follow the guidelines used by other commentators. Generally speaking, 'coloured' in the South African context refers to people of mixed descent, although there are a variety of sub-classifications within this group, such as 'Cape Coloured', 'Malay', 'Griqua' and 'Other Coloured'. For clarity, Constant-Martin uses "Africans" to refer to those whose mother tongue is a Bantu language. "Blacks" includes all those who were discriminated against by the laws of apartheid: Africans, coloureds and Indians". Martin: *Coon Carnival*, p. 4.

6 Wicomb's collection of linked stories, *You Can't Get Lost in Cape Town* (1987) has received much critical attention for her subtle representation of coloured subjectivity. Wicomb is also an astute cultural critic, and received the CNA award for her novel, *David's Story* (2000). Her latest novel, *Playing in the Light* (2006) deals with those who 'passed' for white.

7 Homi Bhabha: *The Location of Culture*, London & New York, 1994, p. 1; Paul Gilroy: *The Black Atlantic. Modernity and Double Consciousness*, Cambridge, 1993.

8 According to Lionnet, this is achieved by stating that the comparisons are warranted on "the theoretical basis of certain *sites* of literality and textuality" (emphasis in the text). In other words, the focus is on "a performative intertextuality which is a function of the ideological and cultural matrix that

generates the works"; Francoise Lionnet: "Geographies of Pain: Captive Bodies and Violent Acts in the Fictions of Myriam Warner-Vieyra, Gayl Jones and Bessie Head", *Callalloo* 16:1, 1993, 132-152, 136.

9 Cheryl Wall: *Changing Our Own Words. Essays on Criticism, Theory and Writings by Black Women*, Rutgers & London, 1989, p. 9.

10 Anthony Holiday: "The 'living dead' return to haunt the 'new' South Africa", *Cape Times*, 30 July 2003, 9.

11 In fact it has been claimed that this has come to 'symbolise' the current South African transitional novel; according to Meg Samuelson this continuing concern with the trope of miscegenation represents the 'failure of the South African literary imagination' in that this metaphorical use of women's bodies denies and distorts the reality faced by South African women who are subjected to violence and alarmingly high incidences of familial or *intra*racial, rather than *inter*racial, rape (my emphasis); moreover, "it also acts as an anchor securing us to the past and [preventing the nation] from being imagined in terms beyond the all-too-familiar ones of blood and race"; see Meg Samuleson: "The Rainbow Womb: Rape and Race in South African Fiction of the Transition", *Kunapipi* 24:1&2, 2002, 88-100, 97. This explains some of the controversy surrounding *Disgrace*, by the Nobel Prize winner, J. M. Coetzee, in which Lucy, the daughter of the narrator, an English academic who is charged with sexual harassment for raping one of his female students, is subjected to gang rape by a group of black men who invade her smallholding. Lucy, in a gesture read as resignation, reconciliation or regeneration decides to raise the child that is produced as a result, and cedes her smallholding to the erstwhile worker and his family who appear to have harboured the rapists.

12 Sailaja Sastry: "Assuming Identities", *Journal of Literary Studies* 18:3, 2002, 275-283, 279 (emphasis in the text).

13 Helena Maria Lima: "Revolutionary Developments: Michelle Cliffs' *No Telephone to Heaven* and Merle Collins' *Angel*", *Ariel* 24, 1993, 35-56.

14 For instance, Agnes Sam: "Jesus is Indian" (1989), Rayda Jacobs: *Sachs Street* (2001), Farida Karodia: *Other Secrets* (2000), Diane Case: *92 Queen's Road* (1991), Zoë Wicomb: *You Can't Get Lost in Cape Town* (1991), as well as works like Gcina Mhlophe's autobiographical play, *Have You Seen Zandile* (1986).

15 Danticat in an interview with Renée Shea: see Renée H. Shea: "'The Hunger to Tell': Edwidge Danticat and *the farming of bones*", *MaComère* 2, 1999, 2-22.

16 These include Wicomb's award-winning *David's Story* (2000), Achmat Dangor's *Bitter Fruit* (2001), Rayda Jacob's *The Slave Book* (1998), Sello Duiker's apocalyptic *Thirteen Cents* (2000) and *The Quiet Violence of Dreams* (2001) and Phaswane Mpe's *Welcome to Our Hillbrow* (2001) which deals with pressing current social issues such as HIV / AIDS, urbanisation and community, as well as the xenophobia experienced by African migrants living in post-1994 Johannesburg.

17 In his study of the history of the Cape Minstrel traditions, Denis-Constant Martin discusses the role of 'Kaaps', a local dialect of Afrikaans. He notes that originally there were forms of Portuguese creoles used alongside Dutch, and "the Creole that was to become Afrikaans therefore incorporated elements of Portuguese and Portuguese Creoles originating in Asia or in Africa, from Khoikhoi languages and from the at least seven languages originally spoken by Asian slaves". Dutch thus became creolised in this multilingual context, and by the beginning of the 19th century, "the language used by Cape settlers was no longer understood by native Hollanders"; see Martin: *Coon Carnival*, p. 57. Interestingly, the first written text in Afrikaans was in Arabic script, since it was of course the language of the largely Islamic Malay community.

18 Stephan Meyer & Thomas Oliver: "Alternative Modernities in African Literatures and Cutures", *Journal of Literary Studies* 18:1&2, 2002, 1-23, 14. See also Gugu Hlongwane: "What Has Modernity To Do With It?: Camouflaging Race in the 'New' South Africa", *Journal of Literary Studies* 18:1&2, 2002, 111-131, for an overview of these debates.

19 Bruce Woodcock: "Post-1975 Caribbean Fiction and the Challenge to English Literature", *Critical Quarterly*, 28:4, 1987, 79-95, 83.

20 Michael Chapman: *Southern African Literatures*, London & New York, 1995, p. 307.

21 Jane Wilkinson (Ed.): *Talking With African Writers. Studies in African Literature*, London, 1992, pp. 190-191.

22 See Woodcock: "Post-1975 Caribbean Fiction", 84.

23 Carol Boyce Davies: "Afro-Brazilian Women, Culture and Literature: An Introduction and an Interview with Miriam Alvea", *MaComère* 1, 1998, 57-74, 59, 62.

24 Lima: "Revolutionary Developments".

25 Mae Gwendolyn Henderson: "Speaking in Tongues: Dialogics, Dialectics and the Black Woman's Literary Tradition." – In Cheryl Wall (Ed.): *Changing Our Own Words*, London & New York, 1989, pp. 16-37, 17.

26 Wall (Ed.): *Changing Our Own Words*, p. 10.

27 Judith Kegan Gardiner: "Gender, Value and Lessing's Cats." – In Shari Benstock (Ed.): *Feminist Issues in Literary Scholarship*, Bloomington, IN, 1987, pp. 110-123, 112.

28 For a more detailed discussion of these two texts, see Miki Flockeman: "Not-Quite Insiders and Not-Quite Outsiders: The Process of Womanhood in Beka Lamb, *Nervous Conditions* and *Daughters of the Twilight*", *Journal of Commonwealth Literature* 27:1, 1992, 37-47.

29 See Trinh T. Minh-ha: "Not You / Like You: Postcolonial Women and the Interlocking of Identity and Difference", *Inscriptions* 3:4, 1988, 71-77.

30 Daniel W. Ross: "Celie in the Looking Glass: The Desire for Selfhood in *The Color Purple*", *Modern Fiction Studies* 34:1, 1988, 69-84, 75.

31 Farida Karodia: *Daughters of the Twilight*, London, 1986, p. 30.

32 Bill Ashcroft & Gareth Griffiths & Helen Tiffin (Eds.): *The Post-Colonial Studies Reader,* London, 1995, p. 426.

33 Bhabha: *The Location of Culture*, p. 1.
34 Zee Edgell: *Beka Lamb*, London, 1982, p. 161.
35 Bev Brown: "Manson and Matrix: A Radical Experiment", *Kunapipi* 7:2&3, 1985, 66-80, 3.
36 Edgell: *Beka Lamb*, p. 1.
37 Kristen Mahlis: "Gender and Exile: Jamaica Kincaid's *Lucy*", *Modern Fiction Studies* 4:1, 164-183, 164.
38 *Ibid.*, 170.
39 See Miki Flockeman: "Fictions of Home and (Un)belonging: Diasporan Frameworks in Michelle Cliff's *Abeng* and Zoë Wicomb's "Journey to the Gifberge", *Alternation*, 2001, 16-133.
40 Michelle Cliff: "A Woman Who Plays Trumpet is Deported". – In M. C.: *Bodies of Water*, London, 1991, p. 57.
41 *Ibid.*, 58.
42 The Griqua, who have First People status, are people of indigenous Khoikhoi, settler and slave descent.
43 In Eva Hunter & Craig Mackenzie, (Eds.): *Between the Lines 11. Nelm Interview Series Number Six*, Grahamstown, SA, 1993, pp. 79-96, 91 (emphasis in the text).
44 Caroline Rooney: "Living Histories", *South African Review of Books*, Feb / May, 1990, 6.
45 See Carol Boyce Davies: "African Diaspora Literature and the Politics of Transformation", *Alternation* 3:2, 1996, 5-27, 10.
46 There have been a number of local definitions of creolisation: for instance, in her discussion of creolisation in relation to coloured identity, Zimitri Erasmus distinguishes between hybridity and creolisation: "hybridity refers to all cultural formations. Creolization refers to cultural formations historically shaped by conditions of slavery"; Zimitri Erasmus (Ed.): "Introduction: Re-imagining Coloured Identities in Post-Apartheid South Africa", *Coloured by History Shaped by Place*, Cape Town, 2001, pp. 13-28, 22.
47 In Michael Dash: "Textual Error and Cultural Crossing: A Caribbean Poetics of Creolization", *Research in African Literatures* 25:2, 1994, 159-168, 164.
48 *Ibid.,* 166.
49 Graham Huggan: "Opting out of the (Critical) Common Market: Creolization and the Postcolonial Text", *Kunapipi* 11:1, 1989, 27-42, 31.
50 Olive Senior: *Arrival of the Snake-Woman and Other Stories*, Trinidad & Jamaica, 1989, p. 3.
51 Hlongwane: "What Has Modernity To Do With It?", 113.
52 *Ibid.*
53 *Ibid.*, 115.
54 Agnes Sam: *Jesus is Indian and Other Stories*, London, 1989, p. 45.
55 *Ibid.*, 44.
56 *Ibid.*, 45.
57 *Ibid.*

Monika Gomille (Düsseldorf)

Translating the Caribbean: Issues of Literary and Postcolonial Translation

Postcolonial writers have radically redefined traditional concepts of translation; while releasing it from its former instrumental role in processes of linguistic transfer, on the one hand, they have, at the same time, inaugurated a considerable broadening of its scope. Translation is now considered to be the basic activity in any form of cultural contact.[1] My essay will focus on the special status of Caribbean culture and literature in this shift of paradigms. Witnessing the first encounter between Europe and America,[2] the Caribbean represents an archetypical scenario of translation[3] which can illustrate its ambiguous role in history. On the one hand, it was instrumental in the processes of the colonisation and suppression of the newly discovered parts of the world by the European powers during the Renaissance and the eighteenth century; on the other hand, it has, as a creative act, been fundamental to the formation of an independent Caribbean culture and literature established by writers from the former colonies during the recent decades. Present-day definitions of translation, therefore, not only take into account the late twentieth-century phenomenon of mass migration of people from all parts of the former Empire,[4] but also the migration of texts and discourses between the mother country and its former colonies,[5] i.e. the creative reworking of those texts. Rewriting has therefore been thematised as a form of translation.[6]

With V. S. Naipaul's *The Enigma of Arrival* (1987) as paradigm, I will attempt to show that Caribbean literature and culture, being largely shaped by processes of both linguistic and cultural translation, have produced a variety of significant images and metaphors that reflect these practices. Naipaul's fictional autobiography exploits and reworks key images like the ship(wreck)[7] and the journey that have dominated Caribbean writing for decades.[8] What makes his fiction representative of Caribbean writing is not least his re-writing, i.e. translating of the "Mediterranean reference points"[9] connected with the early history of colonialism in the New World. I will show that on this matter his translation of the image of the ruin is central, not least, as I will argue below, because it also concerns the 'sense of place' which has been considered to be a key issue in Caribbean writing.[10]

Homi K. Bhabha characterized translation as "the staging of cultural difference"[11] and thus emphasized its performative nature. This means to privilege spatial over temporal modes of translation. I will argue that Naipaul, in *The Enigma of Arrival*, explores performative and spatial practices of translation. This becomes obvious from the walking tours of the narrator in *The Enigma of Arrival* who creates a spatial pattern, a network of paths which metonymically represent the physical and cultural passages that lead to new translations of the self.[12] The narrator's "nerves of a stranger" (EA, 22), betraying his increased sense of cultural difference, are essential for the process of translation. Roaming through the surroundings of Avebury and Stonehenge, he makes the image of the ruin the vanishing point of his reflections about cultural difference. The reader is lead through a landscape characterised by the aesthetics of the picturesque.[13] As an instance of cultural difference, Naipaul's narrator problematises the nexus between the ruin and melancholy, represented by the landlord, which has dominated the concept of the ruin since the late eighteenth century; in *The Enigma of Arrial*, this nexus is exposed as an element of the 'colonial' aesthetics: "An empire lay between us. This empire at the same time linked us. […] But we were – or had started – at opposite ends of wealth and privilege, and in the hearts of different cultures" (EA, 174). At the same time, however, the narrator's obsession with ruin and decay, his compulsion "to see the possibility, the certainty, of ruin, even at the moment of creation" (EA, 25), is thematised, too; it indicates a specific mentality, a "temperament" (EA, 25) which, as the author repeatedly pointed out, is the result of cultural translation, i.e. the educational system of the former colonies: "The migration, within the British Empire, from India to Trinidad had given me the English language as my own, and a particular education."[14]

The before-mentioned notion of displacement of people, texts and topoi is, in *The Enigma of Arrival*, connected with the notion that "the idea of culture as a set of unchanging and coherent values, behaviours or attitudes has given way to the idea of culture as negotiation, symbolic competition or 'performance'",[15] on the one hand, and the notion of an essential discontinuity between past and present, on the other; this means that translation is thus "not a smooth transition, a consensual continuity, but the configuration of the disjunctive rewriting of the transcultural, migrant experience".[16] Naipaul's emphasis on discontinuity manifests itself by the subversion of linear time characteristic of the modern western view with cyclical structures (nature, the seasons of the year); it has its counterpart in the replacement of the sequential character of (autobiographical) narration by patterns of repetition and analogy that make it difficult to distinguish the beginning of the novel from its end.[17]

An important background to both Bhabha's theoretical and Naipaul's performative conception of translation can be seen in the 'textual turn' of anthropology. While translation had traditionally an important position in anthropology, above all in the transfer of oral material (myths, tales, conversations etc) into written texts, it developed, during the 1980s, into "a metaphor based on the notion of making the meanings of one way of life comprehensible in the language of another".[18] In this connection, the study of the rhetorical and textual conventions of ethnographic writing exposed the constructive character of representation,[19] leading to an increased insight into the important role of translation in the construction of cultures. Naipaul, however, also refers to older concepts of anthropology and translation, making use of the idea of 'survival' central in late nineteenth-century thought. This connects him with authors and thinkers like Walter Pater (1839-1894) who took an interest in the 'survival' of mentalities and emotions of earlier cultures.[20] Pater considered the relationships with the dead as stimuli for cultures;[21] as William F. Shuter wrote: "(he) reflect(ed) on what culture has gained from humanity's persistent efforts to imagine the condition of the dead".[22] Similarly, Naipaul's interest in ancestor-worship is fundamental to his reflections about culture. In *The Enigma of Arrival*, this interest shows itself by the narrator's daily excursions leading him to the landscape of Avebury that is characterised by an abundance of prehistoric grave mounds: "Daily I saw the mounds that had been raised so many centuries before. The number of these mounds! They lay all around." (EA, 23)

In accordance with late nineteenth-century conceptions, he considers cultural artefacts as representations of past world views:[23] "I wanted […] to leave no accessible mound unlooked at, feeling that if I looked hard enough and long enough I might arrive, not at an understanding of the religious mystery, but an appreciation of the labour" (EA, 23). Studying ancient culture and religion, he follows the ceremonial paths and tries to re-enact the cultural practices associated with the ancient grave mounds:

> Daily I walked in the wide grassy way between the flint slopes […] Daily I saw the mounds. (…) Daily I walked in the wide grassy way […] Daily I climbed up from the bottom of the valley. (EA, 23)

The narrator's attempt to recover the habits and feelings of an ancient past by way of the "mnemonics of the body"[24] is mirrored by the practices of the gardener Pitton and Jack, the "remnant of an old peasantry" (EA, 22), whose passion for gardening evokes "a version of a Book of Hours" (EA, 20). Walking and gardening (re-) create an 'inhabited' landscape traversed by innumerable paths that intersect repeatedly and betray the return to the same place; the landscape is permanently altered and continuously revalued and interpreted. Like the gardener Pitton, the walker / narrator considers his movements as part of a greater scheme: "I continued easily in that rhythm of creation and walk" (EA, 156). Landscape, therefore, is not a static concept and an object of viewing but a palimpsest saturated in cultural symbolism,[25] a texture formed by human movement; it has a polysemous character as it is criss-crossed by various narrative structures.

The Enigma of Arrival, therefore, shows that for Naipaul processes of rewriting / translation always involve elements of excavation and retrieval.[26] This connects his fiction with a theoreticial strand represented by Stuart Hall whose concept of the "hidden stories"[27] implies acts of translation and border crossing that imaginatively connect a variety of cultural spaces and historical times;[28] "the wide grassy way between the flint slopes, past chalk valleys rubbled white" (EA, 23) can, therefore, evoke "a Himalayan valley strewn in midsummer with old, gritted snow" (EA, 23). Naipaul's emphasis on processes of excavation brings to the fore a non-western, pre-modern view of landscape. In a landscape seen as cultural palimpsest, a "living space",[29] past life is still present. The narrator thus creates a past that appears as "something one could stretch out and reach" (EA, 170).[30] The palimpsestic character of the landscape subverts the modern (western) view of the past as loss;[31] equally, the idea of translation as the digging out of "hidden stories" in a text seen as palimpsest does not mean to produce, by way of translation, a copy but "to re-enact a relationship".[32] At the same time, the metaphor of the palimpsest implies that the "hidden stories" leading to its coming into being must be re-enacted and revised.[33]

An archetypical translation scenario forming the centre of Naipaul's fictional autobiography puts the before-mentioned concepts of translation in a nutshell. It describes a painting by the Italian artist Giorgio de Chirico (1888-1978) the author-narrator, suffering from illness and fatigue, found by mere accident as a tenant of a cottage on the grounds of a ruined manor house in the county of Wiltshire:

> The cottage at that time still had the books and some of the furniture of the people who had been there before. Among the books was one that was very small, a paperback booklet, smaller in format than the average paperbacks and with only a few pages. (EA, 91)

The narrator's interest is aroused by the painting's title: "I felt that in an indirect, poetical way the title referred to something in my own experience" (EA, 91); he describes it from memory with the following words:

> A classical scene, Mediterranean, ancient-Roman [...]. A wharf; in the background, beyond walls and gateways (like cut-outs), there is the top of the mast of an antique vessel; on an otherwise deserted street in the foreground there are two figures, both muffled, one perhaps the person who has arrived, the other perhaps a native of the port. (EA, 91)

De Chirico's painting, which gave the novel its title, serves as a *leitmotif* of the novel, as it becomes the central metaphor for cross-cultural encounters, i.e. cultural translation. The above-cited passage contains the essential imagery of cultural translation dominating Caribbean writing. The ship and the port are polyvalent images[34] connected with the allegory of the journey of life, a motif that has been considered to signify the "instability of the existence in the West";[35] P. S. Chauhan wrote:

> The arrivals and the departures with which the lives of the characters of the West Indian novel are punctuated, indicate an inescapable desire to flee not only an oppressive past or present but also an oppressing psyche, the need to break out of a choking self that is urgent in most protagonists. The compulsive obsession that frantically drives innumerable people away from their homes and the world of their affections is the hallmark of the colonial psyche, a feature not easily forgotten by the Caribbean writer.[36]

In *The Enigma of Arrival*, the allegory of the journey of life functions as a mis-en-abîme of the author's own life and writing.[37] Its main aspect is, however, on "the mystery of arrival" (EA, 92), illustrated by the "two figures, both muffled" (EA, 91). The painting becomes the starting point of a narrative set in the heart of the Old World: "My story was to be set in classical times, in the Mediterranean. My narrator [...] would arrive [...] at that classical port with the walls and gateways like cut-outs" (EA, 92). The "classical port" is a complex image dominating not only Naipaul's continuing reflections about the "creation of place as starting point for the negotiation of identity and community"[38] but also the vital role of translation in this process. The intricate complexities of the processes of cultural translation are illustrated in the newcomer's overcoming obstacles and symbols of rejection embodied in the "muffled figure on the quayside" (EA, 92). At last he gets access to the territory, i.e. crosses the border: "He would walk past that muffled figure on the quayside. He would move from that silence and desolation, that blankness, to a gateway or door" (EA, 92); his initial triumph, however, "give(s) way to panic" (EA, 92) as he feels the threat of losing his identity. The loss of identity is symbolized by the protagonist's forgetting his task and getting lost in the labyrinth of the dangerous classical city (EA, 93) which, with its bustling activity and its time-honoured stock of knowledge, is, in George Lamming's words, an "ancient mausoleum of historic achievement":[39]

> He would enter there and be swallowed by the life and noise of a crowded city [...] The mission he had come on [...] would give him encounters and adventures. He would enter interiors, of houses and temples. Gradually there would come to him a feeling that he was getting nowhere; he would lose his sense of mission; he would begin to know only that he was lost. His feeling of adventure would give way to panic. (EA, 92)

This scene shows the protagonist's wish to return: (He would want to escape, to get back to the quayside and his ship" [EA, 92]), and initially everything seems to be going as he wants: "At the moment of crisis he would come upon a door, open it, and find himself back on the quayside of arrival. He has been saved; the world is as he remembered it" (EA, 92). However, "only one thing is missing now. Above the cut-out walls and buildings there is no mast, no sail. The antique ship has gone". (EA, 92) As in Lamming's *Pleasures of Exile*, in *The Enigma of Arrival* "the change has been irrevocable, ([...] some identity has quite simply been lost und must be forged anew in new circumstances".[40] This scene, showing both the necessity and the violence of translation, is characteristic of the Caribbean archetype. Like Caliban, the narrator in *The Enigma of Arrival* is a prisoner of "Prospero's gift";[41] as George Lamming wrote with respect to the ambivalence of knowledge characterizing the Caribbean archetype: "It has a certain finality. Caliban will never be the same again."[42]

The central passage in *The Enigma of Arrival* dealing with the ambivalence of cultural knowledge exploits the image of the ship and the vocabulary of navigation traditionally used for the negotiation of (cultural) authority.[43] This means to challenge "the notion of the colony as a copy or translation of the great European original"[44] and to inaugurate a process of "reappropriating and reassessing the term (translation) itself".[45] I will try to show that the afore-mentioned image of the ruin is central in this respect. In *The Enigma of Arrival* it serves as one of the afore-mentioned "reference points to classical antiquity"[46] important for the negotiation of cultural knowledge. Pointing out the significance of classical culture for early colonialism, Hulme argued that classical antiquity became a storehouse of images and myths for the self-representation of the European powers during the phase of their colonial expansion.[47] In Naipaul's fiction, the European discourse of the meditation on ruins[48] functions as one of those "myths". In *The Enigma of Arrival* the ruin is highlighted as a cultural symbol that has structured the European visual memory for centuries. Its development was closely connected with the formation of historical thought which took a decisive turn during the Renaissance.[49] The motif of crumbling walls and disintegrating architecture did not appear before the fourteenth century. In paintings representing the Nativity of Christ, ruins overgrown with plants symbolize a new phase in the history of salvation, i.e. the transition from the Old to the New Covenant. The ruin thus marks a way of considering the past as a form of time fundamentally different from both the present and the future. Its prevailing presence in Renaissance painting is a visible expression of the new conception of time and history in the modern age.

Naipaul's reflections about the "survival", i.e. translation of this new conception of time and history, in other words, the modern hegemony of the European model of historiography with its implicit philosophy of history[50] dominate his fiction. This implies, on the one hand, to translate one historical period or culture into another and, on the other hand, to go past the confrontations of history that have been considered to mark the Caribbean excentricity.[51] This becomes especially evident from Naipaul's early novels *A House for Mr. Biswas* (1961) and *A Bend in the River* (1979), where he is concerned with the "sense of loss" (AD, 144) intricately connected with the European "sense of history" (AD, 144). This "sense of history" transmitted by the colonial educational system forms the background to his almost obsessive dealing with the experience of loss, dislocation, and cultural disorientation. In this framework, in *A House for Mr. Biswas*, the protagonist, the descendent of West-Indian indentured labourers, tries to emancipate himself from his past in the wider framework of the idea of a principal rationality of the historical process and its dialectical relationship with human development. The plot's correlative is Naipaul's orientation, in this novel, towards literary realism and its writing conventions dominated by the teleological model of history.[52]

In *A Bend in the River*, the European view of time and history is subverted by non-western conceptions. The novel exploits the classical topos of the meditation on ruins, considering the ruin as a sign for a past civilization which has a normative function for the present. Father Huismans exposes the evolutionary paradigm closely affiliated with the colonial ideologies and the nineteenth-century view of history:

> He didn't simply see himself in a place in the bush; he saw himself as part of an immense flow of history. […] For him the destruction of the European town, the town that his countrymen had built, was only a temporary setback. Such things happened when something big and new was being set up, when the course of history was being altered.[53]

The West-Indian merchant Salim who, like the author himself, moves between different cultures and thus represents the in-between-ness essential to acts of translation, confronts the teleological model of history and the related concept of memory with non-western traditions which are, from a European perspective, characterized by the dominance of the present, i.e. the "absence" of history:[54]

> But little had changed in the manners or minds of men [...] People lived as they had always done; there was no break between past and present. All that had happened in the past was washed away, there was always only the present. (BR, 18)

As Salim points out, in cultures without a fundamental separation between past and present, the techniques of remembrance must necessarily be different:

> Everyman here knew that he was watched from above by his ancestors, living forever in a higher sphere, their passage on earth not forgotten, but essentially preserved, part of the presence of the forest. (BR, 15)

The "presence of the forest", i.e. the ancestors' "passage on earth" (BR, 15) is remembered in the framework of a spatial structure established by bodily practices, i.e. movement inscribed on the landscape;[55] in other words, in cultures constructing the past in another way, ruins cannot function as material manifestations of historical otherness.[56] This becomes also obvious in Naupaul's *Mimic Men* (1967), where the narrator evokes the ruin meditation as one of the European master narratives:

> I came to the ruins of the famous old slave plantation, the overgrown brick walls of the sugar factory, the bricks brought as ballast in the eighteenth-century ships from Europe. And, oh, I wanted to cry.[57]

The reader's expectations are, however, disappointed, as the narrator changes to the comic mode, mentioning "that this (ruin) was a favourite spot for courting couples as well as rapists and others seeking social revenge" (MM, 79). Similarly, in *A Bend in the River* Salim talks about a ruin connected with the slave trade during the islamic occupation of Eastern Africa:

> There was a stockade on this beach. The walls were of brick. It was a ruin when I was a boy, and in tropical Africa, land of impermanent building, it was like a rare piece of history. It was in this stockade that the slaves were kept after they had been marched down from the interior in the caravans; there they waited for the dhows to take them across the sea. (BR, 18)

As he makes clear, however, the ruin can only function as a sign of remembrance in a culture where there are written records; in cultures transmitting memory orally it has no significance: "But if you didn't know, then the place was nothing, just four crumbling walls in a picture-postcard setting of beach and coconut trees." (BR, 18). In cultures dominated by orality, on the other hand, forms of implicit knowledge are central: "We simply lived; we did what was expected of us, what we had seen the previous generation do. We never asked why; we never recorded." (BR, 17)

In these cultures, bodily practrices are important forms of knowledge and can function as memory systems.[58] In this connection, the afore-mentioned "ceremonies of the body" re-enacted by the narrator / walker in *The Enigma of Arrival* come into play again, as Naipaul's fiction tries to reconstruct "hidden stories", i.e. translates historically and culturally disparate areas and places by imaginative acts of "mapping".[59] He juxtaposes the spatial and performative techniques for the formation of identity and memory characterising the archaic cultures of Avebury and Stonehenge (i.e. the material (re-)structuring and (re-)arrangement of the monuments and artefacts and the related rites and bodily practices that have materialised in an impressive landscape of ruins) with present-day orally-dominated cultures, and the aesthetic practices that have characterized western cultures since the late eighteenth century. Only in the last-mentioned cultures dominated by the written word ruins can function as signs of memory, the memory of a distanced, 'museal' past represented, in *The Enigma of Arrival*, by Stonehenge. This means to translate between a 'cultural' and a modern aesthetic view of the landscape / ruin, i.e. between the conceptualization of the landscape as formed by human (inter-)action, on the one hand, and the aesthetic concept of the landscape that came into being within the framework of a specific construction of the past, on the other. As my readings of *A Bend in the River* and *The Enigma of Arrival* have shown, the ruin can only function as an allegory of a 'dead' past, i.e. the hiatus between past and present dominating the modern western discourse about time; it is only in this framework that the narrator in *The Enigma of Arrival* can describe the landscape as "a vast burial ground" (EA, 24), where the ruin becomes a symbol of *vanitas*, "at once diminishing and ennobling the current activities of men" (EA, 24).

To conclude, Naipaul's fiction is informed by various aspects of translation, as it has shaped Caribbean identities for centuries. In *The Enigma of Arrival*, he presents the central tropes highlighting an archetypal scene of translation: the ship and the Mediterranean port. They are reminiscent of the passage of "Prospero's gift"[60] from the Old to the New World and the violence associated with this initial act of knowledge transfer. Naipaul, however, does not leave it at that but rewrites / translates the Caribbean archetype, the figure of Caliban. The narrator, in *The Enigma of Arrival*, imagines him as a migrant arriving at a foreign port and being overwhelmed by the storehouse of knowledge symbolised by that "classical Roman world" (EA, 92). In *The Enigma of Arrival*, however, Caliban's story does not end with the "seizure of books";[61] as the narrator's double, he represents a storehouse of knowledge, too: the knowledge of the 'other' that he translates, as he carries it from the periphery to the centre. This marginalized knowledge undermines dominant discourses like, for instance, the linear time concept by spatial constructions of memory, identity, and time. He can thus translate the "hidden stories" of a palimpsestic landscape into one another and try to re-appropriate a landscape that has been a purely aesthetic artefact, with the ruin as its central aesthetic symbol, as a space of culture which, in *The Enigma of Arrival*, he identifies, in its original sense, with "labour" (EA, 23), the "labour" of tilling the land and the essential tasks and beliefs associated with it. Thus, the narrator's act of appropriation of a landscape by way of bodily movement is, at the same time, a way of reclaiming the past, as his movements trigger memories of Trinidad.[62] The narrator's repetitive walking over the landscape, followed by a journey to his native island with its "sacred places of […] childhood" (EA, 318), implies acts of constructing identity by way of 'mapping' the land and retelling its story, and his participation in the Hindu rites for his dead sister enables him to keep his cultural heritage alive, to translate it into present cultural practice. It means a new beginning for the writer and the start of a new novel: "I lay aside my drafts and hesitations and began to write very fast about Jack and his garden" (EA, 318).

1 See, for instance, Susan Bassnett & Harish Trivedi (Eds.): "Introduction". – In S.B. & H.T. (Eds.): *Post-colonial Translation. Theory and Practice*, London & New York, 1999, pp. 1-18, 3.
2 Peter Hulme: *Colonial Encounters. Europe and the Native Caribbean, 1492 – 1797*, London & New York, 1986.
3 See, for instance, Marina Warner: *Indigo or, Mapping the Waters*, London, 1992, p. 162. The anagram 'Cannibal' / 'Caliban' can be considered as a foundational act of translation; see Peter Hulme: "Reading from Elsewhere: George Lamming and the Paradox of Exile". – In P. H. & William H. Sherman (Eds.): *The "Tempest" and its Travels*, London, 2000, pp. 220-235, 220.
4 The relationship between displacement, i.e. "the liminality of migrant experience" (Homi K.Bhabha: *The Location of Culture*, London & New York, 1994, p. 224) and translation has been theorized by Homi K. Bhabha: *Location*. Central in Bhabha's conception of translation, which challenged the narrow definition of translation as a purely linguistic process, are the poststructural challenge of foundational concepts (language, subject, nation), i.e. the binary relationships characterizing Western thought since the seventeenth century (see Sherry Simon: *Gender in Translation. Cultural Identity and the Politics of Transmission*, London & New York, 1996, p. 165) as well as the change in the conception of texts and their limits (see Monika Reif-Hülser: "Cross-Cuts – In Lieu of a Résumé". – In M. R.-H. (Ed.): *Borderlands. Negotiating Boundaries in Post-Colonial Writing*, ASNEL Papers 4, Amsterdam & Atlanta, Ga., 1999, pp. 274-289, 275). Bhabha's theory of translation centres on the "third space" between cultures, where acts of signification, and thus translation, take place; see Bassnett & Trivedi: *Post-colonial Translation,* 6.
5 According to André Leferve & Susan Bassnett, "history shows that translation constructs cultures It does so by negotiating the passage of texts between them"; "Where are we in Translation?". – In A.L. & S.B. (Eds.): *Constructing Cultures. Essays on Literary Translation*, Clevedon, 1998, pp. 1-11, 7.
6 *Ibid.*
7 Bénédict Ledent connects the image of the shipwreck with "the Caribbean archetype"; *Caryl Phillips*, Manchester, 2002, p. 68.
8 See, for instance, Judith Levy: *V.S. Naipaul. Displacement and Autobiography*, New York & London, 1995, p. 106.
9 Hulme: *Colonial Encounters*, p. 3.
10 See, for instance, Rocio G. Davis, who wrote that "writers from these locations struggle to construct a viable representation for the self as located self. At stake is here a landscape against which then I can authentically figure"; Rocio G.Davis: "Negotiating Place / Re-Creating Home. Short-Story Cycles by Naipaul, Mistry, and Vassanji". – In Jacqueline Bardolph (Ed.):

Telling Stories. Postcolonial Short Fiction in English, Amsterdam & Atlanta, Ga., pp. 323-332, 324.

11 Bhabha: *Location*, p. 227.

12 Ledent: *Caryl Phillips*, p. 119.

13 The modern view of the ruin / landscape is represented by Richard Payne Knight's theory of the picturesque; see Ann Bermingham: *Landscape and Ideology. The English Rustic Tradition, 1740-1860*, Berkeley, Ca., 1989, p. 72. In *The Enigma of Arrival*, the viewer's imagination is aroused by the grave mounds which can hardly be distinguished from the landscape. This implies an exclusively aesthetic perception of the ruin / landscape. Dominic Head argues that the narrator in *The Enigma of Arrival* "inhabit(s) (a) nostalgic pastoral and undermine(s) it from within"; Dominic Head: *The Cambridge Introduction to Modern British Fiction, 1950-2000*, Cambridge, 2002, p. 177.

14 Quotations are from the following edition: V. S. Naipaul: *The Enigma of Arrival*, London, 1987, p. 52. Further references to this edition will be included in the text (abbreviated as 'EA').

15 Simon: *Gender*, p. 153.

16 Bhabha: *Location*, p. 226.

17 Dominik Head argues that the "achronological manner in which (the narrator's) personal growth is detailed (...) pushes at the boundaries of the genres whilst remaining within them"; Dominic Head: *Cambridge Introduction*, p. 176.

18 Stephen A. Tyler: *The Unspeakable. Discourse, Dialogue, and Rhetoric in the Postmodern World*, Madison, Wisc., 1987, p. 96.

19 *Ibid.*, 90-95.

20 William F. Shuter: *Rereading Walter Pater*, Cambridge, 1997, p. 92.

21 *Ibid.*, 93.

22 *Ibid.*

23 *Ibid.*, 107.

24 Paul Connerton: *How Societies Remember*, Cambridge, 1989, p. 74.

25 Christopher Tilley: *A Phenomenology of Landscape, Places, Paths and Monuments*, Oxford & Providence, 1994, p. 26.

26 Chantal Zabus: *Tempests after Shakespeare*, New York, 2002, p. 6.

27 Stuart Hall: *Rassismus und kulturelle Identität. Ausgewählte Schriften*, vol. 2, Hamburg, 3rd ed., 2002, p. 28; see Reif-Hülser, "Cross-Cuts", p. 281.

28 Reif-Hülser points out that the "'act(s) of imaginary recovery" (*ibid.*, 280) implied here are closely connected with the rediscovery of identity.

29 *Ibid.*, 279.

30 Barbara Bender thematized the grave mounds and the network of ritual paths as a spatially organized system of memory, creating a structure of continuity between past and present; Barbara Bender: "Introduction. Landscape – Meaning and Action". – In B. B. (Ed.): *Landscape. Politics and Perspectives*, Providence & Oxford, 1993, pp. 1-17, 10.

31 Quotations are from the following edition: V. S. Naipaul: *An Area of Darkness*. London, (1964) 1968, p. 144. Further references to this edition will be included in the text (abbreviated as 'AD').

32 Eugene Chen Eoyang: *The Transparent Eye. Reflections on Translation, Chinese Literature, and Comparative Poetics*, Honolulu, 1993, p. 127.

33 For Naipaul's complex relationship to the landscape of colonial Trinidad see, for instance, Davis: "Negotiating", p. 325.

34 Travel by ship has been a recurrent motif in Naipaul's fiction; see Dennis Walder,: "V.S. Naipaul and the Postcolonial Order. Reading *In a Free State*". – In Jonathan White (Ed.): *Recasting the World. Writing After Colonialism*, Baltimore & London, 1993, pp. 82-119, 87.

35 P. S. Chauhan: "Caribbean Writing in English: Intimations of a Historical Nightmare". – In Radhika Mohanram & Gita Rajan (Eds.): *English Postcoloniality. Literatures from Around the World*, Westport, CT & London, 1996, p. 50.

36 *Ibid.*, 50.

37 Levy : *V.S. Naipaul*, p. 98.

38 Davis: "Negotiating", p. 332.

39 *The Pleasures of Exile*, London & New York, (1960) 1984; p. 27.

40 Hulme: "Reading", p. 229. What Hulme writes about Lamming is equally true for Naipaul: "He writes as someone educated in the English literary system, deeply aware of the 'whole tabernacle of English names', 'this ancient mausoleum of historic achievement' whose foundations he is determined to shake. […] the postcolonial response must involve at least a partial disidentification with Caliban on the grounds that Caliban is Prospero's creature, and postcolonial intellectuals, whilst having to recognize themselves in Caliban, should at the same time refuse any full identifiction and find another ground on which to stand"; *ibid.*

41 Lamming: *Pleasures*, p. 109.

42 *Ibid.*, p. 109.

43 Hulme, "Introduction". – In P. H. (Ed.): *Tempest*, pp. 3-11, 5. Shakespeare's *Tempest* is, according to Hulme, "about usurpation and force – and, in Caliban's case, the seizure of books" ("Preface". – In P. H. (Ed.): *Tempest*, pp. xi-xiv, xiii.), i.e. the transfer of cultural authority.

44 Bassnett & Trivedi: "Introduction", p. 4.

45 *Ibid.*, 5.

46 Hulme: *Encounters*, p. 3.

47 *Ibid.*, 35. Hulme considers myths such as the story of Dido and Aeneas as central in this process; *ibid.*, 252.

48 Cf. Vergil: *Aeneid*, VIII; see also Edwards Catharine: *Writing Rome. Textual Approaches to the City*, Cambridge, 1997, pp. 30-40. Naipaul's use of Vergil's *Aeneid* as a central intertext provides another powerful link between *The Enigma of Arrival* and Shakespeare's *Tempest* which is based on the *Aeneid*, too; Hulme, *Encounters*, 109.

49 Moshe Barash: “Die Ruine - ein historisches Emblem”. – In Klaus E. Müller & Jörn Rüsen (Eds.): *Historische Sinnbildung. Problemstellungen, Zeitkonzepte, Wahrnehmungshorizonte, Darstellungsstrategien*, Hamburg, 1997, pp. 519-535.

50 Nana Wilson-Tagoe: *Historical Thought and Literary Representation in West Indian Literature*, Gainsville, 1998, pp. 16-25.

51 Ledent: *Phillips*, p. 173.

52 Cf. Bhabha, “Representation and the Colonial Text: A Critical Exploration of Some Forms of Mimeticism”. – In Frank Gloversmith (Ed.): *The Theory of Reading*, Brighton, 1984, pp. 93-122.

53 Quotations are from the following edition: V. S. Naipaul: *A Bend in the River*, London, (1979) 1980, p. 68. Further references to this edition will be included in the text (abbreviated as ‘BR’).

54 See Johannes Fabian: *Time and the Other. How Anthropology Makes its Object*, New York, 1983.

55 Howard Morphy: “Landscape and the Reproduction of the Ancestral Past”. – In Eric Hirsch & Michael O’Hanlon (Eds.): *The Anthropology of Landscape. Perspectives on Place and Space*, Oxford, 1995, pp. 184-209.

56 Cf. Georg Simmel: *Aufsätze und Abhandlungen 1901-1902*, Frankfurt a.M. 1993, p. 129.

57 Quotations are from the following edition: V. S. Naipaul: *The Mimic Men*, (1967) London, 2002. Further references to this edition will be included in the text (abbreviated as ‘MM’).

58 Connerton distinguishes between “inscribing practice(s)”, typical for written cultures, and “*incorporating* practice(s)” characterizing oral cultures, i.e. the technical skills and the respective habits, movements, and gestures materialising in specific forms of “habit-memory”; *How Societies Remember*, p. 84.

59 See Mike Crang & Nigel Thrift, “Introduction”. – In M.C. & N. T. (Eds.): *Thinking Space*, London & New York, 2000, pp. 1-30.

60 Lamming: *Pleasures*, p. 109.

61 Hulme: “Preface”, p. xiii.

62 The landscapes of the Caribbean, with their exhausted soils on which monoculture has left its mark for centuries, are the dark counter-images of the picturesque landscape gardens of Great Britain; they are represented, for instance, by the hostile environment in *A House for Mr. Biswas*.

Mike Alleyne (Murfreesboro, TN)

Singing the Caribbean: An Introduction to Caribbean Music

This chapter attempts to explain some of the origins of Caribbean music, and also mainly catalogues its commercial development as major record companies have sought to capitalise on its international appeal. During this analysis, it is necessary to make regular reference to cultural conflicts which, I argue, have undermined the unique characteristics of popular music from the Caribbean. I am taking this particular approach because many misconceptions exist beyond the Caribbean region about the ways in which the music is represented as being genuine, when in fact the commercialisation process is a constant threat to notions of authenticity. These ideas surrounding what is 'real' in Caribbean music are essential components in identifying where commerce has overtaken culture by attempting to reshape the music to meet perceived audience requirements, rather than to use the music as a genuine representation of the cultures from which it purports to have come.

Why is Caribbean music important? It is especially noteworthy because its global impact is inversely proportionate to the size of the islands comprising the region, and its collective history as a receptor of colonial domination. So at face value, there is little to suggest that significantly influential music would come from a region deemed as politically insignificant in modern times. Furthermore, the dissemination of this music has given a public voice to the people through some artists expressing views that are muted in wider international political discourse, if they are heard at all. Typically, when Europeans or Americans hear of the Caribbean, Jamaica is probably the first and sometimes the only place which springs to mind. However, having lived and worked in the region for many years (and having parents from Barbados), I have a first-hand knowledge which is useful in examining local and global responses to the region's music and identifying cultural differences in the aural creative expression between islands.

I am creating a chronological overview of key phases in the development of the music, with an emphasis on the English-speaking or Anglophone territories, primarily because until recently they have arguably exerted the most visible international influence. It is worth noting, however, that with the global rise of reggaeton, a Puerto Rican-based streetwise commercial fusion of Jamaican dancehall, urban hip-hop and Latino orality, Hispanic popular music has developed an unprecedently high profile without sacrificing usage of Spanish in favor of English. This in itself is quite a remarkable feat in retaining a high degree of (admittedly hybridized) cultural representation while simultaneously achieving commercial success. However, as the genre's name clearly indicates, its rhythmic source is partially derived from reggae.

Nonetheless, I focus primarily on calypso and reggae because of their comparatively lengthy and well-documented histories of crossing cultures and languages in which these music forms have no indigenous roots. Furthermore, these genres have achieved varying degrees of success in major music markets, thereby making any discussion of their impact more easily demonstrable. However, it is worth noting that a variety of cultural influences are innately apparent in these music forms. For example, if we address the fabric of contemporary society in Trinidad, the traditional home of calypso, we find traces of African, British, Hispanic, and Asian populations all of which syncretically combined to create a nation unlike any other. Although one might find similar cultural combinations in Jamaica, reggae's birthplace, the mountainous geography and the larger land mass of that island are among the factors creating a different type of musical expression which is generally more rebellious in nature.

So Caribbean music is distinctly multicultural, with its West African roots simultaneously colliding and integrating with the cultural and musical practices of the region's many colonizers. The British, the French, the Spanish and the Dutch have all left their marks on the characteristics of Caribbean music, although frequently the channels and chronologies of transmission are less than entirely clear. What is evident from its longevity is that the rhythms and artists are infused with a kinetic energy which succeeds in transcending cultural barriers, even when diluted for commercial purposes.

1.Calypso

The case of calypso accurately reflects this complexity, bearing West African roots metamorphosed by the experience of enslaved displacement and European cultural hegemony in the Caribbean. The virtual extinction of the Caribbean's native Indian population of passive Arawaks and militant Caribs following the European arrival means that this discussion is focused on the Creole populations arising from transatlantic and inter-island relocation. Regardless of the colonial ruler, music was consistently seen as a potential catalyst for social uprising and opposition, with evidence of legislation against dance assemblies dating back to the 1600s in the French Antilles.[1]

Apart from the cultural and historical complexities which I will discuss shortly, calypso is above all a music of celebration. Its lyrics are wrapped in rhythm conducive to annual (and global) carnival activities which underline vitality and cultural colour.

Although in recent years there has been considerable debate about the geographical roots of calypso, it remains undisputed that the island of Trinidad – with its African, Spanish, French, British and East Indian influences – accelerated the cultivation and development of the art form. In this specific case, links between the importation of African Yoruba people to Trinidad in the 1800s underscore the fusion of extra-regional influences.[2] Essentially, calypso fuses abrasive sociopolitical commentary and satire with African derived percussively oriented rhythms. It is, therefore, a distinctly dance-oriented music form, and in the nineteenth century this cultural dimension reinforced the inherently communal nature of its musical accompaniment, as exemplified by the emergence of calypso tents as central performance venues before the 1920s. The satirical aspect of calypso has irritated many Trinidadian politicians and other public figures, offering social critique in an easily digestible and entertaining format.

Despite repeated efforts by the British to suppress public Afro-Caribbean cultural expression in the colonial era, calypso persisted as a vital outlet for the oppressed populace and provided one of the few ways to criticise their social conditions. A key turning point in the history of the region's popular music and specifically for calypso was the advent of the recording industry in America and Europe, and the early efforts to catalogue music from other cultures viewed as exotic. As early as 1912, American labels began recording acts from Trinidad, although the 1930s represented a watershed with the involvement of Decca and Columbia coupled with high profile appearances on American radio by prominent calypsonians such as Attila the Hun, Roaring Lion, and Lord Executor.[3] It was typical for calypso performers in the traditional mould to adopt a grandiose persona, coupled with a name embellished by a title suggestive of power. The idea was to convey mastery of language and storytelling, so there were many other similarly titled calypsonians over the following decades such as Macbeth the Great, The Mighty Sparrow, and Lord Executor. It might also be seen as another dimension of the retaliation to colonial oppression, in effect elevating the value and status not only of the calypsonians, but also all of the 'ordinary' people he represented.

Perhaps the most illuminating example of the genre's intercultural and commercial influences is the multilayered controversy surrounding "Rum and Coca Cola", a hit in America in 1945. The release of this Andrews Sisters version was the result of the misappropriation of its authorship by American comedian, Morey Amsterdam. "Rum and Coca Cola" was proven in court to have been previously performed by Trinidad's Lord Invader, and published under his lyrical authorship in a March 1943 pamphlet in Trinidad two years prior to the Andrews Sisters' recording. Another lawsuit was successfully filed by Barbadian musician, Lionel Belasco, over plagiarism of his chord arrangement, but the melodies on which the hit was based apparently came to Trinidad in the 1890s from Martinique as a folk tune called "L'Année Passée".[4]

Furthermore, the lyrics in the Andrews Sisters' version were altered in ways which undermined the subversive intent of the song in its original form. The Trinidad calypso utilized the mixing of rum and Coca Cola as a metaphor of sexually-based social interaction between Trinidad's female prostitutes and the males at the country's American military base in the closing years of World War II. All lyrical allusions to the trade in prostitution were obscured by the insertion of alternative phrases which also eliminated the anti-imperialist context of the song. In fact, in one vintage recording, Invader's performance is introduced as "the way it was intended to be sung" with reference to the work as "the song which had the world upset". This clearly indicates the importance of authenticity to the calypso makers and audiences in the 1940s. However, the key reason for the appeal and success of "Rum and Coca Cola" in any of its forms is the fusion of simple, memorable melodies and storytelling. It is this combination which has arguably provided calypso with much of its crosscultural impact.

In the following decade of the 1950s, the internationalization of calypso was further propelled by the waves of post-war Caribbean migration to Britain, and the first British recordings by performers such as the renowned Lord Kitchener and Lord Beginner, recording for developing record labels like Melodisc and Parlophone. Kitchener (real name: Aldwyn Roberts) was one of several Caribbean musicians who migrated to England in the 1940s and 1950s, seeking new opportunities. In Kitchener's case, he became one of the most prominent calypso figures in England, which experienced a brief wave of intense interest in the art form in the mid-Fifties.

The unprecedented American commercial success of Harry Belafonte's 1956 album, *Calypso*, released by RCA, signified a marketing apex for the genre despite the fact that the record shared little in common with authentic calypso. *Calypso* became the first million selling record in America by a solo artist, simultaneously raising the music's profile while also indicating its ephemeral presence as an outlet for trendy exoticism promoted by major labels as part of an anti-rock n' roll strategy. By 1957, calypso had lost its commercial strength in America as rock n' roll accelerated its momentum, and its influence in Britain would soon be diminished by the rise of Jamaican popular music coupled with the return to the Caribbean of several prominent calypsonians.

The cultural case of Harry Belafonte in the 1950's accentuates the many serious implications of the "Rum and Coca Cola" precedent. Wallis & Malm, who assess Belafonte's appropriation of West Indian folk songs in detail, cite a crisis of copyright inherent in his achievement of hit status.[5] In relation to several artists, among whom Belafonte figures prominently through his textual reinterpretations, they see "a pattern emerging whereby songs from small countries are often picked up and exploited internationally, with the original collector or publisher claiming the copyright on the "first there, first claim" principle, and with the original local composers or "collectors" getting left out.[6] Belafonte's attainment of international acclaim was largely based on his articulation of a rather clinical, Western commodified representation of calypso. Moreover, in such cases as the situation regarding "Day-O" or the "Banana Boat Song", a Jamaican folk song became a title copyrighted in the name of Belafonte and two others none of whom, it has since been conclusively determined, originated the work in question.[7] We should also recognize that while Belafonte experienced Jamaica first-hand as a child, he was born in New York and spent most of his childhood years there, thus giving his interpretations of Caribbean folk songs an innate intercultural flavour derived from his own life. As rock n' roll took hold in America, despite the efforts of both the political establishment and the record industry's major labels, calypso faded from the mainstream as yet another transient trend.

Calypso's lower profile in the 1960s, especially following the birth and explosion of reggae in the latter part of the decade, was addressed with the emergence of soca in the early 1970s. It derived its name from the calculated attempt to commercially fuse elements of soul and calypso, thereby adding a more attractive rhythm-driven veneer and accompaniment to traditional elements. The birth of soca is usually attributed to the late Lord Shorty (Garfield Blackman), with 1974 recognized as the year of the first soca release. However, in recent years, soca's origins have been disputed, most notably by pop star Eddy Grant who controversially cites his U.K. hit recording of "Black Skin Blue Eyed Boys" with The Equals as the first articulation of the rhythmic framework upon which soca was based.

Subsequently, soca has become the core of carnival activity among West Indian communities around the globe, and its successful production is no longer restricted to Trinidad. Montserrat produced Arrow whose "Hot Hot Hot" (first released in 1983) became an international hit in 1984. The 1990s also witnessed the emergence of soca-oriented performers from islands such as Barbados and Antigua which were previously underrated as sources of popular song. These recordings were embraced and consumed by the Trinidad audience and foreign metropolitan listeners. One key issue surrounding the success of soca has been the decline of lyrical depth and poetic artistry in favor of unimaginative and repetitive party sloganeering connected to high tempo digitally generated rhythms. As a result, some critics have complained that the art form of calypso is nearing extinction in the face of growing commercial demands and their creative consequences.

2. Reggae

Reggae is simply the most widely known and highly regarded music from the English-speaking Caribbean, forcefully speaking in its 1970s heyday to its audiences' spiritual and political aspirations in ways rarely achieved in any genre of popular music. Many writers have noted the peculiarity of reggae's success in spite of its decidedly religious perspectives (most evident in its frequent references to "Jah"), largely embracing the tenets of Rastafarianism and many aspects of its pro-black politics while simultaneously promoting global harmony. In addition, we have this hybrid music form arising from Jamaican society's downtrodden citizens, remarkably finding and connecting with wider audiences despite enormous odds.

The story of reggae cannot be told without broadly outlining the chronology of Jamaican popular music as a whole. Like calypso, the roots of Jamaica's music reside in African cultural legacies. Call and response vocal interaction between the performer(s) and audience, and the ubiquitous percussive character are two of the more prominent features indicating transatlantic cultural transference. The native Indian population was supplemented then replaced as a labor force by Africans, with a large influx occurring in the late 1800s.[8]

The result can be witnessed in Pocomania or Kumina, described as "an African ancestor worship cult emphasizing both singing and dancing" which has also survived in Rastafarian drumming.[9] Many writers refer to the African and European fusion evident in the Quadrille, a folk based interpretation of mid-nineteenth century European dance music. However, the calypso-flavored genre of Mento lies in closer historical proximity to the reggae era. With its emphasis on "narrative and topical commentary" and its basic acoustic accompaniment, parallels with calypso are inevitable. Mento figures prominently in the history of Jamaican popular music primarily as a catalyst for musicians who later adopted more urban oriented styles influenced by American rhythm & blues readily accessible through foreign radio broadcasts. Mento was more popular in rural areas, but the beginning of the 1950s marked the start of a rapid and irreversible decline to the point of becoming a traditional music form performed mostly for tourists by the end of the decade.[10] Nonetheless, Mento represents what appears to be the first indigenous Jamaican music to be recorded, becoming the country's first real popular music form and laying the foundation for a vibrant (though heavily corrupt) recording industry.

American-influenced big bands and R&B combos emerged in the 1940s and 1950s, exerting a distinctly more urban energy, which would later be manifested in the Ska explosion following Jamaica's independence from Britain in 1962. The true internationalization of Jamaican popular music was accelerated by the presence of expatriate West Indian populations, especially in Britain, and the development of export channels from the Jamaican industry itself as well as the inevitable formation of domestic labels to service this growing market segment. Melodisc's Blue Beat imprint became so well associated with its popular ska releases that the term 'blue beat' was also used as an interchangeable description for ska. By 1962, Chris Blackwell had formed the later enormously influential Island Records, though at this point his emphasis was on licensing masters from Jamaica for British release.

The single record which most helped to establish Island's financial viability in its difficult formative years was actually recorded in England. Blackwell organized Jamaican singer Millie Small's ska remake of the R&B song, "My Boy Lollipop", which in 1964 sold six million copies worldwide. In accounts of the era it generally appears that since in this early period the core British audience consisted of transplanted West Indians, no major textual divergence from conventional indigenous representation occurred. However, this reading of the exported Jamaican musical text is somewhat misleading. Jones correctly attributes the commercial impact of Island's first successful venture, the "My Boy Lollipop" single, to a textual formulation based on Blackwell's "attempts to manufacture a more marketable and widely acceptable form of Jamaican music"[11]. Essentially a diluted form of ska,

> [t]he song was recorded by mainly English session musicians and employed a full orchestral backing. It was a highly polished production, its clean treble-oriented sound far removed from the vigorous, bass-dominated recordings emanating from Jamaica during the same period. It was perhaps for this very reason that "My Boy Lollipop" reached number two in the British pop charts in 1964 and went on to become an international hit, selling 6 million copies worldwide.[12]

Thus, the enormous success of this textually reconfigured cultural extract unequivocally "signalled the commercial potential of mass marketing a popularized form of Jamaican music to whites".[13] The Trojan label (owned by Island) subsequently followed a similar route, simultaneously servicing its core roots audience while attempting to dissolve media prejudice towards reggae by releasing "a whole series of pop reggae" productions aimed specifically at a mass white audience.[14]

Before this commercial potential could be fully realized, there were still key phases through which Jamaica's music would pass. As the immediate post-independence fervor diminished in the face of harsh economic conditions and difficult political realities, the music itself began to reflect changes in the social temperament. The kinetic enthusiasm of ska was gradually replaced around 1966 by the slower rhythm of rock steady, which facilitated more instrumental emphasis, especially on bass, and greater room for expressive vocal articulation. This process loosely coincided with a growing consciousness of Rastafarian ideology, further ignited by the 1966 visit to Jamaica by Ethiopian monarch, Haile Selassie, worshipped as the living manifestation of God in the Rastafarian interpretation of biblical prophecy.

This organic interaction of events and circumstances contributed to a deepened national spiritual introspection enabling the music to become even slower and more instrumentally and lyrically emphatic regarding sociopolitical and religious themes. It has, therefore, been suggested that reggae emerged at this time as the most authentic Jamaican popular musical expression, unifying links with traditional folk precedents with the experiential complexities of modern life in the context of distant African historical roots. The recurrent theme expressed in the works of many artists was repatriation, without which spiritual recovery from the displacement wrought by slavery would be unrealistic. While the idea rarely manifested itself in actuality, it promoted a consciousness of Africa unlikely to have flourished under repressive British colonial rule.

1968 is broadly recognized as the year in which reggae made its debut, with Toots & the Maytals releasing the first work to actually use the word, albeit with a different spelling: "Do The Reggay". The music was also based on a dance style with the same name. As previously demonstrated with ska, expatriate markets were crucial to the growth and development of the music. However, the breakthrough attainment of pop singles chart placings particularly in the U.K simultaneously hinted at the commercial potential if the genre were to become more album oriented, and the pressure to compromise the music in favor of pop norms. Most of these hits were released by Trojan Records, an offshoot enterprise of Island Records, and described as one of the U.K's most commercially successful reggae labels.[15] Trojan's hits were often characterized by the addition of strings to recordings licensed from Jamaica, with the intent of making the songs programmable for such bastions of resistance as the BBC. Releases by Ken Boothe, Bob & Marcia, and Greyhound exemplify this overt commercialisation. The transatlantic success of Desmond Dekker in 1969 with "The Israelites" single (sung in Jamaican patois) alternatively indicated the possibilities for achieving popularity with more authentic material, but the reggae had not yet transcended its novelty value.

The 1973 cult movie starring reggae singer Jimmy Cliff, *The Harder They Come*, and its accompanying soundtrack, both funded by Island's Chris Blackwell, marked one of the first steps towards having Jamaican popular culture taken seriously in Europe and America. This was soon followed in the same year by the epochal release of The Wailers international album debut for Island Records, *Catch a Fire*. The cultural and commercial issues surrounding this album remain highly relevant to the mainstream global marketing of Caribbean music today.

Catch a Fire emerged at a time when reggae was not considered an album genre beyond the sale of compilations of already established hit singles, and this album was designed to favorably alter mainstream perceptions of the genre. Chris Blackwell, the founder of Island Records, had distributed singles by Bob Marley in the label's first days in the early 1960s, and had also lived in Jamaica prior to the label's formation. Consequently, he had a directly informed cultural awareness of Jamaica lacking among other industry entrepreneurs as well as a familiarity with the artistic development and potential of Marley, who by this time had become a member of The Wailers. Blackwell's vision of a mass marketable form of reggae seems, in retrospect, coincident with The Wailers dual motivation to find audiences beyond the comparatively narrow and notoriously corrupt confines of the Jamaican recording industry. In any event, *Catch a Fire* represented the first attempt to create an artistically cohesive reggae album which could appeal to the rock market. By all accounts, Marley himself was happily complicit in this process, although the ultimate representational power lay with Blackwell.

This imperative meant that it was the first reggae album with lyrics, critical liner notes and graphic conceptual sophistication linked to the album title, all in one package. The visual packaging of *Catch a Fire* as a reggae album dressed in rock clothing also had serious implications for the production of the music itself. The original recording for the album took place in Jamaica using a limited eight-track studio, and at this point The Wailers could independently determine the shape and sonic texture of the songs even though the modest project funding came from Chris Blackwell. Upon completion, the multitrack tapes and Marley relocated to London where extensive overdubs took place under Blackwell's supervision to ostensibly enhance the album's marketability. Some cultural critics have highlighted several problematic issues related to this phase of activity. While the visual repackaging has already been noted, the aural transformations were arguably far more questionable in nature. A principal point of contention is the emphasis of a treble-oriented mix to appeal to European and American rock audiences, when the sonic substance of reggae was and is derived from the emphatic resonances of lower frequencies, especially those produced by the drum and bass. In this sense, Blackwell's marketing strategy separated core authentic elements of reggae from the material that was supposed to be promoting the genre more widely than ever before. Moreover, in further attempting to appease white audiences which had previously proven highly resistant to reggae, Blackwell hired session men in London to perform prominent roles even though these musicians had never played reggae before. American guitarist, Wayne Perkins, states that when he first encountered the music in the studio it seemed both 'strange' and 'backward', and that he could only find a rhythmic norm to complete his overdubbed contribution by having the volume of the bass turned down in his headphones. Similarly, Texan keyboardist, John 'Rabbit' Bundrick, explained his complete unfamiliarity with the rhythmic accents required in reggae, and that Marley had to articulate these for him.

Simon Jones notes that Marley's voice was brought much further forward in the mix and that the basic tracks recorded in Jamaica were also speeded up as a further commercial concession to the perceived prejudices of the target audiences. U.K-based dub poet,

Linton Kwesi Johnson succinctly analyses the overall character of the album:

> Instead of concentrating exclusively on a bottom-heavy sound with the emphasis on drum and bass, you had on this record more of a 'toppy' mix, a lighter sound. The emphasis is more on the guitar and other fillers. On no other Jamaican reggae recording […] was such a clear cut attempt made to incorporate the modern electronic sounds of metropolitan music.[16]

In view of the scope and significance of the changes made to commercially enhance *Catch a Fire*, the question of the extent to which it can be considered representative of reggae at all has been repeatedly raised. The album's initially poor sales of a mere 14,000 copies in its first year of release clearly suggests that that it did not initially find its audience, although following Marley's ascent to superstar status it eventually became a million-selling release.

It is also worth noting that later sales were achieved at further cultural expense by replacing the artistic subtleties of the original album cover, which featured a Zippo lighter which the listener had to open to symbolically set the musical flame alight. This was supplanted (partly for economic reasons) by a full-frame headshot of Marley catching his own fire by smoking a marijuana cigarette. As cultural critic, Paul Gilroy summarizes Island Records visual portrayal of Marley:

> [H]is record company was promoting him as a swaggering and sexually available Rastaman shrouded by a cloud of ganja smoke. This variety of hyper-masculine representation had been thought essential to the development of Marley's appeal to rock audiences.[17]

Catch a Fire established a marketing template influencing not only Marley's later work, but also almost all major label dealings with reggae artists, leading to a succession of signings like Aswad, Steel Pulse and Third World characterized by calculated commercial manipulation. Despite the poetic and political qualities of Marley's work through which he established his popularity on later albums, they were consistently shaped by Blackwell's sonic marketing strategy and, perhaps rather by coincidence than design, some releases such as *Kaya* (1978) seemed preoccupied with romantic love in ways which undermined the core of Marley's artistic identity.

Further evidence of commercial decision-making divorced from cultural authenticity surrounds the posthumous 1992 single release, "Iron Lion Zion". The track was released to coincide with the 4 CD *Songs of Freedom* boxed set, despite the inclusion of an entirely different 1972/3 version on that compilation. Rather than representing the song in its original temporal context, the single was instead transformed to appeal to the sonic palate of the modern buyer. Several elements of the original recordings roots reggae characteristics were supplanted, for example, by synthesizer bass (never used by Marley), digital drum programming, new and very brightly recorded horns and foregrounding of lead and background vocals. In effect, the single promoted a temporally decontextualised representation only marginally related to the framework of the original recording.

Time magazine has enthusiastically cited Marley's 1977 album, *Exodus*, as the best album of the 20th century:

> Every song is a classic, from the messages of love to the anthems of revolution. But more than that, the album is a political and cultural nexus, drawing inspiration from the Third World and then giving voice to it the world over.[18]

However, the preference for this album is indicative of a mainstream tendency to embrace an artist without recognizing the value of their best work. While *Exodus* has been one of Marley's best-selling releases, its emphasis on lighter melodies and thematic content make it unrepresentative of his recorded catalogue as a whole, and it is certainly not his best album. The musical strength and political potency of *Survival*, released in 1979, is a far better example of Marley's creative genius and overall direction.

A key element contributing to the mainstream success of Marley was the adoption of reggae components or syntax by white pop / rock artists, although significantly they would achieve greater commercial success than almost every legitimate reggae act of the era. Paul Simon, Paul McCartney, Eric Clapton, Elton John, The Eagles, 10cc, The Police, and The Clash are all prominent 1970s examples, though few used reggae beyond the occasional novelty single. Clapton's 1974 cover version of Marley's "I Shot The Sheriff" catapulted reggae into pop mainstream consciousness on both sides of the Atlantic, but it simultaneously reinforced a pop-reggae norm stylistically unrelated to the authentic rhythmic and lyrical language of reggae.

Reggae's emergence in the 1970s was also propelled on a more underground level by the significance of dub, which even The Police utilized on their 1978 hit single, "Walking on the Moon". Dub represents the birth of the remix in popular music culture, arising largely from the desire for exclusivity among Jamaican sound system deejays. First, there was the 'version', an unembellished representation of the song without its vocal component, and this reputedly gained popularity virtually by accident due to a studio mixing error. By the early 1970s, masters of the art form such as King Tubby and Lee Perry had elevated the version to a far more sophisticated sub-genre wherein the instrumental elements were totally reconfigured, inclusive of removing and interjecting musical phrases into and out of the mix, sometimes accompanied by fragments of vocals. In addition, dub was perhaps most readily identified by its liberal use of spatial distortion achieved through the use of delays, reverbs and echoes to create entirely separate soundscapes from the original songs from which the dubs are derived. As such, the selling point for dub releases was not the artist whose performance had been remixed, but the engineer responsible for the remixing.

Although dub also involved and indeed helped precipitate deejay chanting or 'toasting' over instrumental remixes, it is arguable that this very instrumental canvas facilitates dub's greatest sonic expansiveness. The genre never achieved large-scale mainstream support, yet it wielded major commercial impact on other genres. The remix concepts so frequently associated with the disco era of the 1970s were directly derived from dub, as is readily acknowledged by the high-profile dance music engineers and remixers of the time. Jamaican deejay toasting became a direct catalyst for the birth and development of rap and hip-hop in New York, and the sonic spatiality achieved by dub has been wholly assimilated by all of the digitally-driven techno music sub-genres which have had particular commercial success in Europe.

The contemporary popular profile of reggae-related music is most clearly evident in dancehall. The commercial demise of roots reggae followed the death of Bob Marley in 1981, which seemed to symbolize the decline of the spiritual and philosophical ideals of Rastafari in Jamaican popular music, at least temporarily. This also coincided with political changes in Jamaica, moving away from a more idealistic Marxist socialism towards a conservative government ideologically aligned with the United States. Furthermore, the hitherto marijuana-based drug culture was soon dominated by cocaine, and its overall social effect was soon evident in the harshness of the music produced in the early 1980s. This was also a time in which digital music technologies had rapidly progressed and became widely available, thereby democratizing sophisticated sonic reproduction through drum machines, synthesizers and sound processors.

The combination of these factors coupled with the popularity of the newer dancehall style, which was far less complex to create, meant that the producer-dominated Jamaican industry was able to reproduce multiple versions of songs with greater ease than ever before. The song most readily associated with the birth of dancehall is Wayne Smith's "Under Mi Sleng Teng" released in 1985. The song reportedly spawned over 200 versions based on precisely the same digital rhythm. Although other dancehall MCs such as Yellowman emerged earlier, "Under Mi Sleng Teng" is cited as the song which established the digital direction of the genre.

Dancehall has polarized older and newer reggae audiences with its initial explicit emphasis on sexuality (referred to as 'slackness') and violence rather than continuing the 1970s focus on spiritual and political themes, and more idealistic portrayals of romantic love. Consequently, the genre was frequently condemned for being crude and lacking creativity. However, as some writers such as Carolyn Cooper have pointed out, the lyrical and musical codes of dancehall are very much rooted in Jamaican cultural specificities which are virtually impenetrable to outsiders who do not first interface with the wider social contexts. In addition, by the early 1990s with the emergence of performers such as Luciano, offering a blend of old and new reggae styles, some dancehall became more philosophical, although less conscious x-rated lyrics maintained their popularity and were often sung by the same performers. The popular musical emphasis on vocal chanting and orality which dancehall helped to create has also given rise to a series of crossover artists fusing their reggae-related backgrounds with hip-hop, with Sean Paul as the most notable example in recent years.

3. Conclusion

No analysis of Caribbean music can be entirely separate from the social and political circumstances under which it evolved. The historical politics involving global culture and the record industry also add a further analytical context. In my discussion, I've suggested that the very technological media through which we are exposed to the music need to be factored into our assessments. It should also be clear that the history of Caribbean music's dissemination has a directly evident bearing on both its present and future, with the continual impact of powerful commercial forces on cultural norms.

Notes

1 Gordon Rohlehr: *Calypso & Society in Pre-Independence Trinidad*, Port of Spain, 1990, p. 3.
2 *Ibid.*, 16.
3 *Ibid.*, 78; John Cowley: *West Indian Gramophone Records in Britain: 1927-1950*, Coventry, 1985, p. 3.
4 Rohlehr: *Calypso & Society*, pp. 58, 362; Donald R. Hill: *Calypso Calaloo: Early Carnival Music in Trinidad*, Gainesville, 1993, pp. 234-236.
5 Roger Wallis & Krister Malm: *Big Sounds from Small Peoples: The Music Industry in Small Countries*. London, 1984, pp. 190-196.
6 *Ibid.*, 190-191.
7 *Ibid.*, 191.
8 Kevin O'Brien Chang & Wayne Chen: *Reggae Routes: The Story of Jamaican Music*, Kingston, 1998, p. 10.
9 *Ibid.*, 11.
10 *Ibid.*, 14.
11 Simon Jones: *Black Culture, White Youth: The Reggae Tradition from JA to UK*, London, 1988, 58.
12 *Ibid.*
13 *Ibid.*
14 *Ibid.*
15 Colin Larkin (Ed.): *The Guinness Who's Who of Reggae*, London, 1994, p. 272.
16 Stephen Davis: *Bob Marley*, Rochester, 1990, pp. 109-110.
17 Paul Gilroy: "Wearing Your Art on Your Sleeve: Notes Towards a Diaspora History of Black Ephemera", *Small Acts: Thoughts on the Politics of Black Cultures*, London, 1993, 237-257, 243.
18 "Best of the Century", *Time Magazine*, 31 Dec. 1999, <www.time.com/time/magazine/article/0,9171,993039-2,00.html>, accessed 2 March 2007.

Klaus Stierstorfer (Münster)

Laughing Caribbean: Humour in Caribbean Literature and Culture

1. Warm-up: Joking Caribbean

As it probably exists in all cultures or ethnic groups, there is a large reservoir of 'Caribbean' jokes, which has not, however, been systematically collected and analysed.[1] Here is a taste of what such a collection might include:

(1) CARIBBEAN UNITY
A California Highway Patrolman pulled a car over and told the Guyanese driver that, because he was wearing his seat belt, he had just won $5,000 US in the state safety competition.

"What are you going to do with the money?" asked the policeman.

"Well, I gun get a driver's licence", he answered with pride and jubilation.

"Oh, don't listen to him", yelled the Trinidadian woman in the passenger's seat. "He real schupity when he drunk."

This commotion woke up the Bajan guy in the back seat. He took one look at the cop and moaned, "I knew we ain' gon' get far in no tiefin car."

At that moment, there was a knock from the trunk and a Jamaican voice asked, "I man mek it krass the barder yet?!"

(2) WHAT'S IN A NAME?
The policeman on a new motorcycle chased down the motorist speeding on Frederick Street in Port of Spain, Trinidad and made him pull over.

"You've got to be crazy driving like that on this busy street", said the indignant policeman, taking out his book and uncapping his pen. "What is your name?"

"Maximillian Nebuchadnezzar Telemarchus, officer", replied the man.

"Well, [...] don't let me catch you speeding again", said the officer, recapping his pen and closing his book.

(3) DUMB BROTHER

Tessa was injured in a car accident and fell into a deep coma. After six months she woke up and found that she was no longer pregnant. Naturally, she asked the doctor to tell her what happened to her baby.

The doctor replied, "Well, you had twins! A boy and a girl. The babies are fine. Your brother came in and named them."

Tessa became anxious as she didn't think her brother was very smart.

Expecting the worst, she asked the doctor, "So what's the girl's name?"

"Denise", said the doctor. Tessa began to feel a little guilty about how she thought about her brother.

"Not bad", she said. "I like the name Denise."

She then asked the doctor, "What's the boy's name?"

The doctor replied: "Denephew".

(4) THE PATIENT JAMAICAN

An Italian, a Frenchman and a Jamaican were about to be executed and were asked to place their request for their last meal. The Italian requested pepperoni pizza, which he promptly devoured and was then led away to the execution chamber. The Frenchman then requested filet mignon, which he ate slowly and was then led away to the execution chamber. The Jamaican's turn was next. He told the warden that his request was a plate of fresh strawberries. The warden asked in disbelief: "Strawberries?" The Jamaican said, "yes, fresh strawberries." The warden replied: "But strawberries are out of season!" "Soooh?" the Jamaican replied. "I man gine wait."

***

The jokes listed above illustrate at first glance at least three things about Caribbean humour: First, the proverbial liveliness and richness of Caribbean humour is immediately obvious; second, the examples reveal a wry kind of wit often presented as triumphing over other nationalities or cultures and, as in the last example, even taking on death itself in a display of indefatigable vitality; third, the jokes show the Caribbeans' ample capacity to laugh about themselves as much as about anybody else. While the first example works with other nationalities or ethnic groups as well and only gains its Caribbean bearings through its title, the others have a pervasively Caribbean flavour. Sample (2) may also be read as satirizing the illiteracy or laziness of Jamaican policemen (notoriously underpaid), but it derives its main comic impetus from the ludicrously pompous name assumed by its delinquent protagonist. It is hence playing up to the well-known tradition of the great masters of Calypso, many of whom adopted high sounding pseudonyms, such as, famously, "Lord Pretender", "Attila the Hun", "Mighty Spoiler", "King Wellington", or "Mighty Fighter".[2] As in an original calypso setting, the winner scores through his assurance and braggadocio. The policeman is simply overpowered by the imaginative strength and swagger of his opponent; the forces of law and order are symbolically defeated by the Dionysian inventiveness of the calypsonian hero of the episode. What is more, the power of order and limitation represented by the policeman here is traditionally seen as collusive with the (former) colonizers. It is therefore all the more piquant and contributes to the hilarity of the joke that the several names adopted by the reckless driver are mimicries of important names taken from various spheres of Western epic lore and history: Maximilian is the name of several European Emperors; Nebuchadnezzar, the name of two great Babylonian kings, of which the second is also of particular biblical relevance as he led Israel into the Babylonian Exile; "Telemarchus", finally, is an idiosyncratic spelling of Odysseus's son Telemachus, as he appears in Homer's *Odyssey*. Similarly, the fourth example is again built on Caribbean presence of mind and inventiveness, here even in the face of death. While example (2) draws much of its fun from its being told in Standard English, the other jokes use varieties of Caribbean English to great comic effect. Indeed, the third example builds its comic potential almost exclusively on the witty use of Caribbean English.

This essay will explore some of the varieties of Caribbean humour as suggested by the introductory examples, with a special emphasis on its reflections in Caribbean literature in English. Obviously, it is impossible to aspire to any form of comprehensiveness in this format; the subject would be well worth an in-depth study of its own and still remains a desideratum in literary and cultural scholarship. This essay can perhaps provide some impetus towards more advanced studies in this field. Its primary aim, however, is opening the field in an introductory way, broaching some of the more important theoretical and thematic issues it involves and furnishing some examples representative of the cornucopian variety of texts and modes on offer here. Before considering ways in which humour functions in Caribbean contexts, it seems helpful to clarify at least in a working definition what concepts of humour the following discussion will employ.

2. Caribbean Humour as Postcolonial Humour?

The semantic fields of 'humour', 'satire', 'laughter', 'wit' or 'the comic' have for centuries been among the particularly volatile and contested areas in critical terminology. Louis Cazamian, Stuart M. Tave or R. B. Martin[3] with their still eminently readable historical surveys are among the modern pioneers in charting this territory from an historical point of view, although, of course, colonial contexts did not cross their minds as relevant to their explorations. A large body of critical studies on general aspects of humour and the comic as well as in the form of special studies on the functions of humour in the work of individual authors, periods or cultures has continued to appear on the market, but, between them, the two companion volumes no. 57 and 91 in the series "Internationale Forschungen zur Allgemeinen und Vergleichenden Literaturwissenschaft" perhaps assemble the most up-to-date scholarly work in the field and collect the most useful bibliographical data in their various essays. *A History of English Laughter* (vol. 57) is, despite its title, neither a straight-forward history nor is it merely concerned with laughter, as it opens a much wider vista on humour and the comic. It provides a collection of in-depth analyses of mainly British and Irish literature from the Middle Ages to the present, assembling an impressive array of case studies which can be taken as representative for specific forms of laughter or humour and the various cultural contextualizations these concepts have undergone through history. Conceived as a companion volume, *Cheeky Fictions. Laughter and the Postcolonial* (vol. 91) moves the focus to postcolonial studies, again expanding the vision on humour and the comic in general beyond the narrow limitation on laughter suggested by the title.[4] Taken together, the two volumes can be read as a helpful, substantial introduction to the wider problematic of the field.

Contributors to these two volumes, as well as the authors of the large body of critical work they draw on, share the experience that it is notoriously difficult to pin down what 'humour' actually 'is' within one single concept or by means of a hard-and-fast definition. Over time, an impressive collection of more or less stringently formulated 'theories' of humour has accumulated which, quite as much as the humour they attempt to describe, are bound up in specific cultural and historical contexts. Noël Carroll provides a concise survey of such theories of humour in *The Oxford Handbook of Aesthetics*.[5] In his attempt at systematically grouping the various historical views on humour, Carroll establishes three overarching theories under which the individual discussions of humour past and present can be subsumed. The labels he uses have been current in one form or another for a very long time, but they seem particularly apt for this purpose. For one, there is the "Superiority Theory of Humour", that is the "association – found in Plato and Aristotle – of humour with malice and abuse towards people marked as deficient".[6] It has found its classic formulation in Thomas Hobbes's *Leviathan* (1681):

> *Sudden Glory*, is the passion which maketh those *Grimaces* called LAUGHTER; and is caused either by some sudden act of their own, that pleaseth them; or by the apprehension of some deformed thing in another, by comparison whereof they suddenly applaud themselves. And it is incident most to them, that are conscious of the fewest abilities in themselves; who are forced to keep themselves in their own favour, by observing the imperfections of other men. And therefore much Laughter at the defects of others, is a signe of Pusillanimity. For of great minds, one of the proper workes is, to help and free others from scorn; and compare themselves onely with the most able.[7]

Since the eighteenth-century, objections to Hobbes led to a reconceptualization in what has come to be known as the "Incongruity Theory of Humour", as notably propounded by John Locke (not mentioned by Carroll)[8] and Francis Hutcheson. Here, humour springs from a perception of incongruity or unexpected disparity, thus substituting "an intellectual perception for a moral one".[9] This view of humour has found many illustrious supporters; Carroll lists, among others, Arthur Schopenhauer, Søren Kierkegaard, A. Köstler, J. Morreall and, with some hesitation, Henri Bergson.[10] The third variation on humour is based on the idea that humour is a result of the release of some pent-up energy or of a liberation from constraint. It is hence called the "Release Theory". Carroll marshals the Earl of Shaftesbury, Herbert Spencer and Sigmund Freud under this category. Referring to Jerrold Levinson's "Humour" entry in the *Routledge Encyclopedia of Philosophy*, Carroll points to a fourth option[11] where Levinson re-establishes a link between humour and laughter, defining humour as a source, however faint, of engendering a disposition towards laughter, hence named the "Disposition Theory of Humour". How to decide, however, which of these theories is best employed in understanding Caribbean humour?

This quandary is, perhaps, best approached by taking advice from Reichl and Stein's reflections on humour in postcolonial studies, where they note a distinctive "move from the general to the specific", in so far as "recent writing [in postcolonial studies] is more concerned with distinguishing between specific postcolonial cultural practices, experiences and histories".[12] As they convincingly argue, writings on humour share the development in postcolonial studies where overarching theories and universalistic explanatory models give way to local observations and, in Michael Freeman's phrase, to "mini-theories".[13] In that sense, the theories summarized by Carroll need not be taken as competing ontological models which can lay equal claim to explaining 'humour' *tout court*, but as functional alternatives which can either be projected as describing different functions of humour within a given text, as deployed by an author or within a given culture, or as different approaches to humour in a given historico-political context with its specific agenda and vested interests hidden beneath the surface. Indeed, the various theories themselves are open to different functions und interpretations: showing up incongruities for humorous purposes in the sense of the theory of incongruity can be subversive or normative, depending on the specific context. Similarly, the association with malice and the general pejorative slant associated with the superiority theory need not be realized in every situation, as it fits most kinds of satire where the satirist will frequently adopt a superior position to the shortcomings she or he exposes to ridicule; if the butt of this ridicule is, for instance, racism, most people would deny any malice in the laughter involved.

Humour, thus, is not simply a recurrent human phenomenon which we recognize when we see it; neither is it only culture-bound to work and become visible as humour in the first place; it is also open to a broad spectrum of interpretation – trans- or cross-cultural, trans-ethnic, polyvalent and always ready for appropriations – wherever it is observed to occur. What I advocate here, in short, as the most useful approach to humour in the Caribbean, is a quasi-semiotic understanding of humour, where humour and laughter are read as signs that do not carry any specific meaning per se, but become meaningful within contingent processes of signification and interpretation, which include the full range of hermeneutic complications and opportunities. Then the alternative theories of humour we have at our disposal emerge as an array of heuristic instruments to understand and interpret these processes of signification.

3. Humour and the Caribbean Way of Life

Writing from her experience on the Caribbean Lexicography Project, Jeannette Allsopp reflects about a specifically Caribbean brand of humour, which in her view can be traced back to the Caribbeans' specific use of language:

> Luckily for us Caribbeans, humor plays a great part in our daily lives and laughter is generally much more common than a gloomy face. Perhaps this is related to our down-to-earth, often rather unsophisticated use of language, especially at folk level.[14]

She exemplifies this kind of humour with the story about a local councillor who was trying to enforce a strict regimen on public spending and hence opposed spending money on public urinals. His opposition was, it turned out, due to the fact that he did not know the word and, enlightened by another councillor, converted his opposition to fervent backing of the vote, proclaiming eagerly:

> Why y'all didn't put de thing in praper terms? Yes! Yes! I vote for them. And while you buildin' you must put in some *arsenals* too![15]

What Allsopp identifies as a general Caribbean sensibility to broadly humorous uses of language again engages with the European heritage of the language – English in this case. Drawing from a school teacher's collections, she shows how proverbs are creatively reinterpreted according to the Caribbean context and experience, resulting in completions of proverbs such as "*A bird in the hand will* mess on your clothes", or "*One swallow does not make* a meal".[16]

Allsopp's linguistic conclusions on the pervasiveness and popularity of humour in the Caribbean had already been observed and confirmed before in general terms. Thus, James M. Jones and Hollis V. Liverpool started their 1976 book contribution on "Calypso Humour in Trinidad" with a quotation form an earlier newspaper article by Jones, beginning with the statement:

> Humour in Trinidad is a way of life. It is the currency of social exchange and the vehicle of psychological and cultural organization.[17]

However, Jones and Liverpool had taken their argument on humour a step further in a different direction in identifying the archetypal form of Trinidadian humour in the calypso. They set out to prove the "basic thesis [...] that Trinidad humour derives from the calypso humour prototype".[18] Calypso is perhaps the most well-known and wide-spread genre of a set of similar institutions sometimes stemming from or at least associated with colonial sacred and secular rituals, such as, most importantly, Carnival in those islands with strong Catholic traditions established by French or Spanish colonisers, notably Trinidad and Tobago, but also Carriacou, Dominica, Grenada, St Lucia and St Vincent. Islands with a predominantly Protestant colonial tradition have their own institutions, such as "Jonkonnu" at Christmas in Jamaica and the Bahamas, "Christmas sports" in St Kitts-Nevis or the "Gombey" parades in Bermuda.[19]

The origin of the term 'calypso' is uncertain, and Keith Q. Warner provides a list of five theories[20] about it, favouring himself the view that it is derived from the West African (Hausa) term *kaiso*, which already shows the connection to Black traditions in the Caribbean. Although the historical development of calypso is also not clearly established, Gros Jean is generally credited as the first Master of Kaiso. He was given this title by Pierre Begorrat, who had come to Trinidad from Martinique in 1784 and set up as a notable of his own making, complete with court and entourage. Gros Jean's songs were either flatteries of Begorrat or lampoons of his master's enemies.[21] His life was ended by one of Begorrat's wives who poisoned him out of jealousy. Gros Jean would, of course, have sung his kaisos in French patois, which only began to be replaced by English as the predominant Calypso language[22] from the beginning of the 20th century onwards.

Calypso's association with Carnival is probably of a later date than its inception, but the link is an important stage in its progress to one of the most popular and widespread humorous genres in the Caribbean and beyond. As Warner sets out,[23] Carnival changed after emancipation in Trinidad and Tobago (where 1 August 1834 is celebrated as emancipation day, commemorated with a national holiday each year) when the freed slaves added their culture and social impetus to the festivities.[24] A highly creative, mainly urban subculture emerged, particularly in areas of Port of Spain where the Africo-Caribbean population was most numerous, with the calypso singer as one of the local heroes. Tents were set up where Calypsonians would practice in the weeks before Carnival. These tents eventually began to evolve into the actual auditoria for calypso presentations, as more and more spectators had come to these tents to listen to the practicing singers from the time after World War I onwards. Although the Calypso season proper had now moved before the high time of Carnival, its link to Carnival has remained and even been strengthened as the new calypsos of a particular season will form the musical mainstay of the Carnival bands in the following weeks – a custom enforced by commercial interests of record companies who began to see a sound profit in this musical genre.

The first vocal recordings of calypso date from 1914, and singers such as Attila the Hun, Roaring Lion or Lord Invader were the first to make it to the notice of an international auditorium, followed by Lord Kitchener, Mighty Sparrow and others whose renown spread well beyond the Caribbean. Most famously perhaps, Harry Belafonte's "Banana Boat Song", a rendering of a traditional Jamaican folk song, became a best-selling hit in 1956, and the album *Calypso*, where it featured, was the first calypso collection to sell more than a million records. It should at least be noted that, although a predominantly male occupation, there have also been famous female Calypsonians. The first one to sing in a "tent" called herself Lady Trinidad and made her debut in 1935.

In 1947, "Lord Kitchener" opened his own tent, calling it "The Young Brigade", which became the venue of perhaps the most famous series of appearances of famous Calypsonians. It had on its programme such famous names as Nap Hepburn, King Fighter, Laddie, Mighty Sparrow, Lord Coffee, Lord Cobra and Young Killer, Lord Caruso, Al Thomas, Arnold "Bass" Bowen, Errol McLean and "Watap" Bentley Jack. While humour has always been a consistent hallmark of calypso as a genre, the kind of humour displayed and the themes, tone and agenda dealt with in the songs can differ widely, from silly word play to the most serious political criticism, from sexual or erotic bantering to the most incisive personal invective. Here, calypso's link to slavery and post-emancipation culture should, however, be kept in mind, even if it is again uncertain in which ways the early stages of calypso were exactly inspired by African musical traditions. As to the role of humour at that early stage, Jones and Liverpool describe the earliest Calypsonians as follows:

> The social context in which these singers operate was slavery. It seems likely in this context that the humour they produced was cathartic for those slaves who were more restricted. It was also a form of prestige and power within the slave class. It seems likely that humour or laughter served as an aggressive cutting stone like the boxing matches that were common among slaves in America. The winners always received special favours.[25]

After emancipation and the Calypsonians' intimate association with carnivalesque traditions, it is still the case that the Afro-Caribbean element remained the major influence in the development of calypso. In thematic content, their songs retained a satirical edge against those in power, commenting on political events throughout the colonial period and playing an important role in the run-up to independence of Trinidad and Tobago, with the Calypsonians Sparrow, Striker and others as important backers of the People's National Movement (PNM). Arguably, they have retained a role in

Caribbean political and social life to this day, as Louis Regis sums it up:

> All things considered, it was fitting that the calypsonian be the herald of independence because he had long championed the national forces and movements agitating for self-rule and statehood. Over the following 25 years, and beyond, he continued commenting on happenings in the political domain, communicating his views about politics, politicians and power sharing. Twenty-five years of his song have left us a priceless archive of social history which is at once the saga of independence viewed from the perspective of the urban, largely Afro-Trinidadian underclass, and at the same time, the dynamic story of a popular folk urban song form as it developed in a volatile time.[26]

The Calypsonians must, first and foremost, be seen as reflecting and communicating the feelings of the common people. Thus, Sparrow, who had supported Eric Williams towards his leadership of the PNM in 1956, immediately came in with criticism in a calypso of the same year, when costs of living started to soar under the new leadership:

> What I say might be very small
> But I know poor people ent pleased at all
> We are looking for betterment
> That is why we choose a new government
> But they raise on the food before we could talk
> And they raise on the fares so we bound to walk.[27]

Duly, Albert Gomes, who had been defeated by Eric Williams – not least because of the Calypsonians' support for the latter – acknowledged the calypso's political power:

> The Calypso is the most effective political weapon in Trinidad. Thus it is that even when cleverly camouflaged with wit and banter, the sharp tang of social criticism is evident in their songs.[28]

Political and social changes in Trinidad had always produced their humorous and often critical comments in the Calypso Tents. Thus, when Trinidad became a major military base for the Allies in World War II and the Americans came in force, they introduced a new way of life with its advantages (jobs), but also with its problems. One of these was humorously portrayed after the Americans' departure in Sparrow's famous "Jean and Dinah", a calypso which castigates Trindadian women's easy availability for the comparatively rich American soldiers and the hang-over the end of the war produced with them, as the local "glamour boys" from Port of Spain took over again – at much reduced prices:

> Well the girls in town feeling bad
> No more Yankees in Trinidad
> They going to close down the base for good
> Them girls have to make out how they could
> Is now they park up in town
> In for a penny, in for a pound
> Yes, is competition for so
> Trouble in town when the price drop low.[29]

Calypsonians can also be observed to reflect on the cultural and ethnic context where they find themselves located and in which they produce their songs, but again the humorous distance must not be missing, as in Dougla's 1961 song "Split Me in Two":

> Let us suppose they pass a law
> They don't want people here any more
> Let us suppose they pass a law
> They don't want people living here any more
> Every body got to find their country
> According to your race originally
> What a confusion I would cause in the place
> They might have to shoot me in space
>
> Well if they sending Indians to India
> And Negroes back to Africa
> Will somebody please just tell me
> Where they sending for me, poor Dougie
> I am neither one or the other
> Six o' one, and half a dozen of the other
> Well if they serious 'bout sending back people for true
> They bound to split me in two.[30]

The multicultural, multiethnic context of the Caribbean, which the Calypsonian Dougla here described in his song, is precisely what Salman Rushdie advocated in general terms three decades later in defending his novel *Satanic Verses*:

> *The Satanic Verses* celebrates hybridity, impurity, intermingling, the transformation that comes of new and unexpected combinations of hu-

> man beings, cultures, ideas, politics, movies, songs. It rejoices in mongrelization and fears the absolutism of the Pure.[31]

Rushdie's magisterial and seminal passage has been quoted over and over again; when it comes to humour, however, Dougla will still carry the votes of many readers for his playful expression of the idea.

It is true that the absolutist view on humour as a basis of Caribbean culture and the place of Calypso as one of its most prominent folk expressions may not be shared by everyone. As Louis Regis points out in his Preface,[32] not everyone even within Trinidad and Tobago accepts the national importance and representative character of the calypso as the "voice of the people". For some, he reports, it is just "rum music", others see it as bacchanalian and a work of the devil or perceive its influence restricted to around the Carnival season, while others again consider it a phenomenon of Afro-Caribbean culture only. These qualifications may in fact instil caution in the aspiring student of Caribbean humour and invoke the necessary scholarly care when generalizing about 'the Caribbean' or, indeed, about 'humour' in general. Nevertheless it should not detract from the convincing arguments put forward by the authors variously quoted in this section that Caribbean culture has a specific humour of its own; that this specific humour is well-rooted in popular culture and takes its strength from these roots; and that calypso is certainly one of its most notable expressions, reflecting the range and colour of Caribbean humour in general.

The widespread popularity and cultural pervasiveness of Caribbean humour has its impact in all spheres of life. This is also the case in Caribbean literature. Again, the literary presence of Caribbean humour is found in many shades and functions, which will be explored in the next section.

4. Literary Negotiations of Humour in the Caribbean

As Keith Warner has shown in his chapter "The Calypso in Trinidad Literature",[33] the influence of calypso can be traced in direct quotations, parallel structures and thematic similarities throughout much of Caribbean literature, from the early Naipaul to Sam Selvon's short stories and Earl Lovelace's novels, and even to the comic strips in the *Trinidad Express*. These occurrences of Calypsonian references show the rootedness of much of Caribbean literature in local, popular culture; they also spread the Calypsonians' specific kind of humour throughout the literary sphere.

While the brand of popular humour taken up by all of Warner's examples from Naipaul to Lovelace reflects the contemporary Caribbean scene of multicultural and multiethnic miscegenation and "mongrelization" (in Rushdie's positive sense again) as a result of the chequered history of the region, it should at least be noted in passing here that in recent times Caribbean authors have also tried to bring out a type of humour which can be seen as original or primeval to the Caribbean, reaching back to pre-colonial times or engaging colonial, 'Western' concepts with a Caribbean otherness which can also find its expression in a particular kind of humour. There is, for instance, the mythopoeic dimension in Harris Wilson's rendering of the "Sermon of the Leaf" in "The Laughter of the Wapishanas",[34] the humorous approach in the various stories around Annancy and other trickster figures from the Caribbean or, indeed, Erna Brodber's story of "One Bubby Susan".[35] In her short story, Brodber not only offers a delightful send-up of 'Western' cultural cartography of the Caribbean in telling the 'real' story behind what is noted as an Arawak carving in the guidebooks to Jamaica, but also "this women's lib business"[36] as well as religious mysticism associated with India:

> Now I don't know if these Arawak Indians is any relative to the Indians in India but I swear to you, what Miss Susan show me that she was doing, was one of those yoga pose that make a person look like Buddha.[37]

... only that there was nothing mystic about Susan's way of breathing at the mouth of her cave where she occasionally enjoyed the fresh air in this manner as a contrast to the stuffiness of the cave in which she lived. The language of the story's narrator is characterized by elements of the Pidgin English of the Caribbean and produces in the narrator's naïve loquaciousness a dry humour with the most hilarious effects.

Apart from such experiments with retellings or reinventions of 'original', pre-colonial Caribbean humour, however, the greatest part of the humour found in Caribbean literature creatively taps those popular, contemporary wellsprings of which calypso is such a striking epitome. V. S. Naipaul as one of the most prominent Caribbean writers is a case in point, and a brief analysis of the functions of humour in one of his particularly memorable short stories can show this.

Naipaul's "The Baker's Story"[38] is a first-person narrative or, perhaps more precisely, a form of dramatic monologue. The narrator identifies himself as a black Grenadian who had been brought to Trinidad by his mother but given away to be raised by a foster mother. The story opens with what the narrator presents as a riddle or paradox to the reader, followed by his explanation which forms the main part of the story. The paradox is established in the combination of blackness / ugliness and wealth in the narrator's persona, as he says at the very start:

> Look at me. Black as the Ace of Spades, and ugly to match. Nobody looking at me would believe they looking at one of the richest men in this city of Port of Spain. Sometimes I find it hard to believe myself [...]. (BS 165)

With no education and no personal assets to start with, he describes his rise in the world. It had all begun with his occasional work for a Chinese bakery in his Trinidadian neighbourhood, from which he rose to regular employment in this shop. When the Chinese shopkeeper's wife dies and her gambling husband eventually loses the shop, the narrator is left to his own devices. The first part of his 'revelation' how to proceed comes in one of his frequent prayers, when he hears God's call to him: " 'Youngman' – was always the way I uses to get call in these prayers – 'Youngman, you just bake bread'." (BS 170) Unfortunately, however, the bakery he has set up on borrowed money is not doing well. The same customers who had been eager to buy the bread from the Chinese owner for whom the narrator had worked now avoid the bakery under his ownership. Then the second part of his revelation comes in the form of his rich old school friend Percy and his categorical refusal to have, as he says, "black people meddling with my food" (BS 173). Now the narrator understands:

> I see names of bakers: Coelho, Pantin, Stauble. Potogee or Swiss, or something, and then all those other Chinee places. And, look at the laundries. If a black man open a laundry, you would take your clothes to it? *I* wouldn't take my clothes there. (BS 173f)

Now he also understands why he was never allowed to serve at the counter of the Chinese bakery where he worked in his youth, and the recipe for his success is made: while he himself bakes his bread of superior quality, he finds a boy who looks Chinese (although he is half black and half Chinese) to serve at the counter, displays an old Chinese newspaper and paints Chinese characters on his shop sign together with his newly hybridized trade name YUNG MAN BAKER, with immediate results:

> I never show my face in the front of the shop again. And I tell you, without boasting, that I bake damn good bread. And the people of Arouca ain't that foolish. They know a good thing. And soon I was making so much money [...]. (BS 175).

Ultimately, the principle of his success is his recognition of deeply ingrained ethnic stereotypes according to which Trinidadian society functions. The mode in which these are presented, however, can be identified as quintessentially humorous, sharing many features with Stephen Leacock's description of life in Canadian Mariposa, Mark Twain's look at his compatriots along the Mississippi, or, indeed, Dickens' sketches of London life and characters.[39] Looking for indicators of the humorist's disposition in Naipaul's short story, the following aspects will be found particularly noteworthy:

- The fact that the narrator is not arguing from a higher moral or ethical ground and does not pose as superior to his fellow-Trinidadians he describes;
- His good-humoured acceptance of the prevalent ethnic stereotypes, even where they are obviously to his disadvantage: When he explains why it took him so long to understand the reasons for the sustained failure of his bakery, he says: "And was only then that the thing hit me. I suppose that what Trinidadians say about the stupidness of Grenadians have a little truth [...]" (BS 173). He then goes on, however, to utilize the undiminished virulence of such stereotypes to his own profit;
- His jokes are good-humoured and not at others' expense; his assertion that "I make my dough from dough" is not without some pride at his success, but even in his distress in the empty bakery with no customers and rising debts he has a joke for passers-by going to the beach on Sunday that "he was loafing" and then notes their much less benign, more Hobbesian brand of laughter: "They uses to laugh like hell, too. It have nothing in the whole

world so funny as to see a man you know flat out on his arse and catching good hell." (BS 171) Even this *Schadenfreude* at his expense, however, is reported in a non-judgemental way as one of the proclivities of human nature.

- Finally, the ironic passages in his story are not marked as narrator's winks to the reader and thus rather reflect the narrator's guilelessness and naïveté, when, for example, he says that "whenever I in any little business difficulty even these days I get down bam! straight on my two knees and I start praying *like hell*, boy" (BS 166; italics K.St.)

The obvious criticism against the humorist's frame of mind displayed in this story will of course be levelled against its tendency of abetting patent social wrongs – such as the regulation of trade, and hence the distribution of poverty and wealth, through ethnic stereotyping and racial discrimination – and human weakness – such as the glee displayed at someone else's misfortunes. Instead of condemning these social and personal vices and propagating a sense of community in Trinidadian society where everyone has the same chances irrespective of skin colour or ethnic provenance and thus abolishing the unjust left-over of a colonial past, the humorist here appears strangely passive and powerless. This seems further aggravated by Naipaul's choice of protagonist / narrator as a person who has succeeded despite – and some might even say: perversely, because of – his almost insurmountable handicaps in skin colour, national provenance, parents and education, and, to make matters worse, who does not seem at all concerned to improve matters now that he is well-off and hence could make his influence felt.

On the positive side it has to be noted, however, that the brand of humour promoted by this short story is not aimed at passivity in the same way as, for example, Mr. Biswas' reading of Dickens might suggest in *A House for Mr. Biswas*:

> Then it was that he [Mr. Biswas] discovered the solace of Dickens. Without difficulty he transferred characters and settings to people and places he knew. In the grotesques of Dickens everything he feared and suffered from was ridiculed and diminished, so that his own anger, his own contempt became unnecessary, and he was given strength to bear with the most difficult part of his day [...]. [40]

By contrast, the short story's protagonist does not simply endure unjust social handicaps, but turns them to his own advantage and by doing so, it could even be argued, subverts them. The more obvious case of subversion in the short story, however, can be found in its deconstruction of essentialist belief in the ethnic stereotypes it describes. Readers are not only shown how these conventions can be manipulated and turned into profit; they are also confronted with the constructedness of these social labels: it is, after all, a black man who is baking their bread, and customers enjoy it so long as they can harbour the illusion that it is bought from a Chinese (or Swiss or Portuguese), but certainly not a Grenadian baker. Thus, satire's open finger-pointing and corrective, socially committed approach is replaced by the arguably more subtle subversiveness of the humorist's sympathetic portrayal, especially when compared to Naipaul's own, jaundiced look at Trinidadian society in his first novels, which George Lamming had lambasted as "castrated satire".[41] Especially against the background of Naipaul's writing from the safe distance of his British exile, his shift from satirist to the humorist of the Baker short story certainly unhinges the possible reproach of adopting the satirist's superior stance and trying to judge Trinidadian society from yet another, this time 'politically correct' discursive framework, which again would be foisted on people like the Grenadian baker, replacing the old, patently unjust system of ethnic and racial discrimination with yet another, ultimately coercive, cultural framework from 'outside'. The jury, it seems, is still out, which approach is preferable, but the issue remains topical and certainly worth a lively discussion.

The generation or generations of Caribbean writers following Naipaul and other founding fathers (the early writers were predominantly men) of Caribbean literature have largely kept up this humorous vein and adapted it to their own modes of writing. Here, Guyana-born Pauline Melville (born 1948), who has earned an outstanding reputation with two short story collections and a novel in the 1990s, can serve as one example of many. After developing her own kind of irony in *Shape-Shifter* (1990), her first short story collection, she introduced a more philosophical vein into her explorations of humour in her novel *The Ventriloquist's Tale* of 1997. The novel investigates the clash of cultures between the Amerindian population of Guyana and the white colonizers in a brother-sister relationship, but also the nature of fiction and story telling in general. From the narrator's first reflections about his own persona and role in the Prologue, laughter is with a programmatic humour put forward as the underlying 'essence' of the universe. When the narrator quoted a radio programme "about the cosmic noise picked up by radio telescopes – that faint echo of the Big Bang that has spread through the universe over the aeons" and faithfully reproduces the sound thanks to his special imitative gift, his grandmother immediately had an interpretation for it:

> "What people are hearing", she said, "is the final wheeze of an enormous laugh."[42]

For all the seriousness of its thematic approach and its frequent skirting of tragedy, the novel must be read as written against this background of cosmic laughter which finds its way into the various stories which intertwine in this book. Thus, Chofy McKinnon humorously commiserates with his hen-pecked landlord Rohi Peraud by quoting an appropriate couplet from a calypso.[43] In the historic storyline of the novel, to give another memorable example, the missionary priest, Father Napier, decides to introduce the natives to the high art of European culture by taking out his violin and playing Mozart's Sonata K.304 in E minor. The effect, however, is stifled laughter and his metamorphosis into a giant grasshopper in the eyes of the village:

> Aunt Bobo's body stiffened and jerked as she clamped her hand over her mouth to prevent the laughter bursting out. Everybody watched as the priest paced the floor, his body bending backwards and forwards, his right arm holding the bow, sawing at the instrument with gusto.
> Someone remarked that he looked and sounded like a great grasshopper rubbing its legs together and the room fell silent as everybody absorbed this information with some concern.
> Moved by the idea that he was introducing these people to the classics for the first time and convinced, even as he played, that the awed silence proved how entranced they were by the music, Father Napier felt his eyes fill with tears.
> Everyone else in the room, except McKinnon who was just amused, watched with a sort of horror as, before their eyes, the priest turned into a giant, buzzing, savannah grasshopper.[44]

Such hilarious comedy cast against a quasi-philosophical conception of humour can be seen as the hallmark of Melville's writing, which she keeps up through the stories of her next collection, *The Migration of Ghosts* (1998). Here, "President's Exile" ends with the reaction at seeing the funeral oration for the president on screen "that the Lokono Arawak villagers of Hicuri exploded spontaneously into howls of laughter";[45] "Mrs. da Silva's Carnival" has the relevant festive season in the title; even the dry and stunning narration of "The *Duende*" ends with Rosita's "grunting laugh" (MG 62) in answer to being questioned about her spontaneous excursion to town; and "Lucifer's Shank", the tragic chronicle of a death from cancer, still insists on humour as the last resort in the face of human transitoriness and pain:

> Jokes. What a rackety handrail to help us through the blizzard. […]
> For Ellie and me, the last coherent exchange had been a shared joke. (MG 82)

"Don't Give Me Your Sad Stories" has the plea for humour in the title and ends with an explosion of shared laughter. The series could be continued in this fashion showing further variations of humour throughout the collection. In Melville's writing, Caribbean humour can be observed to evolve from a fixed institution in Caribbean culture to a mode that, albeit still culture-bound, expands into a universal, generally human agency.

Indeed, much of the humorous elements in Caribbean writing point beyond the confines of the region, not only in Melville's philosophical extension or in local negotiations with colonial cultures, but also through the fact that much of Caribbean writing reflects situations of exile, which in many cases means Great Britain. Thus, a whole stream of Caribbean humour has become productive in a British context, providing a special perspective on the intercultural situation encountered by immigrants from the Caribbean.

Here, to give at least one example, Sam Selvon's 1957 collection *Ways of Sunlight* is a pioneering work in so far as its stories are collected in two parts, the first one set in Trinidad, the second one set in London. A vein of humour runs right through the book, but receives a different refraction in the new setting in London. Significantly, the second part starts with "Calypso in London" which features a calypso session where Mangohead and Hotboy invent a new song, with calypso again prominent as a cultural mainstay of Caribbean identity and humour. Calypso comes up with another reference in "Brackley and the Bed", when Brackley is in high spirits after having had a good meal which Teena has cooked for him and he softly whistles a calypso (MG, 141). On another level, the whole story "Brackley and the Bed" could, however, be interpreted as a calypso translated into narrative form. Brackley, who shares a flat with Teena, has to spend the nights cold and stiff in a corner as Teena uses the one bed. Desperate, he finally decides to marry Teena to be able to take advantage of the warmth of this bed, only to hear from Teena after a rush to the registry that he will not even be able to enjoy his wedding night in the bed: Teena's aunt is expected to arrive in London that evening and will stay with them for an indefinite period, of course sharing the bed with Teena. The elaborate joke can easily be imagined as transformed into a calypso song for carnival.

Indeed, much of Caribbean literature and hence the humour it reflects is written from a volatile cultural and geographical situation, many writers permanently settling down abroad, but still writing about the Caribbean as their imagined home and place of departure. They share the predicament – which has proved very productive in terms of literary stimulus with many – outlined by David Dabydeen's semi-autobiographical narrator in his novel *The Intended*: While his grandmother admonishes her grandson, "Go and don't look back"[46] as she puts him on the bus which will take him on the first leg of his long journey to England, he has also another piece of advice stuck in his memory from his Auntie Clarice, bestowed on him together with a five-dollar bill as he said good-bye to her:

> She kissed me and put the money in my pocket. As I turned to go she called out a final riddle: "you is we, remember you is we".[47]

And the communal feeling and shared culture which Caribbeans thus feel they carry with them wherever they end up around the world always includes an indefatigable sense of humour all of their own.

1 The jokes reprinted here can be found, with many more Caribbean jokes and further, useful information, at http://www.silvertorch.com/c_humor.htm, accessed 15 February 2007.
2 See, for example, James M. Jones & Hillis V. Liverpool: "Calypso Humour in Trinidad". – In Antony J. Chapman & Hugh C. Foot: *Humour and Laughter: Theory, Research and Applications,* London et al., 1976, pp. 259-286.
3 Louis Cazamian: *The Development of English Humour,* Durham, NC, 1952; Stuart M. Tave: *The Amiable Humorist. A Study of the Comic Theory and Criticism of the Eighteenth and Early Nineteenth Centuries,* Chicago, 1960; Robert Bernard Martin: *The Triumph of Wit. A Study of Victorian Comic Theory,* Oxford, 1974.
4 Susanne Reichl & Mark Stein (Eds.): *Cheeky Fictions. Laughter and the Postcolonial,* Internationale Forschungen zur Allgemeinen und Vergleichenden Literaturwissenschaft 91, Amsterdam & New York, 2005.
5 Noël Carroll: "Chapter 19. Humour" – In Jerrold Levinson (Ed.): *The Oxford Handbook of Aesthetics,* Oxford, 2003, pp. 344-356.
6 *Ibid.*, 345.
7 Thomas Hobbes: *Leviathan, or The Matter, Forme, & Power of a Common-Wealth Ecclesiasticall and Civill* (1651), I.vi, ed. R.Tuck, Cambridge, 1991, p. 43.
8 John Locke: *Essay Concerning Human Understanding* (1690), II.ix.2. Ed. P. H. Nidditch, Oxford, 1975, p. 156.
9 Martin, *Triumph of Wit*, p. 19.
10 Carroll, "Humour", p. 347.
11 *Ibid.*, 353.
12 Susanne Reichl & Mark Stein, "Introduction". – In Reichl & Stein (Eds.): *Cheeky Fictions*, pp. 1-23, 7.
13 Quoted in Reichl & Stein: "Introduction", p. 6.
14 Jeannette Allsopp: "Humor Caribbean Style", *Verbatim* 19:3, 1993, 18-19, 18.
15 *Ibid.*
16 *Ibid.*
17 James M. Jones & Hollis V. Liverpool: "Calypso Humour in Trinidad". – In Antony J. Chapman & Hugh C. Foot (Eds.): *Humour and Laughter: Theory, Research and Applications,* London et al., 1976, pp. 259-286, 259.
18 *Ibid.*, 262.
19 See John Cowley: *Carnival, Canboulay and Calypso. Traditions in the Making,* Cambridge, 1996, pbk 1998, p. 8.
20 Keith Q. Warner: *Kaiso! The Trinidad Calypso. A Study of the Calypso as Oral Literature,* Pueblo, CO, 1982, third printing, revised and augmented, 1999, p. 8. Rafael de Leon even argues for the medieval French troubadours

as the real originators of modern calypso in *Calypso from France to Trinidad. 800 Years of History,* Trinidad, [1986].
21 See *ibid.*, 9.
22 Jones & Liverpool: "Calypso Humour in Trinidad", pp. 265-6, report that it was Norman LeBlanc who is given credit to have first used English lyrics for his calypso in 1897 in a calypso that criticized the British Governor, Jerningham, for his intentions to abolish the Port-of-Spain Borough Council.
23 Warner: *Kaiso*, pp. 10-11.
24 See also Gordon Rohlehr: *Calypso and Society in Pre-Independence Trinidad,* Port-of-Spain, 1990.
25 Jones & Liverpool: "Calypso Humour in Trinidad", p. 264
26 Louis Regis: *The Political Calypso: True Opposition in Trinidad and Tobago, 1962-1987*, Kingston, Jamaica & Gainesville, FA, 1999, p. ix.
27 Quoted in Regis, *The Political Calypso*, p. 8.
28 Quoted in Warner: *Kaiso*, p. 69.
29 Quoted in *ibid.*, 70.
30 Quoted in Regis: *The Political Calypso*, p. 11.
31 Salman Rushdie: "In Good Faith" (1990). – In S. R., *Imaginary Homelands*, New York & London, 1991, pp. 393-414, 394.
32 Regis: *The Political Calypso*, p. ix.
33 Warner: *Kaiso*, pp. 147-165.
34 Wilson Harris: "From The Laughter of the Wapishanas". – In E. A. Markham (Ed.): *The Penguin Book of Caribbean Short Stories*, London, 1996, pp. 3-5.
35 Erna Brodber: "One Bubby Susan". – In Markham (Ed.): *The Penguin Book of* Caribbean *Short Stories*, pp. 48-53.
36 Brodber: "One Bubby Susan", p. 53.
37 *Ibid.*, 50.
38 First published in *A Flag on the Island* (1967); all references in the following text are to the edition in Markham (Ed.): *The Penguin Book of Caribbean Short Stories*, pp. 165-175, abbreviated as "BS".
39 Naipaul himself directly refers to Dickens and Mark Twain, for example, in his second novel *A House for Mr. Biswas*, [1961], London, 2000, pp. 315, 374 and *passim*.
40 Naipaul: *A House for Mr. Biswas*, p. 374.
41 George Lamming: *The Pleasures of Exile*, London, 1960, p. 225.
42 Pauline Melville: *The Ventriloquist's Tale*, New York & London, 1997, p. 8.
43 Melville: *The Ventriloquist's Tale*, p. 69.
44 *Ibid.*, 119.
45 Pauline Melville: *The Migration of Ghosts*, New York & London, 1997, p. 24; all following references to this edition, abbreviated as "MG".
46 David Dabydeen: *The Intended*, 1991, Leeds, 2005, p. 53.
47 Dabydeen: *The Intended*, p. 32.

Contributors' Addresses

Dr. Mike Alleyne, Associate Professor, Department of Recording Industry, Middle Tennessee State University, Box 21, Middle Tennessee State University, Murfreesboro, TN 37132, USA.

Dr. Curwen Best, Senior Lecturer, Department of Language, Linguistics and Literature, The University of the West Indies at Cave Hill, Cave Hill Campus, P.O. Box 64 Bridgetown, Barbados.

Dr. Hubert Devonish, Professor of Linguistics, Department of Language, Linguistics and Philosophy, The University of the West Indies at Mona, Mona, Kingston 7, Jamaica.

Dr. Denise deCaires Narain, Senior Lecturer in English, Department of English and Drama, University of Sussex, Falmer, Brighton, BN1 9QN, UK

Dr. Miki Flockemann, Lecturer in English Literature, Department of English, University of the Western Cape, Private Bag X17, Bellville 7530, South Africa.

Dr. Monika Gomille, Professor of English Literature and Translation Studies, Institut für Anglistik und Amerikanistik, Universität Düsseldorf, Universitätsstr. 1, 40225 Düsseldorf, Germany.

Dr. Jana Gohrisch, Professor for New English Literatures, Englisches Seminar, Universität Hannover, Königsworther Platz 1, 30167 Hannover, Germany.

Dr. Gail Low, Senior Lecturer in English, English, School of Humanities, University of Dundee, Dundee, DD1 4HN, Scotland, U.K.

Dr. Helge Nowak, Professor of English Literature, Department für Anglistik und Amerikanistik, Universität München, Schellingstr. 3 RG, 80799 München, Germany.

Dr. Sabine Sörgel, Assistant Professor, Institut für Theaterwissenschaft, Universität Mainz, Philosophicum, Jakob-Welder-Weg 18, 55099 Mainz, Germany.

Dr. Keith Sandiford, Professor of English, The Department of English, 260 Allen Hall, Louisiana State University, Baton Rouge, 70803, USA.

Dr. Klaus Stierstorfer, Professor of English Literature, Englisches Seminar, Universität Münster, 48143 Münster, Germany.

Dr. Silvio Torres-Saillant, Associate Professor of English and Director, Latino-Latin American Studies Program, Syracuse University, Syracuse University, Syracuse, NY 13244, USA.